PRAISES FOR *STC*

"Wow! Stop Your Crying puts a whole new twist on seeing through someone else's eyes. Faced with harsh and complex life challenges from such a young age, he was able to work through them in a way that is completely unique. Truly it shows how a neurodivergent brain consumes its surroundings in an astonishing way!" Tatiana T.

"Love this book. It is very relatable. The way he is parented feels so genuine and real. It's like a conversation with an old friend." Jacqueline D.

"I wish I never had you" were words that Robert heard throughout his entire childhood and into adulthood. This heartbreaking memoir of abuse, trauma, and difficult circumstances also gives hope to others who suffer. Robert's example of strength, courage, and the uncanny ability of turning negatives into positives will have you cheering him on." Doreen A.

STOP

YOUR

CRYING

HOW ONE AUTISTIC BOY
SAVED HIS WORLD

ROBERT BAUTNER

Library of Congress Data
ISBN 979-8-9887884-0-9

Forest City Publications
Tucson, AZ 85738
https://forestcitypublications.com

DEDICATION
To my children Natalie, Parker, Heidi, Michael, and Christopher

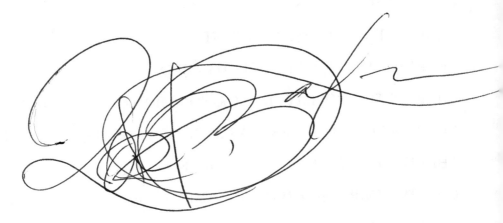

CONTENTS

FORWARD

_____

As I write this forward for my dear friend Robert Bautner, I'm honored by the opportunity to introduce his story of success and perseverance despite life's adversities. I have had the privilege of being a mutual mentor with Robert as he has navigated the process of learning to write and to become a published author. His book illustrates the "human experience" in the pursuit of greater empathy and understanding in our interactions with our fellow brothers and sisters.

This remarkable story emphasizes the importance of cherishing the gifts and abilities of people with autism and to never underestimate them. Often popular culture misunderstands or underestimates the remarkable potential of people with autism. This book illustrates the importance of not counting people out and not judging people based on a superficial understanding.

Robert boldly shares insights from his childhood that have shaped the man he is today. His ability to turn negative circumstances into positive outcomes is worth emulation. I hope you will learn and grow from his experiences as I have.

Christian Mortensen

PREFACE

The accuracy of this story is based on memory over the past 60 years. I share these stories to save lives. It is my desire to connect with others like me who have gone through personal trauma, abuses, and those who have been sexually traumatized. The stories are here to connect to a safe place for those who have had similar experiences. It is also for those in the gay, straight, lgbqt+ communities who feel disenfranchised from their identities and who sometimes question their desire to live. I pray they find, as I did, a dream big enough to live for and turn the negatives in their lives to positives. I also pray they can feel the love God has for them and the peace of knowing He is watching over them as God did for me.

ACKNOWLEDGMENTS

———————————

Writing this book has been a journey, a journey not taken alone. Along the way, I've been supported and uplifted by many individuals who, in their own unique ways, have positively influenced my life and the creation of this book.

I am indebted to my children Natalie, Parker, Heidi, Michael, and Christopher, who have been instrumental pillars of support and inspiration. I'm grateful for your patience, love, and the valuable perspectives you've offered throughout this process. Perhaps most importantly, you gave me the opportunity to fulfill my single most important dream–to be a mom.

A warm thank you to my therapist, Dr. Julia Connelly, whose encouragement and guidance were pivotal in deciding to pen my experiences. It was your belief in me and in the therapeutic power of storytelling that got me started on this path.

To Lara Helmling, my editor, whose keen eye and thoughtful suggestions were invaluable in shaping the final manuscript, I extend my heartfelt gratitude. It was those moments when you would say, "What are you talking about here?" I would close my eyes and think, explaining it as best I could, until you said, "Okay, I think I know what you're trying to say." Your patience, dedication and expertise have helped me better articulate my experiences and emotions, translating the riddles in my head into words that everyone can understand.

I am particularly grateful to Christian and Lisa Mortensen. Your friendship, understanding, and compassionate guidance helped me embrace and understand my autism. Even when I didn't want it to be true, you encouraged me, and walked alongside me, helping me understand that just because I am autistic does not mean I am broken. You were the catalysts for my self-discovery and personal growth, and I cannot thank them enough.

To my dad, I owe a great deal. In a chaotic household, your calm demeanor and accepting nature provided the stability I needed. Your strength and acceptance have been my rock, even now that you are passed from this world.

I want to extend my deepest gratitude to those who took the time to read the early versions of this manuscript and provide me with invaluable feedback. Your input was critical in refining and strengthening my narrative. Special thanks to my dear friend Jan, who encouraged me to delve deeper and express the full range of my emotions in this book. Your push for honesty and authenticity made this work resonate more powerfully. You reminded me that my feelings are the bedrock of this story, and I am so grateful for your unwavering support and encouragement.

Ironically, it was the most traumatic and challenging moments in my life that laid the foundation for the growth and transformation I have experienced. Through adversity, I have found strength and resilience, and for this, I owe a few unusual acknowledgments.

I want to thank God for blessing me with an autistic mind. This unique way of thinking became a shield, protecting me from the full brunt of my mother's animosity. Through it, I found ways to survive and thrive in an environment that should have left me dead, in prison, or addicted to drugs.

A strange gratitude extends to my mother, for not fulfilling your expressed wish to end my life. From surviving your harsh treatment, I found a well of resilience within me, a testament to the power of the human survival instinct.

To my wife, thank you for the pain of divorce. This heart-wrenching loss was a catalyst, flipping the switch that stirred me to write about the dismissed pain of my childhood. You inadvertently gave me the push I needed to confront my past, heal, and grow.

And so, I conclude these acknowledgments with the wisdom of Alfred Lord Tennyson: "'Tis better to have loved and lost than never to have loved at all." Despite the pain and adversity, every experience has been instrumental in shaping the person I am today. They have formed the narrative of my life, a narrative I now have the privilege of sharing with you in this book.

INNOCENT BEGINNINGS

I cried. Curled up on my bed, hands pressed against my stinging face, I sobbed. Tears soaked my pillow in the dark room that I shared with my younger brother. The pain of mommy's[1] fist landing on my jaw burned like fire. It wasn't only the punch that hurt. My heart was shattered.

Mommy stormed into my bedroom. "Stop your crying or I will give you something to cry about!" Just as abruptly she left, slamming the door behind her.

I struggled to stop crying. I hurt my mommy's ears when I cried, but mommy's knuckles hurt my face.

I couldn't count how many times this same scene had played out in my ten years of life.

The next day I made a decision.

I was done with being hit.

I vowed that mommy would never hit me again.

Yet the truth was I was powerless to stop her as long as I lived in my ten-year-old body.

I knew then she would never love me, no matter what I did. I couldn't control that. I couldn't control her hitting me. I couldn't stop her from hating

---

1 Throughout this work, I have purposefully used a lowercase 'm' for mother, because she just doesn't deserve the honor and respect of having a capital letter. This book is a healing journey, and here at the beginning of our path I simply cannot give her that honor. As I wrote this, I wondered if I would ever be able to give her the respect that God indeed wants us to give our parents, considering how she had treated me. I won't spoil the story by telling you how things work out.

me.

But I could control myself.

I could stop crying.

I could stop caring.

I could stop living.

That was the only way to stop her.

I went to the kitchen. Neither mother nor Daddy was home, so I was free to execute my plan. I rummaged through the knife drawer. A knife to the heart seemed the only fix.

I walked to the living room, standing next to the china cabinet, with the knife held in front of me. My four brothers were playing a game, a game from which they had excluded me as usual. I handed a very sharp blade to my older brother Billy, the one who hated me the most. He was the one who would do things to get mother to beat me. He even burned me with lit cigarettes. He was the one most likely to enjoy killing me.

At the top of my voice I screamed hysterically, "KILL ME! STAB ME TO DEATH! KILL ME!"

My older brother Billy paused and turned. He looked me square in the eye, and he laughed. "I'm not going to kill you."

All of my brothers laughed with him.

My heart sank. I stood motionless, staring. I didn't know what to do next.

My brothers returned to the game.

It was as if I wasn't there.

I turned back to my bedroom.

I lay on my bed, defeated and alone. I was still physically alive, but that day was a turning point. I made a decision.

It wasn't the failed suicide attempt or my brother's callous laughter or the countless beatings and screaming from mommy. It was mommy's knuckles to my face. That one action, complete with the pure hate on her face as she struck me, proved to me that she didn't love me. It confirmed what mommy had told me countless times: that she should have never had me, that she should have left me in the cart at the department store or given me away or drowned me in the tub when she had the chance.

Before this point, I had tried to earn her love. I thought maybe I could change her mind. Now I saw that my failure was complete.

Over and over again she had told me this, and now she had proved it to me. Without a doubt, she didn't love me. My brothers didn't love me. Worse, they were cruel to me.

Daddy didn't hate me, but he didn't stop them. He loved me, but he never defended me.

I was surrounded by pain and lovelessness, yet I had a light within me that shone in the darkness. That light was in stark contrast to the world I lived in.

My face still throbbed, a reminder of the undeniable truth.

I needed to be valued, important, and purposeful to others. But now I knew for sure that no one was going to recognize that. Not unless I did something about it.

At that moment I decided to give to others what I had been denied. Value.

I changed, turning negative into positive, bending mother's dominance over me. I turned her clichés of rejection and disdain into a formula for success. I knew I would succeed at something, but I didn't know what that would be yet. I started to practice this by valuing my friends, treating them like I wanted to be treated. In the years that followed, I applied this formula by valuing my customers, treating them with the utmost importance, giving them that which I craved.

It was the way that my daddy treated people. He was kind and compassionate to people, and to me, though in my home mother's cruelty ruled.

Through it all, looking back, I can see that I was blessed with my daddy's disposition to be kind and serve others and also, unlike everyone else in my family, with the desire to know God.

This is my story. It is the story of a boy coming into his own in an environment that did everything it could to stop him...to rob him of his innocence, his self worth, his determination to live.

It is the story of how he used that same environment to persevere, to survive, to thrive, and to overcome. Through years of therapy and self-study, I've learned that my mother was enslaved by narcissistic rage. I've learned that the grip of narcissistic manipulation by a parent can be likened to Stockholm Syndrome, and when that is added to the struggles of a boy on the autism spectrum with homosexual desires, issues like self-love, secrets of the soul, and faith in God enter a creative mix that yields unique and powerful results. In my life, that mix yielded an intense desire to become the mom I never had, a determination to be a successful family man in the traditional sense, and to believe in myself no matter what.

That intense desire drove that decision I made at ten years old. This is the story of how I used that decision to achieve more than I had ever dreamed, how I discovered myself through the riddles of autism, and how God's unwavering love watched over me, even when I didn't see it, even when I didn't know He was there.

CHAPTER ONE

LEMONS, LEMONADE, AND PROPHETS

"Have you been taking your Risperdal?"

I nodded back at my psychiatrist. I can't remember his name now, but I do recall he was an older man with gray hair, a mustache, and small black-rimmed glasses. I replied, "I have."

"Have you noticed anything different?"

"I have."

"What have you noticed that's different?"

"My pee stinks, like after eating asparagus!"

He looked down at his notes, squinting his brow. "Hmmm." He scribbled notes with a pencil on his clipboard. It sounded like fingernails on a chalkboard to my ears. It always has.

I asked, "Why did you put me on Risperdal?" I didn't wait for his answer. I immediately asked another question. "What is Risperdal?"

Answering my last question first, he said, "Risperdal is an antipsychotic drug. It's a mild treatment for schizophrenia, bipolar disorder, or irritability caused by autism."

"Well, I'm not schizophrenic, I'm not bipolar, and I don't have autism!" I asked my first question again, "So why did you put me on Risperdal?"

"You keep talking about this vision you had as a child, building a canyon in detail." He paused, then said, "That's not normal. People don't build canyons. Canyons are formed."

I thought, 'I don't know why he told me that. I know they're formed, but that doesn't mean I couldn't build one. And I had built one.'

I had described my canyon in detail to him, the one I had built at my farm. It was the land I had bought years earlier to build my world in. I had borrowed the earth-moving equipment needed to dig the canyon out of the hillside, but I hadn't stopped there. I told him, "I designed a house using the lay of the land to incorporate a very unusual and unique home. There was an old canal at the base of my canyon, and I decided to use it as a dry moat around the front of the house."

I knew the home would be really unusual.

I described a working drawbridge as a part of the driveway, driving my car across the bridge, over the moat, and through a tall arch. The arch was a part of the house, leading into the canyon. I made a u-turn into the garage. The bridge would be down most of the time, but it was designed to work as an actual drawbridge. That was for the purpose of building it in the first place. If I wanted to close it, I would close it.

I continued, "The front door would be on the inside of the canyon, which meant no salesman would ever knock on my door trying to sell me something I would buy and didn't need. There wouldn't be a door for him to knock on unless he walked across the bridge while it was down. Even if he walked across the bridge, he would have to walk into my canyon and knock on the door to the house. I would be so impressed by his tenacity to make such an effort, if he went that far, I would buy from him whatever he had to sell me, whether I needed it or not, although I thought that was a longshot.

I continued, "The home would have the outer shape of a question mark, again following the lay of the land. The dot would be where I built an enclosed swimming pool overlooking the canyon. Windows would surround three of the four sides of the pool area. The south windows would overlook the canyon below, and in view of the north facing slope of the canyon in the background. A vista of spruce and pine trees I planted would shoot skyward, up the north facing slope of the canyon to its ridgeline. It would be breathtaking!"

People would ask me, 'Is this natural?'

I would tell them, 'No, I built all of this. In a way you're walking inside my mind!'

That might be a scary thought to them, so I would half laugh to ease any tension. The east windows would face the Wasatch Mountains in the distance, and the north windows would overlook the naturally cut of the valley by the River Jordan below. It would be very different and very lovely.

I had told all of this to my psychiatrist in the past. Now, as he was telling me how abnormal all of this was, I stated, "You never asked me why I wanted to build a canyon!"

He relented, saying, "Okay, why did you want to build a canyon?"

"Because the wind blows hard most of the time, and I wanted the canyon to block the wind so the children could go out into the yard and play without getting blown away."

With my clear explanation, he looked at his notes and again said, "Hmmm." Then he added, "I'm going to recommend you stop taking Risperdal and see another psychiatrist in the building. His name is Dr. Keaton."

After seeing him the past two weeks, with no resolution, I was glad to move on again. He handed me a piece of paper to make an appointment with Dr. Keaton. I liked this name immediately. If I wasn't mistaken, there was a Keaton who played Batman in the movies. I liked Batman.

My married life had become an array of mental health practitioners—a parade of psychologists, psychiatrists, and counselors. I was getting used to it. My wife Estie was convinced I had mental problems. I knew I wasn't mentally ill. I was just different. So what if I was different? Nonetheless I was willing to scratch Estie's itch, seeing one mental health professional after another. It had become a way of life for me. More than anything I wanted to save my marriage. I'd seen a long list of people who tried to understand, or at least explain what my problem was. If I even had a problem.

The reason they couldn't find a problem is because they didn't ask the right questions.

I set up an appointment with Dr. Keaton the following week. I was sitting in the waiting room, nervously anticipating Dr. Keaton's invitation to his office. I imagined what his office might look like when I walked through the door.

I envisioned a psychiatrist's couch like the ones I saw in the old movies: an elongated couch with a short curved back, allowing me to put my left arm up against the backside of it while my legs stretched across the cushions. I could pretend like I was a movie star, looking suave and debonair, using my right hand across my forehead like I was in pain or in anguish as I answered his questions. I would interrupt the doctor's question by asking him, "Do you mind if I smoke?"

I didn't smoke.

Dr. Keaton walked into the waiting room and said, "Robert?"

I snapped out of my reverie. "Yes."

He said, "Hi, I'm Dr. Keaton. Follow me please."

I did what he asked.

Upon entering his office he said, "Please, take a chair."

It wasn't what I had envisioned. As I took a seat, I noted it was comfortable even if it wasn't the long couch that I had envisioned.

Dr. Keaton said "Why are you here?"

I told him, "My wife thinks I have mental problems."

Dr. Keaton looked at his notes and said, "I'm going to ask you a series of questions.'"

I said, "Okay."

He said, "Starting at 100, count backwards by 3."

4

I thought, 'I wished he had said by twos. That would be easy.' Nobody ever asked me to count backwards by threes before. I thought, 'I hope I can do this.' I started confidently, "100...97...94...91...88..." I processed the next numbers in my head before the number came out of my mouth. I wanted to come across as I can count backwards by threes, no sweat!...85?" I paused thinking, I hope I get the next one right. "82?...79?"

He stopped me.

I thought he was going to tell me, 'You don't know how to count backwards, start over again.' He didn't. Dr. Keaton asked me two more questions I don't remember, because I was recounting the last question inside my head, hoping I gave him the right answer. I didn't pay attention to his other two questions. Then he gave me his diagnosis. He said, "You don't have a mental problem. Your problem is that you need a woman who loves you!"

I was stunned at his answer. Deep down, I knew he was right.

I left his office, stopping for a brief moment at the marquee on the wall bearing his name behind the glass casing. I wanted to spell his name out in my head, so I had a visual of his name. While staring at the letters 'Doctor Keaton,' I thought, 'He's a good man, just like Batman!'

I never told Estie what Dr. Keaton said that day. I felt if I told her what my doctor said, she would probably say something like, 'Your doctor is right! You should go find someone who loves you!' Whether it was true or not, or whether the whole story was just made up inside my head, the thought of a possible divorce brought back painful memories of my upbringing.

My mind took me back to mother and her rejection of me when I was young. History seemed to be repeating itself in my marriage. I was uneasy with the similarities between Estie's and mother's insecurities. They were eerily similar to me, but why? I still loved both of them, as I understood love. Maybe Estie was hoping one of these mental health professionals could identify what my problem was and fix me. Mother had done the same by putting me in special education programs. Or maybe Estie was looking to have something declared that would justify a divorce, just as mother seemed to daydream about getting rid of me.

It might have all been all in my imagination, but it was real to me. It all brought a queasy feeling to my stomach. I had never wanted mother to abandon me. I didn't want Estie to divorce me now. I decided not to say anything to Estie about what Dr. Keaton had said.

After seeing Dr. Keaton, a new family moved into our church's neighborhood. I asked if I could be the 'home teacher' to the new move-in. The husband was very beautiful to me, and I wanted to be around him. I never told him or anyone about my feelings for him, and I never acted on my attraction. In short order, I was given the assignment to befriend and teach gospel lessons to Christian and Lisa Mortensen along with their family. I was excited to get to know them.

Feeling inadequate, I had surrounded myself with people who were more beautiful than me. Christian was very beautiful to me. My son and I began visiting the Mortensen family monthly. Lisa, expecting twins, always sat on the right side of the couch with Christian on the left. Our relationship between the two families began to grow. Understanding each other's family dynamics sketched out a friendship beyond monthly visits.

I didn't know it at the time, but our relationship with the Mortensens would be crucial to my self-discovery and personal growth. They would be the ones who encouraged me to seek answers about autism. The Mortensens themselves had been studying autism, because one of their children's behavior was different from the others. He was ultimately diagnosed with autism.

Both Lisa and Christian continued to study autism because of their children's diagnosis. My monthly visits to the Mortensens seemed enjoyable, even beyond the gospel lessons. We would spend a good hour with them and their children, talking about our life experiences. I thought stories of my past were interesting, even funny. At that time, I didn't see any of the abuse or any of the trauma. I was oblivious to the social meanings of what I had experienced. I just thought it was normal. It was just how mother was. Sometimes my stories went on for so long, I was invited for dinner. Everyone was getting hungry. As I told more stories, both Lisa and Christian noticed a pattern of behavior. While I talked, I didn't know I was being assessed. Christian and Lisa were tallying up my stories under an autism column. Without me knowing it, they were thinking of how they could help Estie and me in our marriage. They thought maybe an autism diagnosis would help us understand what was happening so that we could have a better relationship.

They mentioned autism frequently because of their son, but I never connected the dots that they were gently hinting that I might have autism. The autism conversations were not directed towards me, so I didn't think the subject was about me. I was wrong.

Years later Lisa said to me, "Your wife introduced herself to me five years ago saying, "You'll meet my husband. He has autism." Lisa laughed. "I was blown away by how she introduced you!"

Christian confirmed what Lisa was saying. "After hearing your stories over the last five years, I think you should go get tested at the University of Utah for autism. They have specialists who can determine whether you have autism or not. Honestly, both Christian and I think you do have autism."

I said, "I don't want to be tested for autism. I don't want to be put on Ritalin or some other psychological drug if it's true!"

Lisa laughed again. "If you have autism that doesn't mean you're going to be put on some psychological drugs at all. All they're going to do is test you to determine whether you have autism or not."

Fearing an outcome I didn't want, I resisted. I said, "That's it?"

Lisa said, "That's it!"

I surrendered myself under pressure. From a self-imposed belief, I still feared I would be drugged if it was determined to have autism. I also resisted because I didn't want to validate the idea that I was broken. Still, I gathered the fee to cover the cost to be tested, set an appointment, and became vulnerable with the results.

Estie accompanied me, waiting to be asked questions about my behavior to validate any misconception about whether I had autism or not. She had experienced years of confusion with me and some of my behaviors. She couldn't fully understand my behavior, and it had brought her nearly to a breaking point in our relationship.

I can't remember now what behaviors she found to be unusual, because they never made enough sense to me to remember. I do recall her saying, "How can you not understand? Everybody would understand what I'm saying. Everyone except you."

In response, I would say, "So there's seven billion people on the earth, so 6,999,999,999 would understand, just not me."

I had no idea that this response was devaluing her by not giving her the validation she needed in that moment. Because of the lack of social context, I couldn't possibly have known that I was hurting our relationship.

I left to go into a separate room to be tested. A psychologist asked me a series of questions. I responded in my fashion. I was given puzzles and odd shapes to put together as the tester observed me. I also found myself irritated with the woman testing me. I felt she was irritated with me, maybe because she looked nine and a half months pregnant. I stared at her pregnant form, thinking she must be miserable. I would be if I was that pregnant. I imagined that she probably wished she wasn't there testing me, but home in a more comfortable environment.

The tester asked me more questions. I became more irritated with her as if I was pregnant, and I expressed my irritation towards her. The tester snapped back at me, confirming my thought. I wasn't necessarily testing her.

I was truly irritated, but I did not understand why. I figured she'd probably go home after testing me and have her baby in a few minutes.

After a few weeks recovering from giving birth, she wrote up my papers. It was a ten page memorandum outlining my behavioral patterns. She found my behavior consistent with an autism diagnosis. She sent it to me by mail.

The suspicions of Estie, Lisa, and Christian were confirmed.

I was newly labeled at 54 as autistic!

I was immediately concerned they would want to put me on medication. I was relieved that the only time they suggested that drugs might be of value would be years in the future, when I got older.

Somehow when they told me that I might only need drugs later in life, I thought they were confirming what I believed from the beginning: I didn't have autism.

Looking back, I know this makes no sense, because the paperwork had just said I had autism. Honestly, throughout the writing of this book I was looking for evidence everywhere that I don't have autism. I have tried and tried to convince myself that I don't have autism. Probably because to me autism means I'm broken, and I refuse to accept that. So the brokenness, really, is in my belief that autism makes me broken.

It doesn't.

I believed that autism was a mental illness.

It isn't.

It is a condition that merely indicates that I have a different way of thinking, a different way of perceiving reality and interacting with the world. If the autistic way of seeing the world was normal, if it was the way the majority of people perceived things, then autism wouldn't be a condition at all. It would be the norm.

At the time of my testing, when I was so annoyed with the woman conducting the evaluation, I thought, 'What will the diagnosis change anyway, if it was accurate? Nothing!' Now I found myself ruminating over this diagnosis, and my mind returned to all the events that had led to this point. I was only there getting the test to save my marriage. I couldn't see how they would tell me anything important or add to my life in any way. I thought, 'So what if I'm different?! Different from what? What is normal anyway?' In my view, being different was normal. I wanted to have the diagnosis rescinded! I had never labeled myself from the comments mother made. "Why do you have to be so different?" "Can't you talk intelligent?" "I wish I'd never had you." I had accepted that I was different and even that people may not understand me, but I didn't let that define me. I accepted it, but I didn't take it any further than that.

And that is the blessing of autism. To this day, I am able to tune out of outer influences to protect my innocence, the pureness of my soul and the core of who I am.

I set up an appointment with the head of the Neurology Department at the University of Utah, Dr. Julia Connelly. I was determined to prove to her that I didn't have autism.

I brought my autism assessment to my appointment with her. I told her, "I want to have my diagnosis rescinded!" I handed her my papers.

She thumbed through them for a moment, looking at what she wanted to see at her discretion. She said, "We'll see."

Leaving the papers with her, we started talking. I was hoping it would be done in one or two visits. Dr. Connelly wasn't so quick. By the end of the first visit I had failed to convince her. She wanted to know more.

I thought, 'She just wants to get paid for my return.' Even so, I returned faithfully each week.

I grew to like Julia. Telling Julia stories about my past seemed satisfying for me, and moreover Dr. Connelly was another female who listened to me. I had a lot to get off my chest and out of my mind, and she was a great help.

I had already been seeing a therapist, Dr. Karen Bellings. I had been seeing her for two years. Dr. Bellings was helping me in my marriage. I had been sharing years of my experiences with mother in order to heal the connection between Estie and me. I told Dr. Bellings, "Dr. Connelly thinks I'm on the autism spectrum."

Dr. Bellings disagreed. "I believe it's trauma, not autism, that is the real issue with your behavior." She continued, "Your upbringing was similar to the people in concentration camps of World War II. It was almost as bad, maybe worse in some cases, because they didn't know the person they were torturing. Your own mother knew who you were, her own son!"

It shocked me that she compared my life to being in a concentration camp. With such a stark comparison, I started thinking about the films I viewed in junior high school history class.

Dr. Bellings's point was well taken with me.

Yet after seeing Dr. Connelly who was convinced I have autism, I began settling into the possibility that it might be true.

But then I was confused.

Dr. Bellings was pretty firm, saying, "You don't have autism, Robert!" I vacillated in the search of my mind for something definitive between autism and upbringing. At times I even became irritated with Dr. Bellings for trying to take away this identity I was starting to relate to.

I switched in my mind from thinking Dr. Bellings was trying to help me to thinking she was someone who was trying to take away my identity.

I found myself mentally protecting my identity as an autistic person more and more. I thought, 'My identity is who I am, straight or gay, autistic or not. God gave me the gift of agency, and He created me in this body and this identity, and my gift back to God is self-control.' I thought firmly, 'Nobody has that right to take away another person's identity!'

Eventually, I realized Dr. Bellings just had a different perspective. I came to the conclusion in my mind that Dr. Bellings was trying to help me, not take away my identity.

Still, I continued vacillating. I didn't 'feel' autistic, whatever that was supposed to feel like.

Autism was beginning to become an identity with some answers I could understand. As I bounced my head at night, I couldn't stop thinking, 'Why did I want to be a mom? How did I survive? What made me change negative into positive so quickly? Why can I still remember all these stories in detail from so long ago? Why did others see me as being so different? What was the answer?' I didn't know anymore. Confusion filled my head.

After a few months of seeing Dr. Connelly, I asked, "Would you ever consider writing a book with me?"

Dr. Connelly replied, "No!"

Stunned at her quick response, I felt uncomfortable the rest of my visit. I let it go, moving onto other subjects. But in the back of my mind, my self-reproach continued. I thought, 'I shouldn't have asked such a dumb question! I don't even know how to read or write. I don't know what an adjective is, a pronoun, or a verb. I don't even know what a structured sentence looks like, let alone know how to enunciate words.'

In the weeks that followed, I relived the uncomfortable feeling of that interaction over and over again, thinking, 'That was such a dumb question. Don't ever ask that question again!'

Why those words came out of my mouth in the first place, I didn't understand. Except I remembered somebody saying to mother long ago, "You should write a book!"

Mother replied, "No one would read it!"

I thought, 'Nobody reads an unwritten book!'

I never brought up writing a book again. I continued visiting Dr. Connelly each week as well as Dr. Bellings. I was trying to comprehend the two dichotomies: with mother, my childhood experiences going into adulthood, and Estie.

Dr. Connelly said, "Do you remember asking me about writing a book with you about three months ago?"

I said, "Yes. I saw the PhD under your name and thought you would give it credibility if I wrote a book with you."

Dr. Connelly said, "It would not be appropriate for me to write a book with you as you're one of my clients. That's why I turned you down."

I understood what she was saying from past experiences with other therapists. I knew she was a good therapist then and there.

Dr. Connelly continued, "I do think you should write a book, Robert! You have a lot of interesting stories inside of you. You talk about your past experience with your mother as if they are all positive. That's not normal for what you've gone through."

I said, "I don't know how to write. I don't know how to type. I don't know how to spell. I don't know how to punctuate. I can hardly enunciate words!"

Dr. Connelly said, "Don't worry about that. That's what editors are for."

With her encouragement I set out to write, but write about what?

After leaving her office with the determination to write a book, I decided I needed to write with a purpose. I had heard there is a high suicide rate in the LGBTQ+ community. Then I learned that the rate in the autistic community is even higher…nine times higher for autistic people than LGBTQ+ people. I was so surprised to hear that. If this was true, I would have a purpose to write.

I asked Dr. Connelly on my next visit if this was a correct assessment.

Dr. Connelly said, "Yes, it is true!" She continued, "It's very prevalent in both communities."

I said, "Really?!"

Dr. Connelly nodded her head, and said, "It is!"

I feel that I found my purpose to write.

As I sat in Dr. Connelly's office I thought, 'I don't understand why people would kill themselves over identity or same sex-attraction when those feelings saved my life, even inspired me. What was I missing? Why did my attractions give me energy and enthusiasm when others viewed them as a death sentence?' I didn't have an answer, but I knew my story, and my story wouldn't let go of me.

My story imprisoned my mind. Between mother, me, and my identity, I was bound by my past. Even though I used my past to turn negatives into positives, my mind was shackled within the frames that mother had created, determining how I viewed life and myself. In some respects, my autism freed me to keep the world at arm's length, and the desire to be a mom gave me direction, motivating me to make the most out of my life.

People thought that if I wrote my story, I would heal. But it didn't heal me, it revealed me to me…me as I really am. It revealed the truth, that I do have autism. For how, except through the innocence of autism, could I have survived what I went through without any consciousness of it?

At the time I was visiting Dr. Connelly, these insights were still beyond my understanding. Yet I kept probing my mind, wondering, why were my experiences so different from others? How would that make a good book? I told Dr. Connelly that I had a lot to think about.

The following week I said to Dr. Bellings, "I'm going to write a book, and you're a part of my life." Dr. Bellings was surprised, concurring it was a good idea for me to write a book, and on the subject I felt passionate about.

It never occurred to me that I could write a book. After all, I considered myself illiterate. But once she opened my eyes to the possibility of having an editor help me, I accepted the challenge with the same excitement and determination I had applied to other impossible dreams–being a mom, owning land–things people told me would never happen, could never happen. Like in the past where I was told, "you'll never own land" or "you'll never make it in the lawn business." Obstacles meant nothing to me. Once I decided to write, once I had a purpose in writing the book, I found a way. I had a bigger purpose than their 'can't.' My bigger purpose propelled me past my own can'ts and theirs, too.

In spite of my inability to write, in spite of being functionally illiterate, I started writing without a computer or laptop. I talked into my phone, and my phone converted it to text. I didn't know how to type, so talking to text worked for me.

I didn't let anything stop me.

Since then I have used writing as a portal to communicate my complex thoughts, my feelings, and in the process I even learned to read fluently.

This is my story.

ROBERT BAUTNER

CHAPTER TWO

NOT ANOTHER ONE

Daddy was born in the village of Homburg in Bavaria, Germany in 1913 and mother was born to German immigrants in Chicago, Illinois in 1919. As for me, I was born in a small house on Stewart Street in Salt Lake City, Utah, the fourth of five boys.

Out in front of the house on Stewart Street in Salt Lake City, Utah, Norm Tabish, our longtime next door neighbor, paced back and forth on the sidewalk with a cigar hanging down from the corner of his mouth. Head low, hands behind his back, he stopped. He pulled the cigar from his mouth, raised his head, and muttered, "Why doesn't that woman have her babies in the hospital like everybody else?" Norm ranted on and on to anyone who would listen. He paced, nervously awaiting the news, and wearing down the sidewalk outside the house.

Inside the house, mother labored for hours.

"PUSH!" the doctor said, "PUSH!"

"I'M PUSHING!" mother exclaimed. "GET THIS BABY OUT OF ME!"

In a frantic cry, as if to say enough is enough, the doctor said, "Focus, another PUSH!"

A moment later, crowning.

"Keep PUSHING! Here it comes!"

The minutes seemed to pass like hours as Norm listened to the commotion inside the house from his well-worn spot on the sidewalk.

"KEEP PUSHING!"

"IS IT OUT YET?" mother yelled.

"There's the head, one more PUSH!"

"IS IT OUT?" mother yelled again.

"Keep PUSHING!"

One shoulder out, then the other, soon revealed the newborn babe to the world.

"It's a boy!" the midwife said.

"A..." Mother took a breath. "Boy." Mother's voice was heavy with disappointment.

"What time is it?" asked the doctor.

"11:06 a.m." said the midwife.

"Another boy!" mother said again, lowering her head. She was exhausted and desperately disappointed. "I was hoping for a girl!"

Mother had had three boys and three miscarriages prior to me. That may have contributed to her disappointment. With three boys in her progeny, a girl would have been a nice finishing touch.

The doctor pinched off the umbilical cord with clamps and handed a pair of scissors to Daddy. With a firm grip and a steady hand, Daddy cut through the tough cord, completing my separation from mother.

While the midwife encouraged the placenta to arrive with a few tugs, Dr. Allred took my vitals and a footprint to verify that I was a live birth on the certificate. "All is well," he said, handing me to mother. "He's the cleanest baby I've ever delivered! He's a beautiful boy. Here you go, mommy." With that, he finished his purpose.

With the breath of life in my soul, I was born June 27, 1961. As mother took me in her arms, she thought immediately, this one is different! Mother would never come to grips with the child whom she just birthed into this world.

Daddy stepped outside the door of the house to tell the neighbor Norm. When Norm saw him, he stopped pacing, pulling the cigar out of his mouth, raised his eyebrows, and looked at Daddy quietly with a clenched mouth. "Well?"

Daddy replied in a calm voice, saying, "It's another boy."

Norm sighed in relief that it was all over, congratulating Daddy immediately. When the coast was clear, Norm and his wife Barbara were invited in to see me. After that, they both retired to their home for Norm to rest from his labors.

Mother had made arrangements for a home birth early on as a result of her negative experiences in the hospital with Frank, their first baby. Saying, "They spanked him so hard that it knocked his hip out of joint. That kept him from walking his first 15 months. Then when I wasn't looking, those bastards put silver nitrate in his eyes before I could tell them, 'NO!' That was the final straw!" Mother was no longer going to have her babies in a hospital after that. Mother had decided the rest of her children would be born at home.

She sought the services of a doctor who specialized in home deliveries, Dr. Rulon Allred. He worked with one of his wives as his midwife. He offered mother the type of service she was looking for. The duo delivered thousands of babies at home with success. Mother was comfortable knowing this and hired them.

Dr. Allred belonged to a polygamous sect in Utah, sometimes referred to as the Fundamentalist Latter-day Saint Church (FLDS). To my understanding there always seemed to be an undertone in the polygamous culture of which polygamist groups had the 'true authority of God' in their line of authority. Dr. Allred was murdered years later by two women who were sent by a rival polygamous leader to kill him. Gunned down in cold blood in May 1977, Dr. Allred had seven wives and was the reported father of forty-eight children.

I never learned how mother knew him or got in contact with Dr. Allred. That information remains a mystery to this day. I was told the story of how Dr. Allred handed me over to mother and said, "He is the cleanest baby I've ever delivered!" Dr. Allred had a special place in my heart. Being born at home made me feel unique, and Dr. Allred's comment made me feel I was important. That was a feeling I needed.

Besides being another boy, mother sensed a noticeable difference in me from the other three boys from day one. Her disposition never softened about wishing I was a girl. Despite her disappointment with my sex, mother kept me and nurtured me the best she could, all the while growing weary of me. She had baptized me into a Lutheran Church shortly after birth, following the same tradition as she had done with the first three boys. But mother never graced the entrance of a church again.

As a newborn I gazed about me as if dazed in hypnosis. I was wide-eyed with a blank stare. Home was the place where mother screamed at my older brothers constantly. She yelled at them, simultaneously beating them, and they cried in pain and anguish in response. I was becoming a part of an uncomfortable but familiar environment of rage. First through sounds, then sight, it was a feeling I didn't understand. I could only process each individual moment, taking it into my mind and processing it through my sensory system. I processed it through the senses, but I did not understand the meaning of the anger before me. They were feelings I couldn't ignore, but I had to continually prepare my mind to cope with them. I was becoming conditioned to view this environment of rage as normal.

Adding to mother's unyielding and unpredictable outbursts of anger, mother became pregnant again almost immediately. Mother had believed that nursing would prevent another pregnancy, but she was wrong. At the age of 43, Mother gave birth again, just 13 months after my arrival, to another boy, Walter. Once again, the girl mother hoped for was denied. When it was all said and done mother had a total of five boys and three miscarriages. It all served to fuel mother's rage.

Vulnerable and innocent at 13 months, I suddenly found myself in the arms of my brothers rather than mother's. Whatever connection I had as the youngest child to mother and my environment was lost. The fragmented society of brothers, each caught up in his own survival, became my world. An innate withdrawal occurred within me. Hearing my older brothers being yelled at, then seeing them beat from a familiar presence, mother. Frank, ten years older than me, was regularly punished for his actions as a young boy. He was repeatedly beaten into submission into a residual alliance with mother's policies.

At nearly two years old, my ears captured the snap of a stick broken over the back of another brother. The sound jumped and startled me. A once calm soul was shaken. Hermann, eight years older than me, was being beaten for disobeying mother's demands and not meeting her expectations. She imposed her will over ours routinely yet inconsistently so that nobody knew what was coming. With each incident I absorbed a barrage of yelling, screaming, and loud voices into my being. My senses within witnessed rage daily, instilling an uneasiness in me.

My body captured the pain as if it was me being beaten. There was no escape. As my mind absorbed it all, I concluded that silence was the only way to combat the hostilities of my environment. I had to protect and manage my feelings, maybe my life, if I was going to survive. If I didn't learn to control my emotions, I believed mother might kill me.

Pooping my pants at the age of two, I became the next target. Mother said, "Two years old and still pooping your pants!" She then blistered my butt with intensity, with the intent to train me in her fashion, for her convenience, under her policies. With each swing of her hand stopping at my butt, saying, "DON'T EVER POOP YOUR PANTS AGAIN! DO YOU UNDERSTAND ME?" With one last swing to my behind, crying louder with each blow, I felt the results of her punishment with the sting of her hand, hearing the angry tone of her voice. Mother's actions wrenched my heart in anguish and spiked the innate fear within as I cried aloud. I was becoming all too familiar with this environment. The blistering of my butt for pooping my pants only added to the physical reality of my mortality.

Blistering my butt again at the age of three, for climbing the fence in the front yard saying, "You ripped a nice little 'L' on the side of your pants just before family pictures!" The tone of her voice and the anger in her countenance reached deep inside of me once again. Without hesitation, out of control, mother beat me, saying, "I'll teach you a lesson!" Each swing of mother's hand stinging on my bum gave me plenty of reason to never climb a fence again.

Even by the age of four, I didn't talk at all. "Hun." Grunting was my only method of communication when I needed attention. Friends of mother said, "Maybe you should have him tested and find out if he is retarded?" It was the normal term they used at that time for anything out of the ordinary. Mother replied to concerned friends and neighbors, "He's not retarded. He's just lazy. He'll talk when he's ready!" Those friends were speechless at her reply, and the subject ended immediately. I never uttered a single word in my defense.

My brother Billy, four years older than me, became another harsh reality of home. He had a devious nature which he turned on me. Yet he was mother's favorite, and mother referred to him as "my pretty little Billy." She probably favored him because of his jet-black hair like Daddy's. Mother spared him from beatings; instead she turned a blind eye to his sneaky, sadistic behavior toward me.

In this environment, it wasn't safe for me to talk, not now. Being mute was an effective way of controlling my environment. Grunting to communicate was my best defense, the best solution I could come up with to protect myself from the environment I was born into. Being muted in silence became my friend for the time being, quieting the turmoil and unrest which filled my mind and penetrated my heart. Mother's uncontrollable anger continued affecting my soul. I needed to protect myself each and every day. My innate security became compromised. Through silence, I was drawn into a safe place inside the innocence of my mind.

CHAPTER THREE

IN VOICELESS SILENCE

Mother's lust to collect was only outdone by her undefined compulsion, fueling a void that was never filled. Knick knacks, one of my mother's favorite compulsions, razzled and dazzled her imagination, filling her eyes with glitter beyond the twinkle of Daddy's eye on their honeymoon night.

Mother amassed a significant collection of knick knacks, antiques and collectibles, everything from an irreplaceable Japanese bowl given to her by the mother of her childhood friend Latta to depression-era glass, unique vases, and other inanimate objects that she deemed worthy of her possession and stature. They were all meaningful to her. They brought her a sense of importance, filling the empty void inside her heart. But the void always returned, emptier than before. Of course, children did not fill mother's void. Children, especially me, expanded her void.

At some point mother decided she needed a place to display her knick knacks, collectibles and antiques, a place that would be out of reach from her children but on display for the world to see, particularly anyone who came to the front door. Mother's love of shopping sent her on a search for such a cabinet. It wasn't difficult to find the cabinet; it was more like the cabinet found her. It radiated 'take me home.' Mother purchased it, having it delivered immediately.

The cabinet fit mother's motif. It fit her style, it fit her personality, it was beautiful, just like mother. An antique tiger oak wood frame cabinet standing about six feet tall with short bold sturdy legs, supporting two thin curved glass windows on either side of a curved framed door. It was a classic, just like mother. The knob, a cute little wooden thing with a tiny wooden button in the center, was pushed to open the door. Hearing the eerie creak of the hinges was adorable. To my eyes and ears, the cabinet was mother to a tee. To this day, every time I hear an eerie creak or see a china cabinet, I think of her. Its full length, silver-backed mirror reflected the backside of mother's collection, adding to its charm, just like mother. It was important to her to place the cabinet front and center as people walked through the front door of the house. It was all about show and tell. It was all about entertainment. It was all about mother.

Items inside the china cabinet, antiques or not, were just as important to mother as the cabinet itself. Mother made herself very clear, "DON'T touch my china cabinet! DON'T even break it accidentally with your roughhousing in the front room. Stay away from my cabinet! Hands off!"

This message was never misunderstood by me. Hearing and feeling the tone of her voice, I felt mother's expectations. "Look with your eyes, and not with your hands, or I will blister your butt!" This was not a faint gesture. Mother had established my loyalty towards her through the innocence of my captivity, first through the tone of her voice, then her actions. I had plenty of experience to know that mother meant what she said, every word of it. There were no exceptions! I never doubted mother, still in my silent cocoon at the age of four. People called me retarded, but I wasn't. I understood mother perfectly and felt her words in every cell of my body. Mother threatened us, threatened me, with the thinnest of margins.

Billy decided it would be fun to open the door to the forbidden cabinet. He turned mother's treasures, all the ones at my height, upside down, intending to blame me for his crime. My inability to defend myself verbally combined with mother's disdain for me was the perfect outlet for his sadistic nature. Making sure mommy was not nearby, Billy pushed the cute little button inside the knob. Then he gave the door a slight tug, freeing it from its resting spot ever so slyly. He slowly opened the door to mask the creak of the hinges from mother's high audible sense of hearing, ever so carefully. While this was happening, I was playing, unsuspecting of what was to come, in the other room.

Billy reached his hand deep into mother's heart, front and center, to further execute his plan. Clasping and turning ever so gently each vase, cup and figurine at my height inside the cabinet upside down or on their side, ever so intently. All the while he listened and looked to make sure mommy was not nearby. Ignoring the beat of his own heart but not his intentions, he eyed mother's prized possession, the Japanese bowl. With the steadiness of both hands, Billy reached into the cabinet, removing the bowl from off its pedestal, setting it to the side of its perch. This was the gem. He stepped back, eyeing his work with glee, leaving the door ajar as a part of his plan to further the evidence against me. His plan was almost finished.

He ran to tell mommy what 'I' had done, nurturing his plan. Finding mother with his heart racing, saying with the utmost concern, "Mommy! Robert opened your china cabinet and turned your things inside the cabinet upside down!"

Mother stopped what she was doing immediately and said, "What did you say?"

Billy repeated himself with the same deep concern, making sure mother heard him correctly.

Mother dropped everything at once to verify what Billy had said was true. Seeing the cabinet door ajar and her things out of place, she verified Billy's story. With fire in her countenance, mother was not going to put up with me disobeying her.

Mother located me immediately, and with the strength of an ox grabbed me by the hand and quickly pulled my arm then my body high into the air from off the floor. I didn't understand what was going on or why mommy was doing this to me. I couldn't defend myself. I couldn't talk. Mother started beating me. I felt the sting of her hand, repeatedly with each blow of her hand on my bum, jumping upon impact with each hit. Putting my free hand to cover my backside to protect myself from another blow only inspired mother to hit me harder. Both my hand and my bum stung with her attack. I was crying and squealing from being hit from out of nowhere.

Mother said while beating me, "I told you!" With another blow and sting of her hand, I cried louder. "Never. To. Touch!" Another hit to my body, crying louder yet. "The china cabinet!" Swinging her hand once again, feeling the impact of the abrupt stop on my bum, I was crying hysterically, but mother didn't stop. She said with a clenched jaw, "Do. You. Un. Der. Stand. Me?!" One last blow to my backside.

Mother stopped hitting me as I freed myself, running to my bedroom, crying in my bed onto my pillow. Mother entered my room a short time later, demanding, "Stop your crying, or I will give you something to cry about!"

Slowly...slowly...I sobered up. I didn't know what had happened. I didn't know why mommy beat me. Billy disappeared from the scene without a word of his involvement or a crumb of remorse.

I was emotionally scarred and devastated, but I recovered. I loved mother. I'd been through this before. I regained my composure. My happiness overtook the pain as I lay on my bed thinking of the world I would build. I turned my head towards the door, staring at the ripples of dents in the knob, wondering what was on the other side of the door for me. I rejected that thought, returning back to my world, a world I knew was safe, a world inside my head, knowing that the world on the other side of the door was a different place than the one in my head and heart.

Eventually, I stood up, placing my hand on the brass latch. Carefully and slowly I twisted the knob as the springs inside the handle began jumping and clicking, breaking the quietness of my world inside of my head.

The sound seemed unnoticeable most of the time, but not this time. The springs were like beating a tin can in my eardrums. The thought went through my head that mommy might hear me opening the door and return to beat me again. I twisted the handle ever more slowly, making sure the knob did not slip from my hand, fearing the sound of the abrupt return of the handle would send an uncontrollable fear to the pit of my stomach which traveled to the core of my heart.

I didn't like that sound or the feeling that followed. I placed both hands on the knob to keep a firm grip. The sound of the knob bouncing back into place was not going to leave without an invitation to disturb mother or capture her attention.

When I couldn't twist the knob any more, I pulled the door open. It stuck for a moment. I put a bit more strength into it, just enough, so that I felt it give and begin to open. I let go of the knob. Then I emerged from my room, cautiously looking around each corner to make sure I was safe. I didn't want mommy to see me.

I didn't fear mother. I just didn't want to get beat again.

ROBERT BAUTNER

CHAPTER FOUR

THE WIDOW'S BITE

Daddy was a lithographer. He honed his craft, becoming a craftsman in the industry, which meant his work was worth its weight in gold. Daddy's work had him criss-crossing the country from Rochester, New York to Denver, Colorado. It was supposed to be a quick stop in Utah then off to California and ultimately New Zealand. If mother hadn't kept having so damn many kids, it would've happened. So mother's temporary stop in Utah continued after my birth and lasted for the rest of their lives.

Being stuck in Utah around Mormons, mother never missed an opportunity to bait unsuspecting prey into her venomous web of conversation. No matter where she was, she would start up a conversation with anyone who held still long enough to listen. Like a black widow spider luring her mate into her purpose, mother lured her prey into conversation to gain a profile of the person who stood before her. She asked innocent and subtle questions in a very calm and pleasant voice. "How long have you lived in Utah?"

As the widow's prey turned to engage her, they came closer to their fate.

Mother continued. "Are you a member of the Church?"

She responded just as calmly. Her prey became that much more comfortable with her, thinking she was a trusted member of their community. Smiles were exchanged.

31

"How many kids do you have?" It didn't matter their answer; mother had just lured her prey into her grasp, gaining their trust. Mother got what she was looking for. Now the widow's bite.

Mother unloaded on them, saying, "Why we moved to this state I'll never know! I had five kids to keep my sanity in the stupid place." This, of course, was a lie. Her real feelings were that she had had too damn many kids in the first place.

Mother continued, "Those Mormons go to their Schoffstall three times on Sunday!" 'Schoffstall' is German for the sheep barn. Mother was relentless, continuing, "They're nothing but a bunch of dumb, conniving sheep." All mother had to do is look for their garment line to keep it simple. But no, mother loved to bait people into her malignant narcissistic conversations, earning her the widow's title.

Mother picked no bones and left–no remorse. Mother was consistent. Within five minutes into a conversation with anyone, mother knew the status of the person who stood before her. How long they lived in Utah, how many children they had, and whether they were a Mormon or not. The person left with a sense of clarity. Mother was not a Mormon, that was the real message. Mother left no doubt in their mind, leaving the conversation empty with her prey wondering what just happened.

Mother found a bumper sticker she couldn't pass up. She showed it to the family first with wrathful glee. She taped it to the inside of the rear window of her car to prevent would-be thieves, 'i.e. the Mormons,' from stealing the sticker or scraping it off her bumper. The black background with orange bold lettering read, "WONDERFUL UTAH, HIGH TAXES LOW WAGES." The sticker glamorized mother's expression of Utah completely. Mother's true personality and every whisper in her head was focused on how to bait people, luring them into a conversation, then attacking them. This was all a part of mother's method of operation.

Like the widow luring her next prey, the bumper sticker in her driver's side rear window left no disappointment. Notes started appearing on mother's windshield that read, "The same road that led you here, leads you out." "Why don't you just leave?" "There's nothing making you stay here!" The notes validated mother's plan for attention and another opportunity to unload on another person. It didn't matter who she unloaded on–as long as she had the chance to be nasty to someone. The bumper sticker captured her prey. Mother read the notes to the family first, then friends. "These Mormons," she said, continuing, "These do-gooders that live in this state, they're nothing but a bunch of hypocrites!" Schtick or not, mother meant every word of what came out her mouth. I listened, I absorbed, I felt it and remembered.

Bonnie Bruns, one of the first people mother met when she moved to Utah, never fell for mother's bait. So mother didn't try to bait her and they became good friends. Bonnie and mother had a lot in common. Neither one of them were Mormons, both wondered how they ended up in Utah. This stupid state with its stupid liquor laws. Mini bottles and liquor by the drink were the only ways to buy alcohol at the time. It was a ridiculous rule to both of them. Bonnie had all girls, mother had all boys. Bonnie smoked like an old fogey stogie. Mother was a party smoker. To mother not being a Mormon was enough in common for her to be someone's friend.

Bonnie became an icon in my relationship along with mother. Standing by mother's side everywhere she went, I loved mother with all my heart.

When people said, "Hello Hedy!"

Mother responded back with a friendly, "Hello."

Turning to me, a sweet quiet boy, they would invariably ask, "Hello, what's your name?"

I didn't respond, still a mute, so mother told them, "His name is Robert. He doesn't know how to talk!" Mother added to the conversation, telling people in front of me, "I wished I never had him! I should have given him away to my friend Bonnie. She only had girls, and she always wanted a boy." Mother continued relentlessly, "I should have left him in the cart at Grand Central!" Mother was baiting me as she did everyone else. But I wasn't an easy one to bait at that time. If she perceived a low response or none at all, mother would add, "I should have drowned him in the tub when I had the chance. He always gets mad at that one!"

Mother laughed then, enjoying my angry reaction at hearing her comment while simultaneously gesturing to the person next to her to convince them she was kidding. Of course, she wasn't kidding, and I of all people knew that. My reaction of anger convinced mother I wasn't retarded. Mother's comment was not a one-time slip of the tongue. She meant what she said. Schtick or not, mother showed contempt towards me in front of anyone she wanted to. And they always gave her a pass. They believed she was kidding, with her sly laugh and friendly manner. They certainly couldn't accept that any mother would say such horrible things to their child and mean them.

Over the years, the constant threat of being given away to Bonnie elevated my observation of Bonnie's mannerisms. I didn't like what I was observing. I concluded that I didn't want to be given away to Bonnie. She had a very raspy voice like phlegm was permanently lodged in her throat. When Bonnie laughed, she choked, clearing her airway before resuming the rest of her laugh until it ended in a gurgle. Bonnie cleared her throat again, but the rasp never escaped her cords. Nearly every visit to Bonnie's house, she repeated the same old story. "It was so cute when Billy, as a little boy, said," talking through her nose, "Bon-nie…can…I… have… some…more… po-ta-tos?" Mother and Bonnie laughed, as if to say, "That's my pretty little Billy!" Bonnie choked, cleared her throat and continued laughing and smiling.

I just listened and observed.

My love for mother never wavered.

Mother visited Bonnie often. One time Billy and I sat in the front seat together of mother's four door 1964 Plymouth Belvedere with its oxidized blue paint. With plenty of horsepower to keep up with mother's mind and every changing thought that went through her head, the car was fast. Mother used every horse it had. I sat in the middle by mommy. Upon arrival at Bonnie's house, mother said, "Stay in the car. I don't want you going in. I'll be just a minute!"

I sat and waited for mommy to return, sitting fidgety, but quietly next to Billy, looking for mommy to return.

Billy stared at the open ashtray. I looked out the window, hoping to see mommy return. Billy noticed the little round knob in the ashtray, the cigarette lighter.

I continued looking out the window, looking for mommy's return.

Billy reached down over me, pushing the button in the tray. In a short moment, I heard a 'POP!' Taking my eye from looking outside the window for mommy, Billy reset the lighter. In short it became a fun pastime. After pushing the lighter three or four times the lighter stopped resetting. Billy pulled out the lighter to see its round orange hot glow. I watched. It was fascinating to me as well as Billy. The glow quickly died out. Billy returned the lighter into its holder to heat up again. Playing with the lighter passed the time away. Mother continued talking to Bonnie inside the house. I kept looking out the window for mommy to return.

Billy pushed the button again. I had lost interest in the lighter. I wanted mommy to return. While looking out the window, Billy pulled the lighter out from its holder again, but this time he started burning me on my arm, pushing the red hot glow into my skin! I was startled with the pain of the burn, and I screamed and squealed out of control. Billy laughed. All I could do is scream louder, crying as the burn intensified. The smell of burnt flesh. I was being branded. It hurt horribly. I screamed louder, finally catching mother's attention.

Hearing me scream brought mother out of the house. She raised her voice above my cry, screeching, "Stop your crying! What the hell are you crying about?"

My cry hurt mommy's ears.

Billy immediately said, "It was an accident, Mommy! I didn't mean to burn him. The lighter slipped from my hand."

I cried from the hurt of the burn.

Mother said, "When we get home, I'll put some mineral water on your burn." She never addressed the fact that he was playing with the lighter.

I was comforted by the idea of the cold mineral water. I felt loved by her, although looking back it seems such a sad expression of love. No hugs, no words of actual comfort like that I've given my children when they were hurt. And certainly no words of admonishment to Billy, her favorite.

Billy never confessed.

I couldn't tell mother what he had done to me, that he had done it on purpose.

I was going to have to start talking if I was going to stand up for myself.

CHAPTER FIVE

STACCATO

I had to be constantly vigilant if I was going to survive. I had to pay close attention to mother's regiment. It had a pattern to it, a skip, a beat which was felt and seen by many in mother's public life. It was easy for me to pick up.

Mother always appeared very spunky, happy, beautiful, and fiercely loyal to those she befriended on her terms. Behind closed doors at home, in mother's personal and private life, it was a different story. It was a plaid of patterns that would have left people in her public life shaking their heads if they had known the vast differences between the two.

If you wanted some level of safety, peace or space, you had to play to mother's rhythm. Learning what her rhythm was became a survival technique from one moment to the next for all five of us boys, even Daddy.

I had to calculate mother's ever-changing mood within her paradigm, which was a pattern of ups and downs, crisses and crosses. One moment this, another moment that. Silence was my friend. Being a mute served me for the most part, except for those times when I had to defend myself but couldn't.

There was a core of similarities between mother and me that created competition between us. Being different then the other four boys threatened mother somehow. Mother was different and so was I. Mother had a unique personality, and so did I. I had a seed of autism in me; so did mother. It's possible mother was autistic herself though she lived in an era where no one would have known the signs. Our similarities became an unspoken chasm between the two of us that mother would never admit.

Staying in my silent cocoon, with the exception of grunting to communicate, controlled mother like a fine-tuned fiddle. Being a mute was instrumental in my survival around mother.

Approaching four and a half, it wasn't safe for me to talk, not yet, but the time was getting close for me to unmute myself. I would have to teach myself how to change from being in my silent cocoon, building my own world, to verbal acquiescence of this world.

Grunting wasn't working out very well in my current environment as time advanced with my brothers taking advantage of my inability to defend myself verbally. I was clearly a target of ridicule by my brothers, creating an irreparable problem. It was imperative that I begin my next phase of survival soon.

Mother's antagonistic attitude towards me bled into my brothers. Along with our similarities, mother's disdain towards me increased, wearing off onto my brothers.

I didn't understand that mother wanted convenience, acquiescence, and compliance, not more work. I displaced mother's time and attention, more than she wanted to give or validate. Not fitting into mother's rhythm caused an additional riff between my brothers and myself.

We all got beaten for not following mother's training, except for Billy. He remained mother's 'pretty little Billy,' mother's favorite. He simply danced to mother's music better than the rest of the boys. He played mother like a fine-tuned fiddle too, but she let him get away with it, and never got beaten!

One of mother's patterns was setting the table. It had to be done mother's way. There were no exceptions. Mother collected an old Franciscan style of china. Apple branches and leaves adorned the edges of the plate with a single apple at the bottom. Mother relished her set of china, using it morning, noon, and night. There was no variance.

Every morning and night, mother set the table according to her food schedule. When dinner plates or bowls were used, the two red delicious apples in the pattern had to be placed at the top of the plate, or bowl. There were no exceptions.

When we helped mother set the table, we were reminded often, "The two apples go to the top!" I learned very quickly that meant exactly to the top, being reminded often to be sure there was no slip in protocol. I did not take any risk of chipping mother's china either. The silverware and napkins were precisely set. Napkins on the left, edges tucked under the plate. Fork on the napkin, the knife's serrated edge inward towards the plate. There were no exceptions.

Mother collected enough place settings for 20 people. There was no such setting on the table as a mismatch of any kind. If at any time it appeared to mother she was running out of plates while serving one of her fabulous parties, the next day mother visited the department store where the china was sold and bought more place settings. Mother was not going to have it any other way—coffee cups, saucers, bowls, platters and more all matching, no variance.

Mother said after each meal, "When you are finished eating, put your dishes in the sink! Stack them neatly and put your silverware in the bucket to soak. I'll wash them and put them in the dishwasher myself!"

Nearly every breakfast and dinner, mother took no chances that we might chip or break a plate accidentally. If by chance we decided to put the dishes in the dishwasher ourselves to please mother and clanked it accidentally against something else, we were notified immediately with mother's keen sense of hearing from the other room. "Who's in there?"

"Me" was often the response.

It didn't matter who it was, mother bellowed out from the other room, "WATCH IT! Don't break my dishes!"

I never broke or chipped a single piece of mother's china. Nobody wanted to find out what the consequences were for doing so, especially me. I knew they were one of mother's prized possessions. She cherished them, like her possessions in the china cabinet. I honored mother's expectations.

During the week it was a different rhythm. "Wash your dishes first then put it in the dishwasher yourself!" was hollered, reminding us nearly every day. "The dishwasher is not a scrubber, scrub your plates first!" Mother checked the dishwasher often to be sure we did what she expected us to do.

It wasn't uncommon to hear mother angrily saying, "Who the hell put their dishes in the dishwasher without scrubbing them first? The dishwasher is not a scrubber!"

I observed mother's patterns and learned them well. Surviving mother's demands became second nature so as to avoid mother's wrath.

Putting the dirty dishes in the dishwasher the wrong way also had its consequences. Mother had a place and a pattern for everything. Mother wanted the dishwasher stacked her way. Anything less than putting the dishes in the dishwasher exactly the way mother wanted it done, and everyone in the house would get an earful!

"Who put their dishes in the dishwasher the wrong way?"

"Who the hell put their drinking glass on the wrong side?"

Mother was not shy. "The coffee cups on the right, glasses on the left!"

No one ever came forward. The consequences could be high. We just heard mother clank the dishes into the correct position.

When mother was mad or upset while washing the dishes, the clank of china had a very angry tone to it instead of its usual rattle. An uncomfortable pitch which shouted, "I'm mad!" Mother had it down pat on how hard to bang a plate without breaking it, sending the message which was necessary to radiate her feelings of disgust.

Like cockroaches fleeing from the scene when the light comes on, everybody scattered when they heard the war drum clank of china.

Mother built that fear in me, maybe the other boys, too. Daddy might come to the rescue, only to hear mother whimpering, "I'm nothing but an old PUTZFRAU!" Putzfrau was a German word which means "an old washwoman." The tone of her voice along with her cry transfused into an uncontrollable feeling. It was a feeling of anticipation, but not like that of anticipating Christmas Day on Christmas Eve. Instead, it was a gut wrenching feeling in my stomach. Would she explode this time? Or would she bring out the brush and find a victim to take out her wrath?

Sitting at the table for any meal with the family was no different. We each sat where we were supposed to sit. That was our assigned seat. No one ever thought of sitting anywhere else. If we were doing homework and dinner time was approaching, we were told, "Sit where you're supposed to sit!" If you didn't move quickly, mother added sternly, "MOVE!" I did what I was told immediately. My brothers did, too.

Everything had its place for mother's purpose. Organized or not, it was orderly for mother's convenience. The children were treated no differently than mother's pots and pans. We had our order, and we better be in order to mother's expectations. Going to a restaurant, mother's expectations were elevated. You'd better sit still and make no noise! Running around in the restaurant was not even a passing thought.

Mother had her order at the kitchen table, for breakfast and for dinner. I sat next to Daddy on his right-side, then Hermann, Walter, Frank, and then Billy sitting next to mother, leaving one place setting open in case of company. That finished the oval back to Daddy. We finished our food, then put our dishes in the sink carefully after we rinsed them off. Mother gave us directions accordingly.

Mother's breakfast was consistent with no variance. On school days and Saturdays, us boys ate together but Daddy ate on his own. Monday, Wednesday and Saturday were egg days. Tuesday was oatmeal, Thursday was farina. Friday was french toast. Every Sunday was like a family reunion.

We all sat at the table together. On Sundays Daddy cooked up pancakes served with real maple syrup, along with papaya concentrate, applesauce, apple butter, pork sausages, lots of butter, and raw apple juice from the health food store. It was a gala in itself.

Sitting in my place where I was supposed to sit, I grunted to communicate like every other time. However, my world, along with mother's, was about to change. I said, "Googie!"

The mutation had taken place.

Everyone stopped eating, and stared at me.

I had said something.

Frank laughed and said, "I think he said Googie!"

In disbelief all of my brothers began laughing, astonished that I had spoken.

Frank continued, "He can talk. He's not retarded!"

I could talk, and I could remember all the feelings of what took place in my life! Like a photographic memory, I had stored them inside my mind.

I needed to talk. I had something to say. While my expressions of emotion were being beat out of me, my feelings were not. They were being beat into me. Mother had overlooked my feelings. I don't think she knew that I had the capacity to feel anything.

Saying the word 'Googie' would be just the beginning.

Frank said, "Googie, that's his new name!"

Everyone laughed again.

Mother spoke up. "I knew he wasn't retarded. I told you, he was just lazy, and he would talk when he was ready!"

Googie became my nickname for the foreseeable future.

CHAPTER SIX

MY HERO

Mother would never have become my hero without me. Mother's relentless onslaught of her words and actions became the catalyst towards the desire in me to succeed in building my own world.

Mother thought she was funny with her cruel wit and constant attempts to bait me. "I should have never had you, left you in the cart at Grand Central, given you away to Bonnie, or drowned you in the tub when I had the chance." She said these things often and in front of many people. By the time I was five years old, it meant nothing to me at face value. I was no longer angered from hearing mother's ill-gotten words. I stopped once I understood that mother liked seeing me angry.

Mother continued telling me, "I should have never had you" for the next 37 years. It was not until I wrote this book that I began to understand why.

Mother's comments became like beads of water falling off a duck's back, leaving an inconspicuous splash which dissipated out of my mind. I became immune to mother's intentions to hurt me, if that was her intent, or if it was her punchline, I didn't laugh.

The ripple from mother's cruel wit of words was a different story. Mother's comments live on in my head. They became a motivational quest. They became a positive statement, a catalyst to become important in my uncanny way. Whether it was just her schtick or not, her words became an empty portrayal of mother's intentions.

Mother didn't know it, and had no clue, but she was setting me up for success. I created formulas inside my head, chemistry I couldn't explain or describe. I wasn't conscious of the process, except in that I observed my environment intently and intelligently. Was it a gift of some sort? Was it a survival technique or a decision on my part, maybe more, maybe less? It might have been mother overdid it.

I began feeding off mother's comments and actions towards me unconsciously, dismissing any feelings that I was unimportant to mother. As hurtful as it may have seemed to the outside world, and as hurtful as the words were, ultimately her comments became passé.

I had lost the difference between affection and beatings anyway. They were just one of the same. Mother's treatment of me was interpreted in my mind as mother's way of caring. 'It was life.' I never hated mother nor developed guile towards her. Happiness radiated from my countenance. I loved mother very much.

Talking in innocence, as a beginner in elementary school, the genie was let out of the bottle. Mother couldn't control my silence. I couldn't control my talking. Like a wind-up toy, I talked and talked. It didn't take me long to embrace verbosity. I chirped away like a canary in a cage. Mother was my sounding board. Every moment I was with mother, I talked to her nonstop.

Mother spent most of her time in the kitchen. I talked while she fixed breakfast, lunch or dinner. When mother was tired and sat on the couch to watch TV to rest, I followed her into the living room and sat with her watching her TV program and talked to her.

"Shush!" she said. "I want to listen to my program."

I sat with mother, quietly watching her program, fidgety, waiting for an available time to talk to mommy. When mother finally got up, I followed her into the kitchen, talking once again. While she was preparing dinner, mother interrupted me in an angry tone of voice and said, "Stop your talking! You didn't talk to you were four and a half and now you won't shut your mouth! Can you please stop talking!"

I stopped talking for a moment, but then continued immediately.

It didn't take me long to start talking in sentences. I enjoyed talking to mother; mother enjoyed my silence. It didn't register to me that I was frustrating mother with my talking. I asked lots of questions and talked away, asking one question after the next. Mother said again, "Stop your talking, you didn't talk to you were four and a half and now you won't shut your mouth! Can you please STOP talking?"

I continued talking to mother.

Sitting at the dinner table while mother fixed dinner, I chirped away.

Frustrated, mother finally lost it, saying, "If you can't stop talking, I am going to tape your mouth shut!"

I continued talking. Mother stopped preparing supper and left the room while I was talking to her. I paused. Mother returned a moment later with a roll of masking tape in her hand. I started talking upon mother's return, staring at the roll of tape she was holding. Mother began spinning the roll of tape in one hand, using her fingernail to feel the click under her nail with the other hand. Unsuccessful in locating the edge, mother reversed the roll, applying her fingernail again, repeating the same process until she felt the click.

Finding the edge, mother scratched the tape as if it was a seven year itch. Pulling three long strips from off the roll, mother placed the spent strips on the edge of the table. I continued talking to mother while mother spun her intentions.

Mother took a step closer to me and said, "Stop your talking, close your mouth, and hold still!"

I stopped talking and held still.

Mother placed one strip of tape over my lips, then another one below my nose connecting to the first strip to the second one, another one above my chin, connecting all three strips together.

I just stared up at mother with blue eyes, like Daddy's. Mother firmed the tape against my skin with her right hand. "There!" She said, "No talking for five minutes!"

I took mother's intention in stride. I hadn't gotten this far in life to let a little tape hold me back. I waited for what I thought was five minutes, then began wiggling my chin back and forth. The tape immediately lost its grip against my oily skin. I grinned, loosening the rest of the tape from off my mouth. I pulled the tape from off my face, smiling from ear to ear.

Mother said quickly, "Oh, for Pete's sake, has it been five minutes already?"

I smiled, staring into mother's eyes. Mother looked exasperated. Mother was clearly frustrated with me. That aside I was hungry. I wanted to eat.

I compared myself to no one. I had no one in my life to compare to anyway. To think it could be any different was never a thought. I had no reason to look, nor did anything register inside my mind, other than I was fortunate and life was good! The chemistry inside my head was simple. I was happy, a happy boy at my inner core. Ultimately I gave myself what mother couldn't give me–attention!

The feeling of hopelessness, sadness, or disappointment never took root. My mind never allowed me to believe anything less than mother loved me. My imagination began to grow. I dreamed dreams from visions inside my mind. I built a world from the innocence I stored inside of my inner thoughts.

The cocoon I lived in the first four and half years of my life was not wasted time, but a positive necessity, like a caterpillar spinning its future. Life would be beautiful!

A new family moved in across the street. They had one boy near my age, Tony. Mother told me he was adopted from Mexico and that they were Mormons. I was learning about Mormons. I learned that they went to church three times on Sunday, and almost as bad, mother heard their barking dog. Then mother saw all their kids, lots of young kids.

Mother asked me, "I wonder if she knows where kids come from." I didn't know the answer to mother's question. After another breath, mother asked me another question very vocally, "When is she going to have her tubes tied?"

I didn't know the answer to that question either. I didn't know what tubes were.

Other than friendly gestures, mother talked very little to Tony's mother and father. I felt agitated when I was around Tony, so I avoided him as much as possible. I don't know why, but mother's attitudes toward Mormons could have been the reason.

Mother and Daddy had their children in their mid to late thirties and forties, and that did not offer opportunities to socialize with other families with similar age children, just older people whose children had come and gone. We were socially isolated in the middle of the city, surrounded by Mormons and no relatives.

As a family sitting at the kitchen table, if the subject came up as to why we didn't have relatives, mother was quick to say, "You don't know how lucky you are not to have relatives!"

I believed mother. I knew nothing else. I guess I was lucky? I was told so.

I had never heard the words uncles, aunts, cousins, nieces or nephews, even Grandma or Grandpa. Those family terms were never used or spoken of. The understanding of how these people fit into a family dynamic didn't exist for me. I wouldn't know what they meant nor understand any time soon. I did have Oma, my grandmother on mother's side, and Omi, my grandmother on Daddy's side. It was many years before I connected the idea of Oma and Omi with having grandmas. My family always used the German words. Even my Aunt Martha was never called 'aunt,' only Martha, and I was well into my thirties before I understood what they were. Perhaps it was a function of my autistic brain that the idea of these family relationships

47

was so foreign to me. By the time I was born, both of my grandfathers were deceased. I didn't know what 'grandpa' or 'grandfather' might be in German. I only knew the terms that my family used: 'Omi' and 'Oma.'

Maybe mother was right. I was lucky not to have relatives. I had no one to distract me. At least no relatives to speak of. Mother had a sister Martha and her son Butch who lived in Chicago, Illinois on the other side of the country, far away.

Mother and her sister had a falling out years ago and never spoke to one another. I didn't know why they had a falling out at the time. Martha's son Butch visited my older brothers in Salt Lake City a few times, but Butch was never identified as a cousin to me, only as Martha's son Butch.

Mother's mother 'Oma' was still living in Illinois then. Oma was developing senility, so Daddy added onto the house for Oma to come live with us. I guess Martha didn't want to take care of her mother with the onset of senility.

Oma had immigrated to America from Germany some 60 years earlier. Oma never learned or spoke English. She only spoke in her native language, German. Having Oma come live with us gave mother a last attempt to build a relationship with her mother from a lifetime of disconnection and discontent between the two of them, but time was fading fast.

As I look back on this time of my mother's life, and then compare that to my own, I see that an uncanny repeat of history was unfolding before me. I was, even at that tender age of five, experiencing the same disconnection and discontentment with my mother that she had with hers. I, too, wanted that connection and contentment more than anything.

Daddy had an addition built onto the house.

With the onset of senility and the language barrier, I never conversed with Oma. Oma shuffled around the house, pausing when she passed, raising her cane and shaking it, saying something in German I didn't understand. She then continued shuffling. It sounded angry, so I moved out of her way.

Mother never translated what Oma said.

Oma wore a dull dingy dress which hung over her body like a worn-out drape. Oma's socks bunched up around her ankles just above her depression-era black shoes. Oma was very old looking to my young eyes. I stared at the whiskers which protruded from her chin. Topped with a gray hair bun, I was scared of Oma and stayed clear of her. I never said hello. I figured she wouldn't understand anyway.

Daddy's mother Omi immigrated to America from Germany, too, right after World War II and before 1950. Omi was the complete opposite of Oma. Omi always came across as sweet, loving and caring. She radiated a pleasant disposition, but like Oma, Omi never learned English and I never learned German. Mother and Daddy thought if you live in America, you should speak the language of the country you're living in. Not teaching us German was convenient for mother and Daddy to converse with one another without having to leave the room when they didn't want any of us to understand the conversation they were having. I never had a conversation with Omi either, but Daddy did translate what Omi said and vice versa. Omi always expressed to Daddy in front of me how proud she was of me and all five of her grandsons.

Omi and mother never got along. Mother protested that Daddy served his aged mother hand and foot.

Mother said often, "I feel put out, that old YUCK!" Mother wanted all of Daddy's attention.

When Omi called to talk to Daddy, Omi always said, "Hanzal!"

When I answered the phone, I knew it was Omi, because that was the only word she spoke that I understood.

When mother answered the phone, Omi said the same thing, "Hanzal?"

Mother slammed the receiver of the phone down hard on the countertop, hoping to hurt Omi's eardrum. Mother mimicked Omi, depressing her tongue in the front of her top teeth, "Hanzal! Hanzal! Hanzal! Yuck! I can't wait till she's dead!" I thought mother's reaction to Omi was just mother's personality.

We lived on Richards Street, a dead end road with ten houses on the street. The east side was stable and the west was transient. We lived three houses down on the east side. Mother socialized a little with the Catholic family two houses further down the road on the same side. Although Mary and Eddie were Americans, they primarily spoke Spanish. In my mind, they were like my Omi and Oma who only spoke German, though they were Americans. The fact that Mary and Eddie were staunch Catholics and not Mormons was to mother's delight. Mother and Mary had plenty in common. They both hated Mormons, and that was enough to be considered worthy of mother's friendship.

Their daughter Emily was my age, but she was a girl. I interacted with Emily at her home, playing house and best of all I liked playing with her dolls. I was the mommy. Emily had a very kind voice, speaking gently with kind words. Mary, Emily's mother, was always nice to me, too, but I could tell by the tone of her voice when she was angry. It sounded like firecrackers coming from her lips. It was all in Spanish, which I didn't understand, but the percussion was not misunderstood. My ears felt it.

Emily and I lived in similar environments. Her dad Eddie was born in Mexico and never spoke English. He sounded mean when he spoke in his native tongue. Emily talked about getting hit by her dad's belt, but I didn't ask any questions. I was scared of Eddie because he yelled and he smoked cigarettes. I stayed away from him.

Mary asked me a question while driving down the road to meet mother for lunch one day. I didn't know the answer to her question. She asked, "Why do people eat? I mean, all they do is just poop it out!" I was embarrassed she asked such a question. I stared out the window, shrugging my shoulders. I thought to myself as I sat in the passenger seat of her car, 'why would you ask me that question?' I just remained silent. I was very uncomfortable with the subject, let alone I didn't know the answer to her question.

It might have been because when mother pooped in the toilet, she hollered with enthusiasm and excitement, "Come in here quickly!" I ran into the room mother hollered from, not exactly expecting it to be the bathroom. I pinched my nose with my fingers. Mother stood by the toilet as if she had just pooped out a trophy. Anything she pooped out that seemed to be more than 18 inches long was worthy of show and tell. Mother said, "Take a look at how big my poop is. Boy, is that a big sausage!" I stared for what seemed an eternity, but it was only a few seconds. I thought, 'this is what you were excited about?' I went back into the front room to finish watching cartoons, trying to get mother's poop charade out of my head. After the fourth time I wasn't interested in seeing mother's poop anymore. Mother eventually lost me as a participating audience member. My brothers were still willing, but I stopped running into the bathroom. The next time mother hollered with enthusiasm, "Come in here quickly!" I didn't.

Mary's question didn't stand a chance for me to answer it.

Conversations around our dinner table seemed to have a familiar ringtone from one dinner night to the next. The topic of religion always seemed to be at the top of mother's list. Mother seemed to be the judge, jury, and executioner on the subject. Mother picked no bones over religion. She told it like she saw it.

Mother said often around the table, "Religion is all bullshit, no matter how you spin it. I'm an Atheist!" It took mere seconds for mother to recount her statement. "I'm nothing!" She corrected herself. Adding to her rant, "Atheism is a religion, too. I want nothing to do with religion! God does not exist, Jesus is a lie, Mormonism is all made up! One bullshit story after the next."

I sat and listened, not interrupting mother's speech. It was a repeat of her feelings from last week.

When mother talked, overbearing or not, I listened to her as if I was the student. I learned what a prostitute was and what it meant. Mother always referred to Omi as "That old prostitute!" Before my grandfather went to war in World War I, thinking he might not come back alive, he made a deposit into Omi, leaving something behind just in case of his demise. He did return, but he never married my grandmother. Omi's passion in her younger years gave birth to Daddy. Right after the war, she had another child with another man. A second boy who died in the '30s of appendicitis. Eventually, Omi did marry a man named Adolph Schilfarth who would adopt Daddy.

A massage parlor moved in at the front of Richards Street. We were now living in the red light district, as mother referred to it. There were always police cars at the top of the street with policemen at the massage parlor. My curiosity prompted me to ask mother, "What are they doing?" Mother never held back any details on any subject, regardless of my age. I paid attention to every word that came out of mother's mouth. Mother told me about prostitution. I became educated by mother.

After several failed attempts of learning how to ride a bicycle in the driveway, I finally learned at the age of six. I was still a bit shaky and was gaining confidence riding a bicycle without training wheels. The edge of the driveway had a short drop off to the lawn below. Flood irrigation was used at one time to water the lawn. That edge was important to control the water, but it was a huge dropoff for me.

I stared at the edge, hoping not to fall off, but my eyes guided me off of the driveway, crashing my bicycle and falling to the lawn below, about 5 inches. I got back up onto my seat and I continued riding my bicycle on the driveway, gaining confidence. As I approached the edge again, I closed my eyes tight in a squint, hoping not to fall off yet again. A moment later, I opened my eyes. I was in the middle of the driveway. I hadn't fallen off the edge! A voice came in my head from out of nowhere. It was very distinct and crystal clear! Soft as a whisper, but with the roar of a lion. "I'M

WATCHING OVER YOU." I didn't know what to do or think about what I just heard inside my head, but it never left my thoughts.

ROBERT BAUTNER

CHAPTER SEVEN

RICK AND THE RATTLE

Mother's anger limited her immediate vision but not her insight. One moment mother was happy, the next moment mother was unhappy and angry. Extremely angry. In the next moment mother would go back to being clear and calm about what she wanted done, but then she flipped back to being enraged with no warning. One moment I understood what mother wanted, but the next moment I didn't understand what mother wanted and mother was upset.

What mother said, what mother wanted, and what mother meant were three very separate expectations, and it was very confusing. It was a guessing game at best. One moment mother inspired me with her gift of wisdom, and the next moment I was getting yelled at. Mother told me often, "You're beautiful," and in the next breath, "Don't let that go to your head!" Then in the next breath I was reminded, "I should have never had you."

I felt mother showed me her love by not giving me away to Bonnie. I processed mother's moods moment by moment with little success, but it was all I knew. To survive, I escaped into the world I'd been building inside my head for years. Mother gave me every reason to retreat there. It was a safe place inside of me that gave me mental consistency and stability.

I talked to mother often, sharing my thoughts and asking many questions. I talked and talked and talked, but mother didn't want to listen. Yet I didn't stop talking. I remember many times when I was talking and mother became very angry. I had now learned to talk in sentences, but mother was done listening to me before I began. She said time and time again, "Stop your talking! You didn't talk till you were four and a half, and now you won't shut your mouth. You talk in riddles! I can't understand anything you're saying anyway! Can't you talk intelligent? Can you say anything that makes sense? I just don't know what you're saying." All of these statements would flow out of her mouth in one fell swoop! It didn't bother me. It was just what mother said. I couldn't understand why mother said I talked in riddles. It made sense to me.

Mother never explained how I talked in riddles; she just told me I did. I clearly frustrated mother, but I didn't mean to. Maybe mother was busy thinking about her TV shows. Maybe my disposition of happiness overrode mother's disposition of anger. Mother reminded me often that she had enjoyed my four and a half years of silence.

I stared at the TV daily to escape from the reality of life. I knew there weren't people inside the console, because the TV screen was black and white. Therefore I knew it wasn't real, but I couldn't figure out how it worked. I asked mother, "Where are the people I'm seeing in the TV?"

"They're actors," mother said. "They're standing in front of a camera."

I asked, "Where are the people who are laughing?"

Mother replied, "It's canned laughter, I can't stand it! It sounds so artificial."

When she said "canned," my mind went to a soup can mother asked me to open up with a can opener. Mother complained often that her hands hurt. She said her hand always hurt from hitting us. That's why she got a heavy wooden stick with broom bristles on it, but that didn't stop her from using her hands. I think she got it from the Fuller Brush Man. He visited mother once a month. We called it the radiator brush, and it hurt when mother used it on my back.

From that time on, whenever I heard laughter on the TV, I thought it was actually in a can. I listened intently to the canned laughter on the TV thereafter.

56

One day while I was watching TV, mother came into the house and said, "Somebody's moving into the old white house across the street." She added with little hesitation or reservations, "I hope they are not Mormons." Mother expressed little tact or finesse in her comments. Mother would make it her business to find out their religious status the moment she met them. Within five minutes of meeting anybody new, mother found out their religion. Mother was consistent. I paid attention.

After a person's religious beliefs were identified, next on mother's concern list was the Vietnam War. The War took its toll on mother's psyche. She hated war! Managing her five boys was tormenting enough, let alone thinking about whether her boys might have to go to war or not. Keeping us in order was a high priority, so high that she was willing to exact violence against us. Yet she feared that we would be forced into the violence of war. It was very confusing.

Daddy had built onto the house for mother's mother to come live with us.

Mother said, "Oma is coming down with senility, and I will be taking care of her. You boys need to behave yourselves."

I was proving to be more work for mother than the other four boys combined. Mother didn't like having me on her list of to-dos. It only increased mother's resentment towards me. So it was easier for mother to tell me than the other boys, "I wished I never had you!"

Mother walked across the street to meet the new neighbors, returning shortly thereafter. She said upon her arrival, "That's a relief, they don't have a dog, no young children." Mother paused to scratch her head. I watched mother's wig move back and forth. Mother continued, "And they're not participating Mormons!" That was as good as a non-Mormon to mother. Mother continued, "We don't need another religious zealot on the street, one zealot is enough." I didn't know what a 'zealot' was, but I remembered the word because mother thought it was important. Mother said all their

57

children were grown, the youngest being 19, but they all lived there except for the oldest daughter Larae. And that daughter was moving into the duplex to the south of the old white house. So she would be living next to her parents. Mother added that she hoped that daughter and her family weren't Mormons either.

Larae, married with two children, did just that. They moved into the back part of the duplex next door to the old white house. I soon met Lonnie, Larae's oldest son. I found out he was five years old and his sister Lauri was three. I didn't care about his age being two years younger than me. With two new families on the street, Richard Street was becoming a family affair. Finding a friend on the street that was a boy my age or close to my age was hard-pressed. Lonnie and I became friends immediately.

Mother soon verified that they were not participating Mormons either. Lonnie and I played together. Mother's public position with Lonnie was nearly the same as her private position: mother liked Lonnie, and his family too, but she seldom talked to them. As long as they weren't practicing Mormons, mother was satisfied, so no further conversation was necessary. Mother had her own clutch of friends anyway.

Mother welcomed Lonnie into the family from the beginning. It didn't take long for mother to give Lonnie a nickname, saying it with mother's charm, enthusiasm and joy, "I'm going to call you Butterball!"

Lonnie laughed, and so did I.

Life was good. I had a friend.

Lonnie's happy personality matched mine, and we became the best of friends. When Daddy took us to the park, Lonnie came with us. Lonnie slept over at my house, and I slept over at Lonnie's house. We never fought or argued over anything. We talked and played together with the greatest of ease. With Lonnie's Grandma living next door, along with his aunts and uncles, Richard Street became alive with people.

The old white house Lonnie's grandma lived in was a convenient few steps away in either direction of both my house and Lonnie's. The dirt driveway at Lonnie's grandma's house was a toy playground for tractors and cars alike, and it was big enough to fill my imagination. The possibilities were endless, playing in the dirt. Their side yard was big enough to play baseball in, Lonnie's favorite game. A garden in the other corner of the yard gave way for Lonnie's grandpa to grow a big garden like Daddy's.

The old white house, built after the depression in the 1940s, was a small wooden framed home with just the basics to raise a family in. The single pane of glass in the southside door sat loose in its frame, rattling with the simplest knock or when someone closed the door. The vibration created a reaction inside of me each and every time. I turned my head and looked towards the house each and every time, wondering who just went in or who just came out.

Walking north down Richard Street towards my home, out of the corner of my eye I caught a sparkle in the dirt from the sun's reflected light. I ran over to Lonnie's grandma's house to find what had caught my attention. The sparkle in the dirt was a tiny toy car. I pulled it out of the dirt, thinking this must be Lonnie's car. I wiped the loose dirt from the car and onto my pants. I thought, 'I'm going to clean it up and return it to Lonnie as if it was brand new!' I was very excited to clean it and return it to Lonnie.

I quickly went home to clean the car, turning on the water at the kitchen sink. I washed the dirt off every corner of the car I spotted. Eyeing the car front and back, top and bottom, side to side, I wanted to be sure every grain of dirt was removed. Drying the car on mother's hand towel, I left a little film of dirt on the towel. I didn't worry about mother hollering, "Who wiped their dirty hands on the towel again?" I could hardly wait to return the car to Lonnie.

I ran to Lonnie's home with the car firmly in my hand and knocked on the door, waiting for someone to answer. Staring at the car in my hand, I waited for someone to answer, but no one answered. I knocked again, glancing at the car, still no one answered. My pent-up excitement turned to disappointment. I couldn't return the car to Lonnie.

Walking off the porch to go home, the thought came to me as with the breath of life, maybe he's at his grandma's house. I hopped the short fence separating the two properties, running to the old white house, leaping up the stairs to the front door. I knocked on the door. The rattle of the window passed through me over the anticipation of Lonnie inside the house.

Staring at the door handle, the knob began to move, the springs in the handle clicked in my ears as it turned. I immediately thought, somebody's home! I held the car tight in my hand, quickly looking at it.

The door hinge opened all the way and Rick, Lonnie's nineteen-year-old uncle, answered my knock. "Come in," Rick said.

I walked into the house, which was the kitchen area of the home. Standing against the wall by the handle of the door, I stood firmly on my two feet as Rick began closing the door upon my entrance. The window rattled with its closure.

With the door closed, I noticed Rick had a friend leaning against the stove to the right of me. His arms were folded against his chest and his right leg crossed at his left ankle. I immediately asked, "Is Lonnie here?" I didn't wait for Rick to answer. Rick stood a pace away. Rick and his friend stared at me as I chirped away, telling them about the car I found, holding it outward in the palm away from my body. I showed the car to Rick and his friend with the innocence of a seven-year-old's anticipation.

I told Rick and his friend, "I was walking down the street." I took a breath and continued, talking with excitement, "I saw a sparkle in the dirt, it was this car, I picked it up out of the dirt, took it home and cleaned it up." I was so proud of my work. It was clear in my voice. I continued telling Rick and his friend, "I want to return this car." Taking a breath and continuing, "I think it's Lonnie's."

Rick interrupted me saying, "Yeah, it could be."

I thought nothing of Rick holding his hand at the fold of his pants by his zipper. As Rick took one step towards me, he exposed his erect penis. I had never seen one like that before. Rick pushed his erection to the right side of my nose, squishing my nose against the skin of my face, my head hitting the wall behind me. Rick took one step backwards, and Rick and his friend started laughing. My mind scrambled to process what had just happened.

As Rick and his friend continued to laugh, I realized I was the brunt of some joke but didn't understand what just happened exactly. I took the back of my right hand and wiped away the smell and moisture from my nose. I still held the car tightly in my right hand. Rick backed up, both continuing to laugh. I twisted my torso towards the door using my left hand to turn the knob. While the car was held tightly in my right hand, I opened the door. My mind was still processing what just happened as I walked out of the house.

The rattle of the window seemed insignificant this time, but I heard the rattle just the same as I slammed the door shut behind me. Their laughter faded from my ears as I jumped down the flight of four steps with the car still held tightly in my hand. I walked quickly past the location where I had found the car an hour earlier in the dirt. I walked across the street, opened the front door to my house, sat down and watched TV as if nothing had happened at all.

But it had.

I entered back into the flow of my daily life at home. Evening was approaching. Mother always retired early for the day and wanted the house cleared of friends or neighbors. Evenings were mother's time. If mother didn't speak up, Daddy did, saying often, "It's time for your friends to go home." It didn't matter who said it, whoever was left in the house went home. Mother wanted her time to be a relaxing time, so anything that took place during the day was over. Mother didn't want anybody to see what mother looked like when she took off her wig and dressed in her silk nightgown. With an application of cold cream applied on her face, nobody was going to see mother without her façade.

Ready for the couch, mother didn't want to be disturbed. If somebody came to the door while mother was stretched out and comfortable, mother was quick to say, "Go see who's knocking on the door." That gave mother time to put on her wig immediately, then look into her hand-held mirror to be sure the cold cream had vanished into her skin. Mother always had her wig nearby for such emergencies.

If Daddy was working in the garden late into the evening, mother asked me, "Go get Daddy and tell him to come in. Tell him I want my feet massaged."

I went and did as I was asked.

I returned to sit with mother on the couch in front of the TV before Daddy came in. I wanted to be with mother. I was learning not to interrupt mother while she watched her evening TV programs, too. While mother and I sat on the couch, I had some questions with what I saw on the TV, but I waited for a commercial. Mother said that's when I could talk.

I asked mother during a commercial, "Can I go on TV?"

Mother replied, "NO! Only important people go on TV, people who have accomplished something important, or people who are actors."

I thought I hadn't accomplished anything important. I knew I was only seven. Besides, I didn't feel important, and I wasn't an actor. I understood what mother was saying. Mother said, "Go tell Daddy to come in here again!"

I never looked at TV the same way after talking to mother. I enjoyed watching it, listening for the canned laughter in every program. I began to process that what I viewed was not real. I had more questions after watching 'Gilligan's Island.' I asked mother, "Is Gilligan acting dumb or is he really stupid?" Mother said, "NO! He's not stupid. He's the smart one, you have to be really smart to act dumb." I liked what mother said, and I thought a lot about mother's comment that dumb people are smart. That's not what she meant, but that's what I heard.

I separated out information, understanding that nothing was real with what I viewed on the TV and dismissing any comparisons to my life. Separating content from entertainment, I listened intently, just like I did to mother.

Mother's comment, "Dumb people are really smart" stuck in my head. Mother's beatings stuck in my head, too. They were real. Hearing mother screaming and yelling was real. Being told, "I should never have had you" was real. Hearing, "I don't understand anything you're saying" was real. Daddy's silence was real. Mother was right, I did talk in riddles. That was really dumb, but that might mean that I was smart. Mother never allowed my spirit to be integrated with her spirit or with her soul, so mother's comments never withdrew my spirit from within me, but added to my experience of this world.

Mother's comments and actions were in a plaid of patterns. Mother didn't understand that I was listening. When mother said, "Can't you talk intelligently?" in my mind, mother never seemed to realize that her next comment conflicted with her other belief, 'dumb people are smart.' It created a conflict of understanding inside my head. Mother never hesitated to say, "intelligent people are some of the ssss-tupidest people!" Mother always emphasized the 's' on stupid.

Her comments spun inside my head. I had a lot to figure out, and I used the process of elimination. I thought to myself, putting the two together, if I told myself I was dumb, then I would be smart. I was beginning to understand this life in my own innocent way. Mother gave me no value or reason to be smart or intelligent. I must have felt I would have been attacked by mother's words if I showed signs of being ssss-mart! I kept it simple in my head. I didn't want to be a stupid boy. I wanted to be a smart man one day. I said nothing about this; I just listened to the tone of her wisdom and to the content of mother's comments.

Daddy came into the house to massage mother's feet. That meant it was time for me to leave their presence. Mother laid on the couch while Daddy massaged her feet and they both watched TV. It was time for me to go to the bedroom. I gave mother her expected goodnight kiss on her cheek before I retired to bed and told her, "Goodnight mommy, I love you!" I did this lovingly every night.

While mother and Daddy watched the nightly news in the living room, sometimes I pulled up a chair, sitting on the backside of the jamb between the kitchen and living room out of mother's and Daddy's sight. I listened to the news and learned what was happening in the world.

The evening was mother's and Daddy's time together with no children to distract mother from Daddy's attention. Mother expected Daddy to massage her feet nightly. Mother would often yell at the TV, because with three teenagers, two of her sons were getting closer to draft age. Mother was worried about them being drafted into the Vietnam War. She yelled at the TV, outraged at the possibility of her son's going off to war. Mother's concerns flared up daily.

I tried making sense of the news with what the man on the TV was talking about. He was talking about "guerrilla warfare." I asked myself, 'Why are gorillas fighting in a war, killing, and wounding people?' I pictured long black-haired gorillas doing this. I couldn't understand. I processed the ingredients of information, concluding no answer, and couldn't get the image of gorillas out of my head.

The Vietnam War, tie-dye, and rock-and-roll ruled the three oldest boys, and that outraged mother. Worse still, they loved acid rock. I didn't understand any of this either, including why my brothers were boiling shirts in a pot on the stove with rubber bands tied around them in different spots.

Acid rock disturbed my brain. Mother was hard-pressed to understand all of this type of music, too. I felt I was mimicking mother. It was another way for me to experience my love for her. Mother yelled, "Turn that crap off!" Mother's yelling at their music, the Vietnam War, at me, and at whatever else was bothering her in the moment faded in my mind into a collection of angry rants. Mother ranted, "They're fighting over oil! That's what this war is all about! My boys are not going to war to fight over oil! They are not going to put my sons at risk. I hate war! Soldiers are nothing but a bunch of trained killers!"

Mother left no uncertainty in my head. As I processed mother's words, I learned terms like "conscientious objector," "draft dodger," and I learned what it meant to desert to Canada. To mother, all of these became viable options for the oldest two boys. In my mind, this told me mother cared about us. The war raged on as did mother's outrage, leaving her with few options.

What took place with Rick sat silent in my subconscious mind for 50 years. I said nothing to anyone until I wrote this book. I didn't want to remember.

In 2018 I called Lonnie to say hello and ask about Rick. I told him nothing about my experience 50 years earlier. Lonnie told me that Rick had died in June of 2017, six months earlier.

Lonnie did not know the purpose of my call yet he shed light on my earlier experience. Lonnie said, "Rick was a drug addict and a pervert. He spent his life exposing himself to little girls."

I wasn't surprised. I said to Lonnie, "I know one little boy he exposed himself to–me!"

Shocked, Lonnie said, "You gotta be kidding me!"

I wasn't.

ROBERT BAUTNER

CHAPTER EIGHT

I DREAM OF PURPLE

Although I erased Rick's aggression from my mind, the effects of his actions had just begun. Worse, it increased mother's aggression towards me. Looking back, I see this clearly. It hasn't ceased to be a shock to my system, to think of how one moment in time can change everything.

Yet to my seven-year-old self, since there were no further incidents, I had no reason to give Rick any thought. I found no reason to tell anybody. In my conscious mind he took no power from me, and I didn't give him any to take from me. At least any power I was aware of.

In reality it wasn't that simple. Seeing an erect penis flipped the sexual switch in my brain. I didn't understand the ramifications of it, but still, it was there. This incident, the one I seemingly pushed away as unimportant, had been absorbed into my identity, my sense of self.

Mother's contempt towards me prepared my mind to survive life. My conscious mind thought one way, my subconscious mind thought another, leaving my body caught in the middle. My body had begun to wake up to the way it was designed to work when its sexual switch became engaged. While my body's sexual switch was turned on with Rick's action, my mind hadn't caught up to its function. My soul had a conflict of interest between the two that I wasn't aware of.

The divide between my mind and body became an advantage with inconspicuous victories along the way. I never agonized over defeat, not even from mother's actions or words towards me. Defeat never entered my mind nor did it take root into my being. I had decided to become somebody important years before, so I viewed everything in life as a step toward my victory. Thus, victory in my mind started years before Rick. A different type of Pollyanna, maybe? I had my body, and my body had me, there within I had many victories between me, myself and I. My body and mind were set to become inseparable friends. Rick's actions towards me jump started my body's sexual journey early on, leaving my mind open to innocently engaging in behavior that became a riddle for my body and me to unravel.

Riddles had become the way that I saw the world.

"You're talking riddles," mother would say. "Can't you talk intelligently?" Mother didn't understand my intellect. "Can't you say anything that makes sense?"

I had absorbed mother's assessment of my thinking in riddles, and I applied it to everything in my life. Making sense out of life never stops.

"I just don't understand what you're saying!" mother stated so often.

Mother and I spoke the same language with a different dialect.

It seemed the more negativity I was fed, whether it was from mother, life in general, or Rick, the more positively I spun it. My decision to love myself and get the attention I needed outweighed mother's or Rick's actions towards me.

It was after what happened with Rick that I began hiding. Deep below the surface of my awareness, I knew I had been violated. I hid from neighbors, people who drove down the street, and people in general. In a panic, I hid from anyone who passed my house when I played in the yard or when I had control of my space. I ran and hid myself behind the closest tree, car, bush, even running inside the house hoping not to be seen out in the open. I felt exposed and vulnerable. Rick's house seemed to be in the background of my mind. Anytime I heard the slam of any door thereafter, I flinched, my subconcious mind returning to Rick and what he had done.

Prior to Rick I slept through the night, waking up dry. This was no longer the case. I began wetting the bed.

Awakened again by the cold in the wet of night, I hurried to clean up, hoping to hide my wetness from mother. In the morning, I greeted mother with happiness. I said, "Good morning, mommy." I said it in a happy tone, hoping mother wouldn't ask me if I peed my bed again last night.

"Did you pee your bed again last night?" mother asked.

"Yes, I did, mommy." In the subtleties of my mind, I wished mommy hadn't asked me that question.

"Put your sheets in the utility room, and your peed clothes, too. I'll wash them later!" Mother spoke with frustration, adding, "If you can't stop peeing your bed I'm going to put you back into your crib!"

I thought silently, 'I hope mommy won't put me back in my crib.' I finished gathering up the sheets and wet clothes, putting what seemed to be a mountain of bedding on the floor of the utility room where the washer and dryer were. After I dropped them from my arms, I stared at the pile for a moment, thinking of all the words mother might say to me as I walked away to wipe down the protective film on my bed.

Peeing the bed changed mother's routine in the morning with a new greeting each school day by opening my bedroom door when I didn't wake up on my own saying, "WAKE UP! It's time to get ready for school!" followed with, "Did you pee your bed again last night?"

My heart pulsated with the sharpness of mother's voice. I felt an electric current inside my heart, within my body's state of slumber, from mother's question. A feeling in my heart I never grew fond of, I checked my mind quickly to answer mommy's question, not knowing if I should answer 'yes.' I felt as if I was going to be electrocuted with my answer if it was 'yes.'

Fully awakened from my deep sleep, my mind engaged with my body to answer mother's question. I reached my hand down under the sheets I laid beneath, feeling the top of my t-shirt on my chest, sliding my hand down onto my stomach, then feeling to the top of my underpants to gain information that I could report back to mommy quickly.

Mother probably knew the answer before I responded to her question, hoping I would say, 'I'm dry mommy!' I would smile with my answer and feel victorious. It wasn't to be this time, as it was no different from last night. I didn't know that my body was reacting to Rick's intrusion.

I answered, "Yes, mommy, I'm wet!" I heard the disappointment from the breath of my words.

"You know what to do!" mother said with frustration, never passing the jamb of my door and leaving my door ajar. I laid in my bed with my eyes closed for the moment, holding as still as I could. Any movement brought a cold chill to my body from the wetness which invaded my warmth overall.

My mind was calm in the moment, slowly crossing my arms over my wet body to hold the blankets down at my shoulders. The top sheet held in the grasp of my hands, I tightened the blankets around my neck, hoping to keep the smell at bay and the warmth to my body inside the blankets...but with little success. The scent of pee vaporized out the top of my blankets into my nostrils from the heat of my body.

I was distracted from the cold and the smell with the sound of mother in the kitchen clanking her morning together with her pots and pans, dishes and silverware, setting the table. These sounds rang in my ears with mother's routine as I visualized her setting up morning breakfast. The sound of plates with their particular thud helped me identify if it was Monday, Wednesday, or Friday. I had to think, pushing the thought of pee out of my head, as mother set the table. I laid still in the bed thinking of the food of that morning. The smell of brewed coffee overrode the smell of my pee for a moment. I needed to get up before mother's return. The thought came simultaneously with mother returning.

"Come on, get up!" mother snapped.

I knew the pattern. With mother gone I reached my hand to the outer edges of my aura on the bedsheets below me and the blankets above, feeling the extent of my expansion from my body's release. I threw the sheets off from around me, the rushing air chilled my body, a feeling like being in a breezeway.

My body shivered as I pulled down my underwear, slowly at first from around my waist, not wanting to touch the pee. Pushing harder between the pinnacle of my legs, my wet underwear stuck to the skin of my thighs, rolling itself together like the twist of a candy cane on the way to the floor. As I pushed downward, my underwear caught on my ankles. My body shivered, feeling frustrated. I felt shackled. I freed one ankle then the other by kicking my underwear off the rest of the way. I danced from one foot to the next to create warmth, pulling my t-shirt away from my chest in a hurry. I wanted to keep the wet from touching my face as I lifted my shirt from around my neck, dropping my shirt to the floor by my bed.

Naked, I ran into the bathroom next to my room and closed the door fast. Mother's words always went through my head, 'Don't lock the door! If you die we can't get in!' I pulled a drawer out right of the door, blocking it from being opened by someone on the other side wanting to enter my space. Family didn't knock; they just walked in unannounced. I wasn't comfortable with people seeing me naked. I did what mother asked me to do, not locking the door. I felt safe with the drawer blocking the door.

My mind drifted as I touched my body with a warm washcloth wiping off my pee.

Mother opened the door unexpectedly, startled with the door hitting the drawer.

I flinched from out of my daze, from the bang in my ears.

"Who's in there?" mother demanded.

"It's me, mommy."

"Why are you blocking the door again?" Mother continued, "If I had to get in there in an emergency I couldn't with the door blocked!"

"I'm almost done giving myself a sponge bath, mommy," speaking loud enough to carry my voice through the jarred door.

"Hurry up!" Mother yelled. "Don't forget to pull the skin back on your penis when you wash it," mother said in a tone that sounded like she was concerned.

"I will, mommy," I said. I pulled the skin back on my penis. I noticed my body's reaction to my touch this time, different than before. The warmth of the washrag touching my penis sent a slight tingle to my brain I hadn't felt before. I dismissed the tingling.

Mother followed up, "Did you give yourself a sponge bath?"

"Yes, mommy, I did."

"Did you pull the skin back on your penis?"

"Yes, mommy, I did!"

"Did you put the wet sheets and clothes in the utility room?"

"No, mommy, I did not."

"Put them in there right now!" Mother said. "You need to stop peeing your bed or you need to start washing your own sheets. I'm tired of washing your peed sheets again!"

I said, "I don't know how to use the washing machine."

Mother snapped, "Learn how to use it!" Mother reminded me again, "If you don't stop peeing in your bed, I'm putting you back into your crib. There will be less sheets for you to wash!"

I didn't know how to stop peeing my bed.

I didn't doubt mother's intention. No matter what I told my mind, I couldn't stop peeing the bed night after night, never asking myself why or what changed.

Disappointing mommy weighed on my mind. As I passed by the laundry room, I stared at the pile of peed sheets I plopped down on the floor again earlier, wondering what I could do to avoid mother's questioning me about whether I peed in my bed or not.

"Meow," the cat softly sounded.

Mother was quick to tell the cat, "Meow yourself, go catch a mouse!"

With twenty-one house cats roaming in and out of the house, there was always a cat that peed on the carpet. It got me thinking.

Mother yelled when the cat did, "Oh for Pete's sake! Put the cat outside and get the baking soda, the cat just peed on the carpet again!" Mother specifically told this to one of the older boys.

I listened to the tone of her voice as she spoke. It sounded angry, just like after I peed in my bed. Mother sounded the same with the cats peeing out of place as she was with me peeing out of place.

I thought if I put baking soda down on my mattress after I peed my bed, I could save mother from washing my sheets everyday and that might help her stop asking me if I peed my bed again last night. I felt mother was always looking for reasons to yell at me. I was looking for ways to avoid mother's questions about peeing the bed.

One option I thought of was to tell mother before she asked me, "I peed my bed again last night mommy." Another option was to sprinkle baking soda down after I wet the bed. I tried that method first. I thought mother would be pleased, not having to wash my bedding again. I was hoping to avoid mother's question. I was wrong. Mother continued asking me, but I told mother, "I'm going to sprinkle baking soda down on my bed, mommy." I thought that was a good idea. Mother said, "Scrub it in." I did what mother asked me to do. I wasn't successful in avoiding mother's questions, but at least she didn't have to wash my sheets every day.

I started sprinkling baking soda down over my wet spot in the bed, letting it dry all day. After school I felt my sheets, and they were dry! I lay a clean bath towel down over the compromised area on the mattress. My bed was ready for me to sleep in again. I didn't have to change my sheets or burden mother with washing them, and I didn't have to learn how to work the washing machine, not yet.

Mother's disgust for me peeing the bed bled into my brothers. As I walked in the room my oldest brother Frank mocked me as I walked by him, making the sound, "Pssssssss."

I knew he was mimicking me peeing my bed.

Other brothers mocked me in their own way, calling me, "Pissy bed, pissy bed, pissy bed, did you pee your bed again last night, pissy bed?"

I yelled, "Stop calling me a pissy bed and leave me alone!"

They replied, "Okay, Googie, stop peeing the bed and we won't call you pissy bed anymore and we'll leave you alone!"

I couldn't stop peeing the bed. I was excluded from playing with them in their activities. They didn't want me to touch them. They said, "If you touch me, then I'll pee my bed, too!"

I learned to do things on my own.

Mother potty-trained her boys early in life, but she never asked me why I was peeing my bed again when I was dry before. I peed my bed nearly every night, not understanding my body was reacting to Rick's invasion of my privacy. As introspective as I was, Rick's actions only added to the riddles of my mind.

My mind needed to escape the boundaries of what happened. There was something brewing inside my head towards my body. I turned my pillow lengthways under my chest, raised my arms above my head clasping my left hand onto my right wrist and started bouncing my head on my pillow, face first. Nonstop. It felt so good for my face to feel the softness of my pillow.

I slept on my stomach from that time on. Wetting my top sheet almost never happened again. I laid on my stomach, bouncing my head face first into my pillow. It became a nightly ritual. Night after night, year after year, bounce after bounce. I counted each bounce in my mind, one at a time. Two in less than one second, I counted to one thousand, then to two thousand, then to three thousand, four thousand, then five thousand, I bounced my head till my side hurt. It was another ramification of my privacy being invaded, but I had no clue. Bouncing my head felt so good!

My pillow became personal to me. It had to accommodate my head bouncing. I experimented with different types of pillows, both foam and feather. Foam pillows blocked my airways by expanding immediately after the release of my bounce. It was a feeling of being suffocated, and it bothered me. Pillows filled lightly with feathers seemed to work the best, leaving an opening for me to breathe in the cavity of my pillow that formed with my face after the bounce.

Feather pillows had their drawbacks, too. Quills of the feathers stabbed me in the face. I wouldn't know it till morning, seeing a braille of blood on my pillow. I had to awaken my senses to the cool air on my face, only then did I know I needed to shift my pillow to prevent being stabbed by another feather's quill.

I did more than just count my bounces. I dreamed while I bounced my head. I was expanding the world inside my mind. I processed solutions, images, and thoughts in 3D. My mind ignored the hurt on the right side of my body until I couldn't ignore the pain any longer. I stopped bouncing, shifted my body to fall asleep until mother's words awoke me in the morning. "Wake up!"

After cleaning myself from the sponge bath, I dressed to get ready for school. I had a question brewing deep in my mind. I thought about it all day long. I somehow associated purple with strangulation. I asked mother because of my sincere trust in her, hoping to hear a yes or no answer to my question, "Is it normal for the head of my penis to be purple?"

Mother said, "Let me see."

I immediately replied, "NO, I'm not going to show you my penis!" I never thought mother would ask such a question. I dropped the subject immediately. I thought, I will never bring up that question again. Then I wondered if mother would ever come in the middle of the night to check to look at my penis. I tried to remember my room setup before falling asleep, but I concluded that mother never looked at me while I was asleep. I trusted mother.

Scan the code above to hear a recording of me bouncing my head. To me, it sounds remarkably like a heartbeat, like a baby's heartbeat through an ultrasound. What does it sound like to you?

CHAPTER NINE

ERASED FROM MY MIND

"If you don't stop peeing your bed, I'm going to put you back in your crib!" True to her word, mother had one of my older brothers dismantle my full size bed, removing it completely from my room and setting up my old crib in its place. With the drop of the mattress between the slats, my crib was one step closer for me to sleep in.

Mother put the sheets on the crib and said, "This is your bed now! When you stop peeing your bed you can sleep in the top bunk of the new bed that we just set up."

I didn't argue with mother. I complied.

My younger brother Walter and I shared the same room by now. We had been in the same room since Daddy added on to the house a couple years earlier for Oma to have her own room. Daddy had the carpenter turn the only window in the bedroom into a doorway which led into Oma's room, the new addition. Oma shuffled back and forth throughout the day through my bedroom to get to her bedroom. My room was more like an extended hallway than a bedroom.

The builder never tied in the new roof with the old roof properly. Each time it rained, rain water leaked through the roof dripping onto my ceiling, then onto the floor. This caused the plaster to fall off from the ceiling. Daddy went up into the attic, placing pans and buckets to catch the rain before the water dripped into my ceiling. I followed Daddy to watch, but the damage was done to the ceiling and was never repaired. Plaster had fallen off of the ceiling and left different formations of characters for my imagination to explore.

Mother sent me to my room often to get me out of her way, sometimes for ten minutes, other times for the rest of the evening. Mother wanted her peace and quiet without me around. "Stop talking and leave me alone!" mother said. "I need my peace and quiet, go to your room!"

I did what I was told and went to my room. Mother needed her space; I gave it to her.

I laid on my bed, staring at the ceiling, identifying shapes like clouds in the sky between what had fallen off and what was still in place. My imagination filled in the pieces. Woody Woodpecker was up there, a clear caricature of his outline in the ceiling near the light and fading into the undamaged ceiling above. It was the stain of a raindrop that never fell to the earth, transforming itself into a new formation as a stalactite above my crib. My imagination was vivid, alive and full of life. I never thought mother didn't love me for sending me to my room. I still thought, what can I do for mother? I wanted to please her.

With a new bed waiting for me, I stared at the top bunk, thinking what mother said, "As soon as you stop peeing your crib, you can have the top bed!" I continued peeing my crib. The top bed did not prove to be a motivating incentive for me to strive towards. In a short period of time, mother's odds and ends began piling up on top of the bed that waited for me, becoming a storage area for mother stuff. Mother's intentions did not yield the positive result mother was hoping to obtain.

Somewhere in the depths of my mind I've been conditioned. Negative became positive, positive became nothing inside my head. Years of being told, "I should have never had you" had its effect in a way somehow inside my thinking processes; negative was transformed into survival.

"You can sleep in the top bunk bed when you stop peeing your crib."

This encouragement from mother died in my head as soon as I heard it. I peed relentlessly, the same as I did in my full size bed. Even going to the bathroom prior to going to sleep, it was to no avail. I practiced using baking soda and towels day after day to kill the smell, but it turned into a stench. Mother's "encouraging" words as she passed through my room to Oma's room were, "Pee-Yew, change your sheets, it stinks in here." I learned how to use the washing machine and wash my own sheets.

I moved my crib from the far corner in my room closer to the door of my bedroom. Before going to sleep, I did what comforted me every night in my other bed. I rolled over on my stomach, adjusted my pillow under my chest and started bouncing my head thousands of times as I did the night before. My body reached almost from headboard to the footboard of my crib, so placing my feet between the mattress and the footboard gave me the clearance I needed above my head.

I gauged my growth by placing my right hand in a fist, then placing my fist between the crown of my head and the headboard to check my clearance. I still had a fist full of clearance to grow before I grew out of my crib. I didn't care about how much space I had as long as I could bounce my head. With all the clearance I needed, I started bouncing my head, counting into the thousands.

I bounced my head with delight, enjoying the feeling of each bounce of my face. Counting. It felt so good. But then the background noise came forward; I couldn't ignore it. The squeak of the springs and the slates holding up the rails of my crib, began echoing in my ears as I bounced my head. My crib rocked back and forth, creating a constant squeak that wasn't there in my full size bed. Before moving back into my crib, I could reach my arms high above my head to bounce, but now it was different. The sound of my crib squeaking interrupted my counting momentarily as my thoughts were displaced. Sometimes I had to start over again.

As I bounced my face into my pillow, my hair was hitting my right wrist.

I was feeling the softness of the strands of hair, gentle brushing against my body. It felt so soft. It was a feeling I hadn't felt before. Like petting a kitten, my mind drifted towards the softness of its touch. My hair felt so nice to the touch of my body. My mind was filled with the greatest of ease, bouncing. I was so pleased; life was good.

Mother and Daddy slept in separate beds. Daddy's room was closest to my room. When I moved my crib closer to the door and left my door ajar, it proved to be a problem for me the next morning. It was Saturday and Daddy was still in his bed. He must have been awakened by the unusual sound echoing down the hallway into his room from mine. Daddy got up to see what all the noise was about. My crib was squeaking back and forth, squeak, squeak, squeak, squeak, squeak, squeak. Daddy was watching me bounce my head on my pillow. He reached down into my crib and gently hit me on my head. Startled, I stopped. Snapped out of my world, I looked up to see who hit me. It was Daddy standing above my crib.

Without me saying a word, Daddy said, "Cut it out, I'm trying to sleep."

I shuffled my pillow and continued bouncing slightly, touching the pillow with my face so as to not let the bed squeak. The next day I moved my crib back into the corner where it was before, and I made sure that my door was closed to help deaden the sound.

Sunday morning seemed to bring peace and calmness into the home. Unless the neighbor was cutting their lawn or there was a barking dog in the neighborhood. Mother would be outraged, ready to call the police if that was the case. Mother hated the sound of the lawnmower early in the morning on Sundays. Mother knew the noise ordinances and would call the authorities to turn in the offender often, even writing them an unflattering letter telling them how inconsiderate they were for making noise early Sunday morning. In that case mother woke me up with her yelling as it made mother as mad as a disturbed hornet! "These inconsiderate people making noise on Sunday before 10 a.m.!" Mother said aloud. Mother could hear everything from afar.

This Sunday was a quiet morning. I woke up on my own with anticipation of what Sunday morning brought, Daddy's pancakes! I could hardly wait for Daddy to cook them. I carefully and quietly stepped out of my crib to keep the squeaks of my crib at bay and to avoid waking Daddy or my brother. I went into the bathroom to clean myself up. I'd been thinking while bouncing my head in between counting, what could I do to please mommy? I thought I would set the table. Mother loved all of her dishes, and I did too. Thinking I would be praised by mother for setting the table, I began.

I muscled the kitchen chair from around the table, setting it close to the bottom cabinet below where the dishes were placed above. I climbed quietly onto the chair then kneeled on the countertop. I opened the cabinet door slowly, moving my body backwards to miss the swing of the door. I resumed my position thereafter to quietly remove each plate from the cupboard, setting them on the countertop one by one without a sound. I hopped down from the countertop quietly. Placing each plate with the apples on top on the table one of the time, back and forth till the table was set with plates. I folded napkins on the left with the crease on the outside.

I inched the right number of forks and knives from the drawer, making sure they did not rattle against each other. As mother had taught, I placed the forks on top of the napkin on the left, knives on the right of the plate, seared edge inward. I knew how mother wanted the table to be set. I placed coffee cups on the saucers with the handle on the right side of the cup for mother and Daddy's convenience. I put drinking glasses in front of everyone else's plate. I knew the table was almost set. I put a fresh cube of butter on the butter dish. I brought out the real maple syrup leaving the applesauce in the refrigerator to stay cold. I was almost ready to go tell mommy I set the table.

A powerful feeling of anticipation for setting the table entered my thoughts, hoping mommy would be pleased. I walked to mommy's bedroom from off of the living room to tell her, placed my hand on the door knob, listening to the springs inside the handle click as I twisted the knob slowly and quietly. I carefully opened the door, taking one step inside mommy's room. Daddy's head popped out from the blankets! I was shocked, thinking, 'Why is Daddy in mommy's bed?' I've never seen this sight before. I was taken back by this anomaly. I closed the door as quickly and quietly as I had opened it. I walked past the set table on the way to my room. After changing my sheets, I laid on my bed and stared at the ceiling to take my thoughts away from seeing Daddy in mommy's bed. I needed to erase this thought out of my mind and never think about it again.

I waited in my room for breakfast to begin, staring at the ceiling and laying on my mattress, dreaming of the shapes above me.

CHAPTER TEN

MOMMY MENTOR–SON MENTEE

"Circumcision, it's barbaric!" mother said to me. Mommy's statement sounded like she was angry, but she might have been passionate or concerned about the subject. One sounded like the other. Mother continued, "That skin was put there for a reason! It should never be cut off!" Mother said it in the same matter-of-fact tone. Mother sounded like an expert. I started thinking about what mother was saying about penises, and extra skin being cut off. This all intrigued me, but my lips clamped shut. I remembered my last question about the head of my penis being purple and mother wanting to see it. I wasn't going to ask any questions that might lead up to the wrong answer again. I listened. I believed without a doubt, mother was so smart. Mother continued, "That skin was put there to protect the head of the penis!" I sat quietly thinking more about my penis and continued thinking, 'What would be different if it was cut off?' I listened as mother's conversation built curiosity inside my mind.

The subject of circumcision was just one of the conversations spoken around the kitchen table on a regular basis, usually at dinner time. Mother had no hesitation, guidelines or limitations to her subjects. I stopped talking when others were around and listened to mommy. I felt comfortable talking to mother. It was one-on-one learning in my eyes. What I felt this time was a powerful feeling inside of me. I didn't know how to explain, but it was in my tummy area. The feelings in my gut I couldn't ignore, like being hungry.

My gut was telling me something. I had to sift through what it was saying, like hot coals from the ashes. I didn't understand what was happening inside my body.

Processing all of mother's conversations inside my mind was a full-time job. Making the wrong decision or misunderstanding mother left me few options. At the very least I was yelled at, hit with her hand, or I got the radiator brush on my backside. Using intuition, past experiences, and common sense, any knowledge was helpful to make a wise decision around mother. Mother used words like "propaganda" often, explaining its meaning usually when it came to religion or politics. Mother threw the term around when referring to those she disagreed with, but she would never use "propaganda" to describe her rhetoric. She was a propaganda machine at its finest. Mother taught me what she felt inside her heart from her life's experiences, but mother's life experiences were not mine.

I paid attention, learning from the feeling inside me an innate desire to survive. I learned it from the very person who told me over and over again, "I should have never had you!" I needed to be watched over from something bigger than me, if I had a chance to live.

Immunization shots were another regular subject around the table, a topic like most topics that set mother on fire. Anytime mother heard about a child dying of leukemia or diagnosed with cancer, mother associated their sickness with immunizations. Mother was quick to say, "It's criminal what they do to babies, giving them shots! A pure bloodstream would never lend itself to death like this!" She continued, "My sons will never be immunized!" And she reminded us at the dinner table, "Those bastards who put silver nitrate in Frank's eyes as a baby!" I believed mother, but mother didn't leave it at that.

Mother was appalled at the very word 'immunization.' It conjured up death, poor health and decay to a person's body. She was passionate and clear her sons would never get shots. Telling me year after year, "If you ever get shots, you will die! Don't ever get them!" Immunization shots weren't going to happen under any circumstances with her boys. Mother enforced the belief I would die receiving shots, and it became deeply ingrained into my mind.

The beginning of the school year brought this subject up annually. Mother signed papers that stated if there was an outbreak of disease her children would be first to leave school. Mother's feelings were that if there was an outbreak, she would want her child out of school. I couldn't discern what shots were lethal and what shots were not. From mother's point of view, all shots were poisonous.

The kitchen table conjured up a narrow array of topics regularly repeated. "I tried five times for a girl and ended up with five boys." Then she would say, "Boy, am I glad I didn't end up with a girl, all she would have done is come home pregnant!" I thought of each time mother made that comment, 'Why wouldn't you teach your daughter not to get pregnant?' I never said a word. Mother was very consistent about being inconsistent, saying, "I had five kids to keep my sanity in this stupid state" in one breath and following it with, "Because of you damn kids we were poor!" in the next. It was a conflict of interest inside my mind. Which one was it?

Mother was raised in a family of all girls. The culture was that one of the children, usually the daughters, would take care of the parents as the parents aged. With five boys in her progeny, I felt that mother wondered who was going to take care of her in her older years. Mother started teaching her boys at a very young age to tend her in her older age, telling all of us at the dinner table with a whimper, "You're just going to put me in a nursing home when I get older and let me rot!"

Mother took exceptional pride in her German cooking from scratch. Mother had a special sauerkraut recipe nobody else had. Her hot and cold German potato salad was another favorite. She painstakingly made rouladen, gurkensalat, rotkohl, and other delectable dishes. She purchased the ingredients from the German delicatessen: white herring, celery root, rutabagas, cow's tongue, German wieners, and of course bratwurst! We didn't starve. We all grew up in the culture of German cuisine. We knew nothing else. Mother was a very good German cook even though she had not grown up in Germany. We never complained once. I didn't even complain about eating cow's tongue. I just put a lot of ketchup on it, which was a no-no in German culture. Mother said, "Ketchup is strictly American."

While mother fed us her cooking, mother also reinforced her beliefs on us. She never passed up an opportunity to manipulate us into her thinking. After telling us about putting her in a nursing home to rot with poignancy at the dinner table, Mother added, "Don't get married, don't have children. If you do get married and have children, don't come around here! Move to China."

WHAT!? Move to China? None of us wanted to move to China and eat Chinese food. Mother's German food was too good to move. I listened to mother's wisdom and Daddy's silence.

Mother's view on religion was just as heated and filled with anger as any other subject, and it too was a regular topic at the dinner table. She had a built-in audience. Mother constantly made herself clear about her feelings towards the Mormons–and any other religious group for that matter.

"Religion! It's all fictitious!" Mother drilled this into her children's heads for the umpteenth time as I sat at the table. "It's all made up to control people," mother said. "Joseph Smith did not have visions; he had seizures!" Mother yelled out with authority.

I continued to listen and learn.

"There is no God! If there was a God, why would He let that airplane crash, killing all those people?" Mother's voice elevated, as if she felt the death of all those people who died on the airplane. "Oh," throwing her right arm down towards the floor, she said, "You'll never catch me on an airplane!" Here she built a belief in my mind between airplane crashes and no such thing as a God. The only other reference to God was when she swore. The term "Jesus Christ" was often used as a swear word.

Mother continued to work herself into a lather. "Religion should be abolished!"

My older brother Hermann chimed in at that moment, "Yeah, look at all the wars that are fought over religion!"

I sat and listened, not saying a word. A thought came into my head, after my brother's comment, "Look at all the wars that are fought over religion." I thought to myself, "Religion must be very important!" I remained quiet with my thought, keeping it to myself so as not to get involved with the conversation. As usual, I had a different thought process inside my head.

Mother told me time and time again, "You have a brain and a conscience, USE IT!"

I knew I had a brain, but I wondered what a conscience was. I didn't ask. "Smart people are dumb and dumb people are smart!" This comment of mother's also went through my head, melding with my understanding of her, her beliefs, and my developing view of the world. As I processed mother's words, my mind went to the TV show *Gilligan's Island*, thinking of Gilligan being smart because he was dumb, and the Professor who was dumb because he was smart.

Mother said often, "You're beautiful, but don't let that go to your head!" This was another inconsistent comment from mother. I felt I knew what beauty was, but the next part, "don't let that go to your head," I didn't understand. When I told her the truth as I saw it, her usual response was, "Oh, you asshole!" That I understood. The other things she said were a puzzle. "Stop talking!" "You talk in riddles!" "I don't understand anything you're saying!" "Can't you talk intelligently?" "Can't you say anything that makes sense?" "I should have never had you!" "You don't know how lucky you are not to have relatives." Mother's words spun in my head.

I stood by mother's side listening from one conversation to the next, cross-referencing all of what mother said from one piece of information to the other. Mother had no idea I would pay so close attention to what came out of her mouth.

Mother talked to the neighbor over the fence, Gerri Taylor. Gerri and mother were two women who got along just fine–no barking dogs, no noisy kids, and neither one of them were Mormons.

Gerri commented to mother, "With your five boys, you could farm them out for a stud service!" Gerri saying it with a little cackling laugh under her breath.

Mother said, "I could!"

I stood by mother's leg and thought, 'why would you agree with what she just said?' Thinking of the massage parlor up the road, red lights, police and prostitution. I couldn't understand mother's thinking.

Life was a confusing muddle with mother as I tried so hard to find the patterns. For the most part I accepted it as normal, but there were times I saw through it. One day while mother drove home from the delicatessen store my younger brother and I hopped back and forth from the front seat to the back seat of the car.

"Sit down and hold still!!" mother said while she was driving the car.

I ended up in the front seat after all the jumping back and forth. I turned to look at mother as she steadfastly focused on driving the car down the road. "I'll never marry anybody like you, mommy!"

My younger brother Walter stuck his head in the front seat of the car, and said, "Yeah, me either!"

I returned to silence as mother continued driving down the road. Mother was silent, too.

After a minute or so, I looked over at her again. There was a tear running down her cheek.

Mother turned to me for just a moment, saying, "You'll be sorry you said that one day!"

I was flooded with guilt. I'd never seen a tear in mother's eye, let alone see a tear roll down mother's cheek. I felt bad for what I said!

In school, with my last name starting with the letter 'B,' I got to sit in the front row or behind a classmate whose last name started with 'A.' I liked the front row this time. I was falling in love with my second grade teacher. Mrs. Devine, she was beautiful. She was only a few years older than me and unmarried. I knew because I asked her. I sat and listened to her while she taught, standing in front of the classroom.

Mrs. Devine asked a question, "What are some words that rhyme with gray?"

Students started raising their hands. I heard, "I know, I know."

I raised my hand, too.

Mrs. Devine called on me. "Robert, do you have a word that rhymes with gray?"

I shook my head yes. I said, "Stray!"

Mrs. Devine looked at me with what I interpreted as a bewildered pause. I thought immediately, is that a bad word? I didn't know what it meant. Mrs. Devine processed my answer for what seemed a long moment to me, as if to say, 'how do you know to use that word?' If she asked I wouldn't be able to come up with the answer, except I heard mother say often, "there's another stray cat!" 'Stray' rhymed with 'gray' in my head as far as I was concerned.

"You're right!" Mrs. Devine said, then gave a short explanation of the word for the rest of the class.

I was pleased that I contributed. I felt important.

Then something shifted inside my head, drawing my attention away from Mrs. Devine. I didn't understand what was going on inside my body, inside my pants. Why was my penis irritating me? I didn't know what was happening. What was going on with my body? Why was my penis doing what it was doing? My penis was erect and pushing against my pants, creating a pressure that was hurting me. It bothered me beyond my understanding. With no comprehension, I was just annoyed by it. I started hitting myself while simultaneously silently saying in a whisper, "Go away, go away, go away!" I continued hitting myself, hoping Mrs. Devine wouldn't see what I was doing or what was happening to my body.

Mrs. Devine saw me hitting myself in my pants. I couldn't hide what was irritating me.

She said "Robert!"

I froze! A breath of thought entered my head, she saw me! I felt my face become flush. I was embarrassed. I ran out of altitude, airspeed, and ideas all at the same time; my head went blank. I laid my head on my desk, wondering what just happened. I didn't know what to think. I just wanted whatever it was to go away and stop hurting me. As quickly as it came, it dissipated, but not from my mind. My head processed, I am not going to raise my hand again. I stopped talking and kept to myself. I was confused. I continued to remain quiet as a student, keeping my comments to myself thereafter.

I could no longer focus in school. My penis was overtaking my thoughts. I was falling behind the other students. My teacher noticed me falling behind, so a decision between mother and Mrs. Divine was made on my behalf. That decision was for me to attend a Special Education class. I needed help catching up to the other students. I couldn't comprehend what I was reading very well, because words were a bunch of letters in some random order I couldn't decipher or understand. This led to my inability to write. I couldn't sound out letters to spell. I barely could do arithmetic, unless it was simple.

I recall another day when Mrs. Devine had a substitute teacher filling in for her. I became very fidgety. The teacher said, "It's time to take a bathroom break and go to the lavatory!" I was relieved at the moment she said that. I needed to pee really badly, but it was too late. I peed my pants on the way to the bathroom. I looked down at my pants, at what looked to me like western chaps. I was soaked, and I was embarrassed. I stood in the hallway by the bathroom. I didn't need to go inside the lavatory anymore.

I stood wet in the hallway with other students walking around me. I was very wet. I thought, I don't live very far from school, I want to go home and change. At the same time, my substitute teacher walked over to me, put one hand on my shoulder, her other on my chest, leaned over and whispered into my ear, "You're going to be okay."

I listened to every word she said. It sounded as if it was the most beautiful music that had ever played in my ears. I heard the gentleness in her voice, the softness of her tones, a sound of music that set me free inside. I noddedmy head yes.

I had never heard such beautiful words whispered into my ear before. Her kindness engaged me in an awareness I was not familiar with in a woman, especially after I had an accident. A gentleness, a whisper of greatness, a sound of beauty entered my soul, transforming itself in my being, the whisper of her words etched in the caches of my mind. I would never forget the beautiful heartfelt tone of her voice: "You're going to be okay."

CHAPTER ELEVEN

A WINK IS AS GOOD AS A NOD TO A BLIND MULE

Mother went through cars like water through a sieve. Daddy could only afford used cars for mother to speed around town as she did her shopping for the family. My positive disposition and happy countenance fueled my desire to connect with mother, spending as much time with her as possible. It may seem to have been in vain, but it wasn't to me. I traveled with mother everywhere, learning about life. I wanted to experience life for myself, not be taught.

Lickety split, away we went in mother's 1964 Plymouth Belvedere. Mother seemed to love colors that were oxidized. It was the common color mother had in all her cars. In this case it was called Oxidized Blue.

I went with mother to every delicatessen store on her route, from one to the next, visiting all four of them in an all day affair, coming home exhausted at the endl. The aroma of the car smelled wonderful, as if the delicatessen store followed us home. It was mother's favorite day of the week and mine, too. Visiting all the different shops, I remained with mother, listening to her even if I couldn't understand what she was saying because it was all in German. Mother had her clutch of friends to chat with. It never bothered me that I didn't understand. I just wanted to be with mommy.

I listened to their conversation closely, picking up phrases that weren't in the German language. From the tones in their voice fluctuations as they embellished their stories and from their gesticulations with body and

93

arms and expressions on their faces, I pieced together their conversations, gathering the gist of what they were talking about. Sometimes I asked mother, "What were you guys talking about?" Mother told me. I continued gathering information for myself.

Friday was Delicatessen Day, as every Friday was. But this Friday was different. I hopped into the car with mother as she rushed off to the store. Mother had an open lane on the outside as if cleared for takeoff. Making her way to the freeway, mother sped off! With mother's shopping route in her head, she stepped on the pedal, speeding down the road, off and running, free as a bird. Sighting a clear path to the freeway entrance ahead of her, she drove speedily out of sight of our street. I sat in the front seat, sitting sideways, talking to mommy with my left leg kneeling on the seat and my right leg on the floorboard. The front passenger seat was the one mother called "the death seat." With two lanes of stopped traffic to the left of her and no cars in front of her, mother's determination mounted to make it onto the freeway before somebody pulled in front of her to slow her down. From the corner of her left eye, mother caught someone weaving through traffic towards her!

"WATCH OUT!" mother yelled. Mother's arm became my seatbelt. Mother slammed on the break, locking the wheels. I heard the screech of the tires, all one second of it as it played in my head like the skip of a broken record. I reacted immediately with my right arm reaching out to catch myself, bracing my body so as not to hit the metal dashboard that was quickly coming my way. My eye caught as if it was the snap of a shutter on a camera, a boy on a bicycle! BAM! The car finished its screeching halt. He was gone from my sight.

Mother reacted quickly, slamming her brakes, leaving a lengthy skid mark behind the car on the road. It all happened in the blink of an eye. The thought went through my head, 'did mother run over and kill the paperboy?' He was gone from my view!

Mother was scared, saying loudly, "I think I killed the paperboy, go check!"

I reached for the door handle, pulling it backwards fast, hearing it ricochet back into its position, pushing the tight door open with both hands hopping out of the front seat of the car and onto the road. I ran to the front of the vehicle to see what I saw a moment ago. He was lying on the road with two broken legs, but I couldn't see him from where I was. Rolled newspapers were strewn in front of the car, my sight was limited from where I could see. I hollered back, "You did run over the paperboy!

It was years before I realized the insanity of having your seven-year-old go check on the presumably dead body of the paperboy.

Mother sat in the car for a moment, not reacting in the driver's seat, fearing the worst, thinking she killed him!

Then I hollered to mother, "He's alive!"

"Are you okay?" I asked the boy.

Other people hopped out of their cars immediately to check on him, too. Some of them were gathering the newspapers that were scattered through the road from the impact, tossed out from the saddlebags tied to his bicycle. The bicycle was bent under the car. The paperboy was lying on the road, alert but what seemed to be dazed. "I can't move my legs!" the boy said.

I heard the sirens in the background. It didn't take long for the police and the ambulance to arrive. More people gathered, and I moved out of the way, staring at the adults who were handling the scene. The ambulance took the boy to the hospital, the police inspected the bicycle, and others measured the length of the skid marks with a measuring wheel. I stood and watched it all. Mother retold the story to the officer as he wrote down her statement. Mother seemed upset, saying what she remembered–seeing him come from the corner of her eye and slamming on the brakes.

The officer pulled the bicycle out from under the car, inspecting it closely. The officer noticed that the car happened to hit the frame of the bike at just the right spot, pointing with his finger to the bent section on the frame. "The boy was lucky," the officer said. "It looks like the car hit the frame first instead of his leg. It probably spared his leg from being crushed."

Mother got the name of the boy from the officer and where he lived. It turned out he lived just a few blocks away from our house. Hancock was his last name.

Mother and I continued on our way after it was all over, mother saying to me, "I seldom have a clear shot to the entrance to the freeway, but this time I did and look what happened." Mother shared her experience with some of her clutch of friends as it was getting late due to the delay of the accident. With limited time, mother picked up her shopping on Saturday where she left off on Friday.

Mother visited the boy in the hospital. He was in a cast from his waist down with two broken legs. Mother brought the boy treats, flowers and gifts, and I went with her as she visited his family regularly over the next two to three months at their home while he healed. I just listened while the tone in the air seemed more jocular than when I saw him on the ground weeks earlier. The boy showed us how he got around in his cast. The boy said, "I don't think I'm going back to deliver newspapers anymore." After we left his home, I thought of mother's generosity to somebody who she hardly knew, and I made a mental note as the thought passed through my mind. I dismissed it, because that was mother.

Mother had a colorful array of words for her fellow drivers while driving down the road. The lucky occupants of those cars never got a chance to hear what mother said to them when they got in her way, but I did. "Move over slowpoke!" "Another Sunday driver in front of me!" "Sightseeing! Move over!" "Get out of the fast lane, Granny!" "Insecure driver!"

When words couldn't come out of mother's mouth fast enough to convey her thoughts, the horn worked nearly as good if not better. It was as loud as a train horn blowing through a street crossing. Mother's instinct to lay on the horn never disappointed her, satisfying the feeling towards the other driver who wronged her by simply being in her way.

If I could describe mother in one word it would be 'authoritarian.' Mother established her authority with her five boys as well with Daddy. Mother was the top dog, leader of the pack. Mother established her domain however she needed to be in control of her children's and husband's lives. Mother used her iron fist early on while simultaneously using her anger to intimidate her subjects. I correlated mother's message with pain, and at the same time I relied on mother for sustenance. Mother established her authority using corporal punishment with me from the very beginning of my life, starting when I was pooping my pants at two years old.

Mother may have developed a problem with authority from the beginning of her life with her mother, my oma. Oma established authority over mother using violence. Mother struggled to become important to her mother, caring for Oma before she passed away in hopes of resolving lingering issues between the two of them. Corporal punishment cemented that authority, but in the wrong way, showing no love thereafter. It was just more punishment. 'Stop your crying or I will give you something to cry about.' Mother would rather compete with the most vulnerable then solve the problem, which would weaken her position as an authoritarian. I don't believe there was a whole lot of difference in mother's mind between a soldier in uniform and a policeman in uniform. Both represented overbearingness and power to mother. Exactly what mother was.

If I could describe Daddy in one word it would be 'calm.' Daddy was the complete opposite of mother. Being the opposite of mother fulfilled the law of polarity. Opposites attract.

Police represented authority to mother and rubbed mother the wrong way, unless it was for mother's convenience. Driving westward one day, mother flew over the east side of the 13th South Viaduct to the other side in her very fast car. Police were waiting on the other side to pull over would-be speeders. It was mother's turn as she whizzed by the police!

They estimated mother's speed using sight, the speed gun of the day. With our windows rolled down, I heard the police holler "PULL OVER!"

"What did he say?" mother asked.

I turned to mother and said, "He said to pull over!"

Mother paused for a moment, taking her foot off the gas. Then she hit the gas pedal, off she went lickety split, zigzagging through neighborhoods.

"Are they following me?" mother asked.

I hopped into the backseat of the car looking through the rear view window. "I don't see anything, mommy," I said.

Mother had a location in mind. She continued to zig zag through the neighborhood, making sure there was no pursuit. Mother made it to Ursula's home, a long-time friend, not far away from where this all started. It was a convenient place to hide out. Mother parked in the driveway and knocked on the door to hurry in the house.

Ursula's husband Garrett was busy building an airplane in his garage.

"Go look," Ursula told me.

I had never seen an airplane close up, let alone one being built in a garage. Garrett was happy to show me his work. It was very interesting to me that an airplane would even fit in the garage, as I eyed it from front to the back of the garage space. It was just the carcass of the plane. No wings were attached to the frame at the time.

I asked him, "Where are the wings?"

He showed me to another room in the back of the garage.

I forgot all about the police chase. The airplane fascinated me more.

When the coast seemed clear, mother and I left Ursula's home, feeling confident she lost the police. Mother's trail grew cold fast with her foot on the pedal. The police were not prepared for mother's reactions and had little chance of catching her.

Several months later, mother called me into the living room and handed me the newspaper. The picture on the front page was of the airplane Garrett had shown me in his garage. It was now a pile of rubble on the ground. He had crashed his plane.

I stared at the picture. I gasped. "Did he die?" I asked.

"Yes!" mother said. "Garrett fell out of the sky and was killed!"

My thoughts went back to the plane he so proudly showed me months earlier.

"Garrett was going to ask Ursula for a divorce later that day, after his flight!" mother said. "Garrett took off from the airport without fueling his airplane. He fell out of the sky like a rock."

"What's a divorce?" I asked.

Mother told me what divorce was.

I felt bad for Ursula. I liked Ursula. I stared at the wreckage in the newspaper. The black and white photo of the plane was just a crumpled up pile of metal on the ground. The sight of the photo continued etching into my mind the longer I stared at it.

My mind kept flashing back in time when Garrett showed me his airplane in the garage. The whole experience played in my mind. Mother fleeing from the police, going to Ursula's home, Garret showing me his airplane in the garage...and now he was dead! I drew a very important lesson from the whole thing–don't fly without a sound mind!

I thought to myself, 'He must have been thinking about his problems. A divorce sounds horrible!'

Mother said, interrupting my thoughts, "You'll never catch me in an airplane!" Mother had no control of an airplane's fate. Yet she did go on airplanes when it suited her. Most everything was out of mother's control whenever she got inside one, which wasn't often, but she succumbed to her fears sparingly.

Another time we were driving down Main Street. That was a slower route to downtown so I don't know why mother took that way. Maybe mother had to make a stop between where we lived and the delicatessen store. This time there was another slowpoke in front of her on the two lane road. Mother looked past the car in front of her to make sure no oncoming traffic was approaching. She was getting ready to pass the slowpoke. "They're only going 30 miles per hour," mother said. "The speed limit is 35!"

"What are you going to do, mommy?" I asked.

"I'm going around them as soon as the coast is clear!" Mother was firm in her decision.

"But there's a policeman, mommy," I said. I pointed at the blue car on the side of the road.

"I don't care—the speed limit is 35 and they're going 30. They're going too slow!"

Mother approached the police car from behind, put on her blinker, and zoomed around them.

"You did it, mommy," I said.

I stared at the officers as we passed.

In mere seconds, the lights came on and the siren roared, signifying, pullover! This time mother did not hit the gas pedal. She pulled over and rolled down her window as the policeman approached.

"Do you know how fast you were going?" the police officer asked mother.

"35?" mother said, sounding sheepish.

"Why did you pass me?" the officer asked.

"You were going 30 in a 35 mph zone," mother said, like he was doing something wrong.

"The speed limit is 30 mph," the officer said.

Mother held her index finger up to her bottom lip.

I stared at the shine on mother's fingernail as she answered the officer's questions. Soon the officer handed mother back her registration and driver's license. The officer sent mother off with a warning.

Mother seemed to be just as blindsided by the sudden appearance of an authority figure as a blind mule is to a swat on the butt. A wink is as good as a nod to a blind mule. But neither the wink nor the nod gets the mule's attention. It wasn't until mother was stopped by the officer, without hope of escape, that she became contrite and submitted to the authority of the law.

After a short delay, mother was off and running to do her shopping at the delicatessen store. Returning home, I helped mother put the meat in the refrigerator next to the cigarettes. "Why do you keep your cigarettes in the refrigerator, mommy?" I was curious.

"I am a party smoker. I only smoke at parties," mother said. "I keep the cigarettes in the refrigerator to keep them fresh!"

"Oh," I replied.

My younger brother introduced me to cigarettes at eight years old. He was seven. I liked the smell, but I didn't understand them. I didn't want to touch mommy's cigarettes. The consequences could be too high. I saw my older brother's roll up tiny cigarettes. He pulled the papers from a small package that read 'zig-zag' on the carton. I saw him sprinkle some dried leaves onto the paper and then roll them up. Pinching off the ends, he lit it, then he held his breath. Then he tried talking to me but his voice was funny, like he had to go to the bathroom really bad, and his chest popped out. It seemed kind of odd. It smelled funny, too, much different than other cigarette smoke I smelled. But I had my own idea. I thought if I gathered some broom bristles from mother's broom, wrapped them in paper, just like I saw my older brother Hermann do, I would have a cigarette, too.

Locating mother's broom, I cut a small handful of bristles off of the broom, nothing mommy would notice. I found a piece of paper and placed the broom bristles on the paper, then rolled up, almost the same way as I saw my brother do. It looked kind of fat like a cigar, but I thought it would do. I found some matches and hid myself behind the bush not far from the house and lit my rolled up cigarette.

I took a deep breath and held it in, just like Hermann did, but only for a short moment. I started choking and coughing from inhaling the smoke. When I regained my composure, I thought this was not what I was expecting. I didn't know what went wrong, but I didn't have the same experience that I had with store-bought cigarettes. I decided there had to be a better way, so I went back to regular cigarettes. My brother Walter and I purchased them from the gas station vending machine. I remember Kool, Lucky Strikes, and other brands. The machine was an oxidized light brown color with smoky glass. We would put the money in, pull the knob and the coil above released the pack, dropping it into the slot below.

Billy caught my brother and me smoking and told Daddy. I was calm and collected at the moment. I simply said to Daddy, "I just breathed in what Walter breathed out."

Daddy looked at me uncertainly with my lie.

Meanwhile my younger brother was screaming, "I didn't smoke, I didn't smoke!"

"Let me smell your breath," Billy said.

Walter ran away and hid himself under the kitchen chair. Daddy seemed to believe my story. I was safe, and he didn't say anything more to me. The fear of getting caught cured me of smoking cigarettes, but not from the aroma that a cigarette offered. I love the smell of cigarette smoke to this day.

CHAPTER TWELVE

MAN'S BEST FRIEND

"I can't stand those Mormons across the street with their noisy kids and barking dog." Mother spit her words with anger. "Every time they leave with their umpteen damn kids in their station wagon, they put the dog outside, and it barks all the time while they're gone. They're probably going to church, those do-gooders! They're so inconsiderate of other people!" Mother had scoped out everyone's house who had a barking dog, hoping they would be responsible dog owners and shut their dogs' mouths if they barked. Mother's ears traveled far and wide.

The dog continued to bark.

She turned to me and said, "Go to the door and see if it's their dog that's barking again."

I had heard this all before. I hesitated, unwilling to take my mind off of the TV.

Mother snapped at me. "Hurry up!"

I jumped at mother's request, opening the inside door to walk through it to open the screen door.

"Don't let the screen door slam behind you," mother snapped again.

It was too late. The door slipped from my hand and slammed.

"I told you not to let the door slam!"

"Sorry, mommy, my hand slipped." I spoke through the screen door. I turned around and stepped to the edge of the porch, looking across the street to verify where the barking was coming from. I saw the Mormons' dog barking in the corner of their fenced yard. I turned back around to come into the house.

Mother reminded me again, "Don't let the door slam behind you again!"

I caught the door, making sure it didn't slam this time.

"It's the dog across the street, mommy," I said.

"Close the inside door. I don't want to hear that damn barking dog anymore, yuck!"

I closed the door quietly and went back to watching my TV program.

Mother waved her arms around. "Who let this damn fly in! Go get the fly swatter."

I obeyed. Mother waited for it to land near her. She slapped the swatter onto the hapless fly, mashing it into the coffee table. She handed me the swatter. "Now go put this away."

I obeyed. When I returned, I took up my place in front of the TV once more.

"Will you massage my feet while you're watching TV?" mother asked.

"Yes, mommy, I will." I began to move the pillows from where I'd planned to sit so I could massage mother's feet.

Mother enjoyed laying on the couch in the early evening. It was mother's time to unwind from her day before heading to bed. Mother worked hard throughout the day and wanted her peace and quiet during this time, away from the sound of barking dogs, noisy kids and sirens. With mother's head elevated and laying on a soft blanket, mother had made herself comfortable.

Mother moved her legs back far enough for me to sit down at the foot of the couch to massage her feet. "Here," mother said. Mother took off her wig of curly blonde hair and handed it to me. "Put it on the table. I want to put it on in case someone comes to the front door."

I dutifully took the mop of fake hair from her and put it on the table by the couch.

Mother continued. "Grab a pillow and put it on your lap before you sit down and massage my feet."

I grabbed a pillow from the backside of the couch and sat down and placed the pillow on my lap.

"Do my left foot first." Mother placed her left foot on the pillow that was on my lap.

I began massaging mother's feet, turning to watch the TV. Sometimes I glanced down looking at mother's foot, noticing that mommy's foot hadn't been washed yet. Mother's toenails were yellow and needed clipping. I thought mother's foot seemed old and wrinkly with lots of calluses on her heel and ball of her foot. I didn't say anything. I kept massaging mother's foot.

"Press my big toe," mother said.

I pressed mommy's toe.

"Ouch!" Mother flinched her leg towards her body. "Not so hard!"

"Sorry, mommy," I said. After mother's big toe was sufficiently pressed, mother wanted each of her toes to be pressed gently and slightly twisted like playing a Stradivarius violin.

Daddy played the violin. I remembered watching his hand movements as he wiggled the strings. That's how mommy wanted her toes massaged, with a little twist. That made mother happy, and that made me happy to do it. Sometimes I thought of playing "This little piggy went to market," but I didn't dare. Mother and I didn't share a sense of humor with one another.

Mother asked, "Take your knuckle and press my heel."

"Okay, mommy. Like this?"

"NO, not like that!" She continued. "Press your knuckle in the center and work your way out."

I paused to understand the question, then I coordinated my response. "Like this mommy?" I said. I pressed my knuckle in the center of mother's heel and worked outward. "Like this mommy?"

"Yes," mother said.

Mother's heel wobbled a little bit as I pressed my knuckle into her heel, sometimes slipping off. That's the way mother wanted her heel to be massaged.

"Okay, you're almost done with my left foot," mother said. It had been the better part of 20 minutes.

"Tickle the top of my foot now," mother demanded.

From my position, I looked down at mother's foot. The tip of her toes was the top of her foot. I took my fingers and tickled the top of mother's toes. It seemed insignificant as I danced my fingers across the top of her toes.

"NO!" mother said. "I want the top of my foot tickled, not the top of my toes!"

Mother made no effort to be clear about what she said, what she meant, and what she really wanted done. I had been conditioned to guess what mother wanted at any given time. Once she couldn't feel the tickling sensation anymore, she wanted to trade her left foot for her right foot. I began massaging and tickling her right foot the same way as I did her left foot. Sometimes mother's foot twitched while she dozed in and out of consciousness. I always knew when mother fell asleep because mother snored really loudly, waking herself up with her own snoring now and again. I watched the TV show until it was over. I wanted to be done touching mother's feet. Besides, I was hungry. Mother had decided to be done for the day, but she hadn't fixed dinner yet.

I noticed that mother had dozed off. She was still snoring. I waited patiently. After a few minutes, she snored loud enough to wake herself.

I snatched the opportunity. "Are you going to fix dinner?"

"I don't feel like it," mother said. "There are three refrigerators full of food, go find something to eat yourself!" Mother prepared less food for the family the older we became.

"There's nothing in the refrigerator to eat," I told mother.

"I just bought some lunch meat the other day." she said.

I said, "It's gone bad already."

"Just fry it up."

I wasn't going to eat bad meat. I found something else to eat. Daddy came home from working all day, changed his clothes, and went into the garden to work. It was Daddy's time to unwind from the day before catering to mother. Daddy massaged mother's feet, too, for mother's second go-round.

Eventually mother and Daddy retired to their own bedrooms after watching The Tonight Show. Mother laid on her bed with an open window, listening for barking dogs echoing in her ears. It didn't take much to irritate mother when she went to bed. Even the street lights irritated her. Mother figured out a way to block the light from her eyes. The sound of barking dogs was something mother couldn't block as easily, because she insisted on keeping her windows open for fresh air. She heard sounds far and wide and was unable to block the noise she heard. It was almost like she wanted a barking dog to irritate her so she could be occupied in the process of complaining. It didn't help that the sound of barking dogs in the middle of the night carried further than sound during the day.

Mother could pinpoint the general location of any barking dog in the neighborhood. She would grab her flashlight by the side of her pillow, put on a mismatch of clothes and canvas the neighborhood looking for the barking dog. If she couldn't find it on foot, she got in her car and drove around the neighborhood until she located the dog's residence. She wrote down the address and immediately filed a complaint with the city in hopes that the city would give them a ticket. The city typically did nothing, and she would then complain to the city for not handling the matter.

If the city still didn't do something about the barking dogs, mother took up the matter herself. Mother had her own noise ordinances in place when it came to dogs, and she wouldn't tolerate them being violated.

On another day after school, I sat down to watch TV. I noticed mother was standing by the front door. "What are you doing, Mommy?" I asked.

"None of your business!" After about 15 minutes, mother said, "Here. Stand by the door and let me know when the Mormons leave across the street."

"Why mommy?" I asked.

"None of your business, just tell me when they leave!"

I got tired of standing so I pulled up a chair from the kitchen table to sit by the front door. I could watch TV and look out the door at the same time.

Mother's intuition came to fruition. The Mormon family let the dog out and predictably drove down the road as mother hoped they would. They were leaving in their station wagon with their umpteen kids, as mother put it.

"They just drove by, mommy," I said.

"Go knock on their door and see if anybody's home," mother asked.

"Why mommy?"

"Just do what I tell you to do!"

I walked across the street as mother asked, opened the gate as the dog jumped and wagged its tail at me. I petted the dog as I walked to the door and knocked. Their dog continued jumping around me, happily wagging its tail. No one answered. I left, closing the gate behind me and went back to tell mother.

"Nobody answered the door, mommy," I said.

"Hop in the car!" mother said.

"Where are we going?"

"Just hop in the car, and do what I tell you to do!"

I hopped in the front seat of the car.

"Sit in the backseat!"

"Why mommy?"

"Just do what I tell you to do!" Mother backed out of the driveway. She continued in reverse all the way down the road in front of the Mormon family's house.

"What are we doing, mommy?"

"Go get the dog and put it in the car!"

"Where are we going with their dog, mommy?" I asked.

"We're going to take the dog to a nice neighborhood and let it out!"

"What neighborhood, mommy?" I asked. I petted the dog as it panted, wagging its tail and looking up at me.

Mother drove about 15 minutes away from where we lived into a subdivision where she thought there were lots of children who would enjoy a new dog in their lives. It was the same neighborhood where mother bought her goat milk. A German lady named Mrs. Schultz. I referred to her as the goat milk lady. Mother and I visited her often. I don't remember any of the conversations because they were all in German. Mrs. Schultz milked her own goats then sold raw goat milk mother bought for us. Mother would never allow us to drink cow's milk. Cow's milk was not as close to mother's milk when it came to the size of the animal that was born. Mother told me that it made sense.

Mother told me in the car Mrs. Schultz was a polygamist. Mother explained to me what a polygamous meant. I just listened to what mother said. "Don't say anything to her next time we go there," mother said.

Next time I went with mother to buy goat's milk, I stared at Mrs. Schultz. I noticed how she was dressed. It was very different from mother's way of dressing.

Not far from Mrs. Schultz home was that neighborhood she felt had lots of kids. It wasn't hard to find an area with children. Mormons generally have large families so finding a neighborhood filled with kids was more of the rule than the exception.

Mother stopped in the middle of the road. "This is a good location, let the dog out." Mother spoke quickly. "Hurry up! Open the door and let the dog out!"

I opened the door, and let the dog out. I didn't see any kids in the neighborhood. "Do you think this is a good place, mommy?" I asked.

"YES," she said. "Hurry up, close the door!"

I let the dog out and watched in the back window of the car as mother drove away.

Mother taught me over and over again, "You have a brain and a conscience, use it!" I wondered in moments like this what mother meant.

A few days later, playing out in the front yard of my home by Richard Street, one of the Mormon kids came over to our house and said, "Your mother doesn't have to complain about the dog anymore. The dog ran away." My conscience took a roll check, and the thoughts of everything that took place a couple days earlier ran through my head. I didn't say anything about the dog, but I thought about it. I knew the consequences of telling him about what happened to his dog would not be good for me. I remained silent. I didn't say anything except to say, "I will tell my mom." I searched my brain, trying to understand my conscience.

CHAPTER THIRTEEN

A BIOLOGICAL REACTION

With my three older brothers having passed through puberty, mother often talked about hormones and sex. I hadn't experienced puberty, but the sexual abuse I suffered at seven turned on my sexual switch, and mother's conversation at the table aroused my curiosity and instincts.

Mother's conversations at the dinner table regularly turned to sex.

"There's too damn many kids in the world as it is! People need to stop having sex!"

Daddy answered mommy in German. Whenever Daddy complained about what mother was saying in her conversation, he spoke it in German. I didn't understand what he was saying.

Mother would look disgusted at Daddy's comment. "They're going to learn about it anyway." Mother said more to Daddy, but the rest was in German. After shutting him down, mother continued her conversation to all five boys that were sitting at the table, listening intently. Mother continued, "EW! People are pigs. At least animals have a season for mating. People just do it whenever!"

I just looked at her, bewildered. I wasn't sure how much more I wanted to hear, but I kept present by listening. Mother's comments stuck inside my head with all the other subjects mother freely talked about, having a loose tongue.

As a young boy of nine, thoughts were turning inside my head more than

I felt safe to talk about. I was building a world inside of me that entertained my imagination. Mother helped me build it. The subjects of prostitutes, sex, penises, pulling your skin back, don't get a girl pregnant, puberty–mother was neither shy nor unabashed. Mother's conversations revolved around remaining in control of her disposition. I never let on what thoughts were going through my mind. I stayed quiet, my body connecting ever more with my brain. Mother's frankness helped connect the dots inside my head. Mother's conversation continued with lots of listening.

"Those Mormons had another baby across the street." Mother sounded disgusted. "I hope she has her tubes tied and stops having so damn many kids. All they're doing is increasing the world's population!"

I thought about the fact that mother had increased the population by five, even if it was to keep her sanity in this stupid state. I said nothing.

My older brother Hermann chimed in. "Can you imagine if each of us had five kids ourselves, that would increase the world's population by 25!"

I quickly did the math in my head. He was correct.

Mother expressed her disgust of even the possibility that that would happen, flinging her right arm forward from her head downward to the floor in a disgusted motion, saying, "Ich! Can you imagine that?"

Mother expressed her dominance on the subject of sex as a revolving topic. If mother had anything to do with it, she was not going to have her interests divided by losing control over us boys. Spouses were competition in mother's eyes. "Don't get married, don't have children, and don't come around here if you do. If you do, you can move to China!" She said this over and over again. Mother made herself clear.

I asked my older brother Hermann, "What is puberty?" I felt safe asking him.

Hermann explained, "Not everybody passes through puberty."

"They don't?!" I said, surprised. "I don't want to go through life without going through puberty."

"Time will tell," he said.

Despite mother's obsession with barking dogs, we had a dog of our own. She was a light brown poodle named Fluffy. Mother made sure that the dog kept quiet. Anytime she would bark, mother barked back. "What's she barking about? Shut her up!"

Fluffy came to play a part in my burgeoning understanding of puberty and sex.

One day I walked out the front door of my house onto the driveway, and I couldn't understand what I saw. Why was Fluffy pulling the neighbor's dog backwards down the street? I was afraid of touching Fluffy. I had never seen this before. The cats never got stuck together.

I said, "Come here Fluffy, come here Fluffy!" I was panicking, hitting the top of my legs as I called Fluffy to get away from the neighbor's dog. "Come here, Fluffy!"

My older brother Hermann heard all my commotion and saw how panicky I was.

I kept saying, "Come here, Fluffy."

"STOP!" he said. "Can't you see they're stuck together?"

"I don't want Fluffy to get pregnant!" I said.

Hermann lifted the neighbor's dog back up on his paws so he wouldn't be dragged. Then he placed his hands on both dogs to help settle them down.

I watched in horrified silence.

Hermann turned to me and said, "I hope you get stuck someday!"

My imagination soared through the sky! What could he possibly mean? Did people get stuck?

When Daddy added on the first addition, a bedroom at the back of the house, mother had envisioned all five boys sleeping in a row in the same room. Mother's vision would never come to fruition. Most of the time, there was so much fighting and disconnection between my brothers and myself that mother needed to separate my younger brother and myself from the older boys.

Mother reminded us of our fighting by saying, "Brotherly love, boy, we sure have it!"

I thought to myself, 'mommy, you never fostered brotherly love between us.' But I didn't say anything.

I played with my toy cars on the floor while my brother Hermann laid on the couch, taunting and teasing me. It was the same sofa I massaged mother's feet the night before. I stood up when I'd heard enough teasing and taunting. I told him, looking down on him, holding my toy car tightly in my hand, "Stop teasing me!"

Mother was in the kitchen feeding Oma. When mother heard the frustration in my voice, she hollered from the other room, "Leave him alone!"

Tension continued between us.

Hermann continued to tease me. "You little baby!"

"I'm not a baby!" I said. I was getting madder and madder. I lost control of any happy thoughts I had in my head. In a snap decision I raised my arm that housed my toy car and I threw it at him! It was a dead aim at Hermann, hitting him in the nuts.

Hermann grabbed his crotch, saying, "Oh crap, I'm going to die!"

His voice sounded strained and odd to me. Hermann looked like he was in great pain. I stood still, watching as he gasped for air. It seemed he couldn't think straight as he pushed the pain from his body. I felt his pain too, and I couldn't decide whether I should run away and save myself or stay and have him kill me when he recovered. I stood there and watched, not able to make a decision, but I knew I hurt him. He didn't kill me then, but little did I know that he was already planning his revenge.

My nature to snoop was only second to my curiosity. I spotted a stack of magazines underneath Hermann's bed. I knelt to the side of them, curious of their contents. I pulled the magazines into the light. The front cover revealed more than I'd ever seen before. I stared at the front cover. I looked behind me. Based on what I was seeing, I knew I shouldn't have found them. I didn't want to be caught looking at them. I thumbed through the first pages, then looked over my shoulder again. I put it back as if I had never touched them. I went to check where everybody was, then returned to look some more. My curiosity grew. I looked through more pages, stopping at a naked man. I froze, staring at his body. I put the magazines back and left them behind, but the image of his body was etched in my mind.

I wanted to see more but not right now. I had to process what I just viewed. Days later I asked my younger brother to pull down his pants in the same room I found the magazines.

He immediately said, "I'm going to tell mommy on you!"

I said, "NO!"

Walter ran out of the room to tell mommy.

I panicked. I knew what mother was capable of. I experienced her beatings and felt she was going to beat me for me asking my brother to pull down his pants. The fear of mother beating me gripped me.

I ran to find a hiding spot. On an empty bed in the back room where I found the magazines, mother placed a feather blanket on one of the beds, a bed for guests. A big thick feather blanket layed on top of the bed, thick enough to lay my still body underneath, hoping to remain as inconspicuous as possible as mother came into the room. I held still under the blanket with no movement. Mother hadn't come into the room yet. I had an itch I needed to scratch. It was getting hot, too, and I was running out of fresh air.

I lifted my arm to scratch my itch, a little fresh air rushed into the cavity under the blanket of feathers. The cool fresh air felt good. I scratched my itch with fear inside my body, waiting for the inevitable. My stomach turned, turmoil set in on the unknown inside my mind. How hard will mommy hit me? How painful is this going to be? I kept waiting, still underneath the feather blanket. My body's heat couldn't escape. It kept getting hotter under the blanket. Another itch...mother hadn't come to find me, worse to beat me. It was getting hotter. The thought crossed my mind, I'll never ask that question again. The pain of mother's beatings was too real, the emotional damage too great, the consequences too overwhelming.

I needed fresh air. I couldn't stay underneath the blanket any longer. It was getting so hot. My temperature rose. I lifted it from my body. Fresh air cooled my face as it flooded my space. I took a breath, breathing in quickly and moving out slowly from underneath the blanket, expecting mother to come into the room at any moment. But mother didn't come in.

Eventually, I slid out from under the blankets, tiptoed to the door, and twisted the door handle. I couldn't let the springs in the handle announce my departure.

Mother still hadn't come to find me. I walked slowly but steadily to my room, but I had to pass the open doorway to the kitchen. If mother was sitting in her chair she would see me. Maybe mommy was on the phone? Maybe mommy was napping or gone shopping? Many thoughts ran through my mind. I peeked around the corner. Mother wasn't in the kitchen. I leaped quickly past the doorway to get into my room where I felt safe from mother.

I didn't get beat. What happened to mother? I wasn't going to ask. I climbed into my crib, laying on the mattress and thinking about the pictures I viewed. I wanted to see more, but not the girl pictures. There were feelings inside my body I couldn't explain, a tingling inside my bowels I didn't understand. They were thoughts of the men's bodies I had viewed. But why?

Thoughts of exploring my body came to life. The pictures I viewed occupied my mind. I had no thought of talking to anyone, and I didn't want to tell anyone what I was feeling, what I was thinking...but I wanted to see more. I started bouncing my head on my pillow, thinking and thinking and thinking. Thoughts of my body were going through my mind. I kept bouncing my head, thinking what were these feelings inside of me? I bounced my head until I fell asleep.

Frank moved out of the house, headed for college in Southern Utah, far away from mother's physical grasp. Mother's influence had embedded itself deep into his mind, like the rest of us. We watched him drive away. The whole family stood silently as he went down the road in his green Volkswagen. Frank never looked back, and he would never return to live under mother's roof.

Mother wept a little as Frank made a right turn onto the main road, heading for the freeway. That was the second time I'd seen a tear in her eye. After that, she never showed any other reaction to his departure. It seemed that the only thing that it really meant to her was that she had a new place for her stuff.

Mother was always looking for new places to pile her purchases: clothes, magazines, labor-saving items, and anything that sparkled. The bed that waited for me when I stopped peeing my crib was already filled up with mother's possessions, and now mother had a new storage area: Frank's bed. It didn't take long for mother to pile Frank's bed with her hoard.

The side of the bed near the bedroom wall appeared to be a good hiding spot with what I was thinking of doing. Curiosity had gotten the best of me. My mind was filled with images that I had seen, that were stuck in my head. My breathing was fast then short and deep. I already spent the last year examining myself more closely than before, becoming fascinated with erections as they came and went. I didn't know why they happened. I also didn't understand what was driving me to make my decision.

The magazines had become a tipping point for me. I had to find out what was hiding inside me. I jammed myself between the bed and the wall, an easy hiding place for me. Anybody could walk into the room or come up from the basement and see me on the floor beside the bed, but I had to take the chance. The tingling feeling inside my bowels became more than I could ignore. What was happening inside of me surpassed any feeling of hunger in my stomach, resulting in an erection.

I couldn't ignore the feelings inside of me any longer. Breathing deeper, quicker breaths, I looked and looked again over the bed of mother's hoard. My mind was racing with images I viewed. My body was ready for this unexpected experience. My mind was not. I looked again, nobody was around. Pulling my pants down, exposing myself completely...I was hiding on the floor by the side of the bed. I hadn't gone through puberty. I didn't know what to expect, but I couldn't hold back.

Placing my hand on myself, still scared that somebody could come into the room at any time, breathing deeper, I looked again over the top of the bed. I had to be sure nobody was coming. There was no thought of stopping, I had to go further. What I was about to experience for the first time would change my life forever. It was an unclear anticipation that pushed me physically, then mentally.

An expansion beyond the present took place in my mind. It was an experience that was infinite. It was an experience that never dissipated from my mind. My mind paused with what had just taken place as I laid there on the floor. It was as if I were in a stupor. My eyes were wide open, then closed. My mind displaced the years of burns, blistering, and beatings to my body. The yelling and screaming that were in my head from verbal assaults dissipated, even if it was just for a moment. It was worth it.

The emotional and psychological damages to my mind, year after year of extremes, gave way, melting the jagged edges of ice. My mind soared through a universe of peace and calmness, a beauty I never experienced in this world. If this was love, I just felt it for the first time. Experiencing this feeling had taken me to a place that was infinite in my head. The expansion of that moment never abandoned me.

As I re-entered this world, listening to my breathing, watching my chest expand then contract, beautiful thoughts formed in my head from this experience. The feeling of that moment became etched into my mind. I was set free, if only but for a moment. I could never go back, this feeling had reshaped my world, becoming a life saver. It was a feeling mother couldn't beat out of me!

I needed this calmness and peace to soothe my mind. I hadn't discovered the emotional connection between my mind and body until now. That natural connection had been hidden but was now released through these feelings deep down inside of me that I hadn't known existed. This was the best thing that could have happened to me in the moment. My life at home was loud, painful, confusing, and inconsistent at best. What was going through my head, and what I could comprehend with what was going on in the world, left me with deep insecurities that had taken a strong hold inside of me.

The relationship I had with mother was an ongoing source of fear, intimidation, threats, anger, insecurities, beatings and more. I was not in a safe place with my emotions. I became accustomed to abuse, displacing my feelings within me. My father was safe to be with, but mother dominated everything, including my daddy. I needed to create a place of peace that I could relate to, a reset of my feelings. Masturbating became that connection with my body to resetting my inner peace, calmness, and focus, creating a strength I needed in a world where insecurities set in with me.

The positive effects of masturbating gave me energy beyond my wildest imagination. I was motivated to recreate this calmness within me. I needed it. For this feeling to be inside of me was incomprehensible to what I was used to. To become aware of this treasure, this gift inside of me, became so important, I couldn't stop thinking about this experience and the possibilities in the future. To think it was there all this time, inside my body, was mind blowing.

Touching myself became extremely personal to me. There was no

119

shame, there was no ugliness, no guilt, no feeling of filthiness. It was just an experience that was beautiful. The world around me changed inside of me forever, an expansion beyond description. My body became the key to my survival. My body became more beautiful and a lifesaver at the same time. I had needed this intervention.

Nobody told me, I never heard nor did I ask, that my body was carnal, sinful, weak or that I was going to hell for touching myself or that I would go blind. There was no external conflict of interest. Furthermore, the male body was inspiring and beautiful to me. These feelings were taking root inside of me, becoming a part of my identity. It was something I couldn't ignore.

My attraction to the same sex was developing. I didn't know what to do with this information or the feelings I held in my heart. I pressed forward, keeping a secret that I would take to my grave. Or so I felt at the time.

CHAPTER FOURTEEN

RAINDROPS AND LEMON DROPS

Every night mother required us to perform rituals of love though they were not expressions of the heart. It was part of mother's order in the household. Like the arrangement of china in her cabinet, her children and husband were required to serve her sense of order. I always gave mother a kiss on the cheek and said, "Good night, mommy." If Daddy was present, I said, "Good night, Daddy!" No matter what the day brought, no matter how many beatings or screaming matches occurred, a kiss and a verbal goodnight to mommy and Daddy was expected.

If I had a lapse in judgment, mother would ask, "Do you not love me?"

"Yes mommy I do, why?"

"You forgot to give me a kiss and say goodnight," mother said.

"I'm sorry, mommy, good night," I said. I followed through with a good night kiss with no hesitation.

Mother usually added, "Don't forget to pee in the toilet and brush your teeth." These were always mother's parting words.

"Okay, mommy," I said. I peed in the toilet before going to bed, but I didn't always brush my teeth. Mother never emphasized the importance of hygiene when it came to our teeth. I saw Daddy's toothbrush on the bathroom shelf. Mommy told me that the toothbrush that Daddy used was about 30 years old. It was older than me, that's all I understood. I remembered staring at it on the shelf: each bristle stood straight as a young soldier's back. Except

121

it didn't look young or beautiful. It was a dull dingy color. The handle had its own patina. It must have been a strong brush, I thought. It seemed to hold up well. I stared at it often.

Mother boasted to other people how her children didn't have cavities because she kept the candy away from us, except mother had a drawer she filled up with candy given to her by the owners of the delicatessen stores each week. With each purchase the nice lady put candy into the bag as an extra. When she came home mother put the candy into the candy drawer. I visited the drawer often. I took one piece of candy out at a time in hopes that mother wouldn't recognize the drawer being depleted. I had acquired a sweet tooth, but I seldom brushed my teeth.

I didn't think I needed to use a brush for my teeth anyway, because as I sat and watched TV, I scraped my teeth using a pocket knife I found. Each time I went over my teeth, I scraped the creamy substance off. I noticed the stuff on the blade of the knife each time I scraped, and I stopped when I didn't see any more stuff on the blade.

Once I remember Daddy walked in while I was watching TV and scraping my teeth with the knife. "What are you doing?" he asked.

"I'm cleaning my teeth," I said.

Daddy replied educationally, "That's not a good idea to do that," continuing, "You should use a brush instead. The metal against your teeth will scratch the enamel off."

"What's enamel?" I asked.

He said, "It's the white coating on your teeth."

I knew Daddy had very yellow brown-looking teeth. I looked at them often when he talked to me. I asked him, "Can I use a toothpick instead. It's wood."

"A soft brush would be better," he said.

Daddy told me he always used a stiff bristle brush, because that's all they had back in the day. It was so stiff it scraped the enamel off of his teeth a little at a time. I wanted white teeth, not like Daddy's teeth. I said, "Okay, I won't do that anymore." From that day on, I stopped scraping my teeth with a knife and used a toothbrush instead. I didn't do it regularly, but when I did I used the brush.

I often stared at people's teeth when they talk to me, but I tried not to make it obvious. I became self-conscious of my teeth, because I had big spaces between my front top teeth. I liked the gaps between my teeth. I'd fill my mouth with water and then force it through the spaces, having three streams at once. People I played with didn't expect that. That was the fun part. The downside was every time I ate a sandwich with a tomato in it, I always pulled the tomato out of the sandwich intact because my top teeth gaps fit between the veins of the tomato, not allowing me to bite through the tomato clean. If the tomato was on the bottom of the sandwich I had a better chance for a clean bite, but I never looked into a sandwich to see where the tomato was. I never paid attention, if I pulled it out of my sandwich using my teeth, I just grabbed it with my fingers and tried to bite it off again. I could've grown up hating tomatoes because of how hard they were to eat, but I found a way to work around the problem. So often, I think we form our likes and dislikes based on such things, sometimes without realizing it.

When it started to get late, I wanted to go to bed and bounce my head before I got tired. I climbed into my crib. Resting my torso on my left elbow, I shuffled my pillow underneath my chest and laid my body down on the top of my pillow in preparation to bounce my head. I made myself comfortable by placing my feet over the edge of the mattress and my arms above my head, clasping or touching my hands and started bouncing. I often didn't count the number of bounces, because it was thousands every night. Instead, I revisited my memories of the day and my dreams of the future while I bounced.

Like a recurring tape that played in my head there was a beginning but no end. My past replayed itself over and over again inside my mind, like a loyal dog that followed me around everywhere I went. My past never ran away; it followed me everywhere. It was a constant rotation of events: what I said, what they said, what I did, what they did. The location of the events became crystal clear in detail in my mind, I saw everything in its place. I tried pushing every detail out of my head. Why was this so important to me? I didn't have an answer.

If there was poor judgment on my part, I squirmed as though it happened right now. If I didn't like what I said or didn't understand my actions, I shuddered. I relived the anguish, the pain of that memory again and again as if it had just happened. I paused from bouncing my head on my pillow, holding my head above my pillow for a moment to think about the experience. What would I do differently? I explored options in my head, and I decided how I would do things differently next time. I gathered my thoughts, and I started bouncing again once I had a new response for next time. At this point I could let the past go. It didn't matter...I'd relive it again, maybe tomorrow? And then I'd have another chance to respond and make the correction. I'd try the new way, and then analyze again if it worked. If I needed to make another choice, correcting the correction, I would do that. To this day, I believe that if we look at what has happened in the past and make a different decision, then we are empowered to become better at life. This is what made the difference between what I did and what I see so many others do. I didn't dwell on the past mistake but instead focused on how I could create a positive future for myself and others around me.

I remember one night I replayed my third grade teacher talking to me at her desk. I saw her glistening spit jump out of her mouth like raindrops. The sunlight heightened each sparkle that flew from her mouth. I watched them, sidestepping her spit as they made their journey to the floor. I didn't want her saliva on me. I moved even further back, but I didn't say anything. The teacher left her desk when she was finished talking to me and gave the class an assignment.

She said, "I'll be right back!" She left the classroom immediately.

I looked at the clock as my teacher left, calculating the remaining time I needed before I had to leave for my special ed class. I wanted to be on time, and I had permission to leave when I needed to, but I always asked before I left. My special ed teacher was supposed to help me learn how to read, write, and spell. It seemed, at the time, to be all in vain. I couldn't figure out how to learn what she wanted me to understand. I didn't know what the word illiterate meant, but I was very illiterate. I couldn't enunciate written words. They were just letters written together to make a word I couldn't understand. I had no phonics skills. I wrote missed spelled words in a sentence without any punctuation. I had no clue how to structure a sentence.

I wanted to arrive on time, but my third-grade teacher hadn't returned to give me permission to leave. A few minutes passed. I was excited to learn in my special ed class, but I only had a certain amount of time.

"I hope the teacher comes back soon," I told a girl in my class. "I leave in ten minutes," I told her.

"What are you doing in your special ed class?" she asked.

"It's a mind reading class," I told her.

"No, it's not," she said.

"Yes, it is!" I replied.

"Okay," she said. "What am I thinking of then?"

I replied, "I don't know, I just started the class. I haven't learned how to read people's minds yet."

About the time I finished lying to the girl, the teacher came on the intercom. "This is your teacher. How come you guys are not focusing on the assignment I gave you?"

125

Most of us looked bewildered at one another. She'd been eavesdropping on our conversations. I had a hard time respecting her after that experience though I replayed that event in my mind. Both lying to my classmate and my teacher's strange behavior rattled around in my head. Why did I say, "I was in a mind reading class?" Why did my teacher leave and then admonish us via the intercom? I tried to figure this out.

I jumped out of my thoughts, feeling the pillow on my face, touching the softness of the feathers as I bounced, a feeling I needed. I listened to the sound in my ears brushing against the sides of my pillow. I played with the sounds of my ear against the pillow. I tried to hear musical notes, but I couldn't find any. I continued bouncing my head. I had more thoughts to think about.

It was the end of the school week. The chairs stood on top of the desks. Everybody's arms were folded along with mine as we stood and waited for the teacher to dismiss us. I was anticipating the ringing of the bell as I danced from one leg to another. I had to pee really bad. The teacher talked as I danced back and forth. I heard her in the background of my mind, but I didn't know what she was saying. Suddenly, I couldn't wait any longer. I stopped dancing as the pee poured from the cuff of my pants. No matter how hard I tried, I couldn't stop.

I hoped nobody would see. I looked over at Bonnie, a girl I liked. She was staring at the cuff of my pants. The pee poured like a cloud burst of rain flowing off the roof of a house. My pee poured from the cuff of my pants, puddling around my feet, traveling far and wide under my desk. Bonnie motioned to her friend who sat behind me. She unfolded her arms slightly and pointed downward toward the cuff of my pants. I didn't have to look behind me, I knew what they were looking at. The boy next to me stepped to his left. Everybody around me saw what I was doing. The pee kept flowing.

I finally looked down to see what they saw. I looked over at Bonnie, embarrassed by what they were seeing. I saw Bonnie slightly stick out her tongue, wetting her lips. I had seen her do this before. I mimicked things I noticed if I liked them by doing the same actions. I didn't know it then, but I would soon begin to mimic her.

The bell finally rang and everything around me faded in a blur as I hurried home to change. I didn't want to return on Monday and sit in the same spot anymore. Besides, when I returned there was a big black stain under my desk. I knew where it came from. I asked another student if he would trade me places, anticipating he would say, "no!" But he didn't say no. "I'll trade you," he said. Surprised at his answer, I was relieved and traded places with him.

I kept bouncing my head, feeling the gentle impact on my face. I had other thoughts. I saw the look on Bonnie's face again, her eyes wide as the pee poured from my pant leg. I think she felt sorry for me. I think everyone did. No one laughed at me; no one made fun of me. To this day I'm grateful for that. But they all felt sorry for me.

My mind went back to another time someone was kind to me, an earlier time when I had had an accident at school. It was the time that the substitute teacher had whispered in my ear the soft words of love as I stood in front of the bathroom door, wet as could be.

All thoughts faded...I was getting tired. I turned my head slightly to the right to breathe as I lay face down on my pillow. Ready to fall asleep, I adjusted my body comfortably...and was gone.

My body rested, but my mind did not. Somehow a decision was made inside of me that Saturday morning. Bonnie's stare had changed me. Her pity had flipped a switch in my head just as Rick's abuse had. Rick's actions and his cruelty started my regression into bedwetting while Bonnie's kindness ended it.

I woke up dry! I stood in my crib. I absorbed the stillness of the morning in the dimly lit room. I looked over at my bed that had stood idle for two and a half years. The bed silently, patiently, waiting for me to make this decision. I AM DONE PEEING MY BED!

To this day I can describe every detail of this moment, the moment when I decided that I would never pee the bed again.

I looked up at the ceiling and saw the formations; I noticed the dull colored paint on the walls. I looked down at worn tattered carpet, every exposed thread embedded into my mind. The white dresser that held my clothes to my left. I looked down at my feet, standing inside my crib. I opened my mouth and said aloud, "Mother's stuff is coming off of my bed!" I stepped over the rail of my crib, never second guessing what I just said. I didn't look back. I took my dry sheets off of my bed, placing them on the floor and then transporting them into the laundry room. I walked back into my bedroom, lifted out the mattress from the crib slats, dismantled my crib and set it against the wall. Then I transported it into the garage out of my sight.

I removed mother's stuff from the top bunk bed that had been mine though unused. Mother was stirring in the kitchen by now.

Mother asked, "So where are the other boys?"

"Mommy, I'm done peeing my bed," I told her happily. "I put your stuff that was on top of my bed onto the floor where my crib was."

"You stopped peeing in your bed?"

"YES, I did." I replied.

My older brother Hermann spoke up sarcastically from the other room. "We'll have to hang buckets underneath the bed to keep Walter from getting wet when you pee your bed again tonight!"

I shouted to Hermann. "No, you won't need to!"

He said, " We'll see tonight, won't we."

"Yes, we will," I said.

Hermann's comment was all in vain.

I had made a decision.

There were no more accidents, no peeing out of place, no defeat, no pomp and ceremony. I stood alone, me, myself, and a dry bed, victory for one, victory for me! I found one of the hidden secrets of life that night inside my mind–confidence. I never peed my bed or my pants again. I was a new boy.

ROBERT BAUTNER

CHAPTER FIFTEEN

HALT'S MAUL!

As the old saying goes, when mother was made they broke the mold. Mother was definitely one of a kind. Mother certainly seemed to have a free spirit about her. I don't think mother fully utilized nor understood the power one woman can hold. I saw it, I felt it, I heard it, I tasted it, and I smelled it.

I saw the beauty in mother, even when it was hard to see her beauty. I felt the pain of mother's beatings on my person. They emanated from her lifetime of anguish with her mother (and quite possibly her father). I never met her father, my opa, but I clearly remember hearing Oma's screaming, yelling, and name calling. The words "I love you" never came out of Oma's mouth. I tasted mother's harshness with us. It was a reflection of her mother's with her. Yet I saw both of them being kind to others. And I smelled mother's cooking. Mother was a good cook.

The city wanted to put a cement median down the middle of the newly constructed road in front of Richard Street, but mother was against it. Mother got wind of it and complained to the city. The city people said, "If you don't want a barricade, create a petition and have people sign it. If you have enough people sign up we won't build a barricade down the road."

Mother put together that petition for people to sign. There were only about eight homes on the street so it didn't take much work for her to talk to everyone.

Mother went to every home with her petition. "With a barricade down

131

the middle of the road you won't be able to make a left turn out of the road."
She told everyone in the neighborhood. "If you're driving east and want to
make a left hand turn into our street, you'll have to go all the way around
the block to get into the street."

Mother's efforts paid off. She got everybody to sign the petition, keeping
the city from putting a cement barricade down the road. I paid attention,
observing mother's success.

The local government also wanted to put fluoride in the drinking water.
Mother became outraged and set up a petition to prevent the fluoride from
being added to the city's water system. Mother was not afraid to hop on the
local talk show and let everybody know, "Fluoride is a rat poison, and they
want to put it in your drinking water!" Mother fought against their proposal
and won. Fluoride was never added to the drinking water.

Mother was more of a goat then a dumb sheep, as mother would say it.
Mother was not going to follow the norm.

Getting immunization shots was another big no-no for mother's boys.
None of us were ever immunized. We were all left with a pure bloodstream.
Mother would have it no other way!

Besides mother having her rounds to the delicatessen stores, she had
her rounds to the local health food stores, too. Mother was referred to in
the day as a "health food nut." Mother didn't mind it. She took her slew of
vitamins everyday. Mother always boasted that she had a good set of teeth
and good bowel movements. Thankfully, we were of an age where she no
longer hollered for us to come look.

Mother was very health conscious. I believed mother had the gift of
health, too. I listened to mother carry on with her insights. Mother said
with assurance, "If people ate like they were a diabetic, they would never
become a diabetic!"

I developed a sweet tooth. I liked sugar, but sugar didn't like me. Nearly
every time I took anything sweet into my body, mother's saying about being

a diabetic left me reflecting that I needed to be careful with my sugar intake.

Mother heard of people having their tonsils taken out. After their removal ice cream was a remedy to soothe their throat. Mother said that the very thing they used to treat the aftermath was what had caused the very problem in the first place. "If they stopped eating so much ice cream, they wouldn't have to have their tonsils taken out!"

I believed her. It made sense.

She continued. "Then there is the risk of diabetes on top of that!" Mother added without apology, "What a bunch of dumb bunnies people are!" Mother simply could not understand people's thinking. To mother, all this seemed like common sense. It came to her so naturally. Mother said it over and over again, "People are nothing but a bunch of dumb bunnies!" Mother reserved the term "dumb sheep" for people who went to church. Mother was careful not to mix those two terms up.

I bounced my head at night thinking about all these things. I recalled when I was eight years old, I had become sick with a fever, a poison or toxin of some sort. Mother loved to tell the story to her clutch of friends, "Robert was sick with something inside his body, so I had him lay on top of the kitchen table and I packed him in onions, starting with his feet and up to his calves. It worked! The toxins were pulled out of his body." Mother said, pleased with her success. I could hear her pride in her voice.

She continued in detail on how she did this. "First I bought a hundred pounds of onions and put them through the food processor."

I remember seeing this tall green machine that mother referred to as a food processor. When mother turned it on, it seemed to roar into action.

Mother was just getting started with her story, and I was following along in my memory. "I laid him on the kitchen table."

I remembered this, too, laying on the table and staring into the kitchen light that hung above me. It seemed like I was on an operating table in a hospital. I had never been to a hospital, but I had seen it on TV. In my mind's eye, mother was the doctor.

Mother continued. "I peeled every onion before putting them through the grinder. I cried and cried from all the onions!"

I didn't remember mother crying from the onions, but I believed her. The noise of the machine must have drowned out any of mother's sniffling. The light above me kept me from watching mother at my feet. I laid flat on my back on top of the table.

Mother continued, "I packed him in onions from his feet upwards, and in the short time he laid on the table, the onions turned BLACK!" Mother emphasized the word black. Mother never showed me, but I heard the passion in her voice. I think mother was amazed at how well it worked, feeling that the onions turning black was further confirmation of the success of pulling the toxins out of my body.

After I had laid on the table long enough, mother unpacked me from the onions. I hopped off the table and took a bath.

All cleaned up, I asked Billy if I could sleep in his bed. I didn't feel good and didn't want to sleep in the crib.

He said, "NO! You stink of onions." He was right.

I went into my room to sleep in my crib.

Mother never packed me in onions again, but mother retold the story over and over again. I think it made her feel important. She felt she had saved my life. Her narcissism knew no bounds.

Disappearing was a real thing in my house.

When mother had company, I disappeared, going into my bedroom. I'd been trained.

If I didn't catch on to what mother wanted right away, I was told in one word: "Disappear." I didn't need an interpreter.

Mother and Daddy believed in the old saying, 'Children should be seen and not heard.' Once she told me to disappear, this rule was in effect until she told me I could come out.

I didn't need to be told twice. Trepidation had been programmed into me. I had installed my confidence on my own, counter to her training. Of course, no one knew.

When she had company, I listened from the outskirts of the room. I wasn't seen, but I could hear their conversation and learn, as long as it wasn't in German. I remember one such time I heard mother call me pleasantly, "Robert!"

I ran into the front room where mother was talking. "Yes mommy," I said.

Mother wanted to be proud of my response in front of her guests. Her public persona was gracious, and she was the perfect mother. And I knew the different tones of her voice. I trained myself to distinguish between them so that I could survive. I made no mistake about it, mother expected obedience, especially in front of other people. I knew that to do otherwise would lead to grave consequences.

Mother asked me in her pleasant, company voice, "Could you go get the gallstones out of the freezer for me?"

"Yes mommy, I will." I knew where her gallstones were. I had done this before many times over. Mother had collected her gallstones from a previous bowel movement and stored her gallstones in a baggie, placing them in the freezer. I hurried. That was another part of my training.

I opened the freezer door and reached into the top right hand corner of the door. They were right where they were supposed to be from the last time I had gotten them for her. The yellow twist tie from a spent loaf of bread sealed the bag closed. I stared at the dull olive green, odd-shaped stones through the plastic bag as I quickly walked from the kitchen refrigerator into the front room. I handed mother the baggie.

I stood very still, waiting dutifully for a moment, while mother talked to her friend about her gallstones. I didn't pay attention to the conversation, probably because it was all in German this time. I waited for a few minutes, knowing that mother was going to hand them back to me after she completed her conversation about them. A few minutes later mother handed me the baggie with the contents intact. I put the baggie back in the freezer for the next visitor.

That bag of gallstones was hers and hers alone, but I would fetch it for her on occasion. As I see it now, I always knew that mother's way was hers and hers alone. Her anger, resentment, coldness, and duplicity in front of others was all hers. They weren't mine though they affected me.

In the same way, I came to believe that mother's resentment towards me began long before I was born, rooted somewhere deep inside of her. On some level, I knew this even as a child. I was a lot of extra work for mother that mother didn't want. Mother felt justified telling me over and over again, "I wish I never had you."

At nine years old, the spaces between my teeth represented yet another problem to mother, having to spend money on me to fix them. All the other boys had 'perfect teeth,' but not me. That would require braces which translated into spending money on me. Mother didn't want to spend money on me. Mother wanted to save her money for her fabulous parties and her trips to the casinos.

Mother was a good speller but had no time to teach me how to read, write or spell for myself. Mother would say, "Don't they teach you anything in school?" Mother boasted about how good she was, spelling words I didn't know how to spell. Mother was a walking dictionary. Why would I need to learn how to spell with mother around?

Besides missing teeth in my mouth, I was born pigeon-toed. Mother took me to the foot doctor to see if my feet could be corrected. Running always posed a problem for me. I was a trip hazard. I tripped over my own feet when I ran but also when I walked. Mother took me to a doctor who fitted me for braces inside my shoes. It was far away, but he was the only one in town who worked on foot correction. For all of her faults, mother did spend time taking me there. The doctor was really smart, and he built an insert for me to put into my shoe, a brace-like piece of plastic. He told me I needed to point my feet outward consciously. I did what he asked me to do. I didn't mean to put my hands outward too, but with a little practice I slowly learned to straighten my feet, keeping myself from tripping over me. I just needed to be taught or shown.

Mother had a lot on her plate to handle, and for the last five years mother had been taking care of Oma. Waiting on Oma hand and foot was in itself a full time job. Mother's relationship with Oma was very similar to that between mother and me. Oma didn't like mother despite the similarities between the two of them. Looking back, I believe mother wanted to build a connection with her mother before she passed.

Oma shuffled around the house, wielding her cane, even venturing outside to the gate. Mother had to keep it locked so Oma wouldn't wander off. One time Oma escaped because mother forgot to lock the gate behind her. Oma always tested the gate upon her going into the front yard. The time she got out, mother had accidentally left it unlocked. Mother had one of the boys and even Daddy scour the neighborhood looking for Oma. They found her walking down a busy street off to the side of the road. From that point on, with no more mistakes, the gate would be secured with a chain and a keyed lock.

Mother's friends asked about the lock. One of them wondered what mother would do after Oma died. She said that she would unlock it, except on Halloween when she would lock it up tight again so those brats couldn't get to the door and beg for treats.

When Oma couldn't escape, she stood by the locked gate, hollering, "HELP POLICE! HELP POLICE!" with a German accent and in broken English. Whenever someone drove by or walked down the road, Oma would holler these words. These were the only words I heard Oma speak in English all the time she lived with us. The neighbors commented how bad

137

they felt to see her hollering like that, but they understood Oma had senility.

Mother boasted that every morning she fixed Oma a hot breakfast of four eggs, a half a pound of bacon, a full potato, four slices of buttered toast and a half a pot of coffee. Oma ate everything and headed back to her room.

Mother said to Oma, "Ein bad nehman!" In English, "Take a bath!"

Oma always responded, loudly and angrily, "HALT'S MAUL!" "SHUT UP!" in English. Oma shuffled her way back to her bedroom.

Every morning it was the same. The same meal, the same conversation, the same angry tones.

Tension between mother and Oma never seemed to dissipate. Even after mother had a room built for Oma, they still argued.

I asked mother what stories she remembered about her life with Oma as a little girl. Mother told me, "Oma made moonshine, the best in town!" It was the Depression, and Prohibition was the law of the land. If you were caught making moonshine, you went to jail. Oma was never caught. It was so profitable Oma paid off her house selling her spirits.

Oma had a system. At that time it was common to have a four-party line. A four-party line meant that the phone rang at four homes all at the same time. All four parties could pick up the phone at the same time and whoever the phone call was for, would talk, but the other three could listen in to the conversation. Oma devised a code, if you wanted a pint of moonshine you simply asked for a dozen eggs. If you wanted two pints, the code was two dozen eggs.

People suspected Oma was making moonshine, but none of them was brave enough to ask her directly. They asked indirectly instead. "Why did the preacher call you at 11 at night, and for two dozen eggs?"

Oma responded, "DAS GEHT SIE NICHTS AN!" "NONE OF YOUR BUSINESS!" Oma had a way of killing any suspicion from the conversation immediately!

With a four-party line back in the day, anybody could spread a rumor about anything and it would be easy to pick up. Somebody commented on how dirty Oma kept her pots and pans. She found out who it was and invited him to the house. It didn't take long for Oma to bring up the subject. Oma told the man, "You said I have dirty pots and pans!" She never asked him if it was true that he had said that. Oma didn't wait for his answer. She picked up a pan and showed him how nice and clean and sparkly they were. Then Oma proceeded to hit him in the head with the pan, clobbering him in the head repeatedly. "Don't ever tell people I have dirty pots and pans again, do you understand me?!"

The man left with more bumps and bruises than when he came. I suspect he never said anything about Oma's pots and pans again.

After Oma paid off the house, Oma sold her moonshine equipment to someone else. Mother said Oma's distillery had its own unique smell to it. "She could walk down the street and smell someone cooking moonshine in the neighborhood."

I asked mother, "Did Oma ever get caught?"

Mother said, "NO."

She had a few close calls from inspectors. Oma hid the moonshine equipment in the attic at the house, throwing laundry inside the kettle and dismantling it so that it was not all in one place. An inspector would come and knock on the door. Oma would let him in but he could never find it.

Mother told me of another unique gift Oma had. Oma was very intuitive. Mother explained that Oma told many people that the banks were going to close. She knew it before the beginning of the Depression. She warned people that they should take their money out of the banks right away.

She told so many people that at one point after the Crash of 1929 the Feds came knocking on her door, wanting to know how she knew it was going to happen.

Oma told them, "People talk."

Mother enjoyed telling me the stories. I listened closely as the stories fascinated my mind.

One morning, mother made Oma's breakfast first before going to get her. Oma wanted her breakfast hot and sitting on the table ready to eat when she arrived. Mother kept it warm for her until she came out of her room. This morning, I was watching TV. I looked over to see mother leave to get Oma. Mother went into Oma's to get her dressed for the day and to come out and eat.

Oma argued with mother as she always did.

Mother told her it was time to get dressed.

"I don't want to get dressed," Oma said in German. "Ich will mich nicht anziehen!"

Mother started dressing Oma anyway.

Oma said again, "Ich will mich nicht anziehen!" Oma proceeded to raise her cane to strike mother with it. Oma collapsed, falling towards the floor. Mother caught her as she was falling. She had died! At that moment, Oma simply stopped living. Her last words were, "I don't want to get dressed." Her last act was to try to strike her daughter.

Mother never made the connection she wanted so badly with her mother. No matter what she did, she never felt loved or accepted.

Mother came into the front room to tell us. "Oma just died."

Mother wanted us to wait and not go in to see her. Mother called Daddy at his work to come home which he did. On the way home Daddy brought his mother Omi to say goodbye to Oma. Mother called the mortuary to come and get her. Mother's plans were to have her cremated. By the time Daddy got there, the mortuary people also arrived having Oma on the gurney. Daddy moved the kitchen table out of the way, to make room.

I didn't know what to do. I'd never seen a dead body before. I stood in the background watching.

Omi seemed to be in a pondering state of mind. She walked over to Oma, patting Oma on the right cheek, saying in German, "Wake up, Wake

140

up!"

Oma was wheeled out on the gurney and later cremated. Mother kept her ashes in a brass box and put her in the top dresser drawer. Mother cried, a sight I didn't see often. To a few friends, she said. "I don't know what I would do if Hans died." Hans was my father.

After mother recovered from Oma's death, the urn with Oma's ashes was comfortably situated in Oma's top old dresser drawer. Mother had another show and tell.

CHAPTER SIXTEEN

IIIXOII

When mother set a curfew, mother meant what she said. My older brother Hermann, 8 years older than me, at age 17, once ignored mother's rule. It was three hours past his allotted time. Hermann thought he could outsmart mother. Coming in at 3 a.m., he knew mother would be waiting for him. He crafted an idea. He thought he'd hop the fence in the far corner of the yard far from mother's view…then walk across the side yard, out of mother's hearing…come in the back door, hop into bed…and mother would be none the wiser. 'A fool and his decisions are soon parted.' He hadn't learned what I had years ago. Mother meant what she said and said what she meant!

Mother waited for Hermann on the front porch, waiting for any movement in the dark of the night to be out of place. Mother worried about us on one hand, and beat us up on the other, usually with her right arm. It was strong and stung a lot. Mother got what she was looking for, she heard a little movement in the corner of the yard. Hermann must have forgotten mother's finely tuned hearing. Mother didn't need to see. She just needed to hear. Mother got both as she looked up the road. Hermann's unwashed, shiny blond hair was glowing in the early morning moonlight.

Mother waited on the inside of the back door as Hermann quietly opened the door. He slowly twisted the doorknob to keep it from rattling or squeaking, but it was all in vain. It didn't matter how sly he was, she was there. This was certainly a lapse in judgment on his part. Hermann stepped one foot into the house...and there was mother, standing before him, angry as a wet hen. With her right arm, mother nearly cold-cocked Hermann. Mother was not going to be disobeyed. Tensions between mother and Hermann heightened after that.

Mother taught us, don't get married, don't have children, and don't come around here if you do, but she really didn't have anything to worry about. Mother was instilling a belief in her boys. In fact, only Walter and I ever married (and Walter only briefly), and one of them is a closet homosexual. Why would any of us want to marry a woman if this is what they're like? For me there was a sense of safety in being attracted to the same sex, something that mother would never understand.

Tension between mother and me translated into tension between my brothers and me. The time I hit Hermann in the nuts, he retaliated by hanging me by a rope around my ankles and throwing the rope over a strong branch of a tree in the front yard. Hermann pulled on the rope until I hung upside down like a bat. As I hung upside down, swinging by a rope, mother drove into the driveway. She was coming home from her errands, and just in time.

Mother saw me hanging and stopped the car immediately. She got out of the car, leaving the car door open and said to Hermann, "You put him down right now!"

Hermann argued back. "Why? He deserves to be hanged. Nobody likes him!"

Mother said again, "You put him down!"

With hesitation Hermann put me down, then continued to argue with mother. Tensions rose even higher between the two of them, screaming at each other in the front yard. This time Hermann struck mother.

Mother was shocked. She had been hit by Hermann, her own son. Mother started crying, calling for Daddy to come from the garden to help her.

"Hans!" she cried. Mother never used Daddy's first name unless there was a problem or Daddy was wanted on the phone. This was not a phone call. Daddy heard the commotion from the garden and came over at once.

Mother cried to Daddy in a whiny voice, "Hermann hit me!"

Daddy turned to Hermann saying, "What's going on here?!"

Mother overrode anything Hermann had to say to his defense in that moment. Hermann never got a chance to say a word.

Daddy said softly but firmly, "Leave, take your possessions and go!"

Hermann respectfully did what Daddy asked him to do. He gathered up what he could, putting what little he had into the saddlebags on his motorcycle. He left the house, all within ten minutes. Hermann had purchased a motorcycle against mother's wishes several months earlier. Mother hated motorcycles because so many people were killed riding them. Hermann's motorcycle had two saddlebags, one on each side of the bike. With the clothes on his back and a few possessions that he could stuff inside the saddlebags, Hermann drove away with no place to stay. We had no relatives, no other family, no connection to people close to us. None of those options existed. His fate for a place to stay was under freeway bridges.

Hermann left in such a fury, he left the magazines behind, underneath his bed. I had checked to see if he had taken them after he was gone. To my surprise they were still there. My mind went to work immediately to take them before mother cleaned out his stuff. I looked around to be sure no one was nearby. I didn't think it was good enough to hide them from view. I went into the main bathroom where the towels were kept and pulled a towel out of the cupboard. I planned to wrap the magazines in the towel to transport them to the bedroom.

I did so carefully so as to not rouse anyone's suspicion. I didn't want to be confronted by anybody, especially my brothers who would tell on me in a heartbeat. I didn't have a story or a lie to tell inside my head. I had a focus. I had made a decision that I arrived at unquestioned. I walked, nonchalantly but with a pace, to my bedroom with the magazines wrapped in a towel to the right side of my body, hiding most of what I was carrying. Still, I was nervous to be caught with them in my possession.

I had to walk past the kitchen doorway. Anybody could have seen me. With a bit of hesitation, I stepped past the kitchen's doorway. I would have been deemed guilty based on my behavior if anyone had noticed me. As it turned out, I didn't need to come up with a story. I was not seen or confronted as I closed the door to my bedroom, hiding them quickly under my bed still wrapped in a towel. I had to be sure no one was around before I moved on to my next step. The plan was to get rid of the towel. I was worried that mother would see the towel as being out of place under my bed and ask about it or that mother would investigate. I couldn't take the chance. I got rid of the towel next, putting the stash of magazines underneath my dresser. Most of my fears were brought on by my imagination, but they were real to me. I had plenty of reasons to fear mother. That was in no way imaginary. That was real life. But mother was not nearly as omniscient as I imagined.

Walter moved into Oma's old bedroom now that she had died. This gave me more privacy, except my room was a hallway to Walter's bedroom now. I set a booby trap up in front of my door that would make a sound if somebody opened it. Still, I was nervous. I pulled out one magazine from underneath my dresser and hid on the opposite side of my bed, away from the door, concealing what I was viewing in case someone came into my room.

My thoughts were to scour the magazine looking for all the pictures of men. I bypassed the women's photos. I had no interest in looking at them. I headed for the section that said, "Just for the ladies." Turning the pages, I came across a centerfold of a famous actor I had seen on TV. He was posed with a piece of wheat in his mouth, laying naked on a bear rug. It was Burt Reynolds. I stared at the beauty of his body. My heart melted with emotion. My mind flashed to the thought, what if someone found out? I didn't want anyone to know my deepest feelings of attraction. I tore his picture from the magazine, hiding it under my dresser, an easy reach from my bed. His picture joined my collection of other pictures of men. I saved the other magazines for a later time.

My paranoia about getting caught deepened. I needed a safer place for the pictures. I often went to the Grand Central Department Store by myself to look at things and buy little things. I had the idea to purchase a lock box to put my pictures in. As I entered the store with my mission, the memory flashed in my mind of the many times mother had said that she should have left me in a cart at Grand Central when I was an infant. I wondered briefly which aisle she would have left me in. I brushed away the thought and focused on my mission. I needed to protect myself from what others might think of me, liking men's pictures.

When I came home with the lock box, I put my precious pictures inside of it, hiding the box in my closet. I still didn't feel safe. Mother had half of her clothes in my closet, and if mother came into my room and into my closet, then what? I couldn't leave them inside my closet. I decided to dig a hole in the backyard and bury the box. I searched for the perfect location. I then found a shovel and started digging. As I dug, I periodically stopped to check the size of the hole with the box to see if it was big enough. I kept digging; I kept checking.

I kept digging until finally the box fit in the hole. As I look back on this now, it's funny to me because the location I chose was right out in the open, right in the middle of the garden. There I was, digging in the middle of the garden with this box in full view of anyone who might happen to pass by. Yet I thought I was being stealthy. That is the mind of a 9-year-old, I suppose.

I buried the box, thinking about it for months. The garden was Daddy's domain. What if Daddy found my box? I couldn't get the question out of my mind. I decided I needed to dig up the box and burn the pictures. I did just that, opening up the box. The pictures had melted together in the heat of the Utah summer and the water from Daddy's efforts to irrigate the garden.

147

I found some gasoline from the shed, dowsing the contents of the box with gasoline. I struck a match, lighting the pictures on fire.

The anxiety over my stash was finally at rest, but my thoughts were never settled, nor did they ever rest. My identity might be safe from others' prying eyes, but I still feared that my secret would somehow be discovered. I was sure to say nothing to anyone that might reveal my secret.

Hermann was still in exile, sleeping under bridges and eating ketchup sandwiches that were a luxury and far from mother's German cooking. In my view now, Hermann knew a freedom the rest of us (including Daddy) could only imagine. Later he told me that he was just angry. I saw him as free from mother's clasp, but in reality he wasn't. Mother had such a hold on his mind. Even recently, Hermann told me (to my horror) that he believes that mother's beatings were a sign that he needed more training. Hermann has never married and never had children, though he does have a long-time girlfriend now. He isn't alone in the hold that mother had on his mind–we all have suffered the same. It was like we all had Stockholm Syndrome. Mother made it clear she clothed us, housed us, and fed us, and we were told we better obey her and love her or by God, we would suffer her wrath. Really, it wasn't God–mother saw herself as our god.

Mother worried about Hermann throughout his exile. He hadn't phoned in for months. The Vietnam War raged on, and mother knew he could still be drafted. She worried about both Hermann and Frank who were both of age, but Frank was in college so he was safe for the time being. Hermann was nowhere to be found, nowhere to be tracked down. Without a phone call, mother had no idea what was going on. As we learned later, Hermann was traveling the open roads on his motorcycle. He made his way to Chicago, Illinois to visit our aunt whom he hadn't seen in about 15 years, since he was a little boy. When he arrived in Chicago, Hermann called mother for the address. Mother was relieved that he was still alive. She gave him the address of their old home in Cook County, Chicago, Illinois. Her sister, Aunt Martha, still lived in that house.

Aunt Martha was mother's only living sister. The two of them hadn't spoken to each other in ages because of animosity that had started over the sale of the family home. The home had been valued at $30,000 and Aunt Martha had to pay $20,000 to mother and Oma, but mother had essentially received all $20,000 because she was caring for Oma. Aunt Martha thought this was unfair, but then she didn't have to build onto her house to care for Oma, and she didn't have to endure the daily verbal and emotional abuse and physical exhaustion of caring for Oma's grumpy and senile state of mind. In this, I agree with mother's side. It amazes me how money amplifies dysfunction in a family.

That dysfunction became further amplified when Hermann decided to visit Aunt Martha. Indeed, Mother became even less interested in ever reconciling with her sister when she heard what happened when Hermann knocked on the door of the family home. Hermann reported later on the short sequence of events: Martha answered the door, Hermann reintroduced himself, Martha took one look at Hermann, said, "I'm busy!" and promptly turned around, and closed the door in Hermann's face. If mother had any thought of ever talking to her sister again civilly, that went out the door along with Hermann that day.

Mother told the entire family and everyone in her clutch of friends about what had happened, expressing her full anger each time she told the story. She went on and on about how her sister Martha turned Hermann away after he had traveled across the country to see her, let alone on a motorcycle mother hated. To mother all motorcycles were death traps. Mother said to others with contempt in her voice, "How she could do that to a young man is beyond my understanding." Mother's friends agreed, siding with mother, elevating her yet again to the heroine, the maligned and martyred heroine that crusaded for justice through her endless retellings of stories.

Ultimately, Mother had a lot more to worry about than what Martha did to Hermann. Mother's anger and concern focused on the Vietnam War, and the possibility of her sons being drafted pressed on her mind, intensifying each day that went by. The United States had a draft lottery system that was based on a man's birth date. The random draft number was calculated then issued to the draftee. Mother viewed it as a death number. Mother's worrying never subsided.

The president of the United States, Richard M. Nixon, got elected on his campaign promise to end the Vietnam War, but as the war raged on after his election, mother loathed President Nixon more and more. "He's nothing but a liar, just to get my vote!" mother said. Angry over feeling betrayed, mother said, "I'll bet none of those politicians' sons had to go to war and fight!" Mother retrieved the newspaper every morning to check the draft numbers and read the news, but that angered mother all the more.

Even the arrival of the newspaper each morning caused mother anger. The paperboy threw the paper randomly and didn't place it in the box where the paper was supposed to be placed. Mother called the newspaper agency constantly to complain.

Immediately after one of her complaints, the paperboy would put it in the proper box for about a week, but then it was randomly thrown again. This incensed mother even more. Mother began telling me, "Go out and look for the newspaper!" continuing, "He doesn't put it in the box anymore!" She got me trained to do it. This should have reduced her anxiety. The time she had spent to search for it herself had been yet another source of anger in anticipation of having to search for the fate of her sons within its pages. I went out every morning after that for the paper, locating it, taking it into the house, handing it to mother or placing it on the kitchen table for her to find. Yet her anxiety never diminished. She writhed daily in her own personal hell of anger and anxiety, relieved only by her expressing it outward through her complaining to her friends, through beating us, and through her absolute control over the household.

If I handed the newspaper to mother, mother immediately unfolded the paper, looking through the draft section to see if her boys' numbers had come up. Mother never explained to me exactly how it worked so I never really understood how she would know. She told me it was a lottery system, but I didn't really know what that meant.

I felt the tension in the air as mother searched the paper intently, taking her finger, sliding down column after column, sometimes saying, "Leave me alone while I'm looking!" I respected mother's request and stood silently, waiting for mother to close the paper. Mother said, "Their numbers didn't come up today!"

Mother knew tomorrow brought another worry. The next morning, I went and got the paper again, and the scene was repeated. The Vietnam War was something mother could never control.

Once Walter and I were in grade school, mother began taking part-time work. One of her jobs was to clean the Stylark Beauty Salon inside the Hotel Utah each evening. Mother usually dragged one or two of the youngest boys to help her. Billy had his turn, and now it was mine. Sometimes Walter came along, and other times I brought my friend Lonnie to help clean. It helped to have a friend come along to play instead of work.

Mother began to tell me that the owners of the Stylark Beauty Salon, Rollins and Stewart were "hom...oh never mind," mother said. Mother refrained from saying what she was going to say, but said, "Well," pausing, "you know," lowering the tone of her voice almost to a whisper adding, "They sleep together."

I wasn't surprised. I could feel what mother was saying was true about Rollins and Stewart before mother told me. I knew they were a couple. It didn't bother me; it intrigued me.

Mother added, "Rollins wears a toupee."

I asked, "What is a toupee?"

Mother told me it was a wig for men.

I asked, "Your wig is a toupee?"

Mother said, "No!" continuing, "A toupee is a hairpiece men wear."

"Oh," I said.

After my conversation with mother, I stared at Rollins' hair each time he talked to me. I wondered if his toupee wiggled when he scratched his head.

I liked to go to the hotel with mother. I got to run around, snooping in all the back rooms. There was a second set of elevators behind the three front elevators. I rode the elevators for fun. I met a woman there, learning for the first time what it meant to be an elevator lady was. When my brother Walter and I were together, we liked going to the top floor. We told the elevator lady, "10 please."

I watched carefully how she operated the elevator. She pushed the black ten button. The buttons were black with white numbers on them. She flipped a brass lever with a black knob, spinning it into an up position. The elevator started going up, taking us to the 10th floor. She stood up to stretch her legs. I observed the emerald green fabric on the seat of her stool. She sat back down as we approached the tenth floor.

When we weren't riding the elevator for fun, I snooped on the shelves where the hotel discarded unnecessary items. Each floor had its own set of shelves in the service. I took things if they were of interest to me. I found an old brass desk lamp that had a cracked hood and a 48-star flag that once hung over the south banister of the hotel. Nobody ever stopped us, but I always wondered as we got to the tenth floor if we would get caught snooping or taking things that we weren't supposed to. We never did get stopped or questioned. I always returned to the beauty salon, feeling I was in safe territory.

Mother told me about an experience she had when President Nixon came to town. It happened on the roof of the Hotel Utah. The Stylark Beauty

Salon was located on the 2nd floor of the hotel. It was to the left after getting off the elevator. The beauty salon was at the same level of the stained glass ceiling that adorned the lobby of the Hotel Utah. It was an easy walk onto the roof through the french doors of the salon. I knew I wasn't supposed to be out there on the roof and I never ventured more than a few feet past the door before coming back in. As I stood on the roof, I stared at all the windows that were looking down on me from above. There were a lot of windows glaring at me. I kept seeing people in my imagination as if they were looking down at me from the windows of the surrounding buildings, and that inhibited me from going further onto the roof. I went back inside and closed the door, pushing the couch that normally blocked the door back in place.

Mother was less intimidated by all the windows above her, and when President Nixon came to town mother wanted to see what all the hubbub was about. Mother ventured out onto the roof, eventually leaning over the edge of the banister. Mother wanted to see if she could view the president's motorcade. What she didn't realize is that the Secret Service was watching her. It wasn't that many years earlier that President Kennedy was shot from above. The Secret Service noticed mother out on the balcony, overlooking South Temple Street where President Nixon was coming down the road in his entourage.

Mother was unimpressed with what she saw and went back inside, pushing the couch back in front of the doors. Moments later mother got a knock on the door, a very fervent and distinct even specific knock that was not misunderstood. The knock sounded important! Mother answered the locked door. It was the Secret Service, and they wanted to know why mother was out on the balcony overlooking South Temple.

They minced no words. They let her know if she was carrying anything at all, even a feather duster, they would have shot first and asked questions later. While mother was telling me the story I thought to myself, I wonder if they knew mother was wearing a wig? I thought if she had wanted to kill the president, she could have hidden a gun under her wig. Mother finished up the story by telling me they left a warning not to do that again. Mother seemed to enjoy telling the story. I wondered what life would be like for me if they shot and killed my mommy.

It was around this time that mother loved to tell a certain joke. It was out of character for her to tell any jokes, but during this time she had this one she told to anyone who would listen. Writing on a piece of paper, she asked, "How do you make a jackass out of this..."

I I I X O I I

"...using this?"

\ \

People were stumped. Nobody knew the answer.

Mother always finished her joke the same way...without a word, she wrote in between the two outer I I.

N I X O N.

CHAPTER SEVENTEEN

THE FOLLY OF A FALSIE

Mother was truly worried about my ability to read, write and comprehend. Special ed throughout elementary school was not helping like mother hoped it would. Mother sought other avenues, including summer school, to get me to learn. Autism was unheard of in the 1960's to the average teacher, and certainly no one knew how to educate someone with this disability. In fact, most people at the time thought of it as a form of mental retardation. Being thought of as mentally retarded was the harsh reality of being autistic in the 1970s. I was just different, but the educational system saw me as deficient. For all the faults of today's educational system, things are better now.

Mother enrolled me into yet another program to help me learn, but I had to be driven to this location daily. Mother talked one of my older brothers into driving me there and back home again when my session was over. Talking my brother into taking me freed mother from any inconvenience or interruptions in her shopping appointments. I suggested that I could ride my bicycle to and from the program, but mother quickly squashed my suggestion by telling me it was too far away and I would get lost.

Mother was probably correct, but so what? Riding my bicycle would give me the experience and the opportunity to learn the way I needed to learn, whether mother was correct about me getting lost or not. I needed the parameters to be different for me to comprehend life through trial and error. Mother didn't understand that I was street smart even if I wasn't book smart.

Riding my bicycle down the street, followed by mother in her car, could have given me navigational skills and confidence to understand the world–even if it were for a moment. My mind needed the opportunity to fail or succeed. I learned by sight, by hearing, and by experience. It would have been just what the doctor ordered for me, but mother denied me the opportunity for the sake of her convenience.

The program was truly different from anything I had experienced before...or since. I sat in a room with mechanical monitors. This was in the days before computers so these were just mechanical devices. They had a keyboard and a monitor but no computer memory or motherboard. There were three or four other kids with me, probably with a similar learning disorder as me. A question would appear on each of our monitors individually, and we had to answer the question to the best of our knowledge by pushing the key that corresponded to the answer we thought was correct. It told us immediately whether we got the answer correct or not, and then it automatically moved on to the next question. If someone got a question wrong I usually heard a distressful sound of disappointment from them, including from myself, but the machine moved on just the same.

It was frustrating to get the wrong answer. I felt like the machines never gave me the opportunity to learn but just left me in the dust. Then a miracle happened, so to speak. I learned from one of the other boys that when you got the wrong answer from the question that was asked on the screen, all you needed to do to get the correct answer was to unplug the machine, then plug it back in again and the question would reappear fresh as if it were never asked.

All I needed to do was choose a different answer on the screen until I got the correct answer it was looking for. I crawled under the desk to unplug the machine each time I got a question wrong. The machine did what it was designed to do, and so did I. It worked each time without fail. From this experience, I was taught that every system can be beat with the right strategy.

I never returned after the first session of the program ended. According to the machine, I didn't need to because I'd gotten all the answers right.

Christmas time was approaching, leaving the fall season and going into winter. The word 'Christmas' brought a small flood of memories to me. Mother made it clear that she didn't believe in Christmas. Year after year mother said the same thing over and over again, "How anyone could believe that bullshit was beyond me!" Mother taught only one culture, 'The culture of mother.' Mother was obedient to her conscience, a conscience she defined. Mother put up a Christmas tree with a few lights, because the lights were pretty. Then she complained that she didn't want the lights left on, because it would only keep the power company rich. I helped put up Christmas lights around the window, but only a few, thinking about what mother said. Mother then ran around the house turning out lights in rooms where nobody was occupied, saying the same thing, hitting her hand on the wall with a loud thud, then snapping the light switch to the off position, saying, "For crying out loud, who left the lights on again? Turn them off!"

We were sitting around the kitchen table one day, and I asked mother and Daddy, "What were your earliest memories of Christmas?"

"I don't have any," mother said. She paused, then continued with a story from our early years. "One year when you guys were little, I simply ran out of time to wrap your gifts."

"What did you do, mommy?" one of us boys asked.

"I put your gifts on a table and threw a blanket over the top of them." Mother continued with a little laugh. "You guys weren't very happy with Christmas that year."

I pictured what mother said in my head, a white bed sheet over the toys on a table near the Christmas tree.

Mother painted a very unexciting Christmas Day for me.

I didn't remember the experience mother just told me. But mother's story reminded me of how one year I opened up some of my gifts carefully to see what they were, then sealed them back up again, acting surprised on Christmas Day. That Christmas was not a very exciting day for me, and I never did that again. I learned a valuable lesson for myself: living in anticipation brought an energy that participation spent.

"What was your Christmas like, Daddy?" I asked.

Daddy smiled. I looked into his blue eyes and felt the humility of his countenance before he ever said a single word. "I was 5 or 6 years old, World War I was just over. The country was devastated from the onslaught of war that only war offers." Daddy added, "War is atrocious!b There were not a lot of resources available. Omi was a single mother."

I listened closely.

Daddy continued. "I received a train set for Christmas. After a few weeks of playing with the train set, the train set disappeared."

"Omi took it away?" I asked.

"Yes" he said, continuing, "And the next Christmas, I received the same train set again, and that continued on for many years."

I put myself in Daddy's story, thinking what it would be like to get the same gift over and over again. I couldn't get his story out of my head, maybe because of the humility it offered me.

Billy talked mother into buying an aluminum Christmas tree one year. A Christmas tree in a box. I helped him erect the tree. It was a different experience from other trees mother normally liked. Mother usually liked flocked trees. The flocking made it look like freshly fallen snow on the tree. This time we were poking the aluminum branches into a pole that represented the trunk of a tree. It was a different experience, but it looked pretty when it was finished. The tree sparkled from the reflection of the aluminum. I added colorful pom poms at the end of the branches. We hung a few ornaments on the tree. It looked nice to me. Mother didn't complain, but she said she liked her flocked trees better.

I crawled under the tree to push the button on the stand. The tree immediately started spinning in a graceful circle with a quiet hum coming from the motor. I would push the other button that played music like 'Jingle Bells,' but the sound was such a high-pitched tone it hurt my ear drums. I could only stand to listen to it for about a minute or less and then I had to turn it off. Billy set up the spotlight that came with the Christmas tree. It had four colors on a wheel that spun in a circle, reflecting the light through the lens of the wheel onto the tree. Red, green, yellow, and blue all took their turns, showing their true colors.

It reminded me of when one of the students brought their own color wheel to school, setting it up in my old kindergarten classroom and turning it on. It seemed out of place. It wasn't Christmas time. There was no teacher in attendance. One student ran over to draw the shades, closing out all the natural light into the room. Maybe they liked seeing the color of the light shining through the lens as it rotated, I thought. I liked the pretty colors myself. I watched as the color wheel spun.

It was only a moment before one of the kids pulled out a game board and set it up, pointing the light of the color wheel on the game they were about to play. Another student ran over and turned out the overhead lights.

I asked my friend, "What are they doing?"

He said, "They're playing with a Ouija board."

That meant nothing to me other than it was a new game. I was curious. I didn't know what the game entailed, but I watched from a distance.

There were three kids sitting in a circle on the floor with their hands together, holding something down. One of them said something I didn't understand. I wasn't interested in what they were saying, but I continued watching them as the color wheel shined and spun its colors on the game they were playing.

The feeling in the room changed, and I didn't like it at all. The light of the color wheel wasn't so pretty anymore. It seemed eerie to me. It made me think of a man talking on the news about LSD. Young people were dying

159

because of drugs. That message scared me away from thinking about using any drugs at all.

I thought maybe they were on drugs while playing this game. One of the three kids who was playing the game got up and ran past me into the hallway of the school, screaming and crying hysterically. I lost even more interest in what they were doing at that point. Something had terrified her, but while playing a board game? It didn't make sense. The sound of her terror never left my head. I didn't want to understand any more about what they were playing or what they were doing. I left the room and played on the playground.

I never saw her again.

For Christmas one year, mother bought one of the older boys a Ouija board. I picked up the box and looked at the name. I couldn't figure out how to enunciate the word. I looked at the pictures on the box instead. It showed letters of the alphabet, but that didn't interest me. Neither did the triangly shape with the magnifying glass. It didn't look like a fun game. I set the box back down after looking at it for a moment. I didn't connect the game mother bought for my brother with the game the students were playing on that day in school.

At the time, letters of the alphabet were a fog in my mind that represented a gap in my brain I couldn't fill on my own. I had no interest in learning how to read or write, because it was hard. A school friend of mine I'd been friends with since kindergarten was very smart. His name was Roger. Roger could read and write far advanced for the grade he was in. He was smart in arithmetic too, adding up everything in his mother's cart at the grocery store, even calculating the tax and coming within a few pennies of being right. He did this all in his head before his mother went through the checkout. Eventually they advanced him two grades from the 4th to the 6th grade. Nobody liked Roger except me. They eventually put him back into the fourth grade at his request. He told me, "Sixth grade was too hard." I think he wanted to be my friend and had asked to be put back into the same grade as me. Mother's philosophy that smart people were dumb and dumb people were smart stuck in my head. I didn't say anything, but I thought why did he do that? He could have been finished with school two years earlier than everybody else if he'd continued.

When I wrote something down from an assignment and got an 'F' on it for spelling, Roger read what I wrote, just how I spelled it. We laughed and laughed together with no end at my spelling. It was so much fun. Why would I have any interest in learning how to spell properly? I didn't care. I could read on a 2nd grade level, but I couldn't pronounce or comprehend words I didn't recognize above the grade.

School was a lot of hard work, and I got frustrated in almost any attempt to read any material, even the magazines underneath my brother's bed. The way I learned to understand was to piece together what I could read, getting the gist of what was written, and then guessing the words in between. It was just like listening to mother speak German to her friends. I could piece what was written together enough to understand, kind of.

Some time after getting the Ouija Board, Billy brought it out. Walter and Billy were going to play.

I asked, "What are you guys playing?"

"SHHHHH!" Billy told me. "It's a Ouija board! Don't talk!"

I remembered that name from the day my schoolmates played it.

Billy asked the board a question.

"Look!" he said. "It's moving on its own!"

Billy said aloud the letters that were being spelled.

I watched what they were doing for a few minutes. I understood what was happening now, but I felt no affinity for it. I soon left the room, thinking about the girl who ran past me hysterically screaming and crying that school day. I went and watched TV instead.

I would rather escape the world watching TV. It mesmerized me, and I lost all connection to the world around me, paying little attention to what was going on around me even if it was happening in the same room. During one of these sessions, Daddy put his hand on my shoulder and taught me a very important lesson. He said, "You should not get so involved in a program that you don't know what's going on around you. I said hello to you when I came into the room, and you were so involved in watching TV you didn't hear me come in the room or say hello to you."

I thought about what he said for a moment and said, "Hi Daddy, sorry. I think that's a good idea." I never forgot that day Daddy put his hand on my shoulder and taught me. I became conscientious of my environment from that moment forward with Daddy's instruction in my head.

I wasn't mesmerized when mother hollered, "Robert, Walter get in here right now!"

Mother always sounded very mad.

Walter and I stopped watching TV immediately and ran into the utility room where the washer and dryer were kept. It was also the same room mother hung the radiator brush, a long oak handled broom of some sort. It was the one mother used to beat us boys with. I just knew it hurt when she hit me with it. One time I thought it was a good idea to hide the radiator brush. That was a bad idea. It hurt really bad when it was back in her possession. I never did that again.

Walter and I ran into the utility room, standing against the cabinet where the radiator brush hung. Walter was to my right. We stood before mother who had her hands on her hips. I knew something was wrong, and I wondered if one or both of us were going to get beat with the radiator brush that was behind us, hanging up in the cupboard.

Mother asked a very pointed question. "Which one of you picked apart my falsies?"

I knew I hadn't done anything. I had no idea what she was talking about. Her question immediately relieved the thought that she would beat one or both of us with the brush.

Now I realize that a moment earlier mother had opened the clothes dryer door to pull her clothes out, and little foam pieces fell to the floor. Mother paused for a moment, inspecting where these foam pieces came from. They were from her bosom builders. The foam crystallized from the heat of the dryer, damaging the contents of her bra. Mother didn't understand heat disintegrates the structure of foam. That's when mother hollered for us.

I processed mother's question: *'Which one of you picked apart my falsies?'* Her question left my mind in a stupor. With a household of five boys and Daddy, I didn't know what a falsie was. So I said, "I don't know what a falsie is."

Mother replied very quickly, "My brazier!"

I replied, "I don't know what brazier is."

Mother's anger skyrocketed at my idiocy.

Mother snapped out, "MY BRA!"

I knew what a bra was.

I said to mother, "I didn't do it!"

My brother Walter said the same thing, "I didn't do it either."

With mother's hands still on her hips, one of them holding the depleted bra, mother said, "Well then, the two of you will stand there until one of you tells me who picked apart my bra."

My mind was completely blank on how to defuse this problem. Then an idea came into my head. I said, "Maybe Fluffy did it?"

"Oh," mother said, "The dog!" This only elevated her anger. "The dog is not going to pick apart my bra!"

My mind went blank again. I was very nervous, then fidgety, as if I was standing on pins and needles. My lips were dry. I knew mother meant business.

I stood before mother with my little brother standing next to me when I remembered Bonnie who stuck out her tongue just enough to wet her lips. My lips needed a little moisture right about now. I was very nervous. I wet my lips with my tongue ever so inconspicuously, then swallowed what saliva I still had in my mouth.

In mother's volatile state, she interpreted me as sticking my tongue out at her. "Don't stick your tongue out at me!" Mother shouted, and with her left hand tightly fisted, she swung from behind her body with the back of her knuckles, SMACK! She punched me in the face, right into my mouth.

Faster than my arms could reach up and grab my face from the impact of mother's knuckle, an accumulation from all the years of mother's beatings on my body traveled into my mind. It left me in a stupor of thought, before the pain even reached my senses. Instantly with the surprise of being hit in the face, a feeling of betrayal set in, forming a deep, open wound in my mind against mother. I ran past Walter, holding my hands tightly to my face, crying through the kitchen into the hallway, then into my bedroom. I slammed my door closed. Slamming the door was my act of war, my war drum beat. I laid on my stomach and cried into my pillow.

I felt the pain of mother's knuckles followed by the feeling of total rejection from mommy. Both hurt to the core of my heart. I cried so much that my stomach began to hurt.

After a while, mother had heard enough of my crying from the kitchen. Mother couldn't stand to hear me cry any longer. Mother threw open my bedroom door. I looked up to mother and saw her scowling face. Mother looked down to me, saying once again succinctly in her deepened voice and gritted teeth, "STOP YOUR CRYING! OR I WILL GIVE YOU SOMETHING TO CRY ABOUT!" Then she slammed the door shut.

The slam of the door shattered my nerves. My body flinched as I rolled onto my back, setting aside my wet pillow. My stomach filled with worry after hearing mother's intimidating voice. It was the same voice mother used to ask, "Who picked apart my falsies?" I didn't want to be around mother or even see her. I felt so humiliated over being punched in the face for something that I had nothing to do with. I didn't touch mother's bra. I didn't know what had happened to it in the dryer! And I hadn't stuck my tongue out at her!

I couldn't comprehend any of this, I couldn't categorize it anywhere in my brain or make any sense out of it in my mind. I believed I could turn any negative mother fed me into a positive, but this time I couldn't. I changed in that moment from being confused to angry. How would wetting my lips, mimicking a girl's action I saw in my head, come to this pain and humiliation? I replayed this scene over and over in my head. Mother had hit me in my face! I was done trying to win over mother's love. I didn't care anymore.

I had been a happy ten-year-old until this moment, a happy child who had cried for being punished one too many times for doing something I didn't do. My natural tendency was to be happy, but I stopped feeling happiness after that day. I made an emotional shield over my heart, repressing my nature. 'I'm not going to cry anymore. I'm done crying,' I told myself. It's too painful. Unlike the machine that I could unplug to beat the system at school, I couldn't unplug my emotions and then plug them back in again for a different answer. I simply lacked any interest in crying. I simply repeated mother's words to myself, 'stop your crying,' and I did.

I made a decision as I sobered up. I WAS DONE CRYING! My tears were beat out of me. I no longer had a tear available to exit my eye.

I never gave my decision a second thought.

I was done crying.

Little did I know, that decision cemented within me. Fifty years later, I still have not allowed myself to cry.

CHAPTER EIGHTEEN

THE DAWN OF A NEW DAY

I lost my will to survive. A shift had taken place in my head. Mother's hateful words were an endless loop playing in my mind.

"I should have left you in the cart, you talk in riddles."

"I should have given you away, can't you say anything that makes sense, I should have drowned you!"

"Can't you talk intelligently, shut up!"

"Oh, you asshole!"

"It's because of you damn kids we're poor."

Mother's unending screaming and yelling echoed in my head. "There were too damn many kids in this world," mother always said. I now believed that I was one of them. She reminded me often, "I had to wipe your ass when you were a baby." It was another way to humiliate me. But I thought that was the way it was supposed to be, that parents cared for their children until they could care for themselves. Was I that much of an inconvenience?

I felt the pain of mother's angry beatings from years gone by on my body. Why should I have one more beating to tally up? There would be no more crying.

This life was less than I believed it was, from what I could gather from the outside world. I stopped dreaming my dreams. A shift took place inside of me over the next several days, an overwhelming feeling that stemmed from not being able to regress my experience. They just played over and over

167

again inside my mind, this endless loop, this endless battle. There was no beginning and no end, unless I ended it. My feelings crashed. Neithe drugs nor alcohol were in the realm of possibilities as an option to deaden my pain (even though my younger brother Walter had already begun drinking), but that wouldn't stop me from using a knife to kill myself. Mother hated guns, so there were no guns in the house that I knew of.

An unsettling feeling persisted in my stomach, a heavy pit filled the bottom of my gut. My thoughts and feelings were all over the place. The uncomfortable feeling in my stomach disappeared when I fell asleep, returning when I awakened. That was the only way I knew I slept. The moment I awakened, a myriad of unresolved issues flooded and swirled in my head. I felt it in my gut. I tried bouncing my head on my pillow to create a different feeling, but the pit in my stomach overtook the bouncing on my pillow. Bouncing my head didn't seem to feel as good with the pain in my stomach. I bounced harder to feel the impact on my face, hoping to overcome the discomfort. Then I stopped bouncing, turned over on my back, then again on my stomach. I didn't sleep well. I continued tossing and turning all night. My sheets, like my thoughts, were wadded up in a knot from all the tossing and turning.

Days of thinking and stewing about my thoughts didn't leave better results in my mind. I walked out of my bedroom into the front room and looked around, seeing my brothers playing games in circles with one another. No one included me in their frolicking. So what? I'd been excluded countless times before. Why should this time be any different? It wasn't. I walked back into the kitchen over to mother's knife drawer. I remembered a knife mother used in her kitchen while she did her cooking. It was the knife I was thinking about using to kill myself. It had a very fine point. Just the one I needed to pierce my chest and stop my heart from beating.

I searched through the drawer for that one particular knife I had in my mind. It had a black polished handle with two smooth rivets holding itself onto its shiny steel blade. My hands trembled as I sifted through a myriad of knives until I spotted what I was looking for and pulled it out of the drawer. I knew this was the right one as soon as I found it. It was exactly what I remembered it to be, all the way to the point. I held it tight in my right hand, feeling the point with my left hand. I didn't have the guts to kill myself personally. I needed help. I walked back into the living room where my brothers were playing their games.

My brothers were on kitchen chairs they had brought into the living room to play a game. Billy, Walter, and one other formed a semicircle in front of mother's priceless china cabinet. I interrupted the game as I walked into their circle. They paused, looking puzzled for a moment upon my approach. I looked into their eyes as they looked down at my hand. I knew at that moment they saw me wielding a knife. But they didn't know what I had in my mind. I didn't care what they thought! I stared Billy in the eyes and screamed at the top of my voice, "Kill me!" "Kill me!" With no tears coming down my face, just anger inside of me, I said again, "I want you to kill me! I want to die!"

I handed Billy the knife to kill me.

He took the knife into his possession. I waited for him to stab me to death. With the knife securely in his hand he said nonchalantly, "I'm not going to kill you."

Then both of my brothers started laughing.

My world stopped. I felt alone, isolated, and empty inside. I had no happy thoughts. I was in utter despair. I wanted to sabotage my life and I failed. I turned around and ran to my bedroom. I laid on my bed thinking about what had just happened. I'm not dead. Why not?

I stared at the formations on the ceiling above. While I was thinking, a slight shift took place. I searched for shapes I hadn't seen before. My thoughts went up an octave; my brow softened. I stared at Woody Woodpecker as he stared back at me, and a tear rolled from my eye. I wiped it away. 'I'm not

169

going to cry,' I told myself. The leaky roof in my room had resulted in a stalactite formation beginning at the edge of the wall. Or so I imagined. I followed the line down the wall, checking to see if it was touching the floor. A slight uptick in my mind illuminated my imagination. The world I had begun building a few years before rekindled inside of me. My dreams reappeared, but just for a moment.

I needed to make a new decision. My attempt to kill myself had failed.

I turned over on my stomach, clasping my left hand on my right wrist and started bouncing my head. I bounced vigorously, continuously. My heart started beating faster and my breath was fast, like I was running a marathon. I found such comfort in hitting my head on my nice soft pillow. I didn't feel the pit in my stomach as much as I did before. I felt my pillow's gentle touch against my face.

I stopped bouncing my head for a moment, resting on my pillow for comfort. I adjusted my arms, resting my face on the right side, staring at the inside of my elbow to the left. With my arms above my head, I stared at the veins in my arm on the inside of my elbow. I watched the biggest vein pulsating in the bend of my arm. It was mesmerizing. I listened to the deep rhythm of my heartbeat and watched the pulse of my vein expand, then contract. As long as that blood was pumping through my veins, there was life in me. Listening to my breath exhale then inhale as I laid on my stomach, it all coincided with one another. I felt a bit of life enter my soul, falling asleep with that thought.

I woke up on my stomach in the same position, exhausted. I opened my eyes, staring at the same arm I fell asleep on. My pillow was wet from drool. I must have slept deeply. I wiped my mouth dry. I began thinking. I stopped staring at my arm and started bouncing again. The harder I bounced the better I felt.

While bouncing my head, my energy began to rebound. I was able to gaze through the trauma. I began to understand my feelings. I remembered the first time I played with myself and how the pain of life dissipated, how the shards of ice melted with the feelings my body gave to me. It was a feeling I needed, now more than ever before, if I was to keep going on living.

My thoughts turned to the boys in my class. The feeling I had for them jumped in my heart. I wanted to be with them and feel their bodies next to mine. I liked that thought. I felt like I could relate to boys. I saw only beauty in my eyes. The girls reminded me of mother, and I wasn't interested. Any reference to a girl reminded me of mother, followed by unpleasant thoughts in my mind.

Daddy massaged mother's feet nearly every night, often massaging my feet and shoulders when I asked him to, usually once or twice a month. I related to Daddy and paid attention to the difference between Daddy's touch on my feet and mother's anger on my body. I shied away from mother's style of touch, the painful beatings, to thoughts of Daddy's gentle touch on my feet.

In my mind, then, boys were gentle. The thought of boys brought happiness into my soul, a feeling I liked, but I wondered if the boys could relate to my pain. Maybe they had pain inside of them, like I had pain I had inside of me? I thought of gentle touches. Could they relate to the feelings I had for them? Could they relate any of their feelings towards me? I was afraid to ask and didn't. Questions like this swirled in my head. I wondered what thoughts were going through their minds. Why was I picking up positive thoughts and feeling their energy in my presence? I didn't know what was real and what I was hoping for, but my thoughts and feelings were healing to me. I needed my imagination to be set free in my mind if I was going to live, and I did, but I kept them to myself, feeling the energy inside my soul.

Thinking about the same sex gave me energy so powerful and positive. I couldn't deny it. I became addicted to the energy I was feeling. It was

171

such a strong feeling that radiated inside of me it lit me up. Feelings I didn't get around mother. Why this was all so confusing for me, I didn't know. I talked myself out of asking anyone any questions again, even though I wanted to ask the questions so badly. I felt if I asked the wrong person, the wrong question, they would know my thoughts. I couldn't let my secret out. I had to keep my mouth shut, tight-lipped. I was determined to take my feelings of attraction to my grave. I monitored my behavior so I didn't give myself away. I said nothing, not a word, careful not to even give a clue. My imagination was sublime to me. I hid it all, keeping it to myself.

Besides, there were a lot of slurs if you were accused of being gay. You were quickly labeled. It wasn't something you talked about anyway. It was all hush, hush. The topic of being gay was treated more like you had a mental disease or you were confused. Maybe you just needed a different mindset or you were just mixed up. None of the above was true! There was an air of intolerance, a feeling of disgust. Maybe you would be harassed or abandoned by 'friends,' worst yet by family. In public, death might be your sentence. I already felt the pain of being abandoned, harassed and felt unwanted. I didn't need more pain. I kept silent and lived in my imagination. I never stopped dreaming. I never stopped feeling. I just stopped crying.

I kept my secret life just that, a secret for me in my world. It was a beautiful place inside my mind for me to live my life, to dream, and to believe again. I never felt I deprived myself. I lived in anticipation but never engaged in participation. Masturbation helped me overcome the urge to act on the feelings I had for the boys in my class. The feelings my body gave to me were the answers to my survival. They enabled me to reset my feelings to get the urges out of my system so I wasn't off-balance. I reset my feelings often in order to stay focused on other parts of life that were important, too.

Although I conquered these urges that were in my conscious mind, I didn't want to eliminate the feelings out of my subconscious. I liked the energy I felt, but I had to stay focused on what I needed to become. I wanted to be a mom. To become a mom–not a mommy or not mother–a mom! As I look on this dream now, it is undoubtedly an odd dream for a little boy. But I believe I needed to resolve the past trauma I had experienced at mother's hand, and being a mom would heal the burning pain deep inside of me. I didn't know why at the time, but I had become competitive with mother. Competing against mother on every front, without appearing rebellious, I wanted to be the mom I never had. It was too complicated for my mind to give the details, but I knew I was going to be a mom someday somehow. I will make this happen, I thought to myself. I was going to do it. My mind was set.

The decision to be a mom was very clear to me. I daydreamed about raising my future children. Each of them already existed inside my head, inside my thoughts. I didn't know how many children exactly–maybe just one, maybe three, maybe more.

I didn't want my children to go through what I had gone through. I didn't want them to have to masturbate to feel peace. I could give them peace, and that way they wouldn't have to search for peace elsewhere.

I decided to pay attention to every thought that went through my head. I noticed every action I acted on and every decision I made. I asked myself why did I do that? Why did I think that thought? I wanted to learn and understand my patterns so I could recognize the behavior in my children. I would stop mid-thought or mid-action to ponder these questions. I didn't need the answer right away, but I needed to pay attention to everything that went through my mind.

I made other important decisions in my life. I felt like I needed to be a provider for my family. I pictured holding my future wife up on one arm above my shoulders and our children on the other shoulder, placing the responsibility on my back to take care of the family, never losing sight of being a mom. In my mind, being a dad was the gateway to achieving my dream of being a mom.

My first desire was to become an architect, because I saw somebody on a popular TV program I liked, *The Brady Bunch*. He was an architect. He was a calm, nice man. I liked that about him. I ordered house plans that were similar to the house I saw on the TV. I told Daddy, "I'm going to build a house different from anybody else's house."

Daddy said, "There's a lot of houses out there."

I still believed I could. I would build a house different from anybody's else. I never doubted myself for a moment. I had confidence to do so.

I ordered house plans from a magazine. I checked the mailbox daily, anxiously waiting for them to arrive. I was over the moon the day they came. I opened up the big gray envelope and laid the house plans out on the table, drawing in furniture, arranging planters, fish tanks and decor. I drew in the sunken living room just like what I remembered on the TV show.

It occurred to me that I might die before I built this house so one day I asked mother, "If I die, would you have this house built for me?"

"NO!"

I didn't ask her twice. As I look back, I wonder at the fact that despite everything, I still trusted mother with my dreams.

I figured that I would find a way to build it myself if it came down to it. I felt I could make all this happen more if I was a carpenter, so I decided to study building construction.

I started concentrating on how floor joists were constructed, the webbing to keep floor joists straight. I looked at how walls were built, how support beams were assembled, and why they were necessary. The electrical was the same, understanding what wires went to the water lines and sewers lines–all of it. It was a good decision for me. I learned by observing. I believed I had the ability to learn to do this, and I did.

As I bounced my head each night, I reflected on my dreams for my future. Someday I would be a millionaire. I would buy land. I would build a house on the hill. And it would be different from anyone else's. I would buy a Cadillac. Nothing was beyond my feat.

I bounced my dreams into me as if I already owned them. I hoped this would be a way to heal from my past and support my family as a mom. But through it all, even at that age of 10, I decided I would keep my same sex attraction secret.

My life had completely changed when mother hit me in the face that day.

It was a pivotal moment in my life.

I have never looked back with regret on any of my decisions. With the one exception, I would like to remember how to cry.

The dawn of a new day, one with tears, still awaits me.

CHAPTER NINETEEN

THE MASK OF HUMOR

Mother loved to throw parties. It was all about show and tell. It was all about entertainment. It was all about mother. When mother put on a party, guests just showed up and everything was provided. Even the liquor was all inclusive. Mother wanted to be complimented on her food. She spent days in advance putting it together, mostly working by herself but sometimes enrolling Billy to help as the day drew close. Her need for acknowledgement and accolades was insatiable, and she worked hard for them. Mother prepared anywhere from 10 to 15 courses, everything from Gurkensalat (German for cucumber salad) to lox (smoked salmon belly) with onions and capers. Food was abundant and fit for a king. It was all displayed on the table in a beautiful array of sights and smells.

Mother would greet her guests with an aura of ease, guiding them to the table of delectables with a smile. It's worth noting that the days preceding that moment were anything but restful and effortless. Mother always complained prior to a party, "This is the last time I'm doing this!" Mother said the same thing before every party. She would say the same thing after every party during the extensive clean-up that its aftermath required.

Mother never asked me to help in her food preparation. Maybe she thought I was too young. Sometimes I wonder if it was because she couldn't stand having me around. Most likely it was because she had Billy to help. Billy was her favorite. The food smelled and tasted like the German delicatessen store mother and I visited weekly. Mother's cooking style and the scrumptious smells ingrained themselves into my senses. I passed through the kitchen on purpose to taste the food. Mother would say each time, "Don't touch the food!" When I didn't listen or she caught me, she would follow up with, "Go to your room!" My only access to the food was to sneak it–I wasn't allowed to have any unless there were leftovers after the party.

Mother collected music records, hundreds of them, most from the big band orchestras of the 1940s and '50s. Mother enjoyed listening to the likes of Guy Lombardo, Beer Barrel polka music, and German records that sang with the spirits they drank–the German beer and the camaraderie of friends forever. She played any music she felt she could waltz to, anything that she could play on her Grundig during the party. Mother enjoyed hearing all its oomph-la-la.

Mother prepared a set of records that she wanted to hear during the party, stacking the records near the needle of the record player. Besides serving liquor, Daddy's job was to keep the music going that mother chose. Over and over, time after time, Daddy played the records mother chose. If Daddy put on a record mother didn't choose, mother would know within the first few notes that it was not a record she had picked. She would immediately express her disappointment to Daddy. They would argue briefly in German. I don't know what they said, but mother seemed to surrender to Daddy's one chosen record.

Mother couldn't stand to hear the music of the early 1970's–acid rock, rock and roll, disco–it was all a travesty to mother and her ears. I agreed with mother. I couldn't listen to acid rock or hard rock either. Until disco came along, I listened to calm music more often than not. The screeching guitars of rock and roll with high pitches hurt my ears and rattled my brain. Maybe both mother and I had traumatic childhoods. Disco was different. I didn't like it at first, but I listened to it long enough to begin to like it. It built itself into my imagination. It fit my youthful energy better than the slow waltzing style of Lawrence Welk and Guy Lombardo, although I admit I enjoyed watching *The Lawrence Welk* every Saturday night. I eventually set aside mother's feelings towards disco for my own tastes.

Mother was disgusted by how people danced, saying, "Look how they're dancing. It looks like they're having SEX while they're moving!" Mother emphasized the word sex with a disgusted tone. I looked a little closer after mother brought up the subject. It looked fine to me. Besides, the sight of people dancing dazzled my imagination.

Mother enjoyed waltzing with Daddy at the dance clubs, but according to her he didn't like dancing with her. The dance floor is where Daddy shined. However, Daddy didn't feel mother knew how to dance to his energetic style. He was known as "Twinkle Toes." Mother often complained the next morning, "Oh, Twinkle Toes danced with every other woman but me." Mother would say with disgust, "I'm not going anymore." But the next time would come, and she would go. And when she returned, she would say again that she wasn't going any more. And so it went on for years.

Mother brought a small violin case that held one bottle of liquor that she would set on the table of the nightclub. When mother opened the lid to show it off, it sang, "How dry I am, how dry I am, nobody knows, how dry I am." Mother got a kick out of showing off her little violin case with her hidden spirits. You had to hide any liquor bottles under the table or inside a brown paper bag in case the nightclub was raided. It was against the law to have any liquor bottles displayed.

This was another reason mother was disgusted with Utah. Mother thought its liquor laws were ridiculous. You couldn't display a liquor bottle on the dinner table at the nightclub. Just the idea that you couldn't have a bottle in view outraged mother. I don't believe mother ever drank hard liquor, except a beer now and again, but she was incensed nonetheless. She would say, "Utah is twenty years behind the times!"

Mother convinced me that Utah was a terrible place to live. I suggested to mother, "Maybe we should change the name from Salt Lake City to Salt Lake's Shitty?"

Mother said, "NO!"

I dropped the suggestion, but I thought about it many times, thinking it was a good idea.

Saturday afternoon, hours before a party, mother went into the bathroom to change into what she had picked out days earlier. It was usually a fashionable pant suit. I watched mother get ready. It seemed like it took hours, especially when she started gluing fake eyelashes on her eyelids, cursing and swearing under her breath, occasionally stomping her heel on the floor in frustration saying, "Why I wasn't born with long eyelashes is beyond me!" This was followed by another stomp.

With one eye open and the other closed, mother tried again and again to get it right. Mother's closed eyelid seemed to flutter like a bird's wings on takeoff. It sputtered between slightly open and almost closed. Mother hollered, "Hold still!" She was talking to her eyelid. She carefully applied enough glue to hold her glamor in place, complaining the whole time about having to put them on in the first place. With one last stomp, she would finally get it in place.

Mother gave me the idea of looking closer at my eyelashes. I had longer eyelashes than she, but not like her false ones. When no one was looking, I applied eyeliner, darkening my lashes and eyebrows. In my eyes I looked as beautiful as mother with her liner on. I liked it.

Her lashes never seemed to hold, no matter how much glue she used. I always found it funny, laughing to myself when mother's glue gave out and her eyelashes sprung free. I would stare at the lash that was out of place, not hearing a word mother was saying because my attention was inextricably attached to the sight of her eyelash, waving at me with each blink of her eye. It was as if mother had an extra body part hanging out of place. I learned quickly it was best not to say anything. I just noticed and smiled, staring at this phenomenon. Mother would check the mirror soon enough to see her curse in life.

With mother's eyelashes glued in place, she adjusted her new foam-filled brazier, complaining that her bosoms weren't big enough, and adjusting what was necessary to get the cleavage she desired. I simply listened again, not saying a word. I didn't see the appeal. Cleavage turned me off.

When mother was satisfied with what she had to live with, mother put on her freshly spruced-up sandy blonde wig covering her reddish brown hair that she didn't like and turning it into a blonde beauty. She would adjust her wig like that of a man's hat, turning it a little to the left then to the right. She would finish off her attire with high heels, sparkly earrings, and a fashionable necklace. Mother was dressed to the hilt, as pretty as chantilly lace. She was ready to present herself at the party. Mother was dressed so beautifully to me.

Minutes before the guests arrived mother hollered, "I need help putting food on the table!" It was all hands on deck. Everybody who was at home ran from all corners of the house to put the food on the table for mother. We all knew better than to eat any of it. Mother arranged the food the way she felt it needed to be set up for people's convenience and flow. Mother had her patterns. Mother wanted the right presentation so that it netted her more compliments. That's what mother wanted. Mother had already set out her apple plates, silverware, wine glasses, and coffee cups ahead of time. Everything was set.

Mother asked me to stand by the front door and holler when I saw the first car pull up. I did what mother asked me to do and watched. When the first car pulled up, I ran to Mommy with excitement in my voice. "They're here, Mommy, they're here, Mommy!" I made sure mother heard me. Mother asked Daddy to turn on the Grundig. She flipped the switch to the coffee machine to start it brewing, and the party began.

181

The smell of freshly brewed coffee filled the air with an aroma only coffee will do, along with mother's cooking, the smell of the delicatessen food, the sight of mother's spread of food on the table adorned in her collection of crystal bowls. It looked beautiful and smelled wonderful. Nothing seemed wrong with the world on those days.

The arrival of the first guest was also my sign to go to my bedroom. I knew my place, and it wasn't with the guests that mother invited.

If I was caught snitching any of the food on my way to the bedroom, I was immediately told, "That was for the company, not you! Hurry to your room before the guests come into the house. I did what I was told, I knew I could eat after the guests left.

My bedroom was just around the corner from the kitchen. I heard the people come in: cheerful, jovial, and bursting with laughter immediately upon entering the house. I could tell who was who by their laughter. I'd been around them enough to know. I thought to myself, "That's Mariana!" She was always the life of any party. I heard another familiar laugh, thinking, "That's Fritz!" With mother's music playing in the background, I knew mother's guests were going to have a good evening. It was the epitome of eat, drink and be merry, and merry they were. The sounds and tones of the guests rang in my ears all throughout the evening. The guests seemed satisfied with the atmosphere of the home, and so was I.

A few guests expressed their compliments to mother in English with heavy German accents. I could understand what they were saying, telling mother how they enjoyed the evening, saying, "Hedy, the food, the music, all of it, was wonderful!" Mother grinned as if to say shucks it was nothing, but it was everything to mother. Mother enjoyed every positive affirmation. Mother loved to hear every word of what they said. Anybody who might have even had a suggestion or complained about anything, even the strength of the coffee, were not invited back to the next party.

That is what mother lived for. The party was not for her children, at least not for me. I sat or laid on my bed, listening to the party. I learned how to occupy my time until the party was over. When I was older and could make my way out of the house, I did so without being seen. That worked for mother, too. Mother didn't care as long as I didn't show up at the party until it was over. When the guests started staggering out and the music stopped playing, I knew the party was over and I came out of my room.

Some of the guests lingered long after the party was over, like Elsie. Mother had told me earlier that Elsie had been a prisoner of the Nazi concentration camps when she was a young lady. I was asked not to bring up the subject unless Elsie brought it up herself. One day Elsie did talk about it. As she began, I realized Elsie had a story deep down inside of her that she wanted to tell.

Elsie sat at the table, taking a swallow of coffee, sitting comfortably in her chair, feeling right at home. Elsie seemed to be pondering what to say or if to say anything at all. Finally she spoke up, "I was in the Nazi concentration camps when I was a young girl." She said it matter-of-factly, taking another sip of coffee. My ears perked up as I had been curious about this since mother had told me. After a long pause, she ended her story as quickly as it began, saying, "I can't tell you about it. It was too atrocious."

That's all she would say. I didn't press her. I sat and ate. I wouldn't find out all the details this time, but I would find out later. Elsie was the epitome of a woman who had been scarred in her youth, but she looked past those early years of life to find a deep love for humanity. "Eat, there's plenty of food," Elsie said with the gentleness of charm. I did eat, and I was ready to listen when Elsie was ready to talk.

All the old Germans had a story to tell. Whenever I got the chance, I sat, ate, and listened.

Mother and Daddy's 25th silver wedding anniversary was approaching quickly. Mother wanted a new kitchen for her anniversary. What mother really wanted was to party in style. Daddy sought out the services of a company who specialized in building cabinets. Arrangements were made to measure the existing kitchen. Once the kitchen was measured, drawings were made and a woman came out to explain how the new kitchen layout would look. She was hoping to close the sale.

I saw an unfamiliar car in the driveway, concluding we must have company. I was curious who was at the house. I entered through the front door, walked through the living room into the kitchen where I saw a lady talking to mother and Daddy intently. They were discussing something that seemed important. Daddy looked up and saw me come in, but I wasn't asked to leave. I quietly sat down, unnoticed by the woman in a chair on the outskirts of the kitchen, listening to their conversation.

I stared at the lady, listening without a peep. She was explaining every detail on how the new kitchen layout would look. This conversation interested me. I stared at her beautiful, jet black hair as she was explaining everything. Her hair was piled high on top of her head.

I found my thoughts going back to when mother and I were shopping in downtown Salt Lake City.

Mother pointed out a woman with her hair on top of her head, saying, "See that woman over there?"

"Where?" I said.

"Over there, the one with the hair piled high on top of her head!"

I pointed at the woman I thought she was talking about. "That one?"

"DON'T POINT!" mother said. "She's a Pentecostal. They wear their hair high on the top of their heads."

"Oh," I said.

Mother said, "They're religious fanatics."

"Oh," I said. I stared at the woman's hairdo. It looked more like a beehive to me.

My thoughts returned back to the conversation at hand, wondering if this woman was a Pentecostal. She looked very pleasant to me. She didn't seem like a fanatic. She seemed very polished, wearing beautiful white pants and a blouse. The contrast between her clothes and her hair were stunning to me. The word 'elegant' entered my head. Mother had taught me what the word elegant meant when we went shopping downtown.

Mother enjoyed the downtown department store named Auerbach's. It was finely decorated. Mother pointed out the beautiful chandeliers, saying, "Those are very elegant." I thought they were beautiful. They sparkled with the color of a rainbow. All of them flooded my eyes and imagination.

This woman seemed very elegant to me. Even her mannerisms had a charm. I stared mostly at her hair. It tilted like the Leaning Tower of Pisa, just a little tilt one way then the other as she talked.

She swung her head, explaining to mother and Daddy where the new location of the sink was going to go, saying, "In front of the window." I watched her hair lean into the other direction. I knew mother wanted to look out of a window when she did the dishes rather than being faced by a wall. I thought mother would like the new location as I listened. I continued to stare at her hair.

"You'll have a built-in dishwasher, left of the sink. You won't have to push your dishwasher up to the sink anymore." Her hair tilted the other direction. I knew mother hated pushing the dishwasher over to the sink. She cursed each time, because it was so heavy. I think mother was sold on that convenience alone.

"The refrigerator will have a new location," she continued. "It's going over here." I watched her hair tilt again. "The stove will have a new location. It will be a couple steps to the right of the sink." I continued to watch and listen as she explained the details. "You'll have a built-in desk right there." She turned her head and pointed to where I was sitting.

She looked me right in the eyes and I looked back into her eyes. She looked back at her paperwork and continued explaining where Daddy's bar would be going, then she stopped talking in mid-sentence, looked back at

185

me, and said, "Whoever gets him will be very lucky!" She said it smiling, giggling a little. Her hair jiggled with her laugh.

I had very pleasant thoughts toward her.

Mother smiled and said, "This is Robert, son number four. This is Esther, Esther Johnson. Her husband Paul came and measured the cabinets the other day."

I didn't meet Paul.

Her giggle embedded itself in my ears, but her words, 'whoever will get him will be very lucky' embedded themselves into my mind. My jaw dropped, my face winced, my head turned a little to the left. I felt like I was in an isolated capsule for a moment. Everything faded from my peripheral– everything except for those words. Did I hear her right? "Whoever gets him? Me? Will be lucky?" Her words captured my mind. I was stunned that somebody would say something so nice to me. I thought if mother still wanted to give me away, I would go with Esther.

I bounced my head on my pillow thinking about Esther's words that night.

Over the next several months, Esther visited mother often as the kitchen was being planned and built. Pipes had to be moved, electrical had to be run. All of this fascinated me. I paid attention and watched closely. It seemed to me that a friendship was developing between mother and Esther. Time would unveil the similarities between the two. Neither of them were Mormons. That was pretty standard with mother. She didn't associate with Mormons. Esther liked to drink. So did Mother, even if it was only beer. Esther had only one son. Mother told Esther in front of me, "I should have stopped with one!" I knew I was number four.

Every time Esther drove to the house and I saw her, I ran to greet her. On this visit, Esther was inviting mother to a family gathering at the park. It was Fremont Park, not too far from home. Mother didn't like to travel very far even though mother drove past the park to go downtown. Mother had her

186

routine. Esther invited all three boys that were home and mother and Daddy to attend. We never went as a family to a park. This was my first experience in a family setting outside my home. They had soda pop and potato chips as part of the food. I never had soda before. Mother never bought soda pop. It tasted so good to me. I had fun, running around playing in the water, eating the food, and just being with Esther.

After the party at the park, I asked Esther, "Could I sleepover at your house someday?"

Esther giggled in the way that only Esther could. I think she was surprised I would ask such a question. Esther said, "YES." She paused for a moment, then said, "I would love to have a sleepover."

That brought a smile to my face, grinning from ear to ear. I couldn't wait.

Esther said she would check with mother. Esther did.

Mother was fine with that. Mother said, "You can keep him." Then mother recanted and said, "no."

It didn't matter to me. I would gladly be adopted into Esther's family.

Arrangements were made with mother. Esther said we would go to a movie. I was totally surprised! My thoughts went back to a movie mother took the family to see a long time ago. I think I was five years old. It was *The Sound of Music*. It was playing at the Villa Theater. I didn't pay attention to the movie's plot, but I remembered watching a lady sing so beautifully as she danced across the big screen. "The hills are alive with the sound of music." She captivated me. I was mesmerized, staring at her and listening to her sing. It took my breath away. It was the only part of the movie I remembered. After that I asked mother a million questions. "Could I go to the bathroom?" "Could I have popcorn?" "Could I have popcorn with a treat?" I interrupted mother over and over again as she tried to watch the movie.

After the movie was over, she declared, "I'll never take you to go see another movie again."

Mother was true to her word. Neither mother nor Daddy ever took any of us to the movies again. This was the first and last movie I went to with my family.

When Esther said we would go and see a movie, I was so excited to go. Going to a movie with Esther was the cat's meow, I thought. I used that term because it was what mother said when she appeared happy.

A date was set. I planned my clothes days in advance. I remembered how beautiful Esther was dressed the first time I met her. She was always elegant. Thereafter I wanted to dress beautifully, too. I found a white shirt that fit me. I went through Daddy's ties and found a black tie with the spectrum of a prism on it. It was beautiful and fulfilled the image I had in my head. I asked Daddy if I could borrow it and then asked him to tie it. Daddy stood behind me, flipping and tucking the tie until it became what I thought it should look like: a nicely tied tie. When Daddy was done, it was long, hanging to my zipper, but that was okay.

I found a black pair of pants to go with my white shirt and beautiful tie. I combed my hair, then searched the house for a nice pair of shoes that fit and put them on. When Esther came to the door to pick me up, my mother invited her in. With disbelief and a big smile on her face, she looked so happy to see me all dressed up. Saying with a giggly laugh, "I can't believe you dressed up for me. You look so cute!" That just reaffirmed my love for Esther. I felt her sincerity. I loved her even more. I smiled at her comment. I was glad I dressed up. It was my true self shining forth because of the light of her compliments and her smile.

With my bags packed to stay overnight, I grabbed my suitcase and left my home to stay with Esther for the night. Esther said, "We're going to go see *Jeremiah Johnson*." She thought I would like the movie. Esther was right. I followed along with the plot better than the last movie I had seen six years earlier. But like the other movie, one scene seemed to stand out in my mind. Jeremiah Johnson was exhausted from something, so he stopped, sat down at the base of the tree, and started reading his Bible.

While Jeremiah was reading, Esther leaned over to me and whispered, "He's reading the–" She stopped herself. "Oh, never mind."

I didn't hear the conversation between mother and Esther, but I knew mother's patterns and behaviors. I knew at that moment mother told her everything about her stance on religion and all its 'lies.' Esther wouldn't be mother's friend if she were to ever disagree openly with mother on the subject.

I already knew he was reading the Bible anyway. That moment in the film became etched in my mind.

After the movie, Esther drove me to her home for the planned sleepover. This is where I met Esther's husband Paul as I walked through the door of their house. Their door opened into their kitchen. I smelled the pleasant aroma of food. Paul was cooking dinner that night.

With my suitcase in hand, I said, "Hello!"

Paul said, "Hi, you must be Robert?"

I smiled and said, "Yes, I am."

Paul said, "I hope you're hungry?"

"Yes, I am," I said.

I liked Paul immediately. Paul is my middle name, too, so we already had something in common.

Paul followed up by asking me, "Do you like to go fishing?"

I pondered Paul's question. Nobody had ever asked me that question before. I stared at Paul for a moment. He had thick Coke bottle glasses with large rims. His eyes looked really big, like the moon, as he talked to me. Paul seemed to be the opposite of Esther's refinement, but very old school and very wise in his mannerisms. I told Paul very politely, "I've never been fishing before."

"You haven't?"

"Nope, I haven't," I said.

Paul exclaimed, "Well, we need to go fishing!"

I told him, "Okay, I'll go fishing with you."

Paul seemed to have it all planned out, according to my answer. He said, "We'll go to Strawberry Reservoir!"

Maybe it was his favorite place to fish. I never heard of the place, but I figured it was a big body of water with fish in it.

Esther then walked me down a short hallway to my bedroom, showing me the bathroom on the left. I knew that would be important. Esther opened the door to my bedroom for the night, and the first thing I noticed was the ambience of the room. The lighting was very pleasant. I looked at the bed and noticed how tightly the bed was made. The room was very neat and well kept. It was her son's room, but the room seemed more like a guest room than a child's. His name was Paul, like his father. They called him "Little Paul." He was sleeping over at someone else's house that night.

I looked around the room. There were beautiful paintings hung on the walls.

Esther said, "I painted the pictures in the room."

"Wow," I said. I stared at the details of the paintings even closer. I found it interesting that she loved to paint fruit. Her painting of strawberries stood out in my mind the most. I set my suitcase down near the bed, letting go of the handle.

"Wash your hands," Esther said, "then come in for dinner."

I did so immediately. I was hungry.

Paul's dinner was ready for us to eat when we came in. It was trout. With Paul's interest in fishing, I wasn't surprised.

Esther said, "This is your seat here," touching the chair in front of my place setting.

The table was set with white cloth napkins and bone white dinner plates with no patterns on them. I thought to myself, it wouldn't have mattered how the plates were set. No one would yell about the apples being in the wrong place.

Esther had other paintings around the house, including one on an easel by the dinner table. Esther was currently painting a portrait. It was the face of somebody close to her. I complimented Esther on her work, wondering if I could be a painter, too. I knew the night was drawing to an end, and there was a thought in the back of my head I'd been worried about ever since Esther said I could sleep over at her home. I thought to myself, 'will I pee in the bed or not?' This would be my first experience sleeping in somebody else's bed rather than my own. The mental image flashed through my mind of waking up in a wet bed in somebody else's home. I would be putting myself to the test.

I had packed my suitcase with a clean pair of underwear, a tee shirt, pants, and a pee pad just in case. I was concerned what Esther might think if I peed her son's bed. I told myself that I needed to wake up in the middle of the night to go pee, but I placed my pee pad down just in case. I didn't have pajamas. I just slept in my underwear and t-shirt like at home.

When I turned out the light, I noticed that Esther had put a cute little nightlight in the room. It had a cute little switch on it, too. I flipped the switch once or twice to try it out. That was my first experience with nightlights.

I didn't bring my feather pillow to bounce my head on. I knew I would have to use whatever pillow Esther had for me. I wanted to bounce my head on the pillow. I wondered if I would make too much noise. I didn't want Esther to know I bounced my head on my pillow. But I checked out the pillow with a few bounces. It was a foam-filled pillow so I couldn't bounce my head on it anyway without feeling like I was suffocating. I turned on my back, reminding myself not to pee the bed, and fell asleep.

I woke myself up once in the middle of the night, being very quiet not to be heard. I checked my pants and the pad. I was relieved to feel I was dry. As I walked to the bathroom, I heard Paul snoring in his bedroom. I quietly

191

opened the bathroom door then closed it just as quietly. The bathroom had a little nightlight, too. Turning on the overhead light and squinting at the brightness of the light in my eyes, I lifted both the toilet lid and seat up. Mother taught her boys to lift up the seat. Mother was furious at us whenever she sat down on a wet seat because someone peed on it.

I worried that if I peed directly into the water, I would make too much noise and wake up Esther or Paul. I didn't want anybody to hear my splash. But I had to pee. I decided to pee on the water's edge, hoping to make less noise, but I kept my pee where it belonged in the toilet. Then I pondered, 'should I flush the toilet or not?' 'Should I wait till morning to flush or flush now?' That would be noisy, too. I thought, 'maybe I should have peed in the sink and turned the water on quietly, washing down the edges of the sink.' I decided I made the right decision to pee in the toilet. I flushed, wincing, taking a slow breath in and hoping I didn't wake anybody up.

Confident I would not pee in the bed the rest of the night, I finished sleeping soundly. I woke up in the morning, opening my eyes first, immediately checking my underpants and bedding around me to make sure I was dry. I was dry. I felt like a runner passing the finish line first. I was very happy to wake up dry.

In the morning, I gathered my belongings, neatly making the bed as if I didn't sleep in it at all. Then I went into the kitchen area and I greeted Esther and Paul. "Good morning." Mother expected me to say good morning to her every morning. I knew that was the polite thing to say.

Paul immediately asked me, "When do you want to go fishing?"

"I don't know," I said.

Paul said, "How about next weekend?"

I said, "Okay."

We had our breakfast. I grabbed my suitcase and thanked Esther and Paul for letting me sleep over. I told Paul I would talk to him during the week to be sure I would be ready for him to go fishing next weekend. Esther drove me back home. Upon arrival I immediately ran into the house and told mother how much fun I had and that I woke up dry. I didn't pee my bed, not even a little bit. I thought mother might also have worried about whether I would pee the bed or not.

Throughout the week, I thought about going fishing with Paul. I didn't have any fishing gear, not even a fishing pole. I asked Daddy for some money to go get one. I went to Grand Central Department Store to purchase a tackle box, fishing hooks, sinkers, lures, bobbers, some bait, and last but not least, a fishing pole. It was like I was a fisherman of old. I took home my blue tackle box, excited to fill it. I opened the lid, seeing the trays slide up. I thought that was so cool to see that open like it did. I filled all the compartments with my purchases. I decided to practice throwing a fishing line.

Paul and I communicated throughout the week as to what and when we would go fishing. Saturday was the chosen day, and we would go to Strawberry Reservoir. As Saturday morning approached, I gathered all my fishing gear and set it out on the driveway, waiting for Paul to arrive. I knew the color of Paul's truck from visiting his home. It was an oxidized mustard yellow truck with a trout on each door of the truck. I waited with anticipation for Paul to come down my road, watching for him from the edge of the driveway.

Daddy was out in the yard, watering the garden. While I waited, I ran over to tell him how excited I was to go fishing.

He said, "Be careful and have a nice time."

I told Daddy, "I will."

Daddy added, "Good luck."

I said, "Thank you."

Paul drove into the driveway right then. I ran to Paul's truck, telling Daddy good-bye as I left him. I put my fishing pole and gear in the back of Paul's truck and hopped in the passenger side.

He said, "Are you ready to go fishing?"

I said, "I am" and closed the door of the truck.

Paul was smoking a cigar. It was kind of smelly. He drew in the smoke through his big lips, making a slight sucking noise. I didn't say anything. I just rolled down the window. I didn't talk much. Paul was telling me about his fishing stories. Paul really loved fishing. I didn't have any fishing stories myself, so I just listened. Paul turned his head towards me intermittently while he was driving. I kept staring at his thick, black-rimmed glasses. I was fascinated by his huge, magnified eyes through his lenses. The lenses seemed a little foggy, maybe because of the smoke. I thought they needed to be cleaned, but I didn't say anything. I didn't mention his big lips either.

After a very long drive that seemed to take forever, sitting in the truck and having to be entertained to keep my attention and my focus, we arrived at the reservoir. Paul knew what he was doing. He had brought a couple of folding chairs. He set them in place by the shore. I showed him my tackle box and all the stuff I bought. He thought that was a good idea. Paul showed me how to tie the fishing line on the hook then bait a worm on the hook. Paul's hand shook a little bit as he threaded the worm on the hook. He said, "This is how you keep the worm on the hook so it can't wiggle off." I tried doing it myself, but I didn't like doing it. The worms were all slimy and wiggly. Besides I felt the pain of the worm getting stabbed with the hook.

After the bait was on the hook and the sinkers and the bobbers were secured, Paul showed me how to throw the line into the water. Paul threw my line in first and set my pole in some rocks that were on the beach at about a 45 degree angle. Then he threw in his line. Paul said, "Have a seat. We'll wait and watch for the bobber to disappear under the water." He continued, "When the bobber disappears, grab your fishing pole right away and jerk it toward you. That will hook the fish on your line."

We sat in the chair and waited...and waited. I quickly lost interest in fishing. I felt bored. But then a fish became interested in my worm and my bobber disappeared.

Paul said, "Grab the pole and jerk a little bit."

I did what Paul asked me to do. I caught a fish! After I pulled it in, Paul cut its throat. I lost more interest as I saw the poor fish die. Then Paul put it in a cooler he brought.

I caught two or three fish that day. Paul did the same. Paul decided to call it a day and wrapped it up. We headed back home on what seemed a longer drive home. I was exhausted from doing nothing. Even though I caught a couple of fish, it was boring to me. When we stopped at my home, we divided the fish.

Paul wasn't finished teaching me. Paul asked, "Do you know how to clean a fish?"

"No," I said.

He showed me how to clean a fish.

That was worse than battling the worm onto the hook and cutting the fish's throat combined.

I didn't like cutting and gutting the fish to clean them. I felt its pain, and it was disgusting, too. I didn't like it.

Daddy asked me, "How was it?"

I told Daddy, "I don't want to go fishing again. I didn't like it."

Daddy said, "I'm glad you made the best of it."

I told him, "I did." I was burnt from the sun and tired from doing nothing–or what seemed like nothing to me.

I never went fishing again, but I still hold a special place in my heart for both Esther and Paul.

Esther had fully embraced her feminine beauty, elegance, grace and charm. She had inadvertently told a ten-year-old boy words he needed to hear to validate his existence. "Whoever gets him, will be very lucky." Her words sunk deep into my heart. Esther may have said these words without a second thought, but they were words I needed to hear.

Esther had an abundance of love and compassion for herself and she had given me some of her love and compassion that day. I ultimately gave myself the rest of the feminine attention I starved for, the attention I needed, even if it was in my mind under the guise of wanting to be a mom and compete with mother. Mother had compassion, but she didn't have love within herself to give to me the way I needed it. Esther's words shaped my life through her acts of generosity and kindness, helping me to become the mom I hoped to be.

CHAPTER TWENTY

THE ART OF DOCILE

Mother had hoped that by attending special ed from second grade on and by graduating from the sixth grade, I would have the basics down. I did not. I could read marginally on the second or third grade level, but I couldn't understand what I read. It was very frustrating for me. It was easier for me to avoid reading altogether than stumble my way through a sentence, feeling dumb and then becoming angry with myself. I could comprehend that Sam and Ann ate eggs, but it didn't go much further with me than that. I think there was an assumption among the adults in my life that comprehension would come automatically as time marched on. It didn't. It might have been a part of the curriculum, but somehow I missed it.

I fell through the cracks of the system, because the system was not designed for me. It was designed for those who grew up in what I call an assumptive environment, one that assumes that children will have certain qualities and learning abilities. It is an environment where it is assumed that children will all learn at the same rate and by the same methods, and they will exhibit the same developmental behaviors at the same time and in the same way.

I learned in my upbringing how to survive and flourish in a hostile environment, but my environment did not in any way match the assumptive environment of the school system. If I could survive my home life, I figured I could beat the school system and flourish, but by the end of sixth grade, it still wasn't happening. Yet I persevered. It was the only way I felt that I could get through school and succeed in life. I was determined to succeed at something.

I had a hole to fill in my heart, one that I knew needed to be filled. The hole was where my value as a person should have been, where my place in the world should have been. It was created by the constant verbal onslaught from mother, telling me, "I should have never had you." My awareness of the hole and my determination to fill it was the result of Daddy's stable, silent, yet powerful presence. Although I didn't know what my value or place would look like yet, I knew it was missing. And I knew it was the way to become successful someday. It became a success principle that drove me to gain recognition from others through my work. In my mind, that success would give my life value and enable me to express the beauty deep down inside of me that needed to come out. With little loving support in my home life and no achievement to cling to at school, only I could fill that hole. I would have to figure it out on my own.

Before I could reach that success I so longed for, I needed to do something that made me feel important, something that would fill the hole in my heart, if only temporarily. Humor was one way to fill the hole even though it only masked my pain.

I remember I would run into the house, telling mother, "I almost died today!"

Mother immediately reacted. "Why, what happened?"

Holding my thumb and forefinger very close together, showing mother the thickness of the plastic wrapped around the internal wires of the electrical cord. It struck me that the protective coating was very thin yet it was all that kept me from getting electrocuted. So I said to mother, "I picked up an extension cord today!"

"And you got electrocuted?"

"NO!" I said. "But if the insulation wasn't on the cord, I would have got electrocuted."

Mother said, "Oh you."

Daddy was in the same room and laughed. He knew what I was doing.

I had a lot of pain to cover up, and one of my escapes was finding humor in even the littlest things.

Based on the location of my home, I was to attend a junior high school in my area, the same school my three older brothers attended before me. I asked Billy, "Tell me about junior high. What is seventh grade like?"

Billy said, "There's a creek that flows next to the school."

That seemed nice to me. I said, "Okay," shrugging my shoulders.

Billy continued, "They're going to throw you in the creek!"

An alarm went off in my head. I pictured being lifted by a bunch of people high above their head, then being passed along until they threw me in the water. My attention went back to Billy. I said, "Why are they going to throw me into the creek?"

"They throw all the seventh graders in the creek!"

"But why?" I said.

"Because, they just do. It's a way of initiating you into the school."

"But, what if I don't want to be thrown into the creek?"

Billy repeated himself, "They throw all seventh graders into the water, Ker-plunk!"

"What if I hit a rock on the side of the bank?" I asked.

"There's a bridge that crosses the water. They just take you onto the bridge right into the middle and throw you off the bridge."

"Who are they?" I asked.

"The ninth graders," he said flippantly.

I believed him.

He continued, "You won't need to worry about hitting a rock."

"What if there's a rock underneath the water and I can't see it?" I was becoming more concerned than ever.

"You won't hit a rock!"

Nothing Billy said so far settled my stomach.

I still wanted to know more. "What is seventh grade like?" I asked. "Are the classes really hard?"

Billy said, "Yes, they're very hard!"

"What if I can't read?"

"They will give you an 'F' on your report card, and that means you fail seventh grade and you'll have to retake seventh grade, all over again."

"All over again?"

"Yes," he said. "All over again!"

More unsettling news.

"What about gym class?" I asked.

"Gym class!" Billy shook his head. "You don't want to know about gym class!"

"What about gym class, what am I not supposed to know?"

"The other kids will pull down your pants and rub this stuff all over your balls, and it burns like they're on fire!"

My eyes got really big. "They will?"

"Yes, they will," he said, "and if you get a boner while they're doing it..."

"Then what?" I said.

"Well, you just don't want to get one!" he said.

"But what if I do?"

"They will laugh at you and see everything!"

I felt very uneasy and very uncomfortable.

This was the topic I was getting to in all my questioning. I was scared of how my body might react, seeing the other boys naked. My attractions and my feelings worried me about going to gym class.

Billy continued, "Everybody who's watching you, if you get one, will laugh at you. And then everyone in school will know and laugh at you, too."

I knew I had to create some serious intervention to prevent it from happening to me.

That night I bounced my face on the pillow thinking about what Billy said, replaying it over and over again in my mind. I kept bouncing, picturing myself walking down the hallway, minding my own business. I bounced with more intensity. In my mind's eye, a group of boys surrounded me, grabbed me, and my books fell out of my arms and onto the floor. As I bounced my head from one side of the pillow to the next, I saw myself in my mind being flung into the air, squirming, hollering for them to put me down! It was so real in my imagination. I saw them carry me to the bridge and throw me in the water. It was all real to me. I stopped bouncing, shifted my pillow. The wrinkles in my pillowcase seemed to be bothering me more than usual tonight. I smoothed out my pillow, resumed bouncing, thinking.

The thought of being thrown into the water brought back uncomfortable memories of being wet. I had peed my bed and my pants enough over the years to know it wasn't a feeling I wanted to revisit. I bounced my face dead on into the pillow, feeling its touch on every part of my face. I shifted my thoughts. I remembered Hermann telling me that not everybody goes through puberty. Would I? My thoughts carried me away again. I became anxious from my racing thoughts.

I knew I couldn't hide my erections. What if I lost control? I pictured myself doing so, telling myself, 'NO! I can't lose control over my mind, my body, or my thoughts.' I forced myself to think of mother beatings, feeling the pain of her hitting me, hoping it would shift my thoughts and the erections won't occur. I needed to calm myself down. Thinking whenever I played with myself, the feelings my body gave to me brought a noticeable peace and calmness into my soul.

I stopped bouncing, resting my face on its side, holding still for a moment and noticing the thoughts that went in and out of my head. The thought that I needed to play with myself entered my mind. Then the thought that I

201

was uncircumcised flashed through my head. I didn't want to think about it anymore. I listened to my breathing, feeling my chest expand then contract. I bounced for a moment longer, feeling the mashing of my teeth into the pillow, my thoughts swirled in my head. An itch on my penis needed to be scratched. I stopped bouncing, resting my face into my pillow to scratch.

I reached down into my underpants to scratch. This was my queue. I turned my pillow from underneath my chest, turning it comfortably under my head while simultaneously turning on my back and removing my underwear. I needed to clear my mind, reset my feelings through the sensations only my body could give me. My body did not fail me. I needed the calmness inside of me to come forward, and it did. I rolled on to my stomach, replacing my pillow under my chest, exhausted. Setting my face to its side, adjusting my body comfortably and falling asleep.

By morning I had replayed being thrown into the creek so many times and worried about being pantsed in gym class that I talked myself out of going to that school Billy told me about. I remembered my friend Roger telling me he was going to a different junior high school. Roger's mom parked in a lot next to the school waiting for the first bell to ring before going inside the school. I hopped into the car with Roger and his mother Lorraine.

I told Roger and his mom, "I want to go to the school Roger was talking about last week."

Lorraine said, "The two of you have been friends since kindergarten! It would be a shame if the two of you parted your friendship because you're going to different schools."

I agreed. I asked if he would let me know when they came to sign him up. "I'll go with you, if they'll let me." I knew our friendship would continue if that happened then.

It was agreed.

I did ask Roger one question before I would feel entirely comfortable with the idea. "Is there a creek nearby?"

He said, "I don't think so." He continued, "I'll look on a map and let you know tomorrow."

I never doubted that Roger could read a map. I couldn't. When I looked at a map Daddy showed me, it looked like a bunch of lines going in every direction and meant nothing to me.

Roger let me know the next day. "I couldn't find any water nearby."

I liked the school already.

Roger and I had a unique friendship. I never thought of myself as dumb for going to Special ED, and Roger never teased me about me going to a class that tried to teach me to read and write. Roger never boasted he was smarter than me, even when they advanced him two grades a couple of years earlier. Although the thought went through my head he would have been going into the 8th grade next year, I didn't say anything. I also thought we wouldn't be friends anymore if he had advanced.

I accepted Roger for who he was, and he accepted me for who I was. We had our differences. He expected my 100% loyalty as a friend. Maybe it was his way to control his environment, or me. Every time I talked to another girl or another boy in school, it seemed to affect him. He somehow felt I strayed from our friendship, that I wasn't loyal to him. I never understood exactly why, and I never asked.

I always knew something was up when he felt I was being disloyal. When I hopped in the car, he wouldn't talk to me. He would just talk to his mother. He would avoid me on the playground. I simply couldn't have other friends. Roger only wanted me as his friend, maybe because nobody else would play with or talk to him like I would. We always made up, and we continued our friendship. I remembered mother's words, "Smart people are dumb and dumb people are smart." I was amazed at how smart he was on the one hand, and how his behavior seemed dumb on the other hand. We were two completely different personalities.

I spotted a blue three-ring binder in the trash can at the Hotel Utah after President Nixon had left town. It had a picture of an elephant on it. I liked elephants. I took the binder out of the trash can, emptying its contents into the garbage. I showed Roger what I had found in the trash can the next day, Roger told me I was a Republican. I didn't know what a Republican was. Roger tried telling me what the differences were between Republicans and the other party (I couldn't remember the name), but I didn't understand. I don't know that I cared. I just liked the elephant on the cover. I saved it, knowing I needed a binder for seventh grade. He didn't want to be my friend, thinking I was a Republican. I couldn't understand what he was thinking. I told him, "I'm not a Republican." I didn't know what a Republican was so how could I be one? I just wanted to be friends.

I always saw Roger and his mother walking side-by-side as if holding hands anytime. I saw them often. It always seemed odd to me. But then, mother had never shown me an ounce of affection in my entire life. Instead, she told me repeatedly, "I should've never had you."

Roger's mom Lorraine was unique as well. I never saw Lorraine without her deep scarlet red lipstick. Her hair seemed frozen into a 1950's hairdo. Her hair always reminded me of a pancake or billboard in the front. It looked nice. Lorraine wore a scarf around her neck, sometimes in her hair, tying it in a fashionable knot. I was used to mother and her wigs. Lorraine was always cordial and pleasant to me. She would often remind me of how Roger and I were friends since kindergarten.

The type of friendship Roger and I had was longstanding. I could hold any conversation with Roger even though I knew he was smarter than me. Still, I never talked to Roger about my feelings. I kept those to myself, inside my secret life. Besides, it wasn't a subject that was talked about openly. I remember Roger's mother used the word 'queer' often when she was talking to me. I kind of understood what the word 'queer' meant. It was somebody who was different from somebody else's expectations. I didn't say anything. I just listened to Roger's mom talk, staring at her red lipstick and looking at her hair.

Roger was constantly being teased by his peers. The way he wore his hair, slicked back, the size of his body, were all grist for the bullies' mill. Even his last name was material for them–Jolly. Roger's name was so similar to the Jolly Rancher candy that everybody ate that kids teased him unmercifully, calling him Jolly Roger. All the teasing highlighted his insecurities. He seemed to be a magnet for teasing. Any and every name he could be called he was called. He might have worried about being thrown in the water in junior high, too. I didn't ask, but I think he might have been fed up with the student body who wasn't nice to him. In either case, he wasn't going to the same junior high school I was supposed to go to.

I remained a faithful school friend to Roger throughout grade school and soon into junior high. Roger didn't live on Richard street, but the next street over. His grandparents lived on Richard Street, but they were very old people from Deutschland. Their backyards butted up to one another. Roger was an intellect, so we never played games, ran or played on the playground, but we enjoyed being around one another.

Roger would meet me at his back porch, showing me how he kept track of the weather each day. He would show me the chart, a spreadsheet of sorts, that he had made and used for years to keep track of weather patterns. He showed me what the weather was like a year ago on this date, even two years ago. Roger would say, "Pick a date, any date." I picked one. He looked it up in his notes and read it off his chart. Then he showed me the results on his chart. I thought Roger might become a weatherman. Roger collected coins and stamps as well as weather information. This was all interesting to me. I collected nothing materially at the moment, although I did collect information. I stored it in my head, not on a chart.

At home early one morning, I noticed something different on my body that wasn't there before–pubic hair. My body was maturing as was my

205

mind. I remembered the conversation with Hermann: "not everybody goes through puberty." I never checked on how factual his statement was. I was just happy that I wasn't left out of the process of going through puberty. I thought to myself, "I can get a girl pregnant." Mother would be pleased that I recognized the possibility so I wouldn't get a girl pregnant. I had no idea of the responsibility that came with intercourse. I just knew that mother would be pleased that I knew how unintelligent it would be.

I looked at my uncircumcised body, having a flashback of the magazines I viewed earlier. I thought about how 7th grade was just around the corner and how I would be required to undress in the locker room. I didn't remember seeing anybody in the pictures with foreskin on their penises. I wondered, 'how can I get rid of it?' I examined my foreskin closely, trying to decide whether I could cut it off myself or have it cut off. My older brothers teased the cats about putting a rubber band around the tail and watching it fall off after a few weeks, saying, "It'll cut off the circulation and fall off without any pain to the cat." I pictured a cat with a stubby tail. They never followed through, but I wondered if I could put a rubber band around the skin without damaging the head of my penis. Then I thought I might not get the results I was looking for if there was any mistake. I decided against that idea, but I didn't stop thinking about how I was going to handle gym class looking like a turtle.

I understood the theory behind the process of the rubber band method, but all of my variations of this idea sent a chill down my spine. I thought of finding an ointment that I could rub on to make it fall off. I remembered a commercial on TV that shrank hemorrhoids. I thought, why wouldn't it shrink foreskin? I bought some to find out, only to find out it stunk really bad, and didn't work. I decided to try other things like Icy Hot, but it burned like I was on fire. I thought, well, if I do get pantsed, I'll know what it feels like to burn. I realized the burning sensation was making my genitals shrink from the pain. That couldn't go away soon enough for me! I tried ice water, thinking that might work. I failed at each attempt. I remembered the words mother said, "It was put there for a reason, to protect the head of your penis." Mother may have been right, but I didn't want to look like a turtle when I pulled my pants down in gym class. I wanted to look like a boy. I also wondered if I got rid of the foreskin, would I lose any length? I didn't know the answer to that question. But that question was a motivating thought to leave it alone. I still wanted to try to figure out something, but I didn't know what. The bottom line was that I wanted to look normal to the other boys when I took off my clothes in gym class, but I didn't know how.

I bounced my head that night with thought after thought going through my head. I added pictures in my mind. Scenes were unfolding before me in my imagination. I was so uncomfortable in my anxious thoughts. I kept bouncing, then stopped. Smoothing out the wrinkles in my case, I continued to bounce my face into my pillow. It felt so good. I was starting to feel better. I bounced my head from one side to the next, then back into the middle. I listened to the sound in the air passing my ears as I hit my pillow. I needed to think about other things, but my mind went back over and over to the question, how do I solve this problem?

I listened to the rhythm of the different sounds. I couldn't find one, I felt the pillow mash against my teeth as I hit my face on my soft pillow. I stopped bouncing, turned my head to the left, listening to my breathing going in and out of my nose as if I just ran a race. I felt exhausted. Thinking it was finally time for me to sleep, I listened to the air like a soft ocean breeze in my mind. I adjusted my body to my comfort and fell asleep.

Puberty brought a new era into my life, a dimension of mental pleasure I didn't expect. My body was more beautiful. I was also pleased that I was experiencing puberty at all since my brother Hermann led me to believe that it might not happen. In addition to these benefits, mother stopped beating me. Mother still yelled, slammed doors, and reminded me that "because of you damn kids we're poor." Mother continued reminding me that she should have never had me and so on, but she didn't beat me.

Mother never apologized for any beatings she had perpetrated on my body. Mother justified all of them. Or she denied them. I reminded mother of the time she punched me in the face with her knuckles. Mother snapped, "Oh that didn't happen, you're just making it up!" I remember it as if it was yesterday. It most certainly happened. Maybe mother had beaten her boys so often that mother lost track. They weren't significant to her. I was flabbergasted. How could she deny something that so obviously did happen? I knew the feelings and the pain that followed each beating, to the point of wanting to commit suicide at age ten. But I dropped the subject. It wasn't worth the time of day to try to set her straight.

I still wanted to figure out how to get rid of my foreskin. To my pubescent, worried mind that was worth the time of day. I didn't know what to do. And then the day came: I found myself on the way to 7th grade orientation, to gym class, the class I feared the most. As the class began, the coach stood before the class, sternly lecturing us. "You will participate! You will wear a jockstrap!" My mind paused on that thought. I liked that thought. I liked putting on my jockstrap. The jockstrap was quite becoming in my mind. I practiced putting it on all summer before school started. The added benefit was that I got used to it so it didn't always get caught on my toes. It still did sometimes, but I learned how to fix it quickly.

The coach continued, "YOU WILL SHOWER AFTER THE CLASS IS OVER."

My stomach clenched. Hearing those words was what worried me the most.

He continued, "You will not go through the rest of the school day stinking up your other classrooms! Especially if you have gym class first period. I'll make an exception for you if it's your last period. If you're going home, you don't need to shower if you choose not to. DO I MAKE MYSELF CLEAR?"

I nodded my head yes. Others nodded their heads as well or said, "Yes, you do!"

Coach turned his attention to his paddle. "This is big Bertha," he said, showing the class a long red board with holes drilled in the middle of it the size of nickels. He seemed quite proud of it. "The holes are there to suck the skin on your body through the holes, intensifying the pain!"

My mind went back to mother, hitting me with the radiator brush. I knew how bad it hurt to be hit by mother over my back or on my bum.

The coach continued, "If you don't want to get hit with it, then do what I ask you to do! DO I MAKE MYSELF CLEAR?"

Whether or not I wanted to do what he asked, I knew one thing. I didn't want to get hit with Big Bertha.

I didn't have gym class last period, so my only option was to shower. The moment came, lockers were assigned, and gym class was next. I had seven minutes to change into my gym clothes. I still didn't have a plan. I thought frantically in the last few moments I had left, setting out my gym clothes. I placed my jockstrap on top of my clothes for a fast exchange. I took my shirt off slowly, delaying the inevitable.

I focused my mind on any painful thought I could muster to avoid getting an erection. My word for 'flaccid' was 'docile.' My thought was, 'stay docile, stay docile.' I thought of burning creams, painful beatings. I was ready to pinch myself if necessary, anything to distract my body from having that reaction. I had to find self-control. I removed my street pants, then reached into my underwear as if I had an itch to scratch, pulling back my foreskin to hide it from view, and finally removing my underwear.

That was simple enough. The foreskin stayed back long enough for gym class and the shower. For the time being, I looked normal. I dropped my underwear to my ankles, focusing on staying docile, thinking of pain, staying docile, thinking of pain, staying docile. I grabbed my jockstrap while bent over as if I had a bellyache, hiding my genitals, thinking of pain, staying docile. I stumbled nervously, concentrating on which part of the jock to put my foot through, balancing on one leg to fit my foot through the right part of the strap.

Shifting to the other foot, balancing like a crane on one leg, I focused on getting my other foot into the strap. It caught on my toe, and a pang of anxiety swept through me. What if I fall?! I wiggled my foot nervously to try again. Shaking nervously from the frustration of the delay, I removed the strap from my toe, pulling my jockstrap up my legs and into place. I had practiced at home enough times to make it easier, but this was the first time that it mattered most. I stayed docile, to my heart's relief. Half of the worst part was over. I had worried for days, weeks and months before. I knew showering wasn't far off, but that was after class.

When it came time to shower, I repeated the process, thinking of pain to stay docile. It worked. Now that the anxiety was beginning to ease, I thought of how my body looked. I knew I looked like a boy, like a man even, revealing everything, like the men in the magazines. Now, as a young boy just becoming a man, I enjoyed showing off my body. Showering wasn't as big a concern as I made it out to be, as long as I remained focused on staying docile. I dried off quickly. I was ready to feel the comfort and protection of my clothes. It felt really good. Combing my hair as if nothing happened at all, I went on to the next class.

I bounced my head that night, comfortably running all the details of the day through my mind. When I felt I was finished, I adjusted my body to fall asleep, and did so peacefully.

Left: Frank, me, Billy, Walter, and Hermann. Circa 1963

Right: My mother and me, circa 1969

Below, left to right: ages 7, 8, and 9. To me, these pictures show how I changed from innocence in the first picture to growing sexual awareness after Rick's molestation from ages 8 to 9.

Left: Omi, my paternal grandma, circa 1965

Right: My father as a German soldier, circa 1936

Left: My father's brother Johann in his German passport. He died of appendicitis in the mid-1930's. No one knew what it was.

Above: Omi is in the white dress on the right, 1907, posing with her parents and siblings

213

Above: Left to right, me at 19 years old, my
brother Frank age 29, and mother

Above: A car cigarette
lighter like the one
Billy used to burn me
in 1965

Right: My father and
mother, dancing, circa 1987

Left: The Japanese bowl mother gave me from her china cabinet

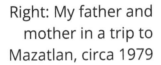

Right: My father and mother in a trip to Mazatlan, circa 1979

Above: My wife Estie holding our youngest son Christopher, Heidi in front, Parker in the center, Natalie behind him, and I'm holding Michael. 1998

CHAPTER TWENTY-ONE

MAKING THE IMPOSSIBLE POSSIBLE

Mr. Davies, my seventh grade history teacher, showed films in class on World War II. I stared at the images and listened intently to the black and white films. I had German heritage after all, and I knew that Daddy had been in Hitler's Army. I was surrounded by Germans. They all had their stories of that era. Most of them had been in Germany during Hitler's reign. One of mother and Daddy's friends, Elsie, had spent years of her youth in a concentration camp as a German Jew.'

I never heard anything negative about Adolf Hitler from mother's other friends, mother, or even Daddy. Elsie was the only one who experienced the evil of Hitler's reign. In the others' minds, Hitler had saved them from the devastating depression that followed World War I and the war reparations.

I imagine they never spoke positively of Hitler in front of Elsie, but I don't know for sure. Elsie had been a prisoner at Dachau Concentration Camp. At one of mother's German parties, Elsie started telling me of her experiences. She began telling me, but then she stopped herself. She said she just couldn't continue, because it was too horrific.

I had heard my daddy say many times that he was conscripted to be a German soldier, and he had marched into Austria. He knew war was not far off. He knew he needed to escape. He said, "I didn't want to surrender my future to somebody else's ambition." His words struck me and stuck with me. These words were indelibly inked into my mind. To this day I wonder how many of us, including myself, have surrendered our agency, our autonomy, our future, our fortune, our secret honor, our day-to-day lives to somebody else's ambitions, even surrendering to the ambitions of a parent, a guardian or an authoritarian figure outside the home.

Now, in school, I was hearing another perspective. I wanted to know more.

I sat in class for weeks, learning and seeing films that showed the strengths of Adolf Hitler and the devastation of his war against humanity. I viewed soldiers on stretchers, wounded or dead. Machine guns firing into other soldiers across the way, tanks rolling over the countryside, shooting their cannon-like apparatus ahead of them. Airplanes dropping bombs. German soldiers marching down the street in a pattern that was described by the narrator as 'the goose-step.' I asked Daddy if he did the goose-step. He said he had. He got up from his chair and showed me how it worked, explaining how uncomfortable it was to walk that way.

In many of the films, Hitler was standing up in a convertible with his arm high in the air, and people were on either side of the road, raising their arms back to him as he passed, in a sign of solidarity. In other films, Hitler was perched on balconies in front of hordes of people that looked like millions to me. He chanted something to the people, and people cheered and applauded whatever he was saying. The film seemed to run faster than life played out. The narrator translated what Hitler was saying but facetiously. The deep voice of the narrator settled in my ears as he described Hitler as "The Dictator." The narrator had my undivided attention.

Neither the crowd nor the 'Heil Hitler' salute shown in the films looked appealing to me. Still, I was fascinated. I thought to myself, 'why were people in a state of compliance? Or were they being forced?' I didn't know the answer. 'Why would anybody want to be there in the first place? Why couldn't they have stayed home?' I didn't know the answer to those questions either.

Perhaps my questions were rooted in my upbringing. Mother wanted my obedience to her overbearing ideology just as Hitler wanted. I complied with mother more than I wanted to admit to myself. I didn't know any different. It was my normal. Maybe there were too many similarities between me and the crowd, between my life and what I saw in the movies. I didn't know the answers to these questions. I felt no clarity in my feelings. I was unsettled watching them. I didn't express any feelings to anybody. What other people would perceive as uncomfortable was comfortable to me. I see now that this was the Stockholm Syndrome people talk about, the same syndrome the German people suffered.

I felt unsettled by the films for many reasons. I thought of myself being in one of those crowds. I felt intensely uncomfortable in an auditorium full of fellow students, let alone a massive crowd like those in the films. I thought about how often I ran and hid behind any tree, car, bush or anything close to me when somebody drove down Richard Street in front of my house. I didn't want to be seen by anybody. I walked fast from class to class at school for the same reason. I didn't want to be seen.

I felt uncomfortable for the people in the film, even if it was years before my time. I struggled to put all of this together and make sense of life–the films' negative portrayal of the Germans, my strong identification with my German heritage, the empathy I had for the people in the films, the atrocity of war and my mother's hatred of war. All of these ideas sparked feelings in me I couldn't sort out. I noticed all of it and took mental notes of how uneasy I felt.

Growing up, there were connotations and comments from mother, Daddy, and their German friends about Hitler and the War. Ursula Ulbrich, a longtime friend of mother, was one of those who talked about it. Ursula lived in Germany under the reign of Adolf Hitler. She said, "Hitler was good for the economy." Ursula paused. "We didn't know what was going on in the outskirts of town, ya." As a very young child, I listened to what Ursula

219

said in her German accent.

Ursula was an odd duck. She had experienced such depressive economic circumstances that rationing had become part of the foundation of her identity. She hosted coffeecake clutches for her friends, and every time she counted each pea on the guests' plates. Mother always complained, "There were six peas on my plate. She must have counted each one of them, the old cheapskate!" Then she would add, "Nobody else had more than I did either." Mother was a natural complainer. To be fair, compared to the twelve course meals at mother's parties, Ursula's servings were chintzy. Mother complained that the coffee was weak, too. On the other hand, mother had not been exposed to the horrors of Hitler and the war or the economic horrors that preceded the war. She had never known that kind of lack. Yes, she had experienced the Depression in America, but that did not compare to the anguish and suffering that happened in Germany during the same time.

I listened to Ursula's comments with an innocent ear. I didn't know the details of Ursula's experience in Germany under Adolf Hitler as she did. I had no comparison at that time. Only after I viewed the films in junior high did I understand what she was actually talking about. In viewing the films and listening to mother's friends, I began to connect the dots between Daddy's involvement in Hitler's Army and the horrors of that war, but I didn't know how involved he was at the time. My curiosity built. I wanted to learn more of the details.

I tuned more and more into the random conversations of the guests at mother's parties as they talked about Adolf Hitler. The words flowed in and out of German and English. Even their English was so heavily accented that it was hard for me to understand. If I heard them say his name, I stopped and listened, perking up my ears, even if the conversation was only partially in English. I strained to understand more. It seemed to be a topic that was often on the old Germans' minds so I had many opportunities to learn.

During one of these parties, I was walking through the kitchen on the way to my bedroom when Fritz Heine, one of mother's friends, drew my attention when he clinked his coffee cup loudly against the saucer. He stood in the kitchen, talking to another guest.

Fritz said, "Hitler was good for the economy." That comment seemed to be a common thread amongst all of mother's and Daddy's friends. It was a sentiment shared by all of the old Germans that lived in Germany at that time. Fritz continued, "What Hitler did for the people of Germany was positive, at least before the war."

I never asked any questions. I was learning more and more about Adolf Hitler as I listened to people's firsthand experiences. I stood at the doorway to hear more of what Fritz had to say. I was ready to leave for my room at any moment, but I lingered to hear as much as possible before mother told me to go to my room.

Fritz's accent was strong and heavy. I had to listen closely.

Fritz continued, "Germany was in a deep depression."

My mind went back to a story mother once told me when she was a little girl. "We were on 'Relief' during the Depression," mother said. "That's what it was called instead of welfare. It was a government program designed to help people make it through." Mother explained there were long lines of people at the soup kitchen.

I tried to understand what it would be like to live through that. I had no comparisons to her experience. Mother's description of the soup line painted a bleak picture in my head. I connected it with what Fritz was saying about "Germany being in a deep depression." Otherwise I'm not sure I would have had a perspective.

Fritz was still talking. My mind wandered back to what Fritz was saying. "The Treaty of Versailles is what sunk Germany into the Depression after World War I."

I stared at his lips. They seemed to protrude out from his face, like a baboon. I wasn't familiar with what he was talking about, but I remembered

221

the words.

Fritz's jowls shook back and forth as he said, "Ya Vol." Fritz paused, taking a sip of coffee, then continued. "The people didn't know what was going on, radio vos bond."

That sounded funny to me. He was saying, "was banned," but it sounded like "vos bond."

He continued. "Information was limited to the people during the war." Fritz said this with wide eyes and without a blink, as if to convey, this is how it was at that time. "After the war we understood what Hitler had done, many including myself felt it was a disgrace to the people of Germany!"

Fritz's sentiments seemed to be consistent among all of mother's friends. I gathered information as best I could to understand what had happened. At least that was my intention. I continued to my bedroom. I knew mother would eventually tell me to go there soon. I thought about what Fritz said after going to bed that night, bouncing my head on my pillow.

I thought about all that Fritz had said after going to bed that night, bouncing my head on my pillow. I recalled the new details I had picked up about the history associated with Hitler. I had learned that he wanted everyone in Germany to have a vehicle. He called it the 'Folks-waa-gen.' That seemed like a good idea to me. I thought, maybe people still traveled in horse-and-buggies at that time? I liked the Volkswagen Bugs. It was Frank's first car. They were cute little vehicles.

There was such a contrast between what I learned at home about Hitler and what I heard at school in Mr. Davies' class. Conversations between mother and her German friends had always seemed positive. I thought nothing of Hitler as a dictator who killed people until I saw the films. I gained new information from the films, and none of it seemed to be from the perspective of the people who had lived under his rule. The films taught me that Hitler worked to create a pure race using German people with blond hair and blue-eyed to populate Germany. This was confusing to me.

Daddy had black hair and blue eyes. I wanted to know how Daddy got out of Germany. How was Daddy involved in the war? Did Daddy see Adolf Hitler? Questions like these swirled in my head while watching these films. I became more interested in Daddy's history and his association with World War II. I had a lot to understand.

In the weeks that followed, Mr. Davies showed my class films about the post-war Soviet takeover of East Germany. This horrified me, too, to see the Germans suffering under another totalitarian regime, even after the Nazis were defeated. In one of the films the narrator explained, "East German soldiers, under the order of the Soviets, strung barbed wire fences across roads that were free to travel the day before. Now they were barricaded off with soldiers armed with rifles, ready to shoot anyone who attempted to cross the fence. They were protecting the new East German domain." The narrator continued as the next scene unfolded before my eyes. "One soldier defected through the barbed wire fence!" To my surprise, I watched as one of the soldiers stopped his guard duties, dropped his weapon and barreled himself through the fence, defecting to the West through a weak spot in the barbed wire entanglement. I pictured that as if it was Daddy. I took the soldier's actions very personally. I was shocked to think about how I was born in America because of someone's actions to escape Germany and maybe a bit of luck...or divine providence.

After watching that scene, Mr. Davies stopped the film to ask the class a question and we had to write down our answer. "How would you feel if you woke up tomorrow morning and there was a barbed wire fence across the street, blocking your passage that you passed through so easily yesterday?" I liked his question! It made me think about exactly how that would happen. I wondered where they would block off the road. Would it separate home from school? Mr. Davies asked a follow-up question. "How would that change your life?" I liked his second question, too! I wrote my answers.

That night I bounced my head, thinking about both questions, my mind floating back and forth between them. As I hit my head on my pillow, these ideas filled my imagination with questions. I turned my attention away from my thoughts and focused on the sensation of bouncing my head. It felt so good and comfortable to me. Then my mind returned to my questions. I kept wondering how I would escape if I was on the oppressed side of the fence. I thought about Daddy being so brave.

I wanted to know more about how Daddy got out of Germany.

Mr. Davies showed film clips of various concentration camps. I was stunned at the films that depicted soldiers shooting people on the edge of a hole–naked, skin and bones, stripped of everything, shot dead. I remembered Elsie saying a little bit about being in a concentration camp. I knew no details about her experience other than she was in one of them. I decided I would ask her to tell me someday. I hoped that she would say something at one of mother's next parties.

At another time I asked Daddy, "Can you tell me your story?"Not waiting for his answer, I asked, "About how you got out of Germany?" Before Daddy could answer, I asked another question. "Did you ever see Adolf Hitler?"

Daddy replied, "Yes, I did. He was a short distance away, inside the playhouse." Daddy supposed I didn't know what the playhouse was, so he explained, "The theater where they did live acting." He continued, "Hitler liked the theater. It was several feet away from where he was standing, but yes I saw Adolf Hitler sitting in the chair at the theater."

I pictured Adolf Hitler surrounded by other people. It always seemed that way when I saw him in the films. I figured they were his bodyguards. I listened more intently as Daddy continued.

Daddy sat down in a chair at the kitchen table. I sat beside him. "Omi was born in 1894. She was 19 years old when she had me in 1913. I didn't know who my dad was. He never came forward to raise me."

I tried to comprehend what it would be like not to have a dad in my life.

I felt Daddy was always there for me. I couldn't imagine not having a dad.

Daddy continued, "I was born in a little village in Bavaria."

I asked, "Was it a city?"

Daddy said, "It was, but more like a group of houses together."

I pictured several houses randomly placed in the green countryside with thatched roofs, chickens pecking in the front yard, and smoke gently rising from the chimneys. I pictured a quaint little village of peace and calmness in my head from what Daddy was telling me. Many years later, I discovered that the authorities listed his birthplace as Munich although I suspect he was born at home in the village.

Daddy continued, "I was born ten months before the start of World War I."

Daddy's birthday was in September of 1913. I did the math. That would mean the war started in June of 1914. When I checked later on, I found that the hostilities actually began in July, but June is when the Archduke Franz Ferdinand was assassinated by a Serbian teenager. Since he was the presumptive heir of the Austro-Hungarian Empire, his death triggered a domino effect of alliances that put the whole of Europe at war.

My thoughts went back to the films I saw in school. Mr. Davies had shown the class films on that war, too. They were very grainy black and white films, mostly showing men in trenches. Mr. Davies had said, "World War I was dubbed 'The war to end all wars!'" I knew that wasn't true because of World War II, and the Vietnam War that was currently raging in another part of the world. Mother was worried about her boys being drafted into war. I returned my thoughts back to Daddy.

Daddy went to get a drink of water on the stove. Daddy only drank warm water. The stove had a pilot light burning all the time. It was there to light the burners, but it also kept a glass of water warm. Daddy said that warm water was better for the body than cold water, because it was less of a shock to the system.

Daddy returned to sit at the table. "War is a terrible time," he said. He paused for a moment. "The village was nearly destroyed, leaving the town in shambles." Daddy stared into space. "Money was hard to come by as well."

I remembered my teacher showing images of a woman pushing a wheelbarrow full of money to buy a loaf of bread. "Did Omi have to push a wheelbarrow full of money to buy a loaf of bread?"

Daddy said, "No, I don't think so, but bread was hard to get."

I nodded my head yes, indicating I understand.

Daddy added, "Milk was hard to come by, too. Omi always thought that's why I was so skinny, because there was no milk to fatten me up." Daddy did look like he was on the malnourished side. I had just thought it was part of Daddy's makeup.

By November 1918 World War I was officially over, and Daddy had another sibling. His name was 'Johann.' Omi gave birth sometime during the course of the war.

I asked, "Was he from your dad?"

Daddy said, "No, I don't know who his father was."

I remembered mother telling me that Omi was nothing but an 'old prostitute.' Mother said it in a disgraceful tone, emphasizing the 'P' and fluttering her lips.

Daddy never told me about Omi's sex life and I didn't ask. I figured it out myself from what mother said earlier.

Daddy continued, "Omi was married a few years later to a man by the name of Adolf Schilfarth. He adopted my brother and me, and we took on his last name. My original dad did not take care of my mother and us at all. Adolf took care of us."

I asked, "If you took on your stepdad's last name, why wouldn't our last name be Schilfarth?"

Daddy replied, "I changed it."

I asked, "How did we get Bautner then?" I didn't let Daddy answer. "How come it's not Schilfarth?"

Daddy said, "I took on my mother's maiden name after the war."

I was thinking about what Daddy said. "What is a maiden name?" I chattered more questions.

"I'll explain more, let me talk!" he said.

"Okay," I replied.

Daddy continued, telling me that by September of 1931 he had turned 18 years old. In June 1935 at the age of 21, Dad was required to enlist into the German Reich Labor Services and serve at least for six months. He said, "I soon found myself drafted into the Wehrmacht being trained as a soldier."

While Daddy was in the military, he got word that his brother Johann had died. He didn't know how at the time and neither did the medical personnel. Years later Daddy learned that he had died from his appendix bursting, poisoning his body. They hadn't known how to treat acute appendicitis in Germany in the 1930s. Johann was only 20 years old.

In 1930 all guns, including bladed weapons, had to be registered. In 1935, The Defense of the Jews was abolished and they were subjected to the arbitrariness and terror of the Nazi police authority. Before long, gun ownership became illegal for German Jews and German citizens alike. If they were not an 'authorized person,' they could not own a weapon. Daddy served in the military of the German army as a soldier, so Daddy was considered an 'authorized person' and could be in possession of a firearm.

Daddy told me about a furniture maker friend of his that owned a Walther pistol. Whether he was German or a German Jew was not made clear to me. He told Daddy, "I cannot own this gun anymore. You might as well have it. I'm not considered a 'reliable individual.' I have to surrender my gun to an 'authorized' person." Since Daddy was considered an 'authorized' person, he handed Daddy the gun.

In March 1938, Daddy found himself marching into Austria in the

Wehrmacht under Adolf Hitler. The relative ease with which Adolf Hitler's army conquered Austria allowed Daddy to request a one-year leave of absence. Daddy instinctively felt world war was imminent, and he wanted no part of it. His plan was to go to America and become an American citizen. He even considered going to New Zealand. That was his future. Daddy said, "I knew the future would not be in Germany anymore." The turmoil and instability of the government and economy of Germany left Daddy with few options. With the looming onset of war, the type of knowledge that causes a heavy emptiness to sink to the bottom of a person's stomach, Daddy made the decision to leave.

Memories of World War I and its aftermath were still fresh in his mind. His future weighed in the faint distance of his mind, ready to be eliminated because of somebody else's ambition. Daddy's plan for his one-year leave of absence was to escape the country and never return.

Daddy knew that if you were important in any way, with any skills whatsoever, the government would not allow you to leave. For this reason, Daddy wrote that his occupation was 'office worker.' Daddy knew an office worker was a non-essential classification. He told me that office workers were a dime a dozen. He reiterated that he had no desire to return to Germany, at least in the near future, and had no interest in staying a citizen of Germany, let alone under Adolf Hitler.

Daddy boarded the 'SS Hansa' for a six-week voyage to America in July 1938, at the age of 24. Daddy had said goodbye to his mother and adoptive father and then visited his biological father to let them know he was leaving Germany to come to America and that he would not be returning.His biological father asked, "Would you stay in touch?" Daddy replied, "You haven't stayed in touch with me all these years, why would I stay in touch with you now?" Daddy left with no argument from his biological father. They never communicated again.

Bringing all his possessions and the Walther he acquired from the furniture maker with him in his 14x24x36 inch trunk, he arrived at Ellis Island, New York that fall. Daddy established residency in Rochester, New York. He was sponsored by an uncle who invented a product for the Kodak film company. That sponsorship allowed Daddy to stay in the United States legally.

The world war Daddy had predicted began September 1, 1939 when Germany invaded Poland, causing Britain and France to declare war against Germany two days later. Daddy wasn't an American citizen yet, so he had the option of going back to Germany. Had Daddy been born in 1912, ten months earlier, it would have been mandatory for him to return to Germany and resume his position as a German soldier. He missed a life-altering event by 10 months, and so did I. Because he was born in 1913, German law allowed him to stay in America. Seeing the films in school, hearing about how devastating the war was and about the ruthlessness of Adolf Hitler, remembering the images of skeleton-like bodies shot and thrown into mass graves, I marveled at how Daddy had made the impossible possible.

While a resident of New York, over the next few years, Daddy learned the lithography trade. Daddy perfected the process of printing, taking a print from start to finish in just a few hours. Prior to Daddy perfecting the trade, a print could take two or three days to complete. Daddy told me of a time when he had gone to a coworker who worked at the lab with him and asked him a question, "How long do you think it took me to create this print?" The coworker responded, "Two days?" Daddy said, "I started it this morning." The coworker replied, "Don't tell anybody. We work by the hour."

Daddy continued perfecting the trade, becoming an expert craftsman in lithography, cutting the time even shorter. His techniques were monumental for the trade and for Daddy. The difference in mentality was striking between those hourly laborers who give no thought to their work and people like my father who took pride in his craft. It was impressive to me, to see how Daddy worked. In November of 1945, Daddy decided it was time to become a citizen of the United States. He also decided that it was time to help in the fight against the Nazis, against the very army that he had been a member of just a few years earlier, the army of his fatherland.

Even though the war was technically over, there was much for the Allies to do as they liberated the concentration camps, arrested Nazi officers, and reestablished a governmental authority amongst the citizens. He enlisted into the Army of the United States in the 606 Engineer Command Battalion, stationed in Chattanooga, Tennessee. By the time of Daddy's enlistment, he had taught himself English.

Daddy served his military regiment in Alaska for a period of time, but then the U.S. needed Daddy to be a translator in Germany for the Americans. Daddy returned to Germany as a US soldier, as an interpreter, serving as a private first class.

Daddy shared one story with me about that time. "I was not allowed to speak to the citizens of the village in Bavaria except to set up dates with the frauleins for my superiors." Daddy paused to drink a sip of water, then continued. "My superiors were worried I could be conversing with the locals and that could turn into an espionage situation."

I asked, "Did the people of the village know you were an American soldier?"

Daddy said, "I couldn't ask them, but I suspect they knew I was a part of the US military since I wasn't allowed to talk to them."

He was told that he couldn't wear his Army uniform while he was in his hometown and he couldn't converse with the citizens there. The officers were concerned that he would be a target because he was with the Americans. Daddy also suspected that they worried he might become involved in espionage since he had emotional and family ties with the villagers.

Daddy argued to his superiors that their fears didn't make sense. "You don't want me to talk to the people of the village, yet you ask me to set up dates with them?" Daddy continued, "That doesn't make any sense to me."

I believe Daddy had a lot of good sense in him.

Daddy's superiors agreed with him, rescinding their previous decision and telling him to carry on with the duties he was assigned as an interpreter.

Daddy did so until his honorable discharge in 1947. It was at this time that Daddy changed his name from 'Schilfarth' to his mother's maiden name 'Bautner.' Daddy said, "I took on the name because Omi's brothers either died in World War I, didn't marry, or only had girls. Those who did marry had no children at all or died. One even drowned in the Rhine River." Daddy paused. "I think it was Conrad who drowned?" He shrugged. "I'm not sure. But I know for sure there was no one to carry on the name. And I liked 'Bautner' over 'Schilfarth' anyway."

I thought about the two names. I'm not sure I would have liked it either, going through school with a last name like Schilfarth. I suspected that the kids would tease me, calling me 'Shit-fart.' I thought Daddy was a wise man on that decision alone!

That same year, in a nightclub in Chicago, Illinois, dancing the night away, Daddy became known as ol' twinkle toes. "That's where I met your mother," he said. Daddy's uncle, the one who had sponsored him when he came to America, discouraged Daddy from marrying this woman. He told Daddy, "If you marry her, I will cut you out of the family fortune!" At the age of 34, mother 28, Daddy defied his uncle and married her on August 23rd, 1947 in Rochester, New York. His uncle was true to his word. He cut Daddy out of his will.

With my dad's experience in the lithograph trade and now married, Daddy and mother waited four years before having children. Daddy said, "We cherished our time alone together." Daddy paused, then said, "Once you start having children, you're never alone again."

I understood what he was saying. I thought to myself, doing the math, I'm twelve, and Daddy's sixty. I thought Daddy lived a long life. I hoped he would be here for many more years so I could get to know him better.

Daddy continued, "After Frank was born in New York in 1951, my family gave us an ultimatum–divorce your mother or leave the state. I chose to stay with your mother. We left New York, traveling across the country, teaching my lithography methods to printing businesses. I taught them my efficient way of printing. That's how we ended up in Utah."

Now there are five children, I thought, and this is where I was created. And now mother feels she is stuck here in this stupid state.

I asked Daddy, "Do you still have that gun you got from your furniture maker friend?"

Daddy said, "Yes, I do."

"Can I see it?"

Daddy got up out of his chair. "Wait here."

I did so.

Daddy went into his room and closed the door tight.

I heard the door close to his bedroom. Now I knew what room the gun was in. After a moment Daddy opened up his bedroom door and invited me in. He had a brown paper bag in his hand.

My next thought was, 'I know what the gun was hidden in.'

Daddy pulled the gun out of the brown paper bag, showing it to me first in the palm of his hand. It was pure black and powerful to me. It was the first time I'd ever seen a gun in real life. Daddy put his hand on the handle of the gun.

The thought went through my head, 'We did have a gun in the house.' The next thought was what mother always said about guns: "Guns kill people. I hate them!" I heard the deep prolonged 'h' in mother's throat when she said the word 'hate.' I thought of the history of the gun, from the time Daddy acquired it in Hitler's Army until now.

As Daddy held the gun in his hand, it occured to me that it was nothing fancy. I thought, 'I'll bet this hasn't been touched since 1938, since Daddy came to America. I didn't ask. I asked a pertinent question: "Is it loaded?"

Daddy replied, "I don't know."

I said, "You should check!"

Daddy did. There was a bullet in the chamber.

I said, "I'm glad you didn't pull the trigger. I was standing in front of the gun."

Daddy and I looked each other in the eyes. I think we were both thinking the same thought.

I asked Daddy, "Can I hold the gun?"

Daddy said, "No, not right now."

"Can I have your gun while you're still alive?"

Daddy said, "We'll see."

At the time, I didn't snoop in Daddy's room looking for the gun. I knew better. I did know the general location and what it was hidden in. I hoped one day, while Daddy was still alive, I would have possession of the gun.

Eventually, I did go looking for it. I found it, but I left it alone. Periodically I checked on it to make sure it was still there. It was. The gun stayed in the brown paper sack for years to come.

In school, learning about World War II, I gained a deeper appreciation for what people went through, coming from the horrendous environment that the war brought. I knew there were more stories available to me that were close at hand, stories from the old Germans that came to our home to mother's parties. I wanted to hear more from mother's friends like Elsie and the other old Germans, but I would have to wait.

CHAPTER TWENTY-TWO

TAMING BUTTERFLIES

I never viewed my family as poor when I was growing up. Once I ventured into the outside world, I didn't feel we were rich either. I always went to bed with a full stomach. I viewed Cadillacs as the image of success. I decided that one day I would own one. I grew up not far from the train tracks. I loved hearing the whistle of the train in the distance as it approached the main street that led to the freeway.

Hearing the train whistle in the distance, I often hopped on my bicycle, riding quickly to the tracks, watching and feeling the roar of the engines as the boxcars whizzed by. I was impressed by the powerful sound and deep vibration. I listened to the clickety clack of the wheels crossing the seams on the tracks, creating its own pattern of sound that changed with the speed of the train. I counted each car losing count after a while.

An occasional squealing wheel hollered 'oil me!' as it wound down the tracks, screaming itself into oblivion. Turning my head, looking down the tracks to see the end finale, was usually a yellow caboose, adding a finishing touch of grandeur of the experience. A man in the caboose would wave to onlookers alongside the tracks and to the cars on the road. It was a friendly gesture from the final train car, passing the intersection, fading into the horizon. The heat of the summer sun gave the distant barren land the glimmer of a mirage, but I knew it was real. I absorbed the energy of the train. I never left disappointed.

By this time my older brother Hermann taught me the game of chicken. We both came at one another from different directions. Hermann on his motorcycle; me on my bicycle. The game was to see who was willing to stay the course or who was going to abandon ship. In this case, who was the chicken? We both circled around, backing away from one another like the old *Gunsmoke* TV show. The duel was on: who was going to draw their weapon first? I came from one direction on my bicycle. Hermann came from the other side on his motorcycle. It looked like one of us was going to get t-boned. I calculated the distances between my brother and slowed my speed down. I suppose he thought I might be intimidated by his motorcycle. If he did, he was wrong. I wasn't intimidated!

We weren't going very fast, but I t-boned Hermann's motorcycle with my bicycle, ripping the pedal pad off his bike. We both stopped.

Hermann got off his motorcycle, looking at his bike to see if there was any damage. He saw the damaged pedal. Picking up the cover from the ground, Hermann asked, "Why did you do that? You ripped my pedal off!" He added, "You swine!"

I knew that meant 'you pig!' I said, "We were playing a game!"

He fixed his pedal the best he could at the location we were at, but he wasn't happy I ran into him. He never asked me again, and I never played that game of 'chicken' with him or any of my brothers.

Playing chicken with a train is for keeps.

Hearing the train's whistle caught my attention every time. I would listen to its sounds to determine whether I could make it to the tracks in time to see the train. There were always four toots of the whistle. Two long, one short, and one long. It was the spacing distance between the four blows of the horn which gave away the direction the train was going–north or south. The northbound train didn't blow the horn because there were no side streets in that direction. Southbound was a different story.

I knew how close each side street crossing was from the next because this was my area, and I had become familiar with my surroundings. The trains and the track became my stomping grounds if you will, and I ventured to know what was around me.

The two side roads were fairly close to one another, and the train blew its horn accordingly. Then there would be a longer pause before the train tootled again as it approached the main road where I viewed the train. I listened for that pattern before venturing out and hopping on my bicycle. I was on alert depending on what I did or didn't hear next.

There was always a pattern with the train going north, too. The train blew its horn just the same, but the long pause before the next side road always gave away the direction of the train without seeing it in person. I could tell the direction of the train based on that pattern, barring a stiff wind to carry the sound away. Usually the train going north had a louder blast of the horn as it approached the main road, adding the longer spacing which verified the direction for me.

I could also calculate the speed of the train by the frequency of the blasts, which helped me determine whether I had enough time or not to get to the tracks and see the train, fulfilling my adventure. It was easy to tell the speed of the train after a while. I listened for the train's whistle every day, and I followed its pattern inside my head unconsciously. Consciously, my calculations were dependent on what I was doing at that moment. If I was in the house watching TV, I would think about how much time it would take to run outside, find my bicycle, and peddle down to the tracks...or if I was already on my bicycle, ready to roll, I would calculate based on that. The distance between whistles gave me that information consistently and accurately.

I learned everything and everyone has patterns. Even mother's intricacies had a pattern which interweaved like the reeds of a basket. Train patterns were no different except they were more predictable and easier to follow than mother's intricacies.

237

The thought came to me to play chicken with the train. I didn't have a death wish. I only thought it would be fun to count how many times I could cross the double set of tracks, pedaling my bicycle back and forth, until the train came rolling by. I also knew which track the train ran on, because I paid attention to the shine of the track. The track that looked shiny like a chrome bumper was the correct track; the other track was otherwise dull or a little rusty.

I wasn't planning on losing to the train. I liked the challenge. It was a dumb thought, but I didn't think so at the time. I hadn't come this far in life, surviving mother, to be hit by a train. Seeing the train coming down the tracks, I listened for the spacing between the toots of the horn. I needed that information to make my calculations. With another glance down the track, I saw the light on the engine coming towards me. The flashing red lights warned motorists to stop. Cars were stopping. I stayed focused.

I pedaled back and forth across the tracks, counting my successful crossings. All the while, I was watching to see the train getting closer. Hearing the whistle blowing, I had the speed already calculated in me. One...two passages...three passages...four. And then my chain came off my sprocket. I was stunned.

I knew the consequences for miscalculating the train's speed, but I didn't calculate having a problem with my bicycle. The train was coming directly at me. I had to figure this problem out fast! I felt confident in my abilities. I reacted, using my legs to push my bicycle across the tracks while staying the seat. I turned my bike around to watch the train go by, feeling the rush of its powerful energy.

Leaving me with an undefined feeling, I decided it was too close a call, and I wouldn't be pulling this stunt again. I never gave a second thought to the people who were sitting in their cars at the railroad crossing, waiting for the train. Surely they had been watching me, perhaps wondering if I had a death wish or if I was just a stupid kid on my bicycle. I didn't know the answer, but they might have thought at the very least, 'what an idiot.' Looking back I would agree with them. But they wouldn't have known I had years of observations inside of me in understanding the trains' patterns. What I hadn't realized, of course, was that the trains' patterns weren't the only factor in my survival. I fixed the chain on my bicycle, put it back on its sprocket, and pedaled merrily on my way back home to wait to hear the next train. I thought nothing more about it.

Another game I tried once was to catch a train as it chugged down the tracks. This experience yielded a different sense of exhilaration than crossing the tracks back and forth. I would run up alongside the train, anticipating the feel of my fingers on the ladder, but something stopped me from following through. The train was within my grasp, but I couldn't close my fist around the metal rung of the ladder to finish the deal. Each time I tried it, I would change my mind. I ran with every intent of catching it, but my thoughts caught up with me every time. Where will the train take me? When will I jump off of the train? How will I make it back home? The future hidden within the adventure was not clear. With no answers within me, I let the train pass from my grasp.

I had a tendency to make the simple complicated and the complicated simple.

I had a friend nicknamed 'Freight Train' who would accompany me on this scheme. In fact, it was his idea. He thought the train would take us towards downtown. Freight Train was out of shape and couldn't keep up with me. I held back, because I didn't really want to catch the train.

When Freight Train caught up with me, out of breath, gasping for air, he said, "Why didn't you catch the train?! You could have got it!"

I didn't have an answer except to say, "I decided not to."

He accepted that answer, and we kept playing by the tracks. I put pennies on the rails, hoping the pennies wouldn't derail the trains. I would come back later after the trains passed to collect the flattened currency. I inspected the flatness of the copper coin then put it in my pocket.

Riding my bicycle up and down the gravel area of the tracks was fun too, but it seemed futile after a while. Little thorns often punctured my bicycle tire. I found myself pushing my bicycle back home to fix the problem many times. Eventually the frequent repairs cured me from riding by the tracks. Fixing my bike caused a lot of frustration: pinching the tube, not checking for thorns in the tire itself, gluing the patch on wrong, setting the tube on fire, and starting all over again. Trial and error slowly taught me.

Another of my favorite train stories happened when Daddy was driving to Omi's house. Over the river and across the tracks to Grandmother's house Daddy drove. It was a track that trains seldom, if ever, used. There were no lights at this track, but there was a small sign.

One day there was a train. Daddy stopped...and so did the train! But Daddy didn't think to stop until the car was halfway across the tracks. Both the conductor and Daddy seemed surprised, but no one was more surprised than me. I was on the passenger side of the car. Seeing the single engine train come to a sudden halt. The train seemed to be prepared for a car crossing, just in case, since there were no flashing lights to warn of a train's passing. The train's braking system worked nicely, I thought. I was glad it worked out so well.

I said, "That doesn't happen every day."

He didn't respond. After a short pause, Daddy continued driving to Omi's house.

Chuck was a friend of mine that lived closer to the tracks than me. I remember a day in school when Chuck surprised me by displaying his emotions. He was crying. He said, "The city came and took away my dog."

I didn't understand why. From my experience at home, I'd become calloused so that I never cried, let alone crying over a dog. I couldn't relate. Then I thought about how mother and I stole the neighbor's dog. I felt bad for Chuck. I asked him if he wanted to go with me to Omi's house. I was being a friend, comforting him the only way I knew how.

Chuck agreed. The next time we went to Omi's, we left with Chuck in the car. Daddy and I drove to Omi's house. Daddy crossed the tracks where the train stopped for him before. There was a man in a blue shirt walking on the tracks. We both saw him walking towards the road. I explained to Chuck how the train stopped for Daddy before.

Chuck interrupted me. "Did you see that man in the blue shirt?"

I said, "Yes, that man by the tracks?"

"Yes," Chuck said. "Do you know who he is?"

I said, "No."

Chuck said, "Stay away from him. He's the kind of guy that will cut off your pee-pee and put it in your mouth!"

Hearing what Chuck just said, I processed every word in shock. I pictured my penis being cut off, being put inside my mouth. I could not understand why somebody would do that to my body, to anyone. I felt the butterflies in my stomach hearing what he told me. I couldn't tame my feelings. I decided, I didn't want that happening to me. I never went to or played by the tracks again. I never jumped on my bicycle to go see the train coming. Each time I passed by the tracks or saw a train, Chuck's story went through my mind. I shuddered to believe anybody could do that to a body, let alone my body.

I continued processing Chuck's information while bouncing my head for hours night after night. I believed Chuck's story. I knew what my penis did for me. I couldn't let anything like that happen to me.

When my 13th birthday was approaching, I told Daddy proudly, "I am going to be a teenager soon."

Daddy replied, "That's good."

I wonder now why I was so happy about that. Maybe there was a subconscious thought inside of me, 'I survived mother,' let alone my innocent wandering around the train tracks.

Struggling with reading in Mrs. Conrad's English Class was a regular occurrence. One day I was stumped by a simple word I could not sound out. Remembering mother's raised voice, 'SOUND IT OUT!' I tried, "Gooo, gooood, gooo." It didn't work. After several attempts, I decided to ask Mrs. Conrad for her help.

I walked up to Mrs. Conrad as she sat at her desk correcting papers. I liked Mrs. Conrad. She was very pretty with similar features to mommy. Mother had auburn hair under her blonde wig. She hated her natural color, but I thought it was pretty. Mother had no gray hair. She just didn't want anybody to see her real self.

I admired Mrs. Conrad's glorious auburn hair, bright red lipstick, and cat glasses, all of which reminded me of mother. Mrs. Conrad glanced up to see me walking toward her. She was looking over the top of her glasses.

I stopped in front of her, my mind focused with curiosity on the mysterious word. "What is this word?" I pointed to the print in the book.

Mrs. Conrad looked through her glasses at the word, then up at me over the top of her glasses. She said, "You don't know what that word is?"

I said, "I don't!"

She replied, "God."

I politely said, "Thank you." I returned to my seat to continue reading, thinking for a moment about how mother had said the word 'God' before. I had heard the word many times, but I had never seen it in print. I continued reading to the best of my ability, feeling appreciative of Mrs. Conrad's gentle response.

Although reading continued to be a struggle, I knew that if I was going to succeed, I needed to somehow learn to read well. I was determined. And I recognized that other people enjoyed reading. I remember Robbie, a boy in my class, was laughing uproariously while reading a book in the library. I was dumbfounded. How could anyone laugh like that over what he was reading? I wanted that experience. And I wanted to succeed in life.

I signed up to be an assistant in the library. One day a book caught my attention that I thought I could read: *Raising the Titanic*. The ship's whereabouts and its content piqued my curiosity. Another book said there was a hidden treasure that I had been left by the Pony Express in a hole somewhere in the Wild West. My imagination was sparked. The treasure might be in my backyard! I dug hole after hole, hoping to find it. The fact that these events had happened so long ago, just a year and a half after Daddy was born, kept my interest.

Once I turned 13, the trains and tracks were in my past. My new dream was that I wanted to be important. I wanted to be a millionaire. I wanted to be successful and beautiful. I wanted to be somebody, but I didn't know who that person was. I wanted to hide that I lived by the tracks, even though others didn't live far from me. I wanted to build the image of success I dreamed about. I knew I could be in the world that I had built within me. I could make it a reality. Living by the tracks wasn't that type of success to me.

Mother bought me a new imitation leather jacket from Grand Central. It made me look like I had style. I needed something different inside my head then what I'd experienced until now. I didn't want to look like I was from the poor side of town. I strutted my stuff as I walked down the hallway of school, swinging my arms with confidence, glancing at people, and hoping they would notice me. I looked at the swag of my jacket and noticed cracks in my imitation leather. I was shocked, then devastated. I did a double take. I was appalled by what I saw. Now I was hoping nobody would see me, let alone see the cracks in my jacket. The cracks look like the floor of a dried lake bed. The cracks in my façade seemed to reveal the cracks within me. I returned the jacket as soon as possible.

Although Roger and I had chosen the same school to be together, we seemed to be distancing ourselves from one another. Perhaps this began because we had no classes together. Roger seemed to be teased everywhere he went, even into junior high school. A new school seemed promising, but it turned out that the teasing found Roger there, too.

Roger seemed to be socially inept in so many ways. Mother's words rang true to me: 'Smart people are dumb, and dumb people are smart.' Roger was undoubtedly very smart, but only book smart. Since I was street smart but not book smart, Roger and I were a good fit for one another. I didn't find any close friends like Roger in school, but we were still distancing ourselves from one another. I found myself thinking, 'I need to let go of Roger as my friend.'

I solidified that decision when I found small notes above the drinking fountains at school, notes that read, "Adolph's goat milk for sale!" I knew it was Roger who placed the notes there above the fountains. I recognized Roger's handwriting style. Roger placed my home phone number at the bottom of the note. I wasn't amused. I took the notes down, throwing them in the garbage.

Roger had done this before. In grade school he used to leave little notes, written in ink, at different locations on the school grounds for people to find. Mr. Smith, the school custodian, had crooked yellow teeth. I took Mr. Smith's teeth personally, because of the spaces and gaps between my teeth. I always stared at people's teeth when they talked to me. I didn't like the spaces between my upper front teeth.

Roger would write a note on the school dumpster front and center for Mr. Smith to read, when he went to the garbage can. The note read, 'Mr. Smith has yellow teeth.' We both laughed as we walked away, but I knew Mr. Smith would read that note soon. I always wondered what went through Mr. Smith's mind when he read it. Seeing 'Adolph's goat milk for sale' brought back a flood of these memories with Roger.

Roger knew that we were distancing ourselves from one another. Roger said to me, "I have a new friend."

I said, "You do?"

Roger said, "I do. His name is Billy."

I said, "Oh."

Roger pulled out a long stick that looked like a miniature baseball bat. "This is my new friend. It's a billy club."

I understood Roger's pun. I had never seen one before, not until now, but I knew what it was. I associated the billy club with the radiator brush mother would hit me with. From then on, I felt uncomfortable around Roger.

A few weeks later I heard a rumor there was a girl walking behind Roger teasing him about something. I learned Roger pulled out his friend Billy and started beating the girl with his club. I thought I made the right decision to move on with our friendship. Roger disappeared from the school. I suppose he was expelled. I wonder now if he had been badly bullied, if he had felt threatened and taken matters into his own hands to protect himself. I only saw Roger on occasion, walking with his mother into the grocery store side by side. I always said hello, but that was as far as our conversation went.

I liked math and thought I was good at it, but I struggled with calculations. After three 'Cs' from each term I realized I wasn't good at math either. I saw the teacher's edition of the math book sitting idly on Mr. Hansen's desk. I saw that Mr. Hansen referred to the side notes in the book when students asked him a question. I knew it had all the answers I needed to improve my grade. Like mother and I stealing the neighbor's dog, when nobody was looking, I stole the teacher's math book.

Taking the book home, the first thing I did was to study its layout. At first I didn't fully understand how the notes read and how they correlated to the mathematical problems posted. I realized the teacher didn't have to know anything about math. All the teacher had to do was refer to the math book that we were being taught by. That's why I observed Mr. Hansen looking in the book on how the mathematical problems were solved. I wondered if he knew anything about math or if he was just there filling a position. I believed it was the latter.

The way I answered my homework would have given away that I was the one that stole the book. Nobody questioned me individually, but another teacher who shared the classroom was not happy that somebody stole the math book. I felt he stared at me while talking to the class. I tried not to take it personally, but I wondered if he was directing his talk to me. My conscience was alive and well, but that was as far as it went.

When the report card came in the mail during summer break, I opened my report card to see if I got an 'A' in math. I got the grade, but I knew I hadn't earned it. I bounced my head that night thinking about how the teacher stared at me. I wondered, through the lens of my conscience that I set aside, if they knew I was the one who stole the math book. It wasn't a feeling I liked, but it didn't stop me. I felt queasy about it, but I learned to live with it. The depth of his eyes staring into mine never faded from my memory. I could never teach the butterflies I felt in my stomach to fly in formation. I never returned the book, but I left it as a reminder of how uncomfortable it was to steal and cheat. It was a reminder that was shaping me.

Between seventh and eighth grade, I found out I needed glasses. I worried that I had made myself go blind so that I didn't have to see the world the way it really was. I pushed the thought aside without telling anyone about my fears.

The benefit of being fitted for glasses is that they made me look smart. Except for the glasses, I didn't know what the image of looking smart was. I knew I couldn't read, write, or spell going into Mrs. Spencer's eighth grade English class. I didn't say anything to the other students that I was illiterate. I didn't want to come across as dumb. Overcoming illiteracy was a bigger challenge than wearing a fancy jacket.

Mrs. Spencer divided the class into groups of six. I looked smart with my new glasses and people wanted me in their group. With my brilliant new façade, students turned to me for the answers from the posed questions. I answered the questions with confidence, except when the papers came back graded, all the answers I gave were wrong, and everyone failed in my group. I was never asked any more questions.

Each term the report card was sent home by the district, addressed to 'The parents of.' I opened the envelope just the same. No Fs. I was glad of that. I had worked hard to beat the system. I didn't expect any, but just the same, I looked down each grade reading from right to left. 'A'...looking to the left...'GYM' class, 'A'...looking to the left...'History.' I received lots of 'H' under the heading of CITIZENSHIP, I looked over at the code on the right side...I read the word, 'Honor.' Honor jumped off the page at me. I thought that meant I was an honor student. By the end of the second term, I had racked up a lot of H's. I was very proud.

In the foyer near the school offices, there was a grooved board on the wall behind a glass encasement. The grooves held white letters, naming the top ten honor students. It was on display for the whole school to see. I read each one of them, one by one. My name didn't appear. I couldn't understand why not since I had received so many 'H's on my report card.

I stood there, utterly puzzled.

The vice principal of the school walked up to me, catching my attention. He asked me, "Are you an honor student?"

I thought of all the honors on my report card, and I replied, "Yes! Quite a few times."

"That's good," he said.

He asked my name.

I told him.

I didn't realize until years later that those H's I received were for good behavior and citizenship, not good grades. The honors student were the ones who had top grades.

The first bell rang, indicating lunch was over. We departed. It was my habit to sprint to my classes, walking as fast as I could. I didn't want to be late but not too early either. I also did not want to be seen by the other students in the halls. It was my way of hiding from my classmates. Of course, my oddly fast walking made me stand out so that I was anything but hidden.

CHAPTER TWENTY-THREE

THE PAST THE PRESENT AND A CUP OF COFFEE

Silent secrets.

Mother started buying beer for her boys when we were in our early teens, even preteens as my brother Walter and I were 12 and 13 respectively. Daddy didn't think it was a good idea. He would say to mother, "I don't think it's a good idea to buy the boy's beer so early in their lives." Mother would just say, "Oh hell, if they want to drink alcohol they will find a way to drink it anyway." Mother's pattern of reasoning was confusing at best to my mind.

Mother had her own self-inflicted beliefs about life. She never changed her position on anything as I grew into being a teenager. She still believed that it was because of us damn kids that she was poor. She said it even more as we got older. But she never hesitated to buy us beer. Her logic didn't compute in my mind. After thinking about mother's comments which invaded the common sense part of my brain, I informed mother that having five boys forced her to buy a bigger house away in the poorest section of town. Mother shot back immediately telling me,"That's not true!" But I knew that it was true.

Mother would have been the same type of person whether she had one child or ten, whether she had five girls or a mix of both. It wouldn't have mattered. She would have complained anyway. It was as if complaining was mother's middle name. Not only was mother entrenched in her beliefs,

I could see she was entrenched in her behavior. Mother never tired of telling me she wished she never had me. She never tired of telling us boys don't get married, don't have children, and don't come around here if you do, and for hell sake don't get a girl pregnant! No one, including me, ever challenged her reasoning. As she spoke I would watch her scratch her head, her wig wobbling back and forth with each scratch. Mother had little to worry about, at least not from the three oldest boys. None of them had any interest in getting married whatsoever. I never saw them bring girlfriends to the house, talk about them, or elude there was any future with a female. I believe whether mother was conscious about it or not that was her plan.

Mother entrenched herself in her hatred towards God and toward any belief that a person's soul might be saved. She said, "When you're dead, you're dead and you're buried six feet under. There is no afterlife. It's all bullshit!" Every religious belief as a whole was dismissed, especially the Mormons! Everything outside of mother's cultural mindset was unsupported.

Buying us beer at such an early age was either part of mother's belief system or her way to 'stick it to any religious beliefs that we may adopt on our own.' I believed mother was herding us into being her friend, hoping it would pay off with dividends later. Mother's attitude of justification was consistent and erroneous at best without any reason. 'They're going to drink anyway.' Walter would later become an alcoholic, blaming our older brother Hermann for his addiction. I personally thought the blame was misplaced. Perhaps he forgot mother's good intentions.

Hermann didn't even live with us when Walter and I were of the age to try alcohol for the first time. Yet I do remember him visiting by that point, a few years after the incident where he struck mother.

By that time, I had developed a sweet tooth. When I tried it, I didn't care for the taste at all. I remember one day Hermann was sitting in the kitchen drinking a beer.

I remarked, "Beer tastes horrible!"

Hermann said, "It's a taste you have to acquire."

Acquired taste or not, I didn't like it.

Walter liked it. He acquired the taste immediately. Early on, I remembered one time when Walter and I were playing ping pong in the basement along with a neighbor, Tony. Tony's family were the Mormons across the street. Walter emptied the second bottle he was drinking. He set his empty bottle of beer down and ran upstairs to get another cold bottle. While Walter was gone, I had to pee really bad. The empty bottle of beer seemed more convenient to pee in than running upstairs into the toilet. Without a second thought, or worrying about the neighbor in the room, I peed in the empty bottle Walter abandoned. I placed the bottle back where I found it.

Walter came downstairs with another bottle of beer. He leaned up against the wall, taking a swig of beer from the fresh bottle. He paused like he was in a daze, staring at the bottle he had just emptied a few moments earlier, except it wasn't as empty as he thought. I saw the look on his face, but I had no idea what he was contemplating. Neither did Tony. Walter grabbed the bottle from off the table, and chugged down my spent pee. I didn't know that he was going to drink from the bottle. But I didn't stop him either.

Walter gagged.

He spit out my pee like a flame thrower. Walter hollered, "Who did this?"

I took off running, leaving the scene, running up the flight of stairs lickety split. I figured he would be angry at me.

A no-brainer. It took him a half a second to realize it was my pee that he drank in the bottle.

I paused at the top of the stairs telling him, "I didn't know you were going to do that!"

He tried splashing what pee was left in the bottle at me as I stepped out of the way. None of the pee splashed on me. I pretended he got some of it in my eye, but he didn't. I prepared myself for a fist fight, just in case, but

Walter never pursued me beyond that moment. I think he was buzzed. Later he told me that he had thought to himself, 'huh, more for me.'

While mother had entrenched herself in her beliefs, I became entrenched in my dream of becoming a mom. My feelings and thoughts strengthened in my early teenage years, becoming a part of everything I thought about. I continued to keep my feelings and thoughts a secret. Silent secrets. I liked my same-sex attraction, protecting my feelings from an environment which had beaten my emotions out of me.

Mother's iron fist was in her style of security, control, and belief that she was making the right decisions. I never second guessed my love for mother. I loved mother regardless, even when I could feel mother's logic didn't connect to my brain. I could only control what I could control and what thoughts were in my mind. I chose to transform mother's beatings and comments into a positive, peaceful place within me, setting aside angry feelings to create a belief that mother was just mother. Negative had become positive for me; I wasn't going to give up on my positive beliefs. I found no reason to be angry toward mother. Instead, I focused on my dreams of the future and my present attention to my body's sexual responses. Day to day, my body rescued me from the pain of life. In a sense, I became addicted to thinking about beautiful men, and I became entrenched in my body's reactions. My body always seemed to come to the rescue to save my mind.

I internalized my feelings of same sex attractions intuitively from the first moment my body responded to my brother's magazine images at nine years old. Without question, I believe my internal desires saved my life. Thinking differently wasn't an option for me to consider. I couldn't get mother to love me, so I loved myself, interpreting my body's feelings as love. I valued my body and the feelings my body gave to me without a price of exploitation. I had so much pent-up energy I needed to release in order to get my mind off of sex so I could do other things. With the spark inside of me and the twinkle of my eye that beamed from my countenance, I masturbated often.

Playing with myself balanced my mind and body, settling my soul for the moment. I felt obligated to find a balance in other areas of life which needed attention from me, like becoming important and succeeding in my life's future endeavors. Bouncing my head at night gave me the time to organize the happenings of the day and process information that had come to my attention.

I never tired of smashing my face on my pillow. The repetitive motion was important and necessary for me to survive. It was just as necessary as masturbating. Bouncing my head helped me center myself. It helped me sort out the swirling thoughts and ideas in my imagination's fertile ground. I planted seeds of expectations in me, building dreams to achieve, laying out plans to obtain them. It helped me sort out my thoughts, feelings and worries. I worried the world was coming to an end, based on television shows that predicted millions of people would starve to death. According to the pundits, the end of civilization within 10 years was inevitable. Mother's comment did not fade for my mind: 'There's too damn many people on this Earth.' I worried where this was going to leave me when I reached the prime of my life. The doom-and-gloom television shows left a pit in my stomach as to a future I had no control over. Bouncing my head helped me detail my plans' intricacies, like building a Swiss watch, while moving forward despite the sorrows of the world.

My cultural experiences were varied from other people's I knew, because of my family's German heritage, and yet my experiences were limited almost exclusively to mother's kitchen and our family home. Outside of visiting the German delicatessen stores in downtown Salt Lake City once or twice a week, there were no family road trips in my life. Just trips to the deli, mother and me. Yet I seldom found it boring. With the way mother drove and how she talked about people, it was always eventful and educational to be with mother. Truthfully, at the time I wouldn't have even known what the term "road trip" meant. The term was never used in our home, and as a family of seven, we rarely (if ever) gathered outside of Sunday breakfast for pancakes. By the time I was 13 years old, several of my brothers had moved out. We never went on a family trip together.

Those few times some of us traveled with mother and Daddy, it was a Sunday afternoon drive, less than a hundred miles round trip, and home in time to watch the evening news. Mother was exhausted from sitting in the passenger seat for more than an hour or two, and Daddy couldn't afford a car with air conditioning. Even with the windows down mother was permanently uncomfortable, complaining, "It's hot in here. I feel like I'm in a cattle car."

I pictured mother in the train car I saw in the movies when Adolf Hitler rounded up people he didn't like, packing them into cattle cars heading for Auschwitz. Without air conditioning, with only the breeze of the wind, mother was permanently hot in the summer. "I'm hot," mother complained again and again. Even when it was cooler, mother was at the age where she had started having hot flashes. Mother always said, "I get these hot flashes all the time!" I didn't know what that meant, except I pictured mother burning up from a flash of fire.

Mother never told us anything about menopause and what happens to a woman when she gets to the end of her childbearing years. I eventually asked and mother explained. After mother's explanation of the time factor, I thought my brother Walter and myself got under the threshold in the nick of time. Mother's outbursts with her hot flashes made knowing more about menopause less interesting to me.

At home mother wanted the doors opened to create a breeze in the evening, then she wanted me to fan her with a piece of cardboard to cool down, but it was still uncomfortable. 'Miss Cleopatra,' mother, laid comfortably on the couch as I fanned her with the cardboard, using one arm, then switching to the other, then using both arms. I kept asking, "Is that enough yet?" My arms were getting tired of fanning mother. I couldn't wait to hear mother say, "Yes, that's enough!" Mother eventually bought an electric fan to replace me.

In the car mother felt hot, cramped, and jostled by every bump in the road. She heard every rattle in the car, constantly wondering if the car was going to fall apart while we were going down the road. These complaints and discomforts were all when Daddy drove. She wasn't in control then. "Sightseeing was a waste of time," she would always say. Her only hope on these trips was only that wherever Daddy was going there would be a good cup of coffee. That usually softened the complaints a little bit. If the coffee was tasteless, mother had no issue filing a complaint with the manager. Mother threatened them, saying, "This is the last time I'm coming here!" But mother had said that at the last restaurant, too. The couch, the TV, and the coffee machine was mother's true domain; not sitting in the front seat of some old hot rattletrap where someone else was driving.

When visitors came from Germany from time to time, they stayed at a nearby hotel, never in our home. There was too much junk and clutter to move out of the way to make room for them. To mother, their presence alone invaded her space and interrupted her routine. Mother couldn't wait for them to leave the house when they visited, closing the door behind them saying out loud, "Am I glad they're gone!" She said that loud enough, I wondered if the people even had gotten down the stairs off the porch. She would then scratch her head through her wig in frustration, eyeing the couch.

Daddy enjoyed these visits with guests, because they gave him an excuse to get away. Daddy would take them on trips to see Southern Utah. If Daddy went without mother, that would only make her more angry towards these visitors. Mother complained loudly and angrily, "I feel PUT OUT!" She would spit the 'P' as she spoke. To mother, this was all very irritating, maddening, and inconsiderate of these people calling upon Daddy to do this. Mother had no interest in befriending these people. Mother had her own tight click of friends and these visitors were intruders. Mother refused to go on these drives with Daddy. She had no interest in sitting in a car with people she didn't know.

The people visiting Daddy knew somebody who knew somebody who somehow knew somebody from some other acquaintance somewhere from the Fatherland. Daddy had been gone from Germany since 1938 with the exception of a brief term during the war. At this point, 35 years had passed. Daddy had no living relatives. Mother had no interest in relatives even if we had some. Quite the contrary, she would regularly remind us how lucky we were not to have any, and told us often.

Mother wanted Daddy to serve her, and when Daddy was gone for the better part of a week, taking his guests sightseeing to Utah landmarks, famous parks and to Las Vegas, she didn't get the attention she thought she deserved. Mother expressed her disgust openly about Daddy's absence, enunciating every word clearly. "Daddy's chauffeuring those people around and won't be back till Sunday!"

Mother wanted to dress down in the evening, take off her wig and put on her nightgown. After she applied face cream, she wanted to have her feet massaged and rubbed with witch-hazel to soften them up, all while she watched late night TV shows. Daddy catered to mother's nightly whims.

When Daddy was gone, mother asked me to massage her feet and apply her foot cream.

I asked mother, "Why don't you have Walter massage your feet?"

Mother said, "I like the way you do it!"

I complained saying, "I don't want to massage your feet!"

Mother would answer, "I had to change your SHITTY diaper when you were a baby!" Mother always emphasized the word 'SHITTY!'

I thought the same thing as before, 'Wasn't that something you just did when you had a baby?'

I didn't argue beyond that point. I massaged mother's feet without further complaining.

When handheld recording devices were available to the public, Billy purchased one and thought it would be funny to record mother's snoring. While I massaged mother's feet, keeping her asleep and snoring away, Billy put the microphone under mother's nose, recording her sounds. I watched Billy and snickered soundlessly in other not to wake her. Mother's snored away, sawing logs! I continued massaging, smiling, and chuckling, wondering how this was going to unfold.

Walter came into the room, witnessing Billy recording mother's snoring and smiled, too. Mother continued. We all tried holding back our laughter the best any of us could as Billy kept recording. I let a little laughter out from my nose, and mother snorted one big gulp of air, waking herself up. We all laughed out loud thinking mother had awoken, but mother was neither coherent nor completely awake.

With one eye open for a moment, mother processed the new information. She saw Billy standing over her and she heard our laughter. She didn't know what was going on. Opening both eyes, she said, "What do you want?"

Billy and the rest of us laughed out loud. Billy said, "I was recording your snoring, Mommy, would you like to hear it?"

Mother didn't know what to expect.

Neither did we.

Billy queued the tape and pushed 'play.' Everyone, including mother, listened intently to the recording. We all started laughing at what we were hearing.

Billy said, "You sound like a gentle ocean breeze with the water lapping along the seashore."

We laughed even harder at that. Mother laughed the most. Billy was right. That's what it sounded like.

Mother said, "Can you save that recording?"

Billy agreed and replayed the tape again and again. Mother had Billy replay the tape to other family members and some friends. It was just as funny the tenth time as the first.

I cared for mother's feet more often than I want to remember while Daddy was gone. This was Daddy's chore, massaging mother's feet. Her feet were hideous. Yellow cracked toenails, bunions, corns, and gnarled toes. Her feet screeched at me like the cries of a seagull on an ocean shore.

Worse, massaging mother's feet was like navigating a regatta.

"Press my big toe."

"Not too hard."

"Ouch, my corn!"

"Stay away from my bunion."

"Don't touch the crack in my heel."

"Press harder."

"Tickle the top of my foot."

"Rub my feet some more."

I did what mother asked.

I hoped mother would doze off, snoring the seven seas, sooner than later. As soon as mother sailed off, snoring into the wild blue yonder, I carefully displaced my body out from underneath mother's feet. Slowly plotting my escape, I moved one leg off at a time, replacing a pillow in my stead, all the while touching mother's feet so she wouldn't wake up. Mother's feet were hideous. Yellow cracked toenails, bunions, corns, and gnarled toes. Her feet screeched at me like the cries of a seagull, on a seaside shore.

Sunday afternoon, when we were not encumbered with guests, we traveled short distances. It wasn't to sightsee, to check out historical sites, go to museums, see priceless art, or understand other cultures from around the world. Daddy drove to a planned restaurant, one that mother had heard about. The taste of the food was iffy. We never knew if she would approve or not. To my autistic mind, the perseveration on the coffee, the food, and the service of each of these new establishments fascinated and consumed me. What would this one be like? It all depended on the strength of the coffee that was served. They had better have real cream or at least half and half to mix in mother's coffee or she would complain loud and long. Any imitation dairy product that was offered as a substitute was the pits, for the birds, and mother wasn't returning.

Mother wasted no time in complaining, nearly from the moment she walked into an establishment, especially if she was not seated after a short wait. Mother wanted the host, the waiter or waitress, to acknowledge her presence and seat her immediately. If mother couldn't get their attention, she complained up the chain of command until someone acknowledged her grievance. If mother's grievance wasn't mitigated soon, mother had no issue telling whomever, "This place is the pits." She would leave in a huff, all of us following her in tow.

If the threshold of service was cleared, and mother was seated to her satisfaction, she proceeded to critique every moment. The service at the table, the taste of the coffee, how hot the food was, how it was seasoned, how quickly mother's coffee was refilled. Then there was the conversation with the server on how long they had lived in this stupid state and if they were a Mormon or not. If the restaurant was to mother's satisfaction, the server was given a tip. Mother's threshold had been met. Mother tipped according to her agenda.

Mother did not vary from her expectations. Every restaurant was judged by the same standards. If the cup of coffee wasn't strong enough to suit her tastes, mother had no problems telling the server, "Your coffee tastes like dishwater!" I imagined that she was assuming dishwater had been tasted by the server?

The noise level in a restaurant was almost as important to mother's experience as a strong cup of coffee. When asked by the host, "Would you like to be seated in the smoking or the non-smoking section?" Mother would take this seemingly simple question and give it a complicated answer that the host wasn't expecting. Mother said, "Just put me where there are no crying babies or noisy kids. Just don't put anyone's crying brats next to me!"

Mother never hesitated to move somewhere else if the host did not take heed to her demand. Mother would leave her seat, passing the unsuspecting noise makers with an angry disgusted look. Her scowl said, "Teach your DAMN KIDS not to cry or take them out of the room if you can't shut them up!" I knew that's what mother was thinking because she always said that before she got up to leave. Mother always wanted the last word, saying, "Those inconsiderate Mormons with their station wagon full of kids!"

Mother liked fine dining and enjoyed the service which came with it. Coffee in upper crust establishments were usually satisfactory and met mother's tastes. As important as the coffee was to mother, silence was equally critical. Any classy establishment that offered a live pianist was almost as bad as being seated next to crying kids. When the pianist played for their patrons to enjoy, adding to the ambience of these fine establishments, mother only heard the plinking of the keys in her ears, never the music. Mother said with frustration, "I wish they would stop plinking on the piano. I can't stand that noise!" Mother always praised the pianist when they walked away, but not for the reason they expected. After the pianist walked away mother was the first to say, "I'm glad they're finished. Now I can eat in peace!"

Part of my cultural experience came from mother and Daddy and their life experiences, and another part came from the array of people mother invited to our home to participate in her parties. These were stories from seemingly ordinary people with extraordinary experiences. When the party was over, I was allowed to leave my room to come out and eat whatever was left over. I sat at the table and listened to whatever mother's guests had to say.

People who escaped Germany with little more than the clothes on their back, surviving to come to America to live their dreams.

I was fascinated by these guests, listening to each of their stories and what they did with their lives since coming to America. Some shared a little, some of them shared a lot. There was Willy and Taya Houmas. Willy spoke German 100% all of the time, but Taya spoke English often. I never heard their stories in full. I knew that Taya was one of the best pastry chefs in all of Utah. She worked for one of the finest hotels in downtown Salt Lake City. Taya would bring some of her creations to the house for mother to enjoy.

Mother hid Taya's cake in the backroom from us boys among the junk piled high. If I found it, I ate some right away, knowing it would be exquisite. Maybe some of the other boys did, too. Mother was always furious if she found that someone had eaten a part of it without asking. She would say, "Who the hell ate some of Taya's cake?" Mother's disgust flowed from her lips to all of us and in particular whoever ate her stash, without mincing her words, "If you want anything for yourself, you have to hide it up your ass to protect it!" Surprised at mother's comment, I pictured her crass words, wondering how it would fit.

Taya's cakes were good for my sweet tooth. Mother never asked me directly if I ate the cake, and I never fessed up that it was me. Mother hid what she didn't want anyone else to eat in a better place, never putting Taya's cake in the refrigerator, because that was too easy of a find. It stayed hidden in the backroom sometimes until it molded. Mother hid many food items that were brought to her, particularly those she considered rare or valuable. Some foods were found by just stumbling across them while looking for something else in mother's vast array of deserted clutter. Later in life I would find myself doing the same thing.

These parties were a pattern in my life, and now that I was 14 years old I listened more intently. Some guests lingered after the party was over. Many times, I would come out of my room to see Elsie sitting comfortably at the kitchen table. Elsie would always invite me to eat, saying, "There's plenty of food." I did so, sitting with Elsie at the table.

Elsie lingered long after the party was over, until Daddy was ready to drive her home. Elsie was a cultural experience in herself and a history lesson at the same time. Sometimes, Elsie would share a little bit of her story, sometimes talking about her experience with only mother and Daddy, and sometimes just me in the room, but never in front of a crowd of people. One day she told her story about being separated from her parents and returning to their home after the war was over but never seeing her parents again. She said, "They never came home."

Elsie said, "My family had been rounded up by the Nazis including my brother, because we were German Jews living in Germany." I could feel Elsie radiating goodness and beauty from within as she painstakingly told even simple parts of her story. I thought of her as a dear woman.

Elsie learned after the war that her parents had been murdered in the camps. Telling me this seemed to be the easiest part of her story. Elsie's brother and she lived through the time at the concentration camp. They were reunited years after the war ended, but by the time that she was telling me about it he had since passed on. He died at an early age due to being experimented on while imprisoned inside the camp. Elsie wouldn't give any further details, except to shake her head in disbelief.

I heard the pain in Elsie's voice. It seemed to emanate from deep within her diaphragm. She raised her hand to her head, swaying her arms slowly at the elbows as if to say 'no thank you,' shaking her head left and right, saying slowly, "I can't tell you anymore." She would pause and then say, "The memories are too painful to talk about right now!"

I could feel and hear the gentleness in her voice and the pain in her heart which never seemed to dissipate. I just sat and listened to whatever she wanted to share.

On another occasion, Elsie talked about ashes that fell from the evening sky, only to end her story as quickly as she started saying, "I can't tell you of the atrocities." Then she said no more.

After hearing these snippets about her time in the Dachau concentration camp, I understood my feelings toward her. I felt Elsie had a story to tell before she passed from this life.

At night I bounced my head on the pillow, feeling the softness of it on my face, thinking about what Elsie said to me that night. I switched thoughts to hear the compression of the bounce in my ear, then going back to thinking more about what Elsie told me, fading out the compression from my thoughts. I processed each word and each hand, eye, and body movement. I wondered what life would be like for me inside of a concentration camp if I was in Elsie's shoes. All I could do was wonder at the moment. I would have to wait to hear more of Elsie's story with mother's next party.

Elsie was a standing invite to mother's parties, the parties that were for mother's friends and moreover for those who complimented mother's food. Whenever I heard the Grundig stop playing, I knew the party was dying down. At the next party, I came out of my room to see Elsie sitting at the table. I hoped to hear more of her story. I wasn't disappointed.

"I pricked my finger to draw blood. I rubbed the blood from my finger on my face to give me some color on my cheeks. Everybody looked so pale. The blood added enough color to make me look healthy, and rosy cheeks made me look more beautiful, too."

I could see the beauty Elsie was talking about. She was still beautiful in her older years. My mind returned to Elsie's story.

Elsie continued. "If you were beautiful, the soldiers were more likely to keep you around, and you had a better chance of living." She paused to take a drink of coffee, setting her cup back down on the saucer. "If you had pimples, you didn't look beautiful to the soldiers and you disappeared. Those who disappeared, we never saw them again. We knew they were put to death."

I processed Elsie's story, taking this part of her story personally. Frank and Hermann both had deep acne scars permanently cratering their face from their teenage years. Billy was confident he would not end up like our two older brothers, but he told me I would end up with deep acne scars, like them. Billy would tell me with certainty, "You are going to end up looking like Frank and Hermann. Your face is going to be scarred with acne and you're going to have big craters in your face!" Billy's deviousness and cruel nature never dissipated as we got older. I thought to myself, 'I like my looks.' His comments worried me. My self-esteem couldn't handle my face being scarred like my two older brothers'.

I imagined myself in the concentration camp, as if I were Elsie. If I had acne back in that day like I did presently, would my life come down to the position of my cheekbones, the form of my body, and the clarity of the skin on my face? I knew the answer in the back of my mind. 'Yes.' I would have disappeared. My acne was a death sentence to me in a concentration camp. All because of something I couldn't control. I wondered, how many people were killed because of acne, out of place cheek bones, or their body form? What more could I have offered to live? I thought, maybe I could do sexual favors. I quickly erased this from my mind.

Elsie continued, "If you were gay they killed you."

Elsie's comment sparked my secrets deep down inside of me more than I was comfortable with at the moment.

Elsie said, "Hitler rounded up the homosexuals and killed them."

My heart sank. I thought, 'It wasn't an option to live as a gay, and I wondered how many men were killed just because of this?' I didn't know the answer. It was a feeling I knew firsthand, a feeling I couldn't control. My mind went blank again.

I turned back into Elsie's voice.

"I think Hitler was gay." Elsie nodded her head. "I wouldn't doubt it!" Elsie offered no smile. Elsie was not joking. "I'm serious," she said, "I think he was."

I wondered about Hitler, but I didn't say anything to anyone. I didn't want to give away any clue to the homosexual thoughts and feelings I had. I felt asking questions could lead to revealing my feelings.

Even though Elsie only shared little bits and pieces of her story, it was relevant to me. I didn't understand why I felt the way I did, though I felt sure I would have been one of those that disappeared or died a horrific death in a concentration camp. I was doomed in Hitler's economy of death, simply because of my acne…not to mention my homosexual feelings. I hid my feelings, as I always did, but I could not have hidden the acne on my face. Elsie was right: these stories were too painful to think about.

Mother slammed the phone down. "Ugh! Those old moochers are coming over tomorrow!"

Mother was talking about Frieda and Fritz. They were two of the first Germans that mother and Daddy met when they moved to Utah. They were also two of mother's regular house guests though they were never actually invited. They would show up like clockwork with gifts for every Christmas and every boy's birthday until we turned 18. They would call the day before, speaking to mother in German. Mother would always say the same thing, calling them "those old moochers." I always knew she was talking about them, although the moniker made no sense.

I was always excited to see Frieda and Fritz. They were kind and I enjoyed their gifts. I felt important because of their generosity towards me.

Their full names were Fritz and Frieda Harold. Fritz was a jolly-looking man who appeared 25 years younger than his age. Round in form, he sat straight in his chair and his face shined, reflecting the light of the window. There was not a whisker of hair on his face. Fritz showed the appearance of youthfulness, making him even more attractive. He sat with his arms folded across his chest, and they rose and fell as he laughed and breathed.

265

Fritz emitted words of wisdom and a sensibility which resonated powerfully in my mind in regards to life and the politics of the day. I liked how Fritz thought. Mother and Daddy never spoke politics with the exception of mother's disgust for Nixon, but I liked the deep conversations Fritz initiated. They stimulated my mind.

Fritz's wife Frieda was more petite. Frieda looked more like a prune. Only a few facial hairs caught my attention on her face from the light of the window. Maybe there were a lot more than a few, but that's what I could see. I tried not to look. Frieda looked 25 years older than she was. She hunched over in her chair just a little bit, arms folded in her lap, her gray hair pulled back into a bun behind her head. She seemed more serious and showed little pizzazz. Even with my young eyes, I saw them as the perfect example of how opposites attract. I asked no questions and made no comments when they visited. I just listened.

I think Frieda understood English, but she never spoke a word of it in all the years I knew her. Only the German language came out of her mouth, although she was typically very quiet. Fritz spoke most of the time while Frieda sat back in her chair. She just listened to Fritz talk to mother, Daddy and myself in English.

I liked hearing Fritz's accent, like all the old Germans. People would tell me, "Your Dad has a German accent." I always replied, "He does?" I couldn't hear it. People were surprised.

As Frieda sat back in her chair, I heard her clicking her dentures. It sounded like she was sending Morse code, moving her mouth back and forth. She must have understood English, but she never spoke it in front of me.

Fritz spoke boastfully in English, embellishing his words in the conversation. It seemed to me when he embellished too much for her taste, Frieda stopped clicking and added to the conversation or corrected what Fritz was saying. Since it was all in German I just paid attention to the tone of her words.

Fritz always replied respectfully back to Frieda in his native tongue, referring to his wife affectionately as "Mama," then resumed telling his story. Frida would nod her head in agreement and continue clicking her dentures. They always sat side by side. Fritz was the driver in their relationship. Even on the road, Frieda never learned to drive. Fritz drove Frieda everywhere, attending to her needs with diligence and care. In their leisure time, they would take weekly drives on Sunday afternoons, touring the canyons, admiring the beauty of the mountains and the lush foliage.

Fritz always seemed to have rhyme and reason to his thinking, and each time they were at the house, I sat around the table and listened to him talk. Even if he spoke of nothing noteworthy, he seemed so confident in the delivery of his words. I don't remember their story. I don't know for sure if they left the fatherland like so many others, with little more than the shirt on their backs, or if they left because they wanted a better life in America, like Daddy. Maybe both knew they had no future in Germany.

Fritz seemed to be someone who had gone through the School of Hard Knocks. My experiences were not the same as Fritz's, but I still gravitated to him, relating to his wisdom as I understood it. I seemed to feel a connection with people who graduated from 'that' school.

Mother's view of them was quite different. She elongated the 'M' in 'moochers' each time they visited saying the same thing. She sounded like a cow in disgust, "THOSE OL' MOO-CHERS ARE COMING OVER AGAIN TOMORROW!"

Even though this comment was directed toward Frida and Fritz, it would have lifelong consequences for me. I wouldn't go over to anybody's house unless I was invited, fearing I would be considered a moocher without a formal invitation.

Mother felt obligated to throw some food together that would be pleasing to them, moreover pleasing to mother. Mother complained about them until the moment they showed up at the door, then it was smiles.

On one occasion, I sat and listened in on the conversation as I had done in the past, but this time Fritz made a comment that caught my attention. Unfurling his arms, Fritz raised his right arm high in the air, a little above his head towards the ceiling, extending his index finger and pointing upward to the heavens. Without hesitation, boastfully, he said, "When we die, we die together!"

I looked over at Frieda, who didn't say a word.

Fritz's statement caught my attention and became lodged in my head.

I wondered what he meant by that declaration. Something about it shocked me. That night as I bounced my head, I processed his statement. I drew no conclusions. "When we die we die together!"

The ol' moochers, Frieda and Fritz, were never invited to mother's parties. At least in mother's estimation, they were never invited, but they invited themselves. Even though they called the day before coming over, mother considered their presence as uninvited. Mother wanted to be in control of who came and when they came.

But the main reason they weren't invited to the parties was that Frieda made the mistake once of not praising mother's food. I learned this from Daddy, having once asked him why Fritz and Frieda were never invited. Instead of complimenting mother, Frieda told her that her mashed potatoes were too chunky. She added insult to injury by buying her a new potato masher. She said it would smash up the potatoes better and make them smoother. Well, if someone wanted to ruffle mother's feathers, all they had to do was tell mother what she was doing wrong with the way mother made her food.

The straw that broke the camel's back between mother and Frieda was when Frieda told mother, "Your coffee is too strong!" The day that Frieda told mother that, I was sitting at the table. I saw the expression on mother's countenance change, like the calm before the storm. From mother's face,

I knew Frieda had again said something displeasing. My eyes moved immediately to Daddy. He kept his head down. I'd been around the old Germans long enough to follow the tenor of a conversation even if I couldn't understand the language. I knew whatever had been said would not go over well.

Mother confirmed what Frieda had said after they left the house. Mother was incensed. Daddy argued with mother's tirade, trying to encourage mother not to get riled up over such a trifling comment. But I knew it would be to no avail. I knew Daddy's comment would be in vain. I knew mother would be turned off. I knew mother.

Another time Fritz told me in a conversation at the table that he was not able to smell. I thought that was interesting. Fritz never offered an opinion on mother's coffee nor her food, except to say that it was all good. Fritz was always satisfied with mother. I wondered to myself if one of the reasons Frieda and Fritz had been married so long was that Fritz never complained about the taste of Frieda's cooking.

Several years later, after my 20th birthday, gifts were no longer brought to the house nor at Christmas time. I thought to myself I should go and thank them for all the years they had brought me and the family gifts. I knew they weren't going to be around much longer because of their age. I made arrangements to visit their home to thank Frieda and Fritz personally for their generosity over the years. I didn't want to have it on my conscience, that I had missed the opportunity to say, "thank you."

Upon my arrival Fritz welcomed me into their home with a warm greeting. As I walked in the door, the first thing I noticed was that Fritz had taken a chair from the kitchen table and cut a round hole in the center of the seat. The chair was tall enough for a 5 gallon bucket to slip underneath. I knew the chair was for Frieda. Frieda came down with Alzheimer's, having lost her faculties. Fritz had engineered a simple toilet for Frieda for her to go to the bathroom without having to go very far. Taking care of Frieda was taking care of Mama.

With Frieda's Alzheimer's worsening, Fritz continued driving Mama around the countryside, enjoying the vistas and the beauty of pristine Aspens with their white trunks and bright yellow leaves, abundant and plentiful in the mountains of Utah. The smell of fresh clean air bespoke the purity of the environment with its abundantly crisp aroma. The mountains rose majestically into the heavens. Steep cliffs with charred edges below made the mountains the beauty they are.

Shortly after my visit, mother showed me a newspaper clipping of a car that had gone over a cliff in the mountains that Frieda and Fritz visited often. Mother said, "It was Frieda and Fritz's car that went over a cliff!"

I was in shock. Then I was grateful that I had stopped and visited to say 'thank you.'

The plunge killed Fritz instantly, but not Frieda! Alive in the hospital, Frieda died a few days later, succumbing to her injuries. I reminded mother and Daddy what Fritz said so many years earlier, "When we die, we die together!" Fritz's words had never escaped my mind but were burned into it.

Daddy cautioned me, saying, "You shouldn't speculate."

I didn't need to speculate. I knew that was what Fritz meant when he had said what he did. I had been around the old Germans long enough to know that when they said they were going to do something, they did it. I bounced my head that night, processing this information of the day, wondering if Fritz's driving off the cliff was a murder-suicide. I came to the conclusion that it was.

CHAPTER TWENTY-FOUR

THE MILLION-DOLLAR QUESTION

Mowing Omi's lawn was my job. I achieved the task with what looked like an exasperated piece of equipment that the cavemen had invented right after the wheel, somewhere about the time Omi was born in 1894. The mower left a lot to be desired. It probably didn't cut much better than a herd of sheep eating the grass and leaving a trail of debris behind them. The old mower shot out a trail of grass that I had to clean up. I pushed the old mower through sparse patches of grass, weeds and dirt, forging a pathway around her house. The sheep might not have been such a bad idea after all.

The wheels on the mower were similar to duck feet, pointing outward. They were the opposite of me, being pigeon-toed. The mower blew out a blue haze that covered the deck in black grease. Its appearance also left a lot to be desired. I muscled the mower through the weeds and dirt of Omi's 'lawn.' In the beginning it was a lot of work for my own muscles, but I forged ahead with positivity.

One time I didn't think Omi would mind, let alone notice with her foggy glasses, if I missed a spot in the back yard behind the garage, but she did. Omi pointed out what I had skipped. I didn't have to be fluent in German to understand Omi's body language, pointing to the area I thought I could get away with not cutting. Daddy interpreted just to make sure I understood Omi knew I had missed a spot. I thought it was a shortcut Omi would never see, but I was very wrong. I decided from that moment on I would cut a

271

lawn as if I was being watched and scrutinized in detail by the person I had to answer to.

Pushing my mower down the road to cut the lawn around Lonnie's dad's favorite bar was a different story. My lawnmower was several steps above Omi's mower. Daddy had just bought it for me to use on our lawn at home. Unlike Omi's lawn mower, the wheels were straight and its brilliant red deck was clean and viable in its entirety. The chrome handle glistened in the morning sun, looking like the shine from the chrome on a Duesenberg in comparison to Omi's four wheel dinosaur. My mower was the top of the line for the day, self-propelled, with a hole on the deck to put the garden hose through to clean the underside of caked-on grass. I took pride in this piece of equipment, keeping it clean and in good working condition after each use, checking the oil and keeping the blade sharp. I got paid $5.00 for mowing the bar's lawn. I felt it was a worthwhile endeavor, and maybe I could become rich mowing lawns, even if I had to split half of the money with Lonnie. He had gotten me the job at the bar, so I only thought it was right to offer him the money.

I bounced my head that night thinking about the money I had earned cutting the bar's lawn. I felt if I worked hard, cutting lawns by myself I could keep all the money in my business. I still believed with all my heart one day I would become a carpenter building homes. I loved building. In the meantime my thoughts carried me away, thinking about starting a lawn mowing business. If somebody was willing to pay me $5 to cut their lawn, what if I had ten lawn accounts? That would be $50 a week, $200 a month. I'd be rich. I had just turned 16, and I had a plan. The beginning of my dreams would start coming true.

I didn't have a driver's license yet or a car, but that didn't stop me from setting up lawn jobs around town. I decided to ask Esther, mother's friend with the Pentecostal-type hairdo, "Do you know anybody I could cut their lawn for?"

Esther said, "Yes, my sister just built a home and needs somebody to cut her lawn."

I thought that would be great. I was very excited.

Esther said, "I will give you her phone number. Her name is Hedy Penney."

Hedy Penney. I thought, 'that's an interesting name.' It reminded me of the fairytale Henny Penny. She was the one who thought the sky was falling and got all her friends to follow her to their deaths at the hands of Foxy-Loxy. She was such a dumb cluck.

Mother's name was Hedwig. Mother had a good head on her shoulders and wore a wig. Omi's last name was Hattwig. Omi never wore a hat nor a wig. I thought, 'Am I glad Daddy changed his name from Schilfarth!' I thought about what would happen if I introduced myself, 'Hi, my name is Robert Schilfarth.' I wondered if they thought I said, 'Robert Shit-fart.' I smiled and laughed to myself, thinking about how I would have to explain my name like this every time. I didn't say swear words, so I knew that wasn't an option. But then what if Daddy had the same last name as Omi did now, Hattwig? Mother would have been Hedwig Hattwig. I laughed again. It got me thinking about the uniqueness of my heritage.

I called Hedy Penney and introduced myself to her. Hedy mentioned that her sister Esther had told her that I would be calling. Hedy gave me her address and asked me to give her a price. There was only one problem, well maybe two, but nothing too serious to my 16-year-old mind.

I asked Daddy if he could drive me so I could talk to Hedy Penney about her lawn. He said he would. I asked Daddy, "Could you keep track of the distance on the odometer reading?" Daddy said he would. I knew Daddy was good at math, because he could figure out bowling scores and keep track of them in his head. I never could figure out how bowling scoring worked. Daddy calculated the mileage to Hedy's house. Hedy lived 8.3 miles away, towards the mountains.

Daddy stopped the car. I looked at the address Hedy gave me and saw this was the place. It was a beautiful new home on the hill. I thought, 'This is where all the rich people live. I could get more lawn accounts!' There were more new homes being built across the street. My mind started calculating the potential profits. All I had to do was work hard. I had a lot of energy to burn off inside me and my ambitions fueled me. A feeling of possibility arose in my stomach. I was breathless, thinking about my future.

I went to the front door and rang the doorbell. Hedy answered. As the door opened, the smell of newness hit my nose, and the sight of Hedy was a spitting image of Esther.

Hedy looked as elegant and beautiful as Esther with her hair piled high on top of her head. Esther's hair was black. Hedy's hair was sandy blonde. Mother's prejudiced thoughts about their hair piled high as a sign of being Pentecostal did not enter my mind. Hedy invited me into her house. My wide eyes took in everything. It was all new. I'd never experienced anything new before. Hedy talked to me for a little while, then walked me through the yard. I gave her a price that Hedy agreed on, and I set a day to start maintaining her yard.

I appreciated the opportunity Hedy gave me and the trust she placed in me. I promised to work hard and I did. I kept her lawn mowed and the flower beds clean from weeds. Daddy was good to drive me and pick me back up. Daddy didn't mind me putting bags of the cut grass I collected in his car, then putting my lawn mower and my equipment in, too. After I was finished Daddy drove me home.

I was so excited about the possibilities life had to offer I couldn't keep it pent up inside of me any longer. I had to tell somebody about my future! I went to my neighbor across the street, Judy Taul, to explain to her how I was going to expand my lawn cutting business and get rich. After Judy answered the door, I said to her, "Judy, I'm going to go into the lawn business and I'm going to make a lot of money!" Without the skip of a heartbeat, Judy promptly said, "The major employer in the city is going on strike next month, and every Tongan and their dog will be out cutting lawns, and you will never make any money!"

I didn't understand at the time the power of negative comments. Mother relentlessly told me, "I should have never had you. I should have given you away. I should have left you in the cart at Grand Central. I should have drowned you when I had the chance! You talk in riddles, I don't understand anything you're saying. Can't you talk intelligently?" Mother had continued telling me these things to that date.

I made the decision somewhere in the back of my head years earlier that I would turn all negatives into positives. It was a lifestyle I acquired in order to survive. After my suicide attempt at 10 years old failed, I chose to live. Then I chose to succeed. I never viewed life again with the thought of failure. I chose to be important, even if I stayed unimportant in mother's mind. I had the quest to be different. When Judy said to me, "You will never make any money!" she couldn't have said anything more positive to me. I never took what Judy said personally. I never thought, 'I'll show you!' That would have netted different results! I did not allow her to place the seed of doubt in my mind. It never occurred to me, nor did I ever doubt, that I wouldn't succeed at something and be important in life at some point in time.

I picked up more lawn accounts as I hoped I would, mowing three other yards in the neighborhood across the street from Hedy Penney. My business was growing. Daddy continued driving me for a while.

But then there was a day when I asked Daddy if he was going to come and pick me up from Hedy Penney's and he said, "You'll have to find your own way back home this time."

I said, "How am I supposed to get back home with all my equipment?"

Daddy said, "That's not my problem. That's for you to figure out for yourself."

All the while I was mowing each of the lawns, I knew ahead of time I would have to find my way back home. I was thinking, 'I could walk home, push my lawn mower, and carry all my equipment. The eight miles would be cumbersome, even if it was all downhill, I still felt it would be uncomfortable and embarrassing. I thought maybe one of my customers would be nice enough to take me back home, but which one? I mustered up the courage to ask such an embarrassing question to one of my customers, Doreen.

I explained to Doreen I didn't have a way back home, and I asked if she could drive me to my house. She agreed to do so happily. I was really appreciative of Doreen, but I realized something had to change if I was going to build my business and make a fortune. I needed to learn how to drive.

Watching mother drive around town gave me the basics of driving. I thought, 'How hard would it be?' "Move over slow poke." "Use your blinker." "Stop sightseeing and start driving!" "Sunday driver!" From mother I knew to honk my horn when people got in my way and speed to my destination, even if I was being followed by the police. What else did I need to know?

At this point the lawn mowing season was nearly over, and I knew I would need to get my license. I wanted to spread my wings, and most importantly, succeed at life, and learning to drive was just one step in the process. I decided I would become a millionaire by the time I was 25 years old. That decision gave me 10 years to figure out how to do it. I had no doubts I could accomplish such a task, even if I didn't have a clear path to accomplish it, except to work hard. I knew being a millionaire would make me important. All I had to do was work hard, very hard. In my mind, my lawn mowing business was the first step. Listening to the old Germans talk around the table had inspired me with their success and hard working attitude. I had turned 16 in June, and my friend Kevin from school asked me if I wanted to get a job at the lumber company down the road. It was close enough I could walk to it in 5 minutes.

With fall approaching I worked to get my license. Daddy asked me if I would wait till I was 16 ½ before obtaining my license. He felt if I waited till I was 16 ½ I would be more mature, making me a better driver. I took Daddy's advice and waited. After all, I respected Daddy. I viewed Daddy as a wise old German. He was always nice and fair to me, and he encouraged me to be a better boy. He was the complete opposite of mother. Daddy encouraged me to save my money, telling me that if I saved 10% of everything I earned over my lifetime and never spent it I could retire years ahead of everybody else. Of all the lessons Daddy tried to teach me, this one was the hardest. Retirement seemed so far away. I thought, 'I have a better answer. I'll just make a lot of money!'

Once I had my license, I decided to get a truck. I kept my job at the lumber company and searched the papers until I found somebody willing to sell a 1950 Chevy pickup truck at a price I could afford. He asked for $500. Daddy said he would pay for half of it. I had $250 in savings. It seemed perfect. I was nervous and excited. I went to look at it. It was exactly what I was hoping for, even if it had a big dent in the passenger's side door. It was simple and easy to maintain, and it was a unique style for me. With a spin around the block, I purchased it. After a few weeks of driving I felt I was a good driver!

I told Daddy as much.

Daddy said, "You'll be a good driver after you've driven a hundred thousand miles!"

I asked Daddy, "What is the average mileage somebody drives in a year?"

Daddy said, "About ten thousand miles"

I thought to myself, 'That's 10 years from now.' I stopped saying I was a good driver. I also decided that I would drive very carefully, being a responsible driver.

Besides the lumber company, I was willing to do any work that was available for me to do with my truck and my abilities. I didn't limit myself. When spring approached, I drove around looking for work, putting an ad in the newspaper. I gave my phone number out to people, seeking someone who was willing to hire me from hauling junk to yard work. I was willing to learn how to build fences if asked; even simple remodeling was not beyond my grasp to learn. I was hungry to succeed and prosper.

I hoped putting an ad in the paper would net me the best results. Just in case, I also wrote my phone number on pieces of paper and handed them out. I felt it would be effective. Cutting lawns on the weekends, working at the lumber company during the week, even a few jobs in between didn't bother me. I was still finding my way into my future.

Before long the phone rang, and mother picked up the receiver. The caller asked for me. Mother set down the receiver and said, "Robert, it's for you!"

I was excited to take the call. I believed that all my hard work had paid off, to have somebody call me to do more work was exactly what I was looking for. I picked up the phone from the counter where mother had laid it down. With anticipation and excitement in my voice I said, "Hello!"

The caller asked me, "Is this Robert?"

I said with enthusiasm, "YES it is!"

He said, "Can we have sex together?"

My heart started racing. Mother was in the room. How was I to answer this question, a question I didn't expect? I knew the answer deep inside of me, but I wasn't going to share it with him. He could have just as well said, 'I know who you are and I know what you've done.' Stunned silence echoed in my head albeit for a moment. He knocked on the door to my secret. My life hit pause. I knew what my feelings were to have a sexual relationship with the same sex as me, but I couldn't bring myself to say yes. My mind froze, replaying his question a hundred times in a blink. I felt so completely blindsided by his bluntness that I couldn't give him a thoughtful answer.

Time waits for no man. My heart pounded harder, louder, faster. I hadn't even uttered a single word. I could hear it in my ears. My chest fell into my stomach. Mother was in my peripheral vision. I felt she might detect any missteps on my part. My breathing had become audibly erratic, and my mind became awash of thoughts with this man's question. I consciously overrode my body's reaction to cover up my breathing patterns so as not to be detected by mother. This man had penetrated my secret, but mother couldn't know. This was too close a call, my feelings were too deep, and I was too vulnerable. I had to pass.

I said, with a shallow breath, "I don't do that!" and hung up the phone.

Mother said, "Was there anything wrong?"

I said, "No, everything's fine" in a calm outer voice. But everything was not fine with my inner voice or with my soul. I had suddenly stopped being the enthusiastic, success-driven young man who was focused on my valuable future and financial goals.

I needed my personality back.

I continued to calm my breathing down, but my heart was still pounding hard in my chest and my stomach was in turmoil. I had to settle down my reaction as I walked back to my bedroom. I felt my erratic breathing might be a red flag for mother to know something was wrong...or it could be the way I hung up the phone...or was it what I said, "I don't do that!" It could have been something as simple as that my countenance changed.

I had to be on guard. I knew if anything was out of place, mother would pay attention to it and be suspicious. The slightest misstep would be noticed by mother. I saw it too many times to be nonchalant about it. I had to protect my feelings, my life, and my soul. What else did I have control of but the privacy of my inner life?

I hid my secret life from mother, and now my innermost feelings were laid on the altar by this stranger. I wasn't willing to sacrifice my feelings because of this phone call. If there was one question I wouldn't want a man to ask me, it was this question. "Can we have sex together?" I continued walking at a normal pace back to my bedroom. I knew what I wanted to do deep down inside me, but I avoided verbalizing it. I decided to deny myself this experience. I wanted to be a mom so badly, nothing else mattered, and even a sexual experience with this man was not going to deter me.

I closed the bedroom door and laid on the top of my bed. My thoughts were as erratic as my breathing. I thought more about his question. I had a lot of reflecting to do.

I asked myself, 'was he someone I gave my number to, or was my number passed on to him?' I retraced my steps. 'What did I miss?' I wondered, 'what does he look like? What did I say that would lead him to believe I was interested, or did I just come across as being weak, vulnerable or easy prey?' I looked for patterns, but it was to no avail. The possibilities were endless. I couldn't identify his profile. I had nothing to go on. I couldn't find anything definitive, except to conclude it was somebody I gave my number to while looking for work.

I needed to get this thought out of my head about having sex with this guy. It was driving me crazy with thoughts I didn't want to act out on. I knew the only one way to move on from this moment was to masturbate. Masturbating always settled me down for the moment. It resettled my mind.

I couldn't masturbate in my room. It was the middle of the day and Walter could come through the room at any time, disrupting the moment by going to his bedroom. Mother could open the door. There was too much traffic through my bedroom that time of the day. My bedroom was not a safe place to take care of my needs that were pressing hard on my mind. I needed to find my space, my personal place, my privacy. I thought the basement would work. There was no traffic down there.

My lower bowels were in turmoil, my mind still able to reason, albeit not for long. My anticipation heightened. I felt it creep up into my stomach. I needed to touch my body. My body was in the location where it needed to be physically and mentally. I blanked out everything around me, setting aside all reasoning. I swallowed, feeling my Adam's apple raise then lower, saliva slid down my throat. My body delivered, allowing me to regain my consciousness, my focus, and my purpose in life. This was the only way I knew how to regain my innocence. Best of all, I did it without drugs or alcohol.

Almost as quickly as my Adam's Apple reappeared below my jawline, my consciousness was reset. I was freed from this moment at hand, resetting my thoughts back into this world like it was before all this started from this man penetrating my secret. In the aftermath, I was ready to move on with the enthusiasm and anticipation I gave myself, and I was looking forward to the next phone call from someone who wanted my abilities rather than my body.

If masturbating became my addiction, I was okay with it. The feeling my body gave me in that moment depicted the world I would have created if I was in charge, and for a brief moment I was. I was in charge of my world, a world that was painless, filled with beautiful bright colors and peaceful feelings at my core. In that heightened moment I recaptured a little of the emotions mother beat out of me from my childhood. The feelings my body gifted me never disappointed me. It always helped me reset my mind into consciousness, even if it was just for a moment. That feeling became a survival necessity, a reminder of how beautiful life was in my world. I gave myself a reason to live for tomorrow, my future, and to become a mom.

I kept an inventory of how I felt inside of me after I played with myself. I knew I wouldn't tell anybody about this phone call, or about my innermost desires. I reinstated my commitment to keep my feelings to myself, taking my feelings to my grave. I knew I had gay feelings deep down inside of me, but I stood steadfast on my decision not to act out on my desires. I needed to dissipate this thought away sooner than later and go back to business. This whole phone call episode had become a distraction for me to overcome. I needed to stay focused on becoming the person I needed to be. I had something to achieve in life. I was driven to become a millionaire, be important, build my world, and to become a mom.

Kevin and I continued working at the lumber company through the winter. I stayed in touch with my lawn accounts for springtime. I didn't know how much I would love lumber, and the building materials in general. I was allowed to drive the big forklifts, and found it challenging, exciting, and they were very powerful. I was never told of the legal age to drive a forklift, but I learned to be careful, sort of. I found out later that I was supposed to be 18, but nobody mentioned it. I moved big piles of lumber. I learned about bunks of wood, what stickers were used for, and I witnessed flies hibernating over winter in between the cracks of wood. The flies fascinated me with interest as much as anything else. I enjoyed the smell of freshly milled wood. The work was steady, and so was the paycheck. I didn't mind the $2.35 an hour as a return. After all, I wasn't planning on getting caught in a job working for somebody else for the rest of my life.

The owner's son Tom, eight years older than me, asked Kevin, "Is Robert on drugs? His eyes are always dilated. They're really big."

Kevin said to Tom, "No, I don't think so."

Tom said, "He's always laughing and smiling!"

Kevin said, "That's what he does all the time!"

Kevin told me about the conversation later, indicating he stuck up for me. But Kevin was right, I wasn't on drugs. I looked in the mirror when I got home, looking past the blue edges of my irises. Tom was right. My pupils were dilated and really big. And I always smiled. I decided to be a very happy boy the rest of my life.

Later on I asked Daddy, "Why are my pupils so big?"

Daddy replied, "It's to let the light in. Your pupils open and close according to the light you're in."

That interested me on how my body worked. I didn't know! He hadn't answered my question on why mine were big, bigger than normal, but I was satisfied with his answer.

After a few months working at the lumber company, Daddy shook me awake in the middle of the night. I was sound asleep. Before I could say anything, Daddy said, "The lumber company is on fire!" I jumped out of bed fully awake, walking quickly to the back windows of the house. The windows displayed the fire's orange glow. I said, "OH MY GOD!" I was surprised that those words came out of my mouth, but I said it.

We lived just three houses away, a few minutes walking distance from the lumber company. I was shocked by the intensity of what I was witnessing. The northern skyline was illuminated with an orange glow like the drama of a sunset, shocking my sight. I heard the sirens of multiple fire trucks in the distance approaching. I had never taken in such a display before in person! Exhausting my view, I went back to bed, wondering if I had a job tomorrow.

Within a day or two, after my emotions settled down, I helped the owner Henry clean up the best I could. I moved lumber that survived the fire using big forklifts. I learned to drive quite well, so I thought. I moved bunks of lumber to a different location adjoining the lumber company.

I drove the forklift into the road, carrying long lumber. Seeing that there was no traffic I dashed out into the road with haste, making a U-turn into the lot to place the lumber. Not calculating the length of the lumber I hit a telephone pole, spinning the lumber off of the forks. I watched helplessly, seeing how I missed calculating my load. The wood came crashing down with a loud noise to the ground, flattening a mailbox in its path.

The dust settled quickly as splinters and fragments of wood scattered everywhere. I looked closely to be sure I didn't crack it. The telephone pole stayed intact. I got scared for a moment hoping nobody saw me, but was even more relieved nobody was walking along the sidewalk when it came crashing down. I hurried and cleared the lumber up from the side of the road. I learned I needed to avoid hasty moments with better calculations. That aside, I had no other accidents. I really liked helping out. But after a couple of weeks, Henry put his arm around me and said, "I would feel bad if I couldn't pay my bills. I need to let you go."

I'd never been fired from a job before. I teared up a little, but I understood. I appreciated the opportunity to work for the lumber company as long as I did, even if it was only about 3 months.

Part of what I missed about the lumber company was I learned how to be a thief. I stole doors, very nice doors, tools, spray equipment, and anything that caught my attention. It became a game, a challenge to me. I disguised my truck as if it was full of debris, lowering the tailgate, so that a void underneath the debris was exposed. I slipped doors and tools underneath and drove away, leaving without question.

Almost no one suspected my ill-gotten gains, except George, the accountant. He was suspicious. As I sat at the contractor counter, I heard George ask the owner Henry faintly from where I was sitting, "Where's Robert getting all these doors from?" I had good hearing like mother. Beyond hearing George's question to Henry, I was never approached.

I had an accomplice inside the door shop. I paid him to help acquire doors and tools for me. I put an ad in the paper selling beautifully finished doors. I sold a few, but it was a lot of work, and I wasn't really making any money for the amount of effort I was putting in. The fire stopped the flow of doors and other ill-gotten gains to me. It was more of a game than a necessity. Stealing the teacher's math book, changing price tags at Grand Central, even stealing $10 out of mother's purse. Stealing was really easy, kind of like the neighbor's dog. It was more of a game about beating the system than anything else. I was become quite proficient at stealing.

This went on until one day I had a change of heart. One of my brothers was looking for something they couldn't find. Hermann said, "Ask Robert, he can get anything!" I pondered his question, wondering if this is how I wanted to live my life. Is that what I wanted to be known for? I felt more like an entrepreneur than a serial thief. I didn't think anybody had noticed. I was wrong. I knew the answer from my conscience deep inside my gut.

I kept a tally of what I stole from the lumber company inside my mind, adding up my acquired inventory. It approached $1,000. That was a lot of money in the 1970's. I tried to displace my guilt, thinking of other things. But the thought of what I stole played on my conscience like the screech of a violin in my ears. I didn't do anything to resolve my feelings or pay restitution for what I stole at the time. But I was thinking maybe I should. I pictured myself sitting in jail, with mother's words screeching across my mind, 'You have a brain and a conscience, use it!' I never justified stealing like mother and me stealing the neighbor's dog, but it still affected me in the back of my mind.

I bounced my head as hard and with fervor as I did every night, filling the need in my mind and body. Except this time it was more painful. I had a zit on the right side of my nose, by my nostril, and it hurt when I bounced my head on my pillow. I turned my head so the impact was on the left side of my face more than on the right side. Except that's not how I liked to bounce my head. I like bouncing my entire face, not one side of it only. I continued bouncing my face the best I could not to impact the zit. It just hurt less, but I kept bouncing. I kept thinking how wrong I was for stealing, but I didn't know what to do at the moment.

I processed as much information of the day as I could until I couldn't bounce any longer. Looking back, I know I needed to hear, "Ask Robert, he can get you anything." It made me look into the mirror of my behavior. Those words spun in my thoughts, even when I wasn't bouncing my head.

Bouncing my head became the catalyst to think outside my comfort zone. When I wasn't bouncing, I processed my body's feelings. My stomach talked to me regularly, like we had a dialogue with one another, but it was all with feelings. I pictured myself in a jail cell, bouncing my head on a foam pillow, suffocating from its expansion, wondering if I could be issued a feather pillow. I thought about how my bouncing would annoy my cellmate, shaking the bed. I imagined that the sound of me bouncing my head would also be irritating. I thought of him saying, "Cut it out!" I came up with no positive conclusion to a life of stealing, no viable results! I didn't want to go to jail. I didn't want to live this lifestyle.

I let the thought and feeling sink in my brain as a remembrance. I had stolen from somebody who trusted me. I was scared to tell the owner, believing I would go to jail. I remembered a story mother had told me. I had asked mother in my youth, "If I go to jail will I get APPLE BUTTER?" Mother said, "NO, all you get is bread and water. NO apple butter!" I wasn't ready to resolve the issue by admitting what I had done, except to stop stealing. I liked apple butter too much. I didn't want to go to jail.

Stealing from the lumber company played on my mind for the next twenty years. Finally, I sat down with them. By that time, the owner was retired so I met with Tom, the owner's son, and his brother Dave. I told them what happened. They said, "Let's get this straight. When you were 16 working for us, you stole $1000 of stuff."

I said, "Yes."

There was a long pause.

I didn't know if they would ask me to pay 20 years of interest. Maybe they would call the police.

It was none of the above.

They said, "Pay it to charity."

Their words reached deep into my soul. It led me to be more forgiving of others, never holding things against others the way that I had held myself hostage to this act so many years before.

Fired from the lumber company, I decided to get another job at a different lumber company until spring arrived.

The phone rang. Mother answered. "Robert, the phone is for you!"

I hustled to the phone. I didn't want to keep the party waiting. I picked up the receiver, saying enthusiastically, "HELLO!"

There was a man on the line. "Is this Robert?"

I replied, "Yes it is."

He said, "I would like to have sex with you."

I was stunned that it was happening a second time. I said, "I don't do that!" I hung up the phone and quickly went back to my bedroom.

My mind raced. This was the second time this man had called me. Who was this? All the thoughts that I had from the first time flooded my mind. My feelings screamed at me inside my body. My mind scrambled to process every thought I allowed myself to think. I couldn't put the voice to a name, nor could I avoid the thought of a relationship. A coup of emotions took over my body. I needed my mind back in control, not my body in control of my mind. Why did this phone call unravel my mind so quickly? Maybe it was so personal? I couldn't dismiss anything I was feeling or thinking. I liked all the thoughts, returning to safe ground and telling myself, 'NO sex with a man. I need to be a mom!' I had spent years raising my children inside my head, leaving me no doubt inside my mind that I could integrate this into reality. I didn't know I was literally integrating my future by bouncing my head on my pillow. This process was so natural for me. I never doubted I would achieve this decision, or any other decision, one day in the future.

I needed to remove the sexual feelings from my mind, not understanding I was bouncing them into me. I was so consumed with these feelings about the same sex, I didn't want to lose control of my destiny. I knew what I needed to do to get my mind back in control of my body. I would only take a moment after finding my personal space. I wondered how much of this was a sense of competition about the size of my penis? Or was it just curiosity about being with the same sex? Or was it my traumatic upbringing? What was going on inside my mind, why was I so distracted?

What was bouncing inside my mind when I bounced my head on my pillow? What wasn't I willing to admit? I became consumed with touching my body for now. I needed my body's reaction to let go of this thought of having sex with my same gender. A cooperative effort was underway, a natural reaction, and a simple fix with a synergistic effect. I needed to think and feel something different and move on from what I was thinking and feeling in the moment, returning my mind back into control, so I could think about other things.

As I did every night I laid on my bed, on my stomach, my left hand clasping my right wrist, and started bouncing. I bounced my head, processing the information of the day. I stopped, face down a little to the side. I opened a pocket in my pillow with my chin to breathe, holding still for a moment. I regrouped my thoughts, listening to my breath hit my pillow, and listening to the beat of my heart. Then I resumed bouncing my head. It felt so good. I focused for a moment on the muscles in my neck, feeling their strength to lift the weight of my head up and down, feeling the energy of a straight back and the curve down my spine. I bounced with synergetic energy with my soul, a fulfillment that only bouncing my head could give me. I didn't understand there were many layers of thinking. There were the conscious events of the day, and thoughts I hid.

The 1950 Chevy pickup truck I had purchased was an old man's vehicle. The truck had style. It was classic. It fortified my persona, a part of who I was inside. It represented a simple, even simplistic life.

My 30-year-old truck gave me the opportunity to learn simple mechanics. I didn't enjoy working on cars, but I thought I needed to learn how to work on vehicles in case I broke down. I needed to know how to fix problems. My old 1950 Chevy pickup truck was the perfect vehicle to learn on.

I forced myself to become familiar with the vehicle's operation. On one occasion, it was the end of a snowstorm, and the streets were slushy and cold. It was a cold where there was a blue hue blanketing the light. Driving down the road in the late afternoon, my truck suddenly stopped working. The fear of being abandoned gripped my stomach, because I didn't have any heat in the truck to keep me warm.

I became petrified with the thought of freezing. I had a jacket but not enough to keep me warm for long. With my truck dead on the side of the road and no heat, I needed to find help soon. I walked to a payphone and called home. Mother answered.

In an anxious voice I said to mother, "Mommy! I need help. My truck is stranded on the side of the road and I'm cold!" By her insistence, I still called her 'Mommy.' It pains me to think of it now, but the fact remains.

Mother said, "I just got off work and I'm tired. I want to lay on the couch and rest!"

"But mom, I need your help!"

Click!

I was stunned that mother had hung up on me.

I really needed her help. Daddy was still at work. Besides, I didn't know Daddy's work number. I had to figure this out for myself. I walked back to the truck. I reached into the engine compartment, trying to identify what the problem was. My fingers were so cold they had lost all feeling.

My brain didn't communicate to my fingers on the exhaust manifold until it was too late. The damage was done. My fingers were burnt from the hot engine. I had no options left. I focused on understanding what the problem was, putting my fingers in snow to slow down the burn. Through elementary deduction I figured out what the problem was. I got my truck started, but I abandoned my intended destination, driving home instead.

Mother was asleep on the couch.

Three months later the phone rang again. I was closest to the phone, so I picked up the receiver. "Hello."

"Is this Robert?" the caller asked.

"Yes," I said shyly.

The caller said, "I want to have sex with you! I'd like to ask you some questions!"

"No!" I said, and hung up the phone.

This was the third time he called. My mind raced. Who is this? How does he know me? Why is he so persistent? The calls brought back a flood of discordant feelings for me. I wanted it, but I didn't want it. The feelings overwhelmed me, taking me away from my goals, even my sense of self. I had to let go of these thoughts no matter what.

With the lumber store burned to the ground, I applied at another lumber company. I really liked working with wood. They had a different system than the previous employer. They seemed more curt, less personable, even unfriendly. They were very strict with their employees and even the customers. They seemed to take a hard stance against the very people who were their lifeblood, both customers and employees alike. It didn't take long to realize this was the wrong employer for me.

One month after I began working for the new lumber company, I decided it was time to leave and build up my lawn business. I decided to let them know that I was leaving after that day's work.

I approached Greg, my manager. "This is my last day."

He was curt and abrupt as usual. He said, "Why didn't you give me a two week notice?!"

I said, "Two weeks after I just started, you would have fired me!"

"That's true," he said.

I left, pondering the strange interaction. 'That was a dumb question,' I said to myself.

I drove out of the parking lot and decided to give all my attention to my lawn business, never giving another thought to working for a lumber company. I never looked back and never questioned my decision.

Eventually that lumber company went out of business. With how they treated people, I wasn't surprised.

Three months passed. The phone rang.

Daddy answered.

The man on the other side of the phone asked, "Is Robert available?"

Daddy said, "One moment." He set the phone down and got my attention.

Before answering the phone I wondered, 'When I say hello, is this going to be that man again?'

I answered cautiously. "Hello, this is Robert."

He said, "Hel.."

I knew it was him. It only took a brief part of a second for me to hear his voice, and I knew what his question was going to be. This was the fourth time over the past year since he started calling me. The pattern was laid out in my head. He was calling me every three months, as if I was on his calendar to call quarterly.

He said, "I want to have sex with you!"

It had become a routine at this point.

I said, "NO!" and hung up the phone.

The feelings inside my stomach weighed heavy, like a basket of rocks. It was a feeling which wouldn't pass. I had to keep telling myself, 'no! I can't engage, no, I can't do it, no, I can't have sex with a man, I've got to get these thoughts out of my head.' It was a relentless struggle of feelings inside my body. My mind wouldn't let go, and the thoughts wouldn't subside except for when I played with myself. Then my feelings would dissipate for the moment. The relief in my body allowed me to think about the other things I needed to think about.

291

I reminded myself over and over, 'I want to be a mom.' That could only happen if I stayed away from these other feelings and desires that seemed to distract me relentlessly. They became embedded in me. I couldn't displace my desire to be a mom anymore than I could displace my sexual desires to be with a man. My mind bombarded me with both thoughts simultaneously. I could only control my actions at the moment, keeping my thoughts focused on being a mom.

On another occasion, I walked into the house, passing through the living room into the kitchen, and a tabloid on the table caught my attention. I recognized the picture of the actor on the front cover. I couldn't read the headline above his picture. "I Q..., I QW, I QU-OT?" I tried to sound it out without drawing attention to my curiosity to read easily.

Both mother and Daddy were in the kitchen. I knew if I asked mother she would say something negative, so I asked Daddy. "What is this word?"

Daddy said, "You don't know what that word is?"

I said, "No."

Daddy's statement caught mother's attention.

"Let me see!" mother said. Mother looked at the word and bellowed out, "I QUIT!" She added with disgust, "CAN'T YOU SOUND IT OUT? Don't they teach you phonics in school?"

I replied, "I don't know what phonics is."

Mother said, "Oh for Pete's sake!"

I learned two new words that day: phonics and quit, but I only learned how to spell quit. The word phonics was beyond my comprehension, let alone how to spell it correctly! The process of phonics that mother explained, 'sounding it out,' was something I could not do in even the best of circumstances. It didn't stick with me. At the time, I avoided reading all together. It was too frustrating.

Three months after the last phone call from a man wanting to have sex with me, I received another phone call. Was it the same man? I didn't know. I could only assume so. He was relentless in calling me. I answered the call, feeling the same way as I did the first time he called me. I continued telling him I wasn't interested, followed by hanging up the phone. My body reacted the same after each call. My heart beat faster, I drew in short shallow breaths, and a feeling of butterflies overtook my stomach. My imagination engulfed me. I learned to rely on my body to save my mind. I separated the two with ease as my body was consistent for me to rely on as it had done so many years ago.

I liked these feelings but they were mixed emotions. I had to displace them. I had to let go of my thoughts to think about my future. I was planning to become a mom. That was somebody important. I told myself, 'I am going to succeed at something. I am going to be a millionaire by the time I'm 25. I am going to do something to make me feel accomplished!' These achievements would make me important. I needed above all to displace mother's words in my head that I wasn't important.

High school was little different to me than grade school when it came to learning, except nobody suggested I attend special ed, and that was okay with me. I didn't want to be teased. I talked to my peers like I had everything together. I taught myself what I needed to learn for me to advance in my life. I became a student of 'their system,' only to graduate with decent passing grades so that I could get a high school diploma.

Beating their system wasn't hard. I didn't place a lot of value in how I was taught from the school system. I'm sure there was value there. It just wasn't for me with what went on in my head. I enjoyed the social part of school, laughing and having fun with my school friends, staying away from the mean kids so as not to get into a fight.

The military kept sending me notices to enlist in the US Army upon graduating. Mother's stance on the military left me with no interest in being in the service. She always said the military did nothing but train boys to be killers. I thought, 'I don't want to become a 'trained killer.' I called up the number on the advertising papers and asked that my name be taken off their mailing list.

The sergeant who took my phone call said, "Okay, what is your name?"

I told him my name.

"What is your address?"

I told him my address.

He said okay, "I'll put you on the subversive list!"

That didn't sound good.

I asked, "What is the subversive list?"

The sergeant said, "If we ever break out into war, you will be the first on the list to go!"

I said, "Oh, why don't you put me back on the other list, and keep sending me information about enlisting then?"

He said, "I won't take you off that list unless you come in and talk to me about it."

I said, "Okay, what is your address?"

He told me. I showed up at the scheduled time.

Upon arrival I met the sergeant.

He said, "It is un-American not to participate in the US military. Hundreds of thousands of people have died protecting your freedom."

I thought to myself, 'I can't argue with what he just said to me. He is correct.'

He said, "I suggest you read a book to help you understand what freedom is all about."

He gave me the title of the book. He said, "You probably won't read it anyway."

I forgot the title by the time he said that. I didn't know how to read anyway. I told the sergeant, "I am a patriotic American. I own a Chevy truck, I like apple pie and motherhood!"

He laughed.

We left on good terms, and I had a new respect for what I didn't understand before.

Congress was talking about reinstituting the draft. Daddy told me that if I went to college, I would be less likely to be one of the first people drafted if war broke out. I took his advice seriously and processed it. I didn't want to be drafted. Daddy told me to look into a trade school. I knew I wanted to become a carpenter. I had been studying construction. It would seem a natural fit for me to get a degree in what I liked to do, and possibly I wouldn't be drafted if it came down to it. But I needed to finish high school first, so there were many months before I needed to make that decision.

Three months later, I received another phone call from the man, just like before. Always towards evening or night time.

Again I answered, "No!" and hung up the phone. Just like before my body tingled in my lower bowels. I swallowed hard, thinking of what was coming next. I knew where my mind was taking me. I felt it in my stomach. My mind cleared itself of all other content. Another swallow, my body began to swell. I started removing my clothes, first my shirt then the rest, catching an escaped drool, slurring it back in my mouth, my saliva slammed against my teeth. I had to swallow quickly or the drool would overflow. I looked down and saw my naked body from above, filling my mind with anticipation.

I was Pavlov's dog.

I breathed heavily with anticipation, hearing each breath enter, then exit. I couldn't change the outcome. I knew where I was heading. It was only afterwards when my body settled down, my restless soul went into remission, and I was about to fall asleep, that my mind was at ease. I felt like I got my mind back in control. I didn't know who the caller was, but he affected my mind each time he called. I didn't know why that phone call was a standing order with me. Why did he keep calling back again and again? I couldn't figure it out. I had no information to go on unless I accepted his offer, and I didn't plan to accept. I had to let my thoughts go in order to fall asleep.

One Saturday I arrived to help my friend and classmate Bruce with his job at the drive-in. I helped Bruce clean up his place of employment, the drive-in theater. I usually helped Bruce and another friend John on the weekends, cleaning the theater grounds. Friday and Saturday nights were a popular time at the drive-in theater and people left quite a mess behind.

I was five minutes late to meet him at his house. I arrived to find a note taped to the door. It read, "Dear Meathead: ...." The note was for me. I took the note off the door and saved it, but I didn't know what a meathead was. I'd heard it on a sitcom, so I knew it didn't have a positive connotation, but I wanted to look up what it actually meant.

I liked helping Bruce pick up the garbage people left behind. I felt I was restoring order. Some of the items people left behind made me wonder if they even watched the movie in the first place. I learned that the winter cold never froze sperm left behind in condoms which were thrown out the window.

Everything had to be cleaned up by 10 a.m. for the swap meet. It was Bruce's responsibility to clean the grounds before the swap meet opened. The swap meets were held each Saturday and Sunday. It was a big event. The swap meet fascinated me. I saw people bring their wares, displaying them for sale. There were people everywhere, engaging in commerce and having a joyful time. I'd been collecting property from people who just wanted to get rid of stuff. It was one of my odd jobs. I thought maybe I could sell the stuff and collect a profit since it didn't cost me anything. I liked my idea.

The phone rang. It was the man with the same question. I had the same answer for him and hung up. I felt the power of energy inside my body, engaging my heart, mind and soul with the thoughts of anticipation. I breathed life into my soul.

It wasn't uncommon for me to enter the house to hear mother on the phone. Mother regularly vacillated in conversation from German to English, then English to German, in the same conversation. Mother's use of English made it easier for me to understand the conversation, especially with the tones of her voice. On one occasion, I entered the room to hear her say, in very clear English and with passion, enunciating the 'P,' "WHAT A PIG!"

Mother ended the phone call shortly thereafter.

I asked mother, "What was that all about?"

Mother was still disgusted and steaming from the phone call she just ended. She said, "Garrett is such a pig! He wanted to have sex with Hilda while she was still on her period. I hope she kicked the bastard in the balls!"

Mother painted a clear picture for me. I'd never been kicked in the balls before, but I remembered when I threw my toy car at my brother, hitting him there. Seeing the pain on his face and how his body reacted to the direct hit seemed relatable to me. I'd been hit there before, just not kicked. I understood the pain that he might encounter if Hilda took mother's advice. It wasn't a pleasant thought. I didn't know mother's friend well enough to ask him if it happened. But mother's picture was painted in my head. I felt squeamish thinking about it.

I felt like I could accomplish anything I set my mind to do, and I did so with unbridled energy. I thought about sex almost constantly, and I used that to propel myself as well. I bounced my head for what may have been hours, but it didn't matter. It felt too good to stop! I reviewed what I would do the next day, what I would accomplish, and what I would someday have, all in the active recesses of my imagination. I channeled the energy of this anticipation from the mental realm into my physical body. I felt there was no end to my energy. My imagination and my thoughts fueled me.

Sometimes I had to stop bouncing in order to process what was going on in my imagination. I couldn't stop what I was feeling so my heart still raced and my breath came fast. I needed to reset my body, letting go of my pent-up energy and giving my mind a rest. Like a bolt of lightning releases energy from an over-boiled atmosphere, I reset my thoughts through my body's natural desire to ejaculate. There was too much energy inside of me not to address.

Since I was ten years old, my decision had been to pay attention to each one of my thoughts. From time to time, this left me to wonder, why was I thinking what I was thinking? What triggered me to feel the way I feel? I didn't have an answer to my questions. I just processed the information, even though I didn't come up with an answer at the moment. Sometimes I wondered what would happen if I acted on my impulses. I wondered what would happen if I engaged in a same-sex relationship. Would I lose my energy's edge? Or would I increase it?

I was too afraid to find out. Mainly, I was afraid that acting on that impulse would change my mental dynamics. More importantly, I thought it would make it impossible for me to be a mom.

I learned through touching myself that participation was a completely different feeling than anticipation. I paid attention to my feelings afterwards. My countenance always seemed to change in me from night to day. I wondered if by participating in a same-sex relationship, would I feel guilty, remorse, or worse, would mother's words haunt me? 'You have a brain and a conscience, use it.' I had to stay focused. I didn't process or question this desire–it was a given.

I had a lot to comprehend, a lot to protect. I bounced my head each night, thinking these thoughts and more that spun in my head.

Helping Bruce clean the swap meet made me think that selling there could be profitable. I felt a connection with very old handcrafted pieces. I placed an ad in the local newspaper, requesting to buy antiques. I thought I could start a business reselling them at the swap meet. I already had a collection of other people's stuff from hauling away their unwanted items, so why not increase my options? I felt a spiritual connection with older people and their one-of-a-kind items, connecting with their craftmanship. Each craftsman had built it by the soul of his hands. I saw the effort and time put into it, and it meant everything to me. My perception was my reality, and antiques brought peace to my soul. It was a feeling of simpler times, and I experienced a glimpse of those moments by just touching the work. It seemed like I became infused with his spirit into my being by just simply touching it. This spirit connection erased the gap of time between then and now.

In exploring the antiques, I had to dismiss mother's stern words, 'look with your eyes and not with your hands,' feeling what mother forbid me to touch. Touching was a connection which I was denied.

I needed to experience that spiritual connection with each antique, mostly by touching it. If I could not, I simply dismissed that it was just old and gave it little value. I didn't gravitate to every piece, even if I could sell it for a profit. I needed a peaceful environment to stay connected with myself, and each piece either facilitated that sense of peace or it didn't.

I felt the same was true of the old Germans I sat listening to around the table at mother's house.

Remembering so many of their stories gave me an invaluable connection to their souls. It seemed like they gave up everything to come to America from the Fatherland. They were people who had given up so much to be here and had gained so much in making that decision to leave, unclear of their fate. They pushed forward. Many of them had overcome insurmountable obstacles during World War II, and it was difficult for me to even comprehend. They had chosen a different path, an unknown path, to come to a different country, regardless of what the consequences were. Whether I was conscious of it or not, I related to them. They pushed through difficulties and I would too. The old Germans who overcame insurmountable obstacles, like Daddy leaving Germany, were like those intricately crafted antiques. It was as if we were cut from the same cloth.

A man answered the ad I put in the paper looking for antiques, calling me up. He said, "I have some antiques for sale."

I asked, "Could I come right now?"

He said, "Yes, you can."

I told him, "I'll be right there."

He gave me his address. I hopped in mother's car and drove to his house. My imagination had no end to the possibilities of what he owned, and what he might be willing to sell to me that I could afford. I dropped everything to meet him.

I rang the doorbell. The old man answered the door. He was nearly bald, and his eyes bulged like a catfish out of water. There were red rings around both eyes. He didn't look really healthy to me, but he was old and I only went there to look at his antiques, not to determine his health. I didn't care what he looked like anyway. I came to see the antiques.

"They're in my basement," he said, showing me the direction. I started walking down the flight of stairs slowly at first. He followed behind me hanging onto the handrail, I picked up speed as I approached the bottom of the stairs. With anticipation coursing through my veins, I reached the basement floor. I quickly surveyed the contents of the area. He was right. He had antiques all over the place. They were on the floor, on the table, on the walls, scattered everywhere. It was one antique on top of another. They were beautiful and available for me to purchase. I only had two hundred dollars on me. I hoped I could afford at least one thing.

I spotted the most beautiful mirror I'd ever seen. An intricately carved frame with columns coming from an ornate pedestal holding up a bold arch above the mirror caught my attention. It was chest high, adorned with intricate carvings, and had a dark stain giving it an appeal that was elegant, beautiful, and heartwarming. The mirror itself seemed the most insignificant part of this art piece. It looked Victorian, at least that's what it appeared to me. As I looked closer I could tell by the reflection of the backing behind the glass, it was very old.

I asked the old man, "How much for the mirror?"

He said, "$100."

I told him, "I'll buy it!" I imagined hanging it on the west wall of my bedroom, at the foot of my bed. The mirror was so beautiful, so ornate, so gorgeous. I felt good about it. I easily pictured myself looking into the mirror. I pulled out my wallet from my waist band since my gym shorts didn't have pockets. I found a $100 bill to give to him. He came towards me to accept the money. I was so excited. He took the $100 bill with his left hand then grabbed me on my crotch, groping me. He asked, "Have you ever gayed?"

I never heard that term before, but I knew what he meant. I swept his hand away with my right hand saying, "No, I don't do that." The endless phone calls soliciting sex passed my mind, and now this old man. My heart raced with short breaths. This is not what I was expecting.

I decided to leave immediately, losing interest in sticking around. I glanced at the rest of the antiques I knew I would never see again. Picking up the mirror, I took it up the stairs and put it in the car, and I drove home. On the way home, I thought about the mirror and how beautiful it was going to be on the wall of my bedroom, giving little thought to the man groping me at the moment.

I was excited to place the mirror on the wall in my bedroom where I was envisioning it would go. It couldn't come soon enough. I could hardly contain my excitement. I set the mirror against the wall on the floor to go find a hammer and a big nail in the garage. I dripped with enthusiasm and excitement, looking for the tools I needed. Locating a hammer and a nail I hung the mirror firmly to the wall. I adjusted the tilt and stared at the workmanship of the frame, absorbing the beauty into my soul, feeling the craftsmanship within. It was beautiful.

Stepping back a few feet to look into the mirror, I realized the mirror had lost its luster. It fell out of favor with my mind, seeing something different then I had seen before in its reflection. I saw the old man's hand on my red gym shorts grabbing me. The ornate beauty melted away as I couldn't dismiss what he did from my mind. The feeling I once had for the beauty of the craftsmanship melted away. I couldn't dismiss the thought. I called him back up and asked him, "Could I return the mirror?"

He promptly said, "NO, I won't give you back your money. You turned me down!" He hung up the phone. A short moment of emptiness filled the void of my mind as to what to do.

I went back into my bedroom, looking at the mirror hanging firmly on the wall, and stared at its deep dark beautiful ornate carvings, one last time. I removed the artwork from off the nail that moments earlier I was excited to pound in place. I turned it around, setting it on the floor, and leaned it against the wall, and took my hands off of the frame. The back of the mirror which once offered no intrinsic beauty to me was now more beautiful than the front of the mirror. It was all too close to home. The craftsmanship took on a different meaning to me. My calmness dissipated into disappointment. Since I couldn't return it, I decided to have a yard sale and sell it. The mirror was the first item sold. I reclaimed my hundred dollars. I knew it was worth more monetarily, but I had peace of mind, and that was worth more to me, and now I was able to move on in my head.

The last day of high school, I decided to attend the senior dance. I had successfully avoided every dance the school offered since 7th grade. To make this conscientious effort to do something different was uncomfortable, sending a pit to my stomach. The DJ played one disco hit after another. I saw dancing as an expression of the soul, but I couldn't wrap my mind around it. I enjoyed watching everybody else on the dance floor moving around, especially the guys. The boys were a beautiful sight to me. Slow dances spurred my imagination, but I was too scared, and very uncomfortable to draw myself so close to the opposite sex. To add to my avoidance, I feared stepping on my partner's feet. Doing so would only add to my inadequacies of the experience.

In my hesitation to ask anybody to dance, I found myself holding up the wall more comfortably. Like prying ice off the frozen tundra, I pushed myself off the wall to ask a classmate I recognized, a girl named Becky. Becky stood near the wall where I leaned. I hadn't built up a relationship with her over the last year because I had no interest in girls. I stared into the crowd of people dancing on the floor as they wiggled and jiggled. I was inspired by their courage. I turned my head towards Becky, figuring I could muster up the courage and ask her if she wanted to dance. If I could start with small talk first, I could lead into a more serious question, like asking her to dance. I could only hope she would turn me down, signaling to my mind I made a half-hearted effort.

I energetically engaged Becky with small talk like, "Hi, how are you?' I didn't remember her answer. I was too nervous to think clearly. I knew I needed to find the courage to ask her a word I didn't want to ask. She told me she was waiting for a boyfriend who was in the military to come home. Becky indicated she hoped to marry him one day. I took her comment as a hint that she wasn't interested in dancing with me. It didn't take much to discourage me since I wasn't interested anyway. I spared the words that I thought of asking her from ever passing the lips of my mouth.

I took that as a hint, never mustering up the courage to say a word about dancing. I excused myself, leaving the dance to go home. Night time had ascended and I drove away. As I drove away I thought, 'That's it? That was my grand departure from 13 years of school?' The further I drove away the more I thought, 'where is your courage?' I drove back, returning to the dance floor to ask Becky if she wanted to dance. I searched the floor and couldn't find her anywhere, figuring she must have left after I did. It was too little too late of a half-hearted effort. I left for the second time to drive home.

The end of the day was approaching, and I was still filled with the desire to do something grand. Instead of turning west toward home, I turned east to find adventure. I drove down a road I'd never driven down before. The lights on my truck illuminated a tall freestanding chimney amongst large piles of rubble. There were bricks everywhere. Later I was told it was where they used to make bricks. It became known as the old brickyard. Staring out of the driver side window, I was in awe of what I saw. I thought, 'this chimney must be about 150, maybe 200 feet tall.' Climbing that structure was exactly what I would consider a grand exit from 13 years of schooling.

The moon and some street light in the background illuminated the surrounding area enough to make this obelisk-like structure appear to be an easy climb. One inch pipes were banded around the chimney like rungs on a ladder to help hold it together. It seemed pretty straightforward: all I had to do was climb from one band to the next. The pipes banding the chimney together appear to be about three feet apart. This seemed very doable to me. Besides, the rubble of the old brickyard was the perfect setting. There was a lot of rubble from buildings that had been torn down at the site. It was scattered in piles ready to be cleaned up. I wondered if they were going to tear down this structure, too. I thought, 'I'll climb it before they do.' I parked my truck a very short distance away from the base of the chimney. I got out, assessing the area to make sure there were no workers nearby. It was quiet. The workers had all gone home for the day. There was nobody to stop me, nobody to question me, and nobody to call the police. If I fell to the ground, I wouldn't be found until the next work day. This adventure was exactly what I was looking for as a grand exit to my school years. Climbing this chimney would be my present to myself. I assessed the structure and decided I could do this, I could climb this chimney on the south side. And to top it off I would spray my initials RB and the date 79 under the rim of the chimney.

My anticipation to climb grew. I located a can of black spray paint in my truck, stretching my back pocket to fit the can in my pants. I walked over to the base of the chimney and grabbed onto the first bar. I shook it. It seemed firm to me. A little feeling of nervousness was felt in my stomach. But I didn't want to focus on the fear that would cause me to change my mind. I needed to focus on climbing the chimney. Grasping the next bar as I scaled upward, it seemed to be a little further distance than the last rung around the chimney, but not beyond my reach. I climbed bar by bar. I looked down only to gauge my distance every so often, then looking up to see how much further I had to go.

I didn't hesitate; I kept climbing. I realized some of the bars were closer and some were further apart. Some of them I could reach completely around the bar with my fingers, and others I could only partially reach my fingertips to my thumb. My knuckles scraped the brick when it was a tight fit. I quickly appreciated the ones that were the easiest to grasp. My shoes felt they had a firm fitting on each rung. My knees shook a little bit, but not enough to distract me. I knew I would need to pay close attention to the next rung, hoping I could get my fingers to touch my thumb. I did not let go of the last bar until I could reach and secure my grasp to the next rung. My breathing calmed down, standing on the rung I just scaled, letting out a small grunt as I lifted myself, free climbing to the next bar. Only looking down for a moment, kinking my head upward to the dark sky, seeing my destination in sight.

I successfully grasped the next bar, stepping up and exhaling a sigh of breath. I stayed focused. I grabbed onto each pipe, wondering if the next will be as strong and firm as the last bar. I thought in the back of my mind, 'I hope this is attached well and won't detach itself from my weight, and pull away from my exerting pressure it wasn't designed for.' With one last rung to climb, I reached my arm over the cap of the chimney. I was startled by the unexpected sound of a flock of pigeons taking flight. My grip loosened. I disturbed their roosting; they disturbed my nervousness. I told myself, 'Hang on! Don't let go!' I hung on tighter, giving a quick glance below me to the ground. I thought, 'that would have been a hard fall straight down.' I didn't expect pigeons could have been so lethal.

With my left leg over the top, I straddled the rim with one leg in and one leg out, facing the east. I scooted myself towards the center of the chimney. The rim was thick enough to sit on easily, but not comfortably. I looked down the center of the chimney only to see a pitch black hole. I could smell the residue of the burn that penetrated the brick from so many years of use, or that's what pigeon poop smells like. My whole body felt jittery sitting on the top of the chimney. The experience was as good as I hoped it would be, not knowing what it would be like until that moment. I looked over the surrounding area, surveying the grounds, thinking of the pigeons that scared me a moment ago. A store parking lot lit to the east. I pulled out the spray paint from my pocket, it was time to tag my initials, and the year. Spraying upside down, I sprayed, "R B 7 9." Wait a minute, 'I think I sprayed the nine backwards?' I looked closer, I did. I sprayed "7 P." This is going to look so sloppy I thought to myself. I painted over the seven and resprayed "7 9" correctly.

I dropped the spray paint can to the ground to make room in my pocket for a souvenir. I thought of taking two cement bricks that were loose, because they had a unique triangle shape to them. They could be identified specifically from off this landmark as proof I climbed the chimney, and not just a brick off the ground. They would become a memento to that specific day I graduated high school. Seeing how loose the bricks were on the top of the chimney I thought, 'This thing would fall down in an earthquake.' I lifted two cement pieces from off the edge and placed them in my back pocket the best I could to keep my hands free. I didn't want to drop the pieces thinking they may shatter on impact.

Swinging my left leg back over the side of the chimney to scale back down the same way I climbed up. After about an hour and a half I reached the ground from where I started, picking up the can of spray paint. I walked to my truck, placing the two cement pieces on the seat of my truck along with the can of paint in preparation to drive home. I turned around, and looked up to the rim of the chimney. There was enough light I could see where I tagged my name. I was satisfied with my grand exit, never thinking twice of the dance I missed. Even as I passed the school on the way home.

I never told mother or Daddy nor any of my family. I just kept it to myself. I brought in the two cement pieces that I had taken off the chimney, setting them on the floor next to my bed. I figured I would find a place to put them in the morning. I wanted to go to bed and sleep. I laid on my stomach and bounced my head with satisfaction. as I recounted the day's events. It had been a grand exit. I shuffled my pillow after a short time of bouncing, I turned my head to the side of my pillow, and fell asleep.

Mother and Daddy drove or often participated in a chartered bus to Wendover, Nevada. They loved the atmosphere of the gambling casinos. Mother loved to call the slot machines 'one-armed bandits,' saying, "Those one-arm bandits stole my money." The trip was just another excuse for mother to spend, a pastime she loved to do most, while Daddy liked to play cards and drink. This was Daddy's escape. The slot machines were one of mother's. They would be gone for the weekend.

I went to bed by 10:30 and fell asleep quickly after bouncing my head. Sound asleep, the phone rang and rang and rang and rang. I could hear the phone ring in the distance of my mind, but when you are asleep it has a different sound to it, a disturbing sound that says wake up! I didn't want to regain consciousness. But there was only one way for me to sleep. I knew I had to wake myself up to answer the phone, so I could go back to sleep. Aroused from my slumber, I made my way over to Daddy's phone in his bedroom. Since Daddy's bedroom was closest to my room, it was the fastest way to end the annoying ring.

Groggily I said, "Hello?"

A man's voice said. "Is this Robert?"

I replied, "Yes it is!" My mind sharpened quickly. I thought it might be the same man that had been calling for the last three years. If it was, I decided if he asked any questions, I would answer them this time. Now that I was 19 years old, I believed I could handle talking to him.

Short shallow breaths proceeded from my body. I was all too familiar with the response my mind gave my awakened body, though I felt more control of it this time.

Butterflies fluttered in my stomach. I knew the next question to come out of his mouth.

He said, "I have some questions I'd like to ask you!"

I knew it! I knew that was what he was going to say. He had asked me too many times before. I said, "Okay, what are your questions?" I wanted to see where this led me.

"How tall are you?"

I told him, "I'm six feet tall."

Daddy had a long cord on his phone. I strung the phone into my bedroom so that I could lay in my bed and answer his questions.

He asked, " What color is your hair?"

I replied, "Light brown."

"What is the color of your eyes?" he asked.

I said, "Blue."

"Do you have a mustache?"

"No," I said. I thought, 'I'm not old enough to grow one.'

"Do you have a beard?"

I thought I knew where this was going. I replied cordially, "No, I do not have a beard. I don't have any facial hair."

My heart beat quicker. I tried not to breathe heavily into the phone as he asked me his questions. If he was listening closely, he would notice I was breathing quickly, with short shallow breaths, almost in an air of anticipation.

His questions continued. "How much hair do you have on your chest: heavy, medium or light?"

I replied, "Light to none." I chuckled. I had no body hair. With the exception of underarm and pubic hair, I was essentially hairless. By now I was just having fun with his questions. I don't think he picked up on my humor.

"Do you have an innie or an outie?"

I had never thought about that before, other than mother had taught me not to play with my belly button so that it doesn't come out. I told him, "It is an innie."

I was pretty sure what the next question was going to be. I thought, 'is he really going to ask me what I think he's going to ask me? Am I going to answer his question if he does?'

He paused for a moment.

I knew he was hoping I would answer him.

Then, where the rubber meets the road, he asked me the million-dollar question. "What is the size of your penis?"

In dead silence, I pondered his question.

My breathing intensified with short shallow breaths. My mind sent goosebumps throughout my body thinking about his question. Should I answer him or not? After what seemed like eternity in my mind, I decided to answer his question, telling him the size of my penis. I knew the answer was a very private part of my body, but boys will be boys.

After telling him, he asked, "Do you want to get together?"

I said, "No." I expanded my answer, "I've been getting these phone calls since I was 16 years old, and now I'm 19. I've been getting them from you or somebody else, maybe someone is passing my phone number around for the last three years." I took a deep breath, and continued explaining, "I've been getting a call four times a year ever since I was 16. Every man has wanted to know the questions you just asked me. 'Do I want to have sex with them?' I usually hung up the phone, or I told them no, then hung up the phone!"

He said, "Let me get this straight, you've been getting this phone call four times a year from me or someone like me since you were 16 years old, and now you're 19, and you don't want to get together?"

I said, "That's correct. I don't want to get together, and I don't want to have sex with you."

He replied, "I'll never call you again!"

Without malice, anger, or frustration towards him I said, "Thank you."

We both hung up the phone simultaneously. True to his word, he never called me back.

Yet my imagination was in full bloom.

I took the phone back into Daddy's room, returning to my bed. I laid on my back thinking of the phone call. My secret was safe. I had kept my feelings of attraction and desires to myself. I thought about the conversation that had just transpired, and the years gone by since that first phone call started, and how I felt inside never letting go of my desire. I was glad I had answered his questions. I felt I was mature enough at 19 to handle whatever he was going to ask me, and I was.

My mind became engaged with thought rather than emotions. I didn't play with myself this time like previous times after the phone call. I let my emotions rest. I kept processing my thoughts, turning on my stomach to bounce my head, perching my body on my left elbow and turning my pillow lengthwise to place it under my abdomen the way I liked my pillow, making sure the open end of the pillow case was by my belly button.

Smoothing out the wrinkles on my pillow case, I laid my body down on the pillow, feeling the cool cover on my face as my head sank to the bottom of the feathers. I clasped my right wrist with my left hand and started bouncing my head with the energy the anticipation gave me. I felt I was on top of the world. I bounced my head with more fervor and intensity, like I was running the one mile race.

Pausing after an unknown amount of time, face down into my pillow, breathing hard, I listened to the beat of my heart pounding in my chest, feeling my lungs inhale then exhale. Feeling my blood coursing through my veins, I was pumped for life. Alive, feelings intact, my butterflies in formation, I dreamed dreams in the secret of my life. They expanded my energy even more. I stopped again, shuffling my pillow and smoothing out the wrinkles, and I began bouncing again. I finally started to wind down to fall asleep, exhausted. It must have been after midnight. I let go of the thoughts in my mind to dream however it wanted to dream, and I fell asleep.

CHAPTER TWENTY-FIVE

SHITEN SHINOLA

Daddy asked me to pick him up at the airport. I didn't expect anything out of the ordinary on the way home, but yet again I was propositioned.

It had become a part of life for me. I was constantly being solicited–not by girls but by boys. I was flattered and I liked it, but I resisted.

This time it happened while driving home, and it caught Daddy's attention.

In the car beside me two young men about my age were gesturing at me. At first I didn't think anything of it. They simply drove alongside me, nothing unusual. Then they were driving in a horseshoe pattern, moving from one side of my car to the other, then back to the other side. After the second time of moving in this pattern, it became obvious to me this was another solicitation. At this point they were on the passenger side of my car. I glanced in their direction.

Holding his hand at the front corner of the window, the driver held his thumb and index finger together like he was holding his penis. My heart started racing when I saw this gesture. My breathing became erratic with quick short shallow breaths. I tried to suppress them.

It seemed to me that this gesture meant, 'I want to hold your penis.' I wasn't taught what it meant, but I could tell what the sign was suggesting. Later I asked my friend John if my intuition was correct. He confirmed it was.

Daddy picked up on the difference in my breathing pattern. It was clearly an audible difference from one moment to the next.

Daddy asked, "What's going on?"

I replied to Daddy, "I don't know." I kept on driving, suppressing my heavy breathing.

Hoping to regulate my breathing pattern, I pushed his question out of my mind and changed the subject. I said, "I'm renting a spot for Saturday and Sunday, hoping to sell my stuff at the swap meet that I've been collecting."

Daddy said, "Good, I'm glad you're getting your collection out of my yard. It's too much at the house."

I thought I had hid it well so that it wasn't so obvious, but maybe not. I said, "I'll sell it."

After turning off the main street, the other car continued on. We made it home without further incident.

I followed through on what I told Daddy. I packed everything I wanted to sell into my old truck and drove it to the swap meet, laying out my wares at the designated area and hoping for sales.

One person after the next walked by.

Some asked, "Do you have any antiques you want to sell?"

I told them, "No, I collect them for myself." I thought of some of the antiques I started collecting years ago.

Waiting for people to come by for a purchase wasn't as boring as sitting with a fishing pole waiting for a fish, but it was close. I liked the interaction with people better than fishing.

A woman came by and picked up a bathroom rug. She turned it over scrutinizing the white coating on the underside. The coating was peeling off. She explained, "The rubber coating keeps the rug from sliding on the bathroom floor." She turned it back over and said, "No thank you." I didn't know the importance of the backing of a rug was to prevent it from sliding on the floor.

314

I remember in particular one man who came to my booth. He had wavy gray hair and a belly that looked like he was nine months pregnant. His face was twice my head, big lips, and huge pores all over his face. He also looked very strong. He was at least 30 years older than me. I assessed everybody I met. He asked, "How much do you want for that box of junk?"

I said, "$10."

He said, "It's not worth $10! I'll give you $5 for it, and that's still too high!"

I considered his offer. I had picked it up for free, so $5 was still $5, and it was more than I had before. I told him, "Okay."

The man said, "I have some stuff you might be interested in trading." He continued, "Do you need tires?"

I said, "I don't know. Can you look at my truck and tell me what you think?"

The man came over and looked at my truck tires.

He said, "They're wearing down pretty well. Winter's coming. You probably need some good tires on your truck!"

I remembered Daddy telling me that 'good tires and a clean windshield will go a long wayg.' Feeling I was a good driver and practiced safe driving habits, I asked, "How much are the tires?"

He said, "I can give you some tires for $20 a piece." That seemed a fair price. I noticed he didn't use the word 'sell.'

I didn't haggle with him.

He said, "My name is Dick Olsen. I have a store up the road on the north side of 33rd South. In big lettering it reads Olie's Tire Supply. You can't miss it. Come by after the swap meet is over and I'll trade you some tires." This time he didn't say $20.

I told him, "My name is Robert."

Dick handed me his address on a piece of paper and said, "I don't have a phone number. It's disconnected. Why don't you meet me up there at 3:00?"

I noticed the address was really close to where I had climbed the chimney. I said, "I'll drive up there after the swap meet is over."

Dick replied, "I'll be waiting for you."

I finished the swap meet with marginal sales, thinking about meeting the man I met. I was motivated to get tires in preparation ahead of the winter snow that was still months away. I didn't procrastinate. I followed up on what we agreed upon and met Dick at 3:00. I could remember his name because his name reminded me of a body part I didn't want to talk about to anyone. I knew Dick's real name was Richard and wondered why anyone would use the nickname Dick.

I met Dick at his store. The faded dirty white dilapidated storefront displayed a faded orange cracked sign that barely read, "Olie's Tire Supply." There were two bays for cars to enter. Neither looked like it had been opened in a long time. I asked him, "It doesn't look like you've been open for business for a while?"

He said, "I closed it down about a year ago, I'm selling the land. I've been in business for 30 years, and that was long enough."

He told me about his plans for the building. He wanted to salvage every timber on the roof, timbers he had put in place himself when he built the store 30 years earlier. He really liked the tire business. He told me everybody needed tires because a car can't run on three of them. He said if business ever got bad, he would just throw roofing nails up the road about a block from his shop. Dick laughed. As people's tires went flat, they would have to pull into his shop, and they'd thank him for his help. He laughed again.

I pictured him doing so in amazement, and wondered if he actually ever really did that. I asked, "So, did you throw nails up the road?"

He said, "No."

Dick laughed again, and so did I. I thought, 'I'm going to like this guy.'

Dick also engaged my mind with questions about my life. "Are you going to school?"

I replied, "Yes." I told Dick the details of trade school. I told him, "I'm learning to become a carpenter." I didn't elaborate with any details.

He said, "Why don't you come to my house. I thought I had tires here, but they must be at my home. You can have any tire store put them on the front of your truck." Dick continued, "Put them on as soon as possible. If you have a blowout driving down the road with your front tire, you can lose control of your truck."

Dick convinced me on that comment alone.

Dick continued, "The worst would be driving down the freeway when that happens!"

I thought, 'That's true, I don't want to lose control of my truck.' I thought more about what Dick said, picturing myself having a blowout while going down the road. I knew that would be very dangerous. I wanted to prevent a blowout because of a worn out tire. I said, "Okay, I'll meet you at your home." I asked, "Do you have any antiques?"

He said, "I do. I have two lamps you might be interested in. My sister married a Bamberger."

I said, "I don't know who that is."

Dick said, "Old man Bamberger started a railroad back in the day. They have money to burn!"

I pictured a big bonfire with them burning money to stay warm. I asked, "What is your address?"

Dick said, "Follow me. I don't live far away."

I followed him to his house. As I arrived I noticed Dick had a lot of stuff under his carport, to the side of his home. Dick invited me into his house, pointing to the lamps in the corner of the living room.

The lamps were as beautiful as I hoped they would be, cut crystal table lamps with no shades. He said, "I'll sell you both of them for $100."

I said, "I'll buy them!" I was excited to add them to my small collection.

Dick took the time to show me everything else he wanted to talk me into. I didn't have the money to buy everything Dick wanted to sell me, but trading was appealing.

After showing me everything in his collection inside his home, he eventually took me to his backyard where he had tires piled everywhere. He rummaged around, finding two tires he thought would fit my truck. Dick added, "They're not a match but that doesn't matter. The only thing you want to make sure is that you don't mix still belted tires with nylon. That will send you all over the road, and you'll lose control."

I didn't know that. It seemed like he had my best interest at hand. I paid him in full for the tires, and the lamps, and I excitedly put the tires into the back of my truck, along with the lamps in the front seat, and went home. I was excited not only because of the tires and the lamps but because I had a new friend, someone who engaged my mind, who took an interest in me.

I had gotten Dick's phone number to call him again, but I soon learned Dick's phone only worked when he felt motivated to pay his phone bill, which only seemed to be about 20% of the time. More often than not, I would simply drive over to visit him.

One day when I was ready to hop in my truck, mother asked, "Where are you going?"

I said, "I'm going to meet a man I met at the swap meet on Sunday a couple of weeks ago. I want you to meet him."

Mother said, "Drive carefully!"

When I arrived, he answered the door disheveled and seemingly just awakening.

He said, "Come in."

This time he had a dog inside his home.

He said, "I found this dog, it came to my house yesterday, he seemed hungry so I fed it."

I asked, "Did you name your dog?"

He said, "I hadn't really thought about it. Maybe I'll call him Perpy." Dick laughed.

'Perpy?' I thought. It sounded like herpes. I didn't think it was a very good name, but it wasn't my dog. I was used to a simple name like Fluffy.

He said, "Let me get dressed, and let's go get a cup of mud."

"What's a cup of mud?"

"Coffee!"

"Okay." I didn't drink coffee and had never heard that expression.

He turned to head up the stairs. He paused and said, "I gotta go see a man about a music lesson first."

I had no idea what he was talking about. Moments later, when I heard sounds emanating from his upstairs bathroom, I realized what he meant. It sounded like he had a bowel blowout.

I sat in his front room pretending I didn't hear what I just heard. It sounded disgusting. I thought of how my mother used to show me her long poops when I was a little boy. I pushed the memory and the sound out of my head as quickly as possible. I waited until he was ready to go.

His hair was combed, but he had a piece of toilet paper on the side of his face. I didn't want to say anything. I was too embarrassed. I didn't have to say anything anyway. He said, "I nicked myself shaving." I thought, 'I'm glad I don't shave.' I didn't have any hair to shave off anyway. He looked better than he did moments earlier when he looked more disheveled.

"Let's just go to JB's up the road."

We hopped in my truck and headed to the diner. Dick told me where to turn to make it to the restaurant.

On the way to the diner, I asked Dick, "How old are you?"

Dick answered, "I'm 48."

I calculated the math. Dick was 28 years older than me.

He told me he was divorced and had two sons. He said he had divorced their mother after she had an affair. Dick said, "My wife talked in her sleep,

319

and she said the man's name! That's how I found out she was having an affair."

He discovered the man was a police officer. He told me more of the story. He walked into the precinct one day asking to see the man. Once Dick found him, he walked up to the desk and confronted him. After talking to him for a moment, a very short moment, he lifted the desk up, turning it over on him, and walked out.

I was spellbound, thinking about what he just told me and what he did to the man. "What did they do to you?"

"Nothing, I just walked out."

I believed Dick. He was a strong man. Probably from moving tires all his life. I had no doubt he could do what he said he did.

He said, "Going through a divorce is harder than somebody close to you dying."

I said, "Why is that?"

He said, "When somebody dies it's over in a short time; a divorce can linger on for a very long time."

I said, "oh." I didn't know anybody who had gone through a divorce.

Dick said, "You might know one of my boys from when you were in high school?" He told me their names. The names seemed familiar. I was never acquainted with either one of them. I looked up their names in the yearbook, putting a face to their name. I remembered seeing them around. Their countenances always looked like they were ready to start a fight at any moment, so I had stayed away from them.

Making a deal always seemed to be the first order of business with Dick. In fact, he would try to make deals with me multiple times throughout any conversation.

I enjoyed our conversation at the diner counter.

When I got home I described Dick to mother, telling her about this man I met at the swap meet.

Mother asked, "Is he a Mormon?"

I said, "I don't know. He drinks coffee." I never thought to ask Dick if he was a Mormon or not. I didn't care.

It seemed to be one of mother's pet peeves that Mormons didn't drink coffee. What drinking coffee had to do with God, or religion, was beyond her understanding. Mother exhausted herself correlating the connection between the two.

I continued, describing Dick to mother. "He likes to do trades on everything. He owned a tire store up the road. It's closed now, and he was selling the land."

Mother seemed interested in what I was telling her. I told Mother what some of the things were that he wanted to trade.

Mother interjected, "He sounds like a wheeler dealer."

I hadn't heard the term before but it seemed fitting.

I replied, "Yeah."

I never gave it any thought. I had never felt I needed a father figure in my life. Daddy and I had a good relationship with one another. But then Daddy and I never played any kind of ball together, we never threw a frisbee back and forth, we never went camping or had deep conversations with the exception of Daddy telling me about his World War II experiences.

Daddy and some of us boys did go on hikes once in a while. We played checkers now and again, and he massaged my feet and shoulders on a somewhat regular basis, but that was pretty much the sum of our interactions together. Daddy was 48 years older than me, so maybe he was just tired. I was just glad as old as Daddy was, he was still alive when I was 19. I would sometimes ponder on age and the passage of time. Daddy was almost seventy yet in very good health. I became used to people who were older than me, learning from some people who seemed to have experienced the weathering of life. I also understood that sometimes older people are just that, older.

Daddy never engaged my mind verbally as much as he did with his touch. Later in life, he became an unofficial reflexologist. He knew all the parts of the foot and how they related to the rest of the body. He would practice reflexology on my feet, telling me all the connections in the body. It was fascinating to me. But Dick engaged me mentally in a different way, and I related to this way of interaction.

On one occasion Dick got his phone working, and he answered when I called.

Dick said, "Let's meet at JB's and talk over breakfast."

I said, "What time do you want to meet there?"

Dick said, "I'll meet you there at 8:30."

I said, "Okay." I had never been a person to sit at a restaurant talking over breakfast, telling each other what the day was going to look like. I just got up, ate, went to work, and moved the day along. Sitting and wasting time in a restaurant, spending money before the day even began, seemed like a bad idea to me.

Dick and I met at JB's at the time we agreed upon. The restaurant was completely full, with the exception of the counter. It was foreign to me, seeing so many people this early in the morning having breakfast. I wanted to get to know Dick, so I pushed back my feelings of awkwardness and uncomfortableness. I never thought Dick might proposition me sexually but in the back of my mind I wondered if he might try to seduce me at some point. I felt I was in a safe place mentally with Dick, but I was prepared from years of experience to change course if necessary.

I listened to Dick. He liked to dominate the conversation. He seemed to be a bit on the crass, even overbearing side, perhaps a bit like mother. I stared at his face as he talked, noticing all the imperfections he had like I did with my face. I had no attraction to Dick visually, nor did he address my visual needs in any way. However, Dick's presence invited a conversation inside my head that I couldn't identify. It was a different type of relationship

I needed that was forming. With a full restaurant, we were offered the last two seats at the counter. Shortly thereafter we ordered our food.

Dick asked, "How come you don't drink coffee?"

I said, "The last time I drank coffee I was about 12 years old. I added lots of cream and sugar to cover up the taste. My dad said to me, 'why bother drinking coffee if all you're doing is adding cream and sugar to cover up the taste?' My dad was right. Besides, I have a sweet tooth. I just never bothered drinking coffee again." I thought about Daddy and his coffee. Daddy liked his coffee straight black. I liked the smell of coffee in the morning air, but the taste was awful.

Dick never tried to convince me otherwise.

Sitting and waiting for the food to come out, the subject of religion came up. Dick asked, "What religion are you?"

I'd been taught by mother all my life about religion, sitting around the kitchen table, including hearing discussions with my brothers for years. Religion was a big part of mother's life, as long as you believed as mother did, that it was all lies. I paid attention. I believed as mother believed and taught. I said, "I don't believe in religion. I don't believe in God nor do I believe in Jesus Christ!" I was pleased with my answer I gave to Dick. I thought, 'next question.'

Dick paused, shifting his weight on the stool, took a slurp of coffee, as if he was in deep thought. He leaned in towards me, then leaned back in his seat. With a slight turn to the left, Dick set his cup of coffee down on the counter, sliding it a little further in from the edge. He leaned forward towards me again, then back square in his seat. It was as if he was mulling something over in his head, trying to figure out how to word what he was thinking.

I felt a little uncomfortable as he leaned towards me the third time.

He looked me square in the eye.

I looked back at him. I saw his oversized big head, bigger than ever.

323

I noticed the skin on his face had the smoothness of an orange peel. I had never noticed until he was so close. Bags adorned the bottom of his eyes which stood out like shriveled prunes. Every wrinkle and groove on Dick's face was amplified as Dick leaned in. I felt this was too close for my comfort. I entertained myself staring at his face, I couldn't pass up how Dick's lips protruded out as part of his face's composition, balancing his oversized head.

Every feature of his face was amplified, for my entertainment. I didn't know what he was going to say, if anything at all, but Dick was uncomfortably close. His face held little expression in the moment, as if he were processing an answer he was about to give me.

Surprised at the proximity of this person to me, I stared back without a blink of my eye, wondering what was next.

Was he going to give me a kiss?

Dick again gave a quick glance to his left, scooting his coffee even further from the edge of the counter, and he leaned his upper body weight on his arm towards me. He said, in a firm, succinct tone, "If you don't believe in Jesus Christ, I don't want anything to do with you!"

I was dumbfounded at his response and was completely thrown off guard. I had never seen mother lose a friend by telling people religion was all for the birds and that she didn't believe in any kind of a god. I didn't want to lose Dick's friendship. I felt I needed to salvage the relationship and salvage it quickly! I thought about all the teachings I had had growing up, and I instantly set them aside. A conversion took place inside of me on the spot, in the blink of an eye. I returned an answer, saying, "I believe in Jesus Christ!"

Dick was satisfied with my answer, and we moved onto another conversation. I didn't know anything positive about Jesus Christ except He was tied with religion, and people who believed in religion were fanatics. Mother had taught me this, and I had believed her. I didn't think Dick was a fanatic at the time, nor at any other time, but in the back of my mind Dick seemed to make mother's point, that religious people are hypocritical. If he was truly religious, he wouldn't have rejected me and told me, "I don't want anything to do with you if you don't believe in Jesus Christ" if he was being truly religious. It was a positive manipulation for me, but it was manipulation.

I knew I was manipulated all the time, by ads on TV, politicians, and salespeople. My brother had told me that the only reason people talked to each other was because they wanted something. Not all of these manipulations were bad, but I had been taught that all religion was an abuse of power, causing all the wars in the world, and that it should be abolished. I wondered then if Dick was a Mormon, mother's most hated religion.

I asked Dick, "Are you a Mormon?"

Dick said, "I am, I'm a 'Jack-Mormon.'" I remembered mother using the term, and she always laughed afterwards. The term Jack-Mormon always seemed to meet mother's approval of a good Mormon, if there was such a thing. I knew a Jack-Mormon was someone who was Mormon in name only. They would drink coffee, they didn't go to church. He didn't practice his faith, but he talked about having faith in God.

After breakfast I drove back, thinking about Dick's comment, "If you don't believe in Jesus Christ I don't want anything to do with you!"

When I got home, I went to find Daddy. He was in the hallway, standing near his bedroom door. I asked him, "Do you believe in Jesus Christ?"

Daddy paused for a moment as if he was gathering his thoughts before answering my question. After a moment, he said, "He was a nice guy, and a good teacher."

I shrugged my shoulders, satisfied with Daddy's answer. I asked no further questions. I had no other thoughts on the subject of religion. I knew Omi prayed at Christmas time before we ate, but it was all in German and I didn't understand the words, only that we were to be respectful and hold still until Omi was done with her prayer. I also knew to say, "Amen," following her lead.

I never brought up the subject of religion again to Dick. I had nothing to add. I had no interest in going to church, giving up a day of work. I knew people didn't work on Sunday if you were a Mormon. Years ago when I was a little boy, the State of Utah had passed a law mandating that businesses were closed on Sunday. It was referred to as the 'Sunday closing law.' Mother hated that law. She wanted to go shopping. I didn't like it either. I thought about people who were forced to not shop or work on Sunday without having a choice. I knew hospital workers, policemen and firemen still worked. It didn't make sense why everything should stop on Sunday. It was just as productive for me as Monday.

I bounced my head that night, processing my conversation with Dick and with Daddy about Jesus. The feathers seemed to be harder than normal, hitting my head on the pillow. My face felt the impact. I didn't stop, but I wondered where the softness of my pillow was. I was processing thoughts in between feeling the hard feathers of each bounce, and with my head unfettered. Trying to dismiss my thoughts on religion, I started thinking of what work I needed to accomplish the next day. I bounced my head until I was clear with my thoughts, shifting my body, finally holding still until I fell asleep.

With Dick's phone out of order again, I drove to Dick's house. I wanted mother to meet Dick, thinking, 'Mother would probably approve of Dick as a Jack Mormon.' I told Dick when I arrived, "I want you to meet my mom and Dad."

Dick replied, "I'm a little uncomfortable meeting your parents. I'm almost their age!" Dick grinned, showing me he was truly uneasy about my request.

I said, "They won't care!"

Dick changed the subject. "What are you going to do with your life?"

I wasn't distracted with Dick's question. I was ready with a response. Without missing a heartbeat, I answered with the energy and enthusiasm of the anticipated dream that I had filed deep inside of me years ago. It had begun after Rick stuck his penis in my face, the day a switch in me was flipped from off to on. It was a sexual switch, driving me to the exploration of my body, and it was an ambition switch, pushing me to have a plan for my life where I would never be a victim. It was a dream I had been planning during years of bouncing my head on my pillow, night after night, a world I'd been building in detail. I said, "I'm going to buy land, acres of land!"

Dick cut me off in the middle of my response, interrupting my answer to him. Standing a few feet from me, Dick took a step closer. It was as uncomfortable as sitting at the restaurant counter when he leaned into me, a feeling I experienced each time Dick entered my space. I held my ground where I stood, wondering what he was going to do next.

Dick flapped his fingers like a sock puppet, a tongue lick away from my face, moving his thumb and fingers as the mouthpiece of the puppet and said, "TALK, TALK, TALK! Talk's cheap, you'll never buy land!" He said it as a matter of fact. He was completely expressionless, pulling his arm back, like a bully drawing a line in the sand.

I didn't hesitate for a moment. I immediately crossed his line in my mind.

Dick could not have said anything better to me. It was that beat of water on the back of the duck, again a negative inconspicuous bead of judgment, jumping into the ripple of life that floated by me years ago with mother's repeated comment, "I should have never had you!" Dick's negative response "you'll never buy land" floated away in my mind, leaving no afterthought that I couldn't achieve what I set out to do. Subconsciously, I turned his negative into a positive.

I had no anger, malice, or ill will towards Dick as a result of his comment. I didn't expect to hear what he said, but Dick said the magic

327

unscripted words I needed to hear to validate my intentions. Dick had just done me a favor without him even knowing anything about me or my past. Not a single doubt entered the space of my mind. I never doubted with a single bounce of my head that I couldn't buy acres of land of what I had been envisioning with millions of bounces into my pillow, night after night. I remained expressionless, processing what just took place. I wasn't mature enough to describe the value of his comment. I said nothing in response.

Without any further discussion, I brought up the subject again of meeting my mother. Dick relented. We hopped in my truck and we drove to my house to meet mother. Mother asked her usual questions. Dick answered mother's questions the way mother liked to hear her questions answered. Dick and mother hit it off. Mother liked Dick because he was a Jack-Mormon, and Dick liked mother because of her genuine spunkiness. Mother offered Dick a cup of coffee, and he accepted. Knowing mother, it was probably a test to see if Dick really drank coffee. Dick liked his coffee black. The two of them talked like they had been friends for years.

Mother asked, "Do you go to church?"

"I didn't go to church last week," Dick said, "but next Sunday I will." He laughed, then said, "I said that last Sunday and didn't go either."

Mother and Dick laughed in acquiescence.

Dick seemed to fit right in, becoming friends with mother instantaneously.

As time went on, he would even visit mother and Daddy when I wasn't around. College slowed down our relationship for a while, but every moment I had available between working or college I spent with Dick.

I continued observing his behavior without saying a word. I felt what I was learning was valuable information even though I didn't practice his philosophy of business, or how he treated people in general. Still, there was more I could learn. What Dick didn't know was what I was gaining from him: experience that I could not have learned anywhere else. The price I paid to stay in this friendship was invaluable to me.

Some of my ideas Dick responded to were met with the comment, "That's like jacking off in the middle of the road." I was too embarrassed to respond. It was too close to home and the visuals were uncomfortable. Seeing Dick talk people out of their possessions, devaluing their thoughts, dreams, and ideas to gain an interest was more than about money, it made me realize that this was his character. I noticed once Dick owned your former possession, thought or idea, the value skyrocketed to the next person. Suddenly the thing he had said was once "worthless" was now good stuff. Without any changes at all, it was worth tenfold, just by owning it himself. It went from 'shit' to 'shinola.' 'Shinola' was the shine in the buff of a well-polished shoe. It was beautiful, valuable, and worth every penny he was asking for and more.

I thought his character was isolated to Dick himself. I didn't find anything wrong with his character personally. I accepted Dick for who he was. It was worth every deal I engaged in with Dick to learn about his character, because I learned to notice the same character traits in others. I listened for keywords that stood out, like "How much do you want for that piece of junk?" It was disguised in many different ways, or it was hidden in less inconspicuous patterns. "High prices, devalued service, that's a dumb idea" was an obvious dead giveaway to me of the same character. It was just different, netting the same attitude to me, in my mind. The ability to notice this manipulation served me well.

I remember once I was asked by a possible customer, "How much will you charge to cut my lawn?" I answered, "$25." They said, "Will you cut my lawn for $5?" It was clear I was standing by someone with the same character traits as Dick. The person immediately devalued my services and time. I knew what to do when I heard key phrases or comments like these. I said to the lady respectfully, "Somebody will cut your lawn for $5 if you keep looking." I knew it wasn't going to be me. I left her standing where she stood and went back to work.

329

As close as we grew together as a father and son relationship, I never told Dick my innermost feelings. I couldn't take any chances that my feelings could be trampled on or have them thrown out with the bathwater along with the baby, so to speak.

I needed Dick in my life. Besides, Dick didn't know what I was getting from him….fun. Dick also occupied my mind, so I wouldn't lose control of my body in an unscripted passionate moment of sex which I avoided. This was invaluable to me. Dick didn't know he was helping me stay on track to become a mom. I didn't seek negative, negative sought me. When it did I was fortunate to turn negative into a positive. Turning negative into a positive was vital for my life.

I started playing simple mental games with Dick, mostly to entertain myself in his presence. Once I stood at the door wanting to leave, but I couldn't muster up the words to say "goodbye." Dick stood in front of me, a few feet away talking and talking and talking. I didn't know how to leave in between his words, so I decided to take a step to the right of me to see what Dick would do.

Dick took a step to his left, still in front of me, front and center. I took a step backwards. Dick took a step forward towards me. I didn't hear a word Dick was saying. I thought to myself, 'What will Dick do next?' I took a step to the left. Dick took a step to his right. I kept entertaining myself by moving around the room until Dick took a long enough breath for me to hear the pause in his voice I was looking for, and I exited his presence. As I drove home, I thought it was interesting that Dick followed my lead like he did.

Dick showed me how to groove tires, deepening the tread to get more use out of a tire which was seemingly worn out and otherwise useless. This was the way he made money. He would convince people they needed new tires, sell them regrooved tires, and then take their old ones and regroove them for the next gullible customer. With Dick's tire groover in just a few minutes it became a valuable tire to a person who couldn't afford new tires. Dick would sell the tire with a deepened tread for $20 or $30, even more if it was a bigger tire. With a little bit of labor, he made a nice profit.

Dick taught me how to rick tires on a truck without tying them down. Any tire lost in travel was money down the drain. Once we arrived at his closed shop, Dick would hop out and recruit me to help him unload the truck. He said, "Roll that tire to me!"

I had never rolled a tire before. I thought, 'How hard could it be?' I pulled a tire off the truck and rolled it to Dick, except it never got to him. The tire weebled and wobbled in a direction away from Dick. It hit something and fell over. I laughed.

Dick said, "Don't you know how to roll a tire?"

I said, "Yes!" I pulled another tire off the truck. The deflated tire hit the ground with a thud. Then I rolled it to Dick. The same thing happened except it rolled in another direction, hitting something else and falling over. This one never made it to Dick either until I retrieved it and took it to him.

Dick said, "You roll tires like old people fuck!"

I was shocked he would say such a word. I never would use that word in my wildest thoughts. I didn't want to think about anything he said. I eventually learned how to roll a tire, but I always thought about his comment thereafter when I touched a tire.

We interacted with one another, talking and playing, some of it was more serious. "Hey," Dick said, "You have an oil leak coming from your tire."

I said, "What? No I don't!"

Dick said, "Come look!"

I looked. Dick was right! I knew the color, consistency and smell of brake fluid and other oils a vehicle used. I stuck my finger in the fluid, touching it, feeling its consistency and rubbing the texture between my thumb and forefinger first. Then I brought it to my nose to smell it. I thought, 'This is serious,' except Dick started laughing. Confused for a moment, I suddenly realized I was touching and smelling Dick's pee. He laughed and laughed. I was so shocked and surprised at his actions, but I laughed along with him. I thought about when I peed in a bottle which my brother drank. Maybe it was karma?

We often scoured the town for opportunities to get something for free. Dick needed some rocks for his landscaping, and I happened to know where some rocks were in a field I spotted while mowing lawns. While putting rocks in the truck he said, "I gotta go take a shit."

I said, "What? There's no bathrooms around."

He said, "I'll just go over there in the trees."

I just kept loading rocks in the truck, not thinking about the situation.

We interacted with one another while working together on other projects that were more intense. Dick wanted to build a shed in his backyard.

I said to Dick, "I found an old barn. Maybe we could tear it down to get the wood?"

Dick said, "Let's go look at it."

We did. I went and talked to the owner of the land.

He said, "Yes, you can have the wood. Just tear it down and take it away." Then the man said, "This was the first chicken coop of Kentucky Fried Chicken. Colonel Sanders used it to raise his chickens in it."

I was surprised at what he told me, and I appreciated the information. I liked history.

The man telling me this brought back memories of going to Kentucky Fried Chicken's first store. It was just down the street from where I grew up. It was in the back of an old building. There were no windows. You just walked to this tiny space, placed your order, waited a few minutes, and you left with a bucket of chicken.

More often than not, there was an old man standing in the corner, watching people come in and out of the store. I later found out it was Colonel

Sanders watching customers enter and leave. Eventually they replaced him with a life-size statue in the same corner. The building had no glamor to it whatsoever. When I learned to read, I read the words on the side of the building. I always appreciated it saying, "Come As You Are" in cursive. It was an indication of the southern hospitality Colonel Sanders felt towards people. I liked it. I decided I wanted a license plate someday that said, "Come As You Are." To me it would be a way to invite people into my life.

In all our interactions and experiences, Dick didn't know the whole story of how I was benefiting from him. I felt I was getting the better end of the deal, just like Dick felt he was with me. It was a win-win friendship.

I was so hungry for a gay relationship. I had to find ways to distract myself. In all our wheeling, dealing, and adventures, Dick occupied my mind with thoughts and activities of life. We became like father and son.

I needed Dick as a father figure, but he also taught me very important lessons about money. Dick taught me 'never spend your seed money.' He said not spending your seed money was vital to financial success. His tire shop as his seed money. He taught me when you buy land to never surrender the trustee's note. He would eventually go on to sell his tire shop three times. Twice people bought the land and then faltered on their promise. The tire shop was his seed money to raise his family, but it was the seed money for his retirement as well. This was very different than Daddy teaching me to save my money.

I applied Dick's lesson on seed money to my lawn business. Working hard cutting lawns helped me gather seed money for investment purposes. I wanted to build a house and then get married so my future wife would have a ready-made home. Dick said it would be better to build a house together.

He taught me that I was buying other people's lunch when I did business with them. Because of this, it was important to minimize the number of people between my product and how that product was prepared and delivered. The more people that I had to pay to bring my product to market, the less control I had and the less profit I would keep. Dick warned me that people will eat your lunch if you let them, if you surrender your profits to them.

Don't pee on my leg and tell me it's raining outside.

When the tire shop was operating, he told me he would occasionally drop a $5 bill on the floor. He was doing his own form of baiting. He wanted to know if the people who were working for him were honest or not. He knew what he was doing.

Dick was more than just somebody I met at the swap meet, he became a surrogate dad I didn't know I needed, filling a hole in the measure of my creation by being a dad like friend. He taught me how to make a deals with people, (even if I didn't like the way he made deals with me), he taught me the best decisions he made were on the spot decisions, not ones that he had to mall over and think about. He took time with me in interactive ways, my dad did not. He taught me how to have fun, my dad did not. As valuable as my dad was to me, Dick was valuable in a different way, never replacing my dad, but interacted with me in a relatable relationship my mind could comprehend. Dick helped me notice how I searched, scanned, and became something from everyone I met or didn't want to become. It was all information that enriched my life, strengthened my mind, and gave me a perspective from their life's experience I couldn't have lived for myself. While Dick took advantage of me selling me his treasures that were somebody else's junk he talked them out of. He didn't know I was getting something more valuable, he helped me keep my identity and dream of becoming a mom intact. I never told Dick I was gay, his gregariousness kept my sexual desires safe in me. I didn't wondering into surrendering to my homosexual feeling even with my close relationship with him.

I needed this relationship in more ways than one.

CHAPTER TWENTY-SIX

OMI

With Omi's health on my mind I walked into the house. Mother and Daddy were sitting at the table, talking.

I interrupted their conversation. "How is Omi doing?"

Daddy stared into my eyes. "Omi isn't doing so well."

I stared back. Daddy's eyes seemed to swell on the edge of blustering with tears, but no tears came. Sick to my stomach I asked, "Is Omi going to die?"

Daddy did not give me a direct answer. Instead he said, "Omi had a pill set aside. If she ever got so old that she couldn't take care of herself, she would take the pill, and die."

Mother interrupted with a cackle. "Except she forgot where she put it!"

Daddy gave mother a look as if to say, 'You're talking out of turn woman.' It seemed to me Daddy didn't appreciate mother's comment, but he said nothing in return. He looked back at me. I listened intently to the rest of mother and Daddy's conversation. As hard as I wanted to deny death, I knew death was inevitable with Omi, sooner than later.

I thought to myself while mother and Daddy talked at the table. Another German who had a death plan, Omi, had a death pill. Fritz had a death plan, Fritz did what he said he would do, boastfully saying at the same kitchen table just a few years earlier, "When we die, we die together!" Driving his car over the cliff, killing the two of them, Fritz did exactly what he said he would do, die together.

Daddy had a death plan too, telling me one time, "When it's time for me to die, I'll just walk off into the woods, sit down against a tree and die!" Fritz, Daddy, and now Omi all had death plans. Even Hitler had a death plan, which history verified. I thought about what it was with these Germans and their willingness to die when they decided it was time to go. These people in my life, not to mention the people I had heard of in German history lessons, would never know how their words had influenced my thought process.

I returned to the moment, wondering what a death pill looks like, and where would Omi keep a pill like that. Would she keep it in a medical bottle, in a drawer, in a cabinet, or in a closet, on a top shelf? What if someone found it and accidentally swallowed it? Would it be out of reach from Omi's grandchildren, or anybody else? I thought, 'I hope she never finds it.' All these thoughts swirled in my head.

While mother and Daddy continued to talk, I lamented the old German conversations in my head. The old Germans meant what they said and said what they meant! I learned when mother said what she was going to do, she did it. When mother said she was going to put me back into my crib if I didn't stop peeing the bed, she did exactly what she said she would do. Mother put me back into my crib. I had no reason to believe these people didn't do what they said they were going to do otherwise.

An uncomfortable feeling always seemed to accompany my thought of Daddy dying the most. I didn't want to think about it anymore. I loved Daddy! I knew he was going to die someday as well. The reality of Daddy being nearly a half a century older than me was daunting. I knew the inevitable would one day happen. Daddy would die, too. My mind was scattered with thoughts. I had to return to the moment with Omi's impending death in the air. This shift in my life was an uncomfortable feeling I found hard to stomach with what the future ultimately would hold.

A couple days after Daddy told me that Omi wasn't well, mother said to me, "Omi's in the hospital."

I wondered if Omi found her pill. I didn't ask. I didn't want to know.

I gasped instead. An uncomfortable feeling in my stomach accompanied mother's comment. I wanted to avoid my next question at all costs, but it was just as painful to not know the answer if Omi died. If she died, I assumed mother would gleefully say, 'Yes, the old prostitute is dead!' Saying it with no sorrow, even worse she would say it with a cackle. This thought persisted, amplifying this horrible feeling inside my gut. I found the courage to ask, "Did Omi die?"

Mother said, "No! Daddy is with her in the hospital!"

I asked, "Is Omi going to be okay?"

Mother said, "I don't know."

I felt hopeful, but my hopes were dashed with mother's next comment, "Omi couldn't find her death pill, so she took a whole bottle of sleeping pills instead. They've pumped her stomach, putting charcoal inside of her."

I knew charcoal helped filter water, but I didn't know if you put charcoal in somebody's stomach it would do the same thing.

I asked mother, "Which hospital is Omi in?"

Mother told me. The LDS Hospital.

I asked for the address and said, "I'm going to go see her." Leaving the conversation, I hopped into my truck, hoping to get to the hospital soon and see Omi alive and well. An uncomfortable feeling arose inside of me as I walked into the hospital. I didn't want to be there under these circumstances. A mixture of healing and death entered my mind. I hoped Omi was alive and healing so that she could return home and everything would be like it was before this whole incident.

I figured I would see Daddy in the room after I found Omi's room number, but Daddy was not there. I looked twice. An old gray-looking woman stood upright in the room before me. I thought, I hope I have the wrong room. 'That's not my grandma!' Where's my dad?

But it was.

I looked into her eyes. Omi stared back into my eyes. My rosy cheek grandma, the one I remembered along with her pleasant countenance, my Omi, was gone. An uncomfortable feeling persisted in my mind and body. I was in denial. As much as I wanted Omi to live, I knew she was going to die. Omi's countenance had a gray hue. It was a gray that seemed to part the veil prior to death. I was feeling the pain my body wouldn't deny me.

Tenderly I said, "Hi Omi." I had no other words beyond, 'Hi Omi.' The language barrier stopped our conversation, but not our communication. I reached out and held Omi's hand.

I thought back to the time when I was eight or nine years old. I walked in Omi's house with Daddy. I had a slight scowl on my face, a crease in my forehead, from squinting in the sun. I didn't know I held my face like that. Omi motioned with her hand across her brow, showing me how smooth her forehead was without any creases.

I didn't understand what Omi was doing or saying at the moment. Daddy was standing next to Omi and interpreted saying, "If you don't have a scowl between your eyes, your skin will stay nice and smooth like Omi's." I looked at Omi's forehead. Daddy was right. Omi had nice smooth skin between her eyes. I decided from then on to make a conscientious effort not to scowl my forehead even when the sun was bright, blinding in my eyes, always thinking about Omi teaching me to have a smooth forehead. I couldn't help but think how much I appreciated what Omi taught me while standing on her porch at such a young age.

A nurse came into the room. Omi wasn't supposed to be standing up. The nurse motioned, wagging her finger as if to say no-no, while saying very lovingly, "You need to lie down in your bed." The nurse patted the bed to convince Omi to return and lie down. I felt I should leave. I said, "Goodbye, Omi!"

After a few days Omi was discharged from the hospital, but she was still not doing well. Daddy stayed with Omi night and day.

Each day I asked mother, "How's Omi doing?"

Mother answered my question, the way I wanted her to answer.

Then one day mother answered the way I didn't want her to answer.

Mother said, "Omi died last night in her sleep. Monday would have been her 86th birthday."

She went on to tell me that the funeral would be on Monday.

I thought, 'What a birthday present, to be buried on your birthday!'

Mother showed no sympathy or empathy towards Omi's passing, saying as many unpleasant comments as she could to get them out of her. She did like Omi's warm potato salad recipe, though she claimed that it was marginal. She said, "That old YUCK! She gave me her potato salad recipe and left out the one ingredient which made it like hers." Mother continued, "I had to figure out what it was without her!"

I asked mother, "What was the ingredient she left out?"

Mother snapped, "She didn't tell me to add lemon juice to the potatoes, and how much!"

I thought, 'It doesn't seem that difficult to me. Perhaps it was just an oversight?'

"Yew!" Mother ramped up her discussion. "Good riddance to the old prostitute!"

I wasn't surprised with mother's comment. I returned no response and showed no emotion towards what mother said.

Mother continued, "The old witch hoped I would die first so that she could be buried between Daddy and me." Mother's thought made her even more angry towards Omi saying, "Ooh! I don't have to hear her say 'Hansel' anymore when I pick up the phone!"

With Omi's passing, mother's desire to have Daddy's undivided attention day and night was fulfilled.

Even though Omi was gone, mother didn't calm down about her. But I was used to mother's rants.

I thought of Omi as a kind, loving, affectionate woman who was proud of her grandchildren. Even though we verbally never communicated with one another, and I never stayed overnight at her home, I thought Omi's actions spoke louder than words.

Omi's funeral was held the night before her birthday.

I asked Daddy, "Are people going to come to the funeral?"

Daddy said, "Omi had no friends here, nobody knew her."

Omi only had Daddy to look after her.

Daddy said, "Only the family will be coming to the funeral."

I knew that included the five boys, mother, and Daddy. We had no other family near or far.

Hermann invited his girlfriend Jenny to come to the funeral. She had become a friend to the family.

Seeing Omi in the casket with her glasses on seemed odd to me, but it was the Omi I remembered. I thought, 'when I die someday, I don't want glasses on me inside my coffin. I don't even want to be seen dead.' Death didn't look pleasant to me. I had a moment where I was planning my funeral, a picture on top of the coffin in a jovial light seemed more pleasant than seeing a dead body.

I reached into the coffin and tenderly put the back of my hand against Omi's once warm rosy cheeks. Omi's skin was cold to the touch. I tried to comprehend death as I touched her. I didn't want to stare at reality very long. I wanted to walk away, but I waited another moment gazing at her upper body. I knew this would be the last time I would see her. I looked at Omi's hands which were placed on her lap. Omi's hands seem to reveal her age more than her face. I reached into the coffin once again, placing my hand on her hands. They too were cold, completely lifeless, and void of Omi's once warm touch. They weren't the warm soft gentle hands I remembered holding in the hospital a few days earlier.

340

Thoughts of Omi's life flashed through my head. I said in a whisper, "Goodbye, Omi." I showed no emotion. I noticed nobody else did either.

After a few minutes I asked Billy, "Can I go home with you?"

Billy said, "Yes."

I thought about Omi as I walked away from the casket. I was thinking about the question I asked Daddy years ago, "How did Omi come to America?"

Daddy had said, "Omi's home was bombed out. She had nothing left in Germany to be there by herself after the War ended."

I thought, 'Omi went through both world wars.'

Daddy continued, "With no family in Germany, Omi had no reason to stay there. Omi answered an ad in a German magazine *Der Spiegel*. The ad asked if anybody living in Utah was willing to be a caregiver, helping an older man until the end of his life."

A German man by the name Ferdinand Koopmann had put in the ad. Arrangements were made and agreed upon through letters and phone calls. Omi asked only that he provide for her with room and board, living expenses, and at the end of his life that he would give her his house and furnishings in his will, free and clear from any of Mister Koopmann's family obligations or children's claims. Mr. Koopmann agreed. Omi arrived from Germany, obtaining her green card to become a legal worker. The first order of business was for Omi to take care of Mr. Koopmann, and the second order of business, the will, was contingent on the first order of business.

Mr. Koopmann had built a house for his children who lived next door to him. There was a cement pathway connecting the two homes. Why did their daddy have to put an ad in the magazine looking for outside help? I didn't know the answer to that question and couldn't figure out the reasoning behind his family living next to him yet not being a part of his life, but that was their arrangement.

As a small child, I walked on the pathway between the two houses, and a woman with a stern look met me halfway. The woman appeared out of nowhere. I looked into her eyes, and she stared back into mine with what seemed to me to be an angry look. A sense that I was not welcome overcame me. My desire to explore immediately ceased. She never said a word, yet I felt her thoughts, as if she were saying 'you're trespassing.' I turned around to go back into Omi's home. Even at that young age, I wondered if there was a connection between Omi being the one to care for Mr. Koopmann and the woman's anger.

Billy and I turned to leave, saying goodbye and heading to the exit. I pushed on the door, holding it for Billy as we left the funeral home. The sun had gone down, and the lights of the parking lot were lit. I walked to the car with Billy in silence, my thoughts of Omi returned. I remembered the conversation with Daddy after I met the angry woman on the pathway. When I told him, Daddy said, "Don't go over there anymore." With her stern look locked into my brain, I listened to Daddy and never approached the house again. Soon after, a fence was erected to divide the two properties. The sidewalk connecting the two properties remained intact, like a snake slithering under the fence.

Mr. Koopmann built a room in the front of his garage where he placed a machine he invented around 1910. Daddy and I stood before Omi on her enclosed porch. Omi was motioning to me, to show me something in the garage, but I didn't know what she was trying to say.

I looked at Daddy.

Daddy said, "Go!" Daddy knew what Omi wanted to show me.

Omi opened the door, turning on the light. The old switch had a distinct snap to it. I followed Omi inside. Omi stopped, carefully closing the door and tugged on the closed shade which covered the window, raising it to let a little more light in the room. A single lightbulb hung from the ceiling on a twisted wire. The pull cord was still intact on the base of the light bulb, causing the light bulb to hang on a slight angle from years of pulling on the string.

The room had been painted white at one time. Now it appeared dull and dingy from years of wear, tear and dust. It was a room smaller than my bedroom, and it had another door leading to the garage itself. The floor was cemented from wall to wall. I witnessed a contraption I couldn't identify along with a smell that I never smelled before. Nothing in my memory helped identify it. There was no thought of familiarity. This machine was very unique in its layout. Omi seemed excited to show me this contraption as if she invented it herself.

It looked like a plain wooden cabinet. It was a converted armoire. Oma also had one at our house and it always smelled like mothballs. Off to the left side of the cabinet there was a drum-looking thing on four stilts. There was also a metal box sitting on the floor to the right of the cabinet. It looked like a large milkbox.

Without saying a word, Omi flipped on the switch, turning on the machine. I flinched, hearing an eerie sound I had never heard before. I saw bolts of lightning flashing out of the bottom of the drum-looking thing. Above the bolts of electricity, a single wire wound around the drum from the bottom to the top, resembling an oversized spool of thread. I looked into Omi's eyes with concern. Omi looked back at me to assure me that I was safe.

I was remembering all of this as I looked for Billy's car. I spotted it in the parking lot. It was a familiar car to me. It has once belonged to Fritz and Frieda. As I walked towards it, I thought of the many times when Frieda and Fritz came to visit mother. Billy bought it from them before Fritz bought the new one and went over the cliff with his wife. My thoughts returned to Omi showing me this machine in the garage.

I felt comfortable in Omi's presence, and I let go of any fear of the sound I was hearing. I was trying to comprehend everything, but I had no reference point for what the machine was doing. The electricity flowed from

343

the cabinet to this drum on four stilts. The sparks coming from the bottom edge of the drum were fascinating. The whole experience was exciting but a little scary. Omi reached down to hold my hand, comforting me. The noise persisted. I didn't feel the need to plug my ears because of its low pitch.

Daddy came into the room. I looked at Daddy with big eyes. He said, "That's the sound of electricity."

Omi turned off the machine. Daddy explained to me that most of the mechanics of the machine were inside the old cabinet. The guts of the machine consisted of a series of wires and what appeared to be silver plates. The electricity flowed through the silver plates, giving the electricity its sound and giving off the unique smell. I stared at the inside of the cabinet with curiosity as I sought to understand how this thing worked. I saw the six silver plates that Daddy had pointed out. They were front and center, lined up like dominoes.

The machine amplified the sound of electricity, giving it a very distinct vibration in my ears. Hearing the sound made this contraption more interesting to me. The smell was strong even when it was turned off. It was a different experience than anything I had ever seen or heard before.

Omi turned on the machine and retrieved a metal cane which was leaning up against the side of the cabinet. Holding the cane to the floor, Omi put her arm to the edge of the drum where the bolts of lightning were emanating. The bolts jumped into Omi's arm!

I was surprised. All I had known before was that an electric current would kill a person. Here Omi had this energy going into her and was fine. I wanted to try it! I stepped toward the machine.

Omi immediately stopped the electricity going into her arm, and motioned to me not to get too close to the inside of the cabinet. Omi walked over, closing the doors while the machine was running and turned off the machine which was a single switch on the side of the wall. Omi showed me more how it worked.

Daddy did, too. Lifting the lid on top of the metal box on the right side of the cabinet, Daddy said, "It's oil."

Daddy told me that the oil took the amperage out of the electricity. It would kill a person without the oil to absorb its energy. I realized it was an important part of the machine's workings.

With feelings of that moment still resonating within me, I waited by the passenger car door for Billy to unlock it. Once he had popped the lock, I immediately opened the door, hopped in the seat of the car, and closed the door with a firm solid clasp, a sound which only seemed to accompany the old cars.

It was as if the present moment was a dream and the past was reality.

My thoughts returned to Omi.

Omi lowered the drum to the floor, then above my head towards the ceiling, ultimately stopping the drum at my height, showing me how the drum raised and lowered with a simple counterweight. Omi watched my reaction as I studied the rope and pulleys. A single rope was attached to the top of the drum which stretched to the first pulley on the ceiling above it. From there the rope crossed the ceiling above the armoire to a second pulley on the right side of the cabinet above the oil container. The rope at the other end held three steel old window counterweights. The old window weights were used to equalize the drum's weight, creating an equal balance. I knew this was no toy. I didn't touch it, but I thought it would be fun to raise and lower the drum.

Omi turned on the machine and the eerie sound pierced my ears once again, but this time I wasn't afraid. Omi then handed me a metal cane to hold while standing at the drum with the machine on. I stared at the drum more intently. The wire was wrapped around it like a spool of thread. It appeared to be painted a faint gray, or maybe it was dust on the edges of the wires that had accumulated over time. I could see up close how tightly the wires were wound. She told me to touch the cane to the floor and keep it there at all times.

I did as I was told. Immediately the lightning bolts started coming out from the bottom edge. I stared in fascination. It was very interesting to my mind to see this up close.

Omi motioned me to put my arm up near the edge like she had done. She directed me not to touch the drum, motioning me again with her hand as her communication method. I understood, and felt safe. I raised my arm next to the edge, watching the bolts of electricity shoot into my arm. I felt several tingles on my skin. It didn't hurt. The lightning bolts were going into me without killing me, or even shocking me. Just a tingle. Omi motioned to me to continue holding the metal cane on the floor, grounding me to the earth. I nodded my head, motioning 'yes, I will.'

Omi took a step backwards from me as I switched hands with the metal cane, placing my right arm next to the drum. Omi grabbed a fluorescent light tube which sat loosely on top of the cabinet. It had no wires attached to it. She returned back to me, grabbed my arm, and held the light over her head. The light flickered for a brief moment, then lit up completely! I smiled as my eyes glowed with amazement, seeing the light illuminated as if by magic.

Omi then let go of my arm and held the light above my head. I looked up to see the light above me come on too, just like with Omi. It shined brightly as if it was turned on by a conventional switch. I smiled from ear to ear. This was all so interesting to my mind, seeing the light glow, made me think electricity was flowing through me. Omi seemed pleased at my reaction. She grabbed my arm again, holding the light above her head the second time. The light turned on again.

Later Daddy told me, "Mr. Koopmann had a business using this contraption to heal broken bones."

Now I understood why it went all the way down to the floor. It was to heal people's broken ankle, foot, or leg. People came from all over the valley and would put their arm or whatever broken bone they had next to the drum, allowing the electricity to heal the bone faster than a body would normally heal on its own.

Daddy continued, "Mr. Koopmann built such a big business with people coming to heal broken bones that he bought land all around him. Then built houses on the land, and sold the houses."

Now I understood why he built the house next to him for his children.

When Mr. Koopmann died, Omi inherited his entire estate, consisting of his home and all his possessions including this electrical machine.

Billy turned on the key, engaging the engine. My mind heard the sound but I remained in my memories of Omi.

Two years after Mr. Koopmann died, when I was about 12 or 13 years old, Omi read an ad in 'Der Spiegel.' A man living in Florida by the name of Adolph Hattwig placed the ad in the German magazine. Omi answered the ad. Before long, Adolph flew out to Utah to meet her. Convinced she was everything she said she was, and he was everything he said he was, a short engagement took place between his plane touching down and the courthouse, and the two were married.

When Daddy heard the news, he said to me, "Omi married Adolph today!"

I said, "What? He just came into town." I was surprised at how fast they had married. I looked forward to meeting my new grandpa. I thought of all the things I would tell him.

Daddy said, "He only speaks German."

I considered this. We wouldn't be having much conversation, I guessed. Like my Omi and Oma, I knew I would just smile and nod. At least I could call him by name. "What would be his name in German?"

"Opa," Daddy said.

The whole idea was novel to me. I had never met either one of my original grandpas, because they had died years before my birth. Mother only told me two stories about her father, one, he died of obesity, and the second was that mother was his favorite daughter. Mother did not otherwise talk about her father, or his life. Daddy being an illegitimate child never talked about his biological father, except to tell me he said goodbye to him when he left Germany. Daddy never told me anything about his stepdad. Otherwise I had no other history on them. Mother always made sure I understood that Daddy was conceived by his mother being a prostitute, therefore being an illegitimate child. I didn't care. I loved my Daddy.

Now married, Adolph and Paula Hattwig prepared to drive back to Florida for an extended honeymoon at Adolph's home. Before leaving, Adolph bought a brand new car for their journey. Parked in the driveway, I jumped into the backseat, experiencing the new car smell for the first time. The seats were still covered in plastic from the factory. I was impressed by the diamond imprint on the plastic. I was excited for the two of them, and I had a new grandpa!

After a few short weeks living in the cold winter of Utah and ready for the long awaited honeymoon in the warm Florida sun, Adolph and Omi drove away. Passing through Evanston, Wyoming on the way, Adolph encountered a snowstorm. He began to drive carefully up and over the bridge. He used caution, but he was not used to icy roads.

Adolph lost control of the car, flipping it on its top, killing him instantly. Omi lived and was in the hospital. I stood in the hall near Daddy's room, listening to Daddy on the phone. His conversation sounded serious.

Billy, wanting to see a reaction from me, wasted no time saying, "Adolph is dead!"

I responded immediately, "NO, HE'S NOT! DON'T SAY THAT, HE'S NOT DEAD!"

Daddy set the phone handle down on the receiver.

I turned to Daddy, looking at him saying, "Is it true, Daddy?"

Daddy nodded his head.

I didn't want to believe it. They just got married. The new car smell was still in my nose. I said, "It's been less than 6 months since they've married!"

Daddy prepared the station wagon to go get Omi out of the hospital in Wyoming. Daddy laid down all the seats in the car, making a makeshift bed for Omi for the two hour drive from Evanston to her home in Salt Lake.

In the present, Billy started driving the car out of the parking lot, stopping before entering the main road.

My mind had returned to Omi.

Omi inherited all of Adolph's estate, including his home in Florida, $100,000 and all his possessions. There was no funeral held for Adolph in Utah. I think his body was shipped back to Florida, or Germany to his family, if there was family. I never learned the details. Omi recovered after a few months, being taken care of by Daddy at the home she inherited from Mr. Koopmann.

Billy pulled the car onto the main road. He asked casually, "What are your thoughts when I say sex?"

His words jolted me out of my fond memories of Omi. I said, "What? What are my thoughts about sex? Is that what you said?"

Billy said, "Yes, that's what I asked!"

Billy had no idea how much I desired to engage in a sexual relationship with a same-sex partner. I considered trusting Billy with my secret, but I decided against it. I also couldn't believe he would ask me such a thing when Omi had just died. I said aloud, "You know it's Omi's birthday tomorrow."

Billy said, "I know."

I was stalling to think of an answer, trying to avoid giving away any information about my feelings or thoughts of being with a man. I said, "This is an interesting subject to talk about. We just left Omi's viewing."

I was thrown off by Billy's question. I didn't know what to say right then and there, if anything at all. After all, I had a secret to keep, and it was near and dear to me. I liked the thought of talking about sex, but I couldn't give any information away that could leave clues about my desire.

I didn't want to lose focus on what Billy was asking me. It seemed Billy had something important on his mind to talk about. But I also knew I had a tendency to say too much once I started talking, to overexplain and dig myself into a hole. I decided not to engage in the conversation.

Without a response from me, we drove the rest of the way home in silence. I continued in a somber mood thinking about Omi. But, I thought I could talk to him in the morning about his question.

Billy lived across the street, so it was a quick walk. I wanted to talk to him further about the subject he started last night. I knocked on the door. Billy answered as usual. Except this time he didn't invite me into his house like he did every other time before. Instead, he came out, closing the door behind him and talked to me on the back porch.

I asked, "Can we go in?"

"No!"

I thought, 'Why doesn't he invite me into his house?' It didn't make any sense to me.

He stepped off the porch, further away from the door.

I followed him. I resigned myself that he wasn't going to let me in, so we talked near the back steps.

Billy said, "You know I go to bars and nightclubs regularly, don't you?"

I said, "Yes, you told me before." I knew he was talking about gay bars and nightclubs. I had suspected for a long time that he was gay.

Billy said, "You should go with me to the nightclub. You would be a hot number there!"

I replayed Billy's comment in my head. 'I would be a hot number at the nightclub?' I liked what he said. I was familiar with being solicited all my life. Yet I knew how I handled myself on the phone, hanging up every time. Even one on one, I rejected every advance. I pushed away the old man's hand. To see a beautiful man soliciting me in person, without any parameters, worried me. It was possible that I would succumb to my feelings, and that worried me.

Would a nightclub setting be too tempting for me? I felt more vulnerable not being able to say no if I was solicited. Anticipation filled my mind, yet I knew I couldn't participate. I knew I couldn't go! But the question kept going through my mind, what if I did go? What would happen?

I became scared of not trusting myself inside my mind. I was afraid of my own thoughts.

Billy interrupted my mental rant. "So do you want to go?"

I paused for a moment.

Billy waited for my answer.

I said, "No, I don't think so, I don't think I should go!" I couldn't bring myself to say a word about my feelings. I kept reminding myself, 'I'll take my feelings to my grave.'

I left the conversation to go home, thinking about what it would be like if I went to the nightclub. I had to let go of these feelings which were overpowering me. I needed to reset my mind. I needed to be at peace with myself. I had to think about other things that were important. My experiences along with my imagination scared me and excited me, sending me into an emotional frenzy. I played with myself to let go of my thoughts.

I bounced my head on my pillow thousands of times at night, digesting this information with each hit of my face. I needed to process my experiences each and every day. Thinking about Omi and these sexual thoughts, mixed with being invited to the nightclub with Billy, all confirmed my decision not to go. Thoughts swirled in my mind. Unable to focus on just one experience, I enjoyed each bounce of my head on the pillow. It felt so good.

Feeling the softness of the feather with each impact, I thought more about my decision not to go to the nightclub. Suddenly, I stopped bouncing. The pillowcase had bunched up to form an irritating crease on its surface. I felt the opening of my pillow. It was upside down. I turned the open end under my stomach, and continued bouncing, feeling the goodness of the bounce until I was ready to fall asleep. Adjusting my body, I laid on my stomach, satisfied with my bounces.

Later Billy told me why he wouldn't let me in.

He said, "I had a man sleeping over last night. He wasn't dressed."

I wasn't surprised. I pondered our conversation, about going to the nightclubs, and being a hot number. Now it made sense to me why we talked at the door.

Billy had no clue that I would remember this information, and quite frankly at the time neither did I.

CHAPTER TWENTY-SEVEN

TANGLED

I was invited to go with friends to a local amusement park to enjoy the rides. I stopped at a kiosk selling roasted corn on the cob. The beautiful amber color attracted my attention. I thought, 'I've never had corn before.' I ordered one. I added salt and pepper while it was dripping with butter and took my first bite into corn at 19 years old. My taste buds erupted from the flavor. It was so good. I ordered another one. I thought, 'I need to ask mother why she never fed us corn.'

Etched indelibly in my mind and on my taste buds, my first encounter with corn was memorable.

When I got home the first words out of my mouth was to mother. "Why didn't you feed us corn growing up?"

Mother said, "Germans never use corn in their recipes. It isn't part of the German diet. When I was introduced to corn I liked it, too, but it's an American food. I cook German food. That's what your father likes."

Mother continued, "I sent corn seeds over to Omi while she was still in Germany. Omi wrote back, 'Why did you send me corn seeds? I have no pigs!'" Mother's explanation made sense to me, so I left it at that.

Mother was no stranger to talking about what was on her mind. Her only obstacle was finesse. Mother said to me, "I never had an orgasm before!" I thought, 'Oh. Why are you telling me this?' I knew mother and Daddy slept in separate bedrooms nearly all their married life...with the exception of five children and some miscarriages. They must have encountered each other somewhere along the way in spite of their separate bedrooms.

One time when I was ten I was asked by the man who ran the beauty salon, "Did your father wear a pathway between the two bedrooms?"

I replied, "I don't know." I pretended not to understand what he was talking about. Besides, I didn't want to have this conversation anyway. I remembered that I only saw Daddy in mommy's bed two or three times, and that was devastating.

Now at 19, mother opened up to me like I was the priest at confession. She told me the details of how Daddy and mommy had sex. I was completely blindsided, I didn't need to know the details. But mother shared the information anyway. It was more than I needed to know, or wanted to picture in my head, but I didn't walk out of the room either. The picture was painted nonetheless. Mother was trying to tell me something, but I didn't know what.

Later I thought, 'This could explain mother's nonchalant, even casual view, regarding a personal experience with sex.' It was personal to me even if I did it with myself. I said to mother, "Thanks for the information" and changed the subject. I asked, "Do you remember how you asked me to go get the gallstones out of the freezer and bring them to you to show your friends who came over to the house?"

Mother said, "Yes."

I asked, "How did you collect those?"

Mother said, "The kitchen strainer."

I pictured this in innocence, thinking mother scooped them up from the bottom of the toilet bowl after they fell out of her butt, rinsed them off and put them in a baggy? Eventually I understood that mother pooped in the kitchen strainer and sifted the stones out of her stool. A grave picture was painted in my head. I thought of all the fabulous parties mother put on, using the kitchen strainer for the food she served her family, and her guests alike. She used the strainer often for her famous sauerkraut, salads, and vegetables. I didn't like the picture in my head that I was envisioning. I ate all of mother's food which she prepared using the strainer.

I changed the subject again to get the kitchen strainer out of my head. It wasn't getting easier to dismiss mother's words about sex. This conversation wasn't really going the way I thought it would. I said, "I'm not going to call you mommy anymore! You've been demanding that I call you 'mommy' and Dad 'Daddy' ever since I was a little boy!"

Mother said, "Oh I have not!"

I said, "Do you remember how I referred to Daddy as 'him' one time?"

Mother said, "I don't remember."

I said, "I do."

Mother said, "You're just making this up!"

I said, "No I'm not, I referred to Daddy as 'him,' and you said, 'who are you referring to as him!' I knew I'd cross the line immediately when I said that word, 'him.' I had to find a lie immediately to cover up my mistake. So I lied and said, "Hermann!"

Billy was standing in the room next to me and was quick to say, "Liar! He meant Daddy!" I lied again, saying, "No, I didn't!"

I'd been conditioned. It was a slip in protocol, and I knew better. I persisted. I said, "At the time I felt the wrath that I knew you were capable of inflicting on me." I wasn't finished telling mother of my experience. "I felt the tone and threat in your voice, and I knew I had better change my reference immediately."

Mother said, "I didn't threaten you!"

I said, "That's how I felt."

Mother said, "Why are you making this stuff up?!"

I said, "I'm not making this stuff up, you just don't remember." Except for the gallstones, I couldn't understand why mother wouldn't acknowledge what I was saying. Why were they so clear in my head and not in mother's?

I continued with another unresolved irritation stored inside me that I wanted to resolve. An irritation with deep feelings attached to them. I asked, "Do you remember lining Walter and me up against the wall in the utility room when I was ten and Walter was nine? You asked with your hands on your hips, 'which one of you picked apart my falsies?!'"

Mother said, "No, I don't!"

I said, "I do, and you did!"

I continued, "You opened the dryer door, and what was once your bra's foam padding had crystallized from the heat and fell to the floor in little pieces. You didn't understand that heat disintegrates foam, which caused the foam to break down and fall apart. Neither Walter nor I picked apart your bra. It was your lack of understanding that heat disintegrates foam which caused them to crystallize and fall apart."

Again mother said, "You're just making this up!"

I said, "No, I'm not. You just don't remember, but I do!" I was hoping for some acknowledgement of a mistake on mother's part. I tried jogging mother's memory further. "Do you even remember hitting me in the mouth with your knuckles?"

Mother said, "No, I never hit you in the mouth."

I chuckled under my breath and shook my head in disbelief. I continued, "I was nervous, standing in front of you, so I wet my lips mimicking a girl in the fourth grade. You immediately said, 'Don't stick your tongue out at me.' Then you hit me in the mouth with the back of your hand with a full onset swing!"

Mother quickly replied, "I did not!"

I said, "You did. I ran to my room crying, then you told me after crying for a while 'if you don't stop crying, I'll give you something to cry about.'

Mother said, "How do you remember all this stuff?

I said, "I don't know. I just do!"

Mother saying, 'How do you remember all this stuff?' could have been interpreted as an acknowledgment, but it lacked empathy for me to connect. Empathy, an emotion I myself had been beat out of, feeling completely numb. I traded my emotions for survival long ago. Besides, emotions lacked all logic for my brain to process.

I was getting nowhere with my haphazard interrogation. I decided to drop this particular subject of her hitting me in the mouth. I felt mother was uncomfortable with me putting her on the spot. But I was surprised I couldn't get mother to remember any details whatsoever.

I wanted to tell mother more in the aftermath of being hit in my face. Like, I had made the decision never to cry again, and that I handed Billy a knife to stab me to death, hoping he would kill me, or this was the very moment I decided to be a mom and that I was gay. Except, I made too many promises to myself not to reveal the deepest thoughts and feelings my body gave me. I didn't need them trampled on too. If I could have had my mental faculties together, I could have been more expressive like telling her, "This very moment of being hit in the face changed my life forever, it became a moment frozen in time, and unlike any other moment this incident became indelibly etched into my 10-year-old brain, because I had failed to win over Mommy's love."

I didn't know why I'd been cast out of her life. I got nowhere with mother. I wondered if mother saw me as she saw herself, or was I just an obligation, a threat, or an insurmountable chasm in her life? I didn't know the answer.

'Why did she never include me in her heart?'

I had one more pressing comment on my mind.

I said to mother, "I'm not giving you a goodnight kiss anymore. You've been requiring me to give you a goodnight kiss every single night before I go to bed, ever since I was a little boy."

Mother said, "Stop it, why do you keep saying this stuff?"

Mother didn't like what I was saying, I could feel it.

357

She said, "I knew I should have never had you!"

I was no stranger to hearing mother say this for the umpteenth time. For the first time I replied back, "You lost control of me when you birthed me!"

Mother was not pleased at my comment and was about to reply when Billy walked into the room, interrupting our conversation. "How's college going, Googie? Are they teaching you how to read yet?"

I reacted immediately, saying, "My name is Robert! That's what you can refer to me from now on!"

Billy was puzzled at my reaction. I don't think he expected my firm response. Billy didn't reply back. He might have told all my siblings after my comment, because all of them started calling me by my given name from then on. I was never referred to as Googie again.

I didn't return to the subject of mother's loyalty kiss. I didn't feel I needed to clarify any further. I knew I wasn't going to do it anymore, ending mother's manipulation and dominance over this dimension. It was like 'one small step for man, one giant leap for mankind.' It was one giant leap for Robert. I was freeing myself from mother's clutch. It was a leap in the right direction.

Mother had no response to Billy's comment.

I made my point, and my intentions.

Mother cast me out of her life, then reeled me back in at her convenience, then cast me back out, then reeled me back in, like I was a fish on a fishing line. My emotions, my feelings, my desire to love mother, were all cast out. Mother had no interest in connecting with these feelings with me.

I saw this behavior over and over again with how mother treated other people in her life, like long time acquaintances, close friends, and neighbors. She would cast people out of her life when they disagreed with her view on God, Mormons, Jesus Christ, religion in general, barking dogs, noisy kids, how she made her coffee, or a simple off the wall comment. Then she'd reel people back in, not out of convenience but out of appearing nice, if it suited her. Mother had no loyalty, except to herself.

Mother never saw her inconsistencies as a detrimental way to communicate, or her actions as a tangled web of confusion, and there was no value in pointing them out. They just became a part of mother. Confounding statements that never made sense, except in a weird way they did. But only because they came from mother. Telling me things like, "You are beautiful," and on the other hand saying, "But don't let that go to your head." Other times she'd begin, "It's because of you damn kids we are poor," and then she'd swing back in the other direction and buy us beer, justifying it to herself by saying that we were going to buy it anyway.

Then there were the times when she said, "I tried five times to get a girl," as if girls would have been the cat's meow, but in the next breath saying, "Oh, I'm glad I didn't have a girl. She just would have come home pregnant."

"I'm glad I had my five boys, but I should have stopped with one."

"The world has too many damn people on it," she'd say. Then she'd turn around and say, "My five boys kept my sanity in this stupid state!"

The zigzag of comments, opinions, emotions and intelligent statements were all mixed up in a bundle of information. I had to decipher which was true, which was overbearing, which was hostile, which made sense to my mind, and which one I had to dismiss. Day after day, one moment to the next, mother was relentless.

I was in the boat one moment, cast into the water to fend for myself the next, with hook, line, and sinker.

Mother's character was consistent in its inconsistencies, finding me offensive somewhere in the back of her mind. I wonder now if Mother wishing she never had me was only a cutting remark because I reminded her of something she had cast out of her life and didn't want it reeled back in. Giving birth to me reminded mother of something deeply unresolved in mother's past. There were the same views of life which made sense to me one minute mixed with insane rage the next. I had resigned myself long ago to her ways, saying out loud to myself, 'That's mother.'

Mother's behavior came at the expense of her five boys. It was brought to my attention that we had all suffered at her hand when a mature friend of mine talked to my brother Frank for a few minutes and came back to me and said, "He's a 30-year-old teenager!"

What he said sounded right, thinking more about what he told me. I wondered, would I be a 30-year-old teenager when I'm 30? I made what I thought were mature decisions at 19. I knew that in a few years I would be viewed as an adult. I liked my brother, but I didn't want to be like him. Frank was into viewing women in miniskirts, go-go girls and listening to music on his collection of 8-track tapes. These were the least of my interest. We were all stuck in mother's cycle of abuse, and we each responded in our way. I needed to pay attention, make a conscious effort that I didn't want to get stuck in adolescence if it was at all possible. I got stuck in innocence, turning negatives into positives and denying my true feelings about what was happening around me, just to survive the moment. Mother's tangled web of behaviors reached deep into each of our minds in their own unique way.

That night and the nights that followed became ongoing conversations inside my head, bounce after bounce. Yet in the middle of my thoughts, the kitchen strainer returned with mother's gallstones being extricated out of her stool. I tried to bounce the thoughts of the strainer and gallstones out of my head, not to mention all the meals that had been prepared since using that strainer. What could possibly be more tangled than that?

No matter how hard or how often I bounced my head on my pillow, comfortable or not, I couldn't bounce mother using the colander for her bowel movement from my thoughts or my imagination.

CHAPTER TWENTY-EIGHT

BIRDS, BEES AND UNCOMFORTABLE REALITIES

My last year of high school I walked down the hall to the next class, Social Studies. A boy who had the same class as I did walked a few steps in front of me. His laughter caught my attention.

I had a tendency to stare. Walking behind him, I noticed his clean hair cut, shapely body, and a laugh which resonated deep with me. His laughter sounded very inviting to be around. He seemed to be a happy boy. His friends frolicked around him. I walked alone, talking to no one. I didn't mind. I stared at the back of his body, thinking how beautiful he was. I was perfectly happy inside my world.

I had never said 'hi' to him. I didn't know his name. He didn't know me. We had no reason to know each other. Besides, I was too shy to say a word, though I quietly observed his mannerisms, taking notes inside my mind.

We entered class as any other day, sitting in our assigned seats. He sat two rows to my left and up one seat. It was testing time in social studies. The teacher had twenty five questions surrounding current events.

"Write down your answers," the teacher said. "Question nine, who is the president of the Church of Jesus Christ of Latter-Day Saints?"

Living in Utah, that was a simple question, and I knew the answer. I wrote down, 'Mr. Kimball.'

The questions continued.

At the end of the test, the teacher said, "Be sure your name is on your paper."

I did, passing my paper to the front of the class. The papers were then passed two rows to the left, then redistributed back down the rows for us to grade each others' work. I didn't know it at the time, but this happy boy got my paper.

The teacher went through the list of questions and answers. When she got to question nine, she said, "Question nine! President Spencer W. Kimball."

The happy boy let out an audible laugh.

He said, "Who wrote Mr. Kimball?" Laughing, he looked around the class, then back onto the piece of paper. Noticing my name, he said, "Who's Robert?"

I laughed, knowing that was my answer. I supposed I was the only non-Mormon in the class and the only one to answer 'Mr. Kimball.' I didn't know any different. I said, "I'm Robert."

He said, "That's you?!"

I said, "That's me."

He said, "I have never heard anyone reference the Prophet of the Church as Mr. Kimball." He laughed again, saying, "It is a different way of saying his name that I have never heard before!"

That one interaction began our friendship. He said, "My name is Brian."

In a short time, Brian introduced me to some of the friends he frolicked with while walking down the hall. There were three main friends: Mike, Greg, and Richard. Brian eventually told me he was a Mormon.

I told him, "I'm not a Mormon."

He didn't seem to care if I was or if I wasn't. He never pushed his religion onto me in any way. I'd been given a lot of anti-Mormon information based on my experience with mother. I didn't push any of mother's anti-Mormon views onto Brian.

The other friends didn't seem to care either. We started talking regularly on the phone and in person. I finished up my last year of high school, graduating a year before them.

Comfortable with our friendship, even after I graduated I would go back to the machine shop during school hours when I knew Brian and Mike were in shop class. Mr. Larson, the machine shop teacher, let me visit my friends during school hours. He never told me I shouldn't be there after graduating.

I brought some magazines I had saved from underneath my brother's bed to show Brian and Mike. The pornographic pictures I thought would be interesting for them to see.

Mike said, "Whatcha you got there?" Mike looked through his safety glasses at first, then lifted them up to get a more unobscured look at what I was showing him.

Brian stepped to his side, looking at the pictures for a brief second.

They weren't really interested in what I was showing them. The shop teacher looked too, but only for a brief moment. The teacher didn't seem interested either. I could read his feelings based on his actions, because he walked away.

Brian expressed to me in a gentle voice, "We don't look at that kind of stuff, it's not good for your brain."

I respected what Brian said and closed the magazines. I was okay with his decision. I thought, 'I guess I shouldn't have shown them the pictures.' The pictures did not affect our friendship. I threw the magazines away in the dumpster behind the school afterwards, walking to my truck. I valued my friendship with Brian over the magazines I'd saved. Brian's lack of interest strengthened our relationship, because he was honest with me without rejecting me. The girls' pictures didn't do anything for me anyway.

Mother spent my childhood inviting people over to the house, feeding her guests German food, and now it was my turn. I invited Brian, Mike, Greg, and Richard over to my house to enjoy mother's food, piggybacking off of one of mother's parties from the night before. I set out the food like mother

363

except it was outside on the picnic table. I thought, 'I hope they enjoy the food.' I knew it would be different for them.

I set out mother's sauerkraut, cooked up the bratwurst, served potato salad, and introduced them to goat's milk. Like mother, I wanted to serve my heart out. They seemed to enjoy the food, but I wasn't sure.

Greg said, "It was very different, especially the goat's milk."

I appreciated his comment. It gave me a sign that I was appreciated. I was glad they liked it. I was hoping they would.

If they didn't, it would have been hard not to take it personally. I had learned that from mother, too.

By this time I had gotten to know the families of my new friends. Their moms and dads were very nice to me. Brian returned the favor by sending me an invitation to a party with Mike, Greg and Richard. As I perused the invitation, I saw the letters, 'BYOM.' I couldn't understand what 'BYOM' meant. I was familiar with BYOB, bring your own bottle! I had no idea what BYOM was. I called Brian to thank him for the invitation, and I asked, "I know what BYOB means, but I don't know what BYOM means."

Brian laughed. "I thought you would know what that meant."

I said, "I've never heard of it before."

Brian said, "When people throw parties the meat can be kind of expensive, so BYOM means bring your own meat."

I laughed. It was so simple. I said to Brian, "Mother never had anybody bring their own food in any way, not even their liquor to a party!" I thought, 'I don't know anything about this culture.' I had no idea people brought food to a party they were invited to.

As instructed, I brought my own meat to the party.

Brian called me the day after the party and asked, "Do you want to go camping with us?"

I said, "I've never been camping before, not even with my dad, but yes I'll go!" I hung up the phone and picked out a suitcase suitable for the situation. I was ready for the adventure.

When Brian arrived, he saw my large suitcase.

I said, "My suitcase is packed and ready to go!"

Brian asked, "What do you got in your suitcase?"

I said, "Thing's for the camping trip."

Brian said, "Well, let's just take a look and see what you got inside that puppy."

I unclasped my suitcase, showing Brian the contents of my camping equipment. This consisted of mostly household stuff to set up a kitchen and six razors.

Brian said, "Why do you have a razor in your suitcase?"

I said, "So I can shave!"

I moved some stuff around to show Brian, saying, "I'm bringing six razors!"

Brian laughed. "Why are you bringing six razors?"

I said, "In case you or one of the others need to shave?"

Brian laughed again, saying, "We're going camping. Nobody will be around us, and no one will care if anyone shaves or not!" Brian swung his hands at his waist in a horizontal chopping motion, still chuckling. "Let's take those out of there. They won't be necessary."

I said, "Can I bring one for me?"

Brian consented, saying with a smile, "You can bring one razor for you!"

I smiled. I got to bring a razor for me.

I had a fun time camping. Brian's actions led me to understand how much they cared about me. He was playful, calm, and treated me nicely. He treated me like I existed and moreover like I was important.

Sitting in his driveway at his home, enjoying the calmness of the moment, Brian said, "I think I'll be going on a mission for my church, to serve God."

He sounded a little hesitant to me.

Brian continued. "I'll be gone for two years."

I thought, 'Two years, that's a long time! I'll be 21 years old!' I thought, 'I hope he'll change his mind and not go.' But I didn't say anything.

Brian said, "I won't be able to talk to you for those two years."

Surprised, I said, "You won't?"

He nodded. "That's the rules. I can write you a letter though."

I said, "If that's what you do. I'll read your letters."

I felt we had become close at becoming friends!

Still I'd hoped he would change his mind and not go on a mission.

A few weeks later, after the other boys had already left for their missions, Brian said, "I received a letter in the mail telling me where I'm going to go on my mission."

I said, "You did?"

Brian said humbly with a smile, "I'm going to the Leeds England mission!"

I was happy for Brian at the moment because he was happy, but I was thinking, 'He'll be gone for so long.'

Bouncing my head that night, I thought about Brian leaving and these new friends in my life. It made me happy to think of them, though I would miss Brian. I bounced like I always did with intention, thinking a myriad of thoughts. I remembered a conversation I tried to dismiss but couldn't. I had overheard it in my last year of school. "If you put a noose around your neck like you were hanging yourself, but not to the point of death while you masturbate, you'll heighten the experience tenfold." What I heard sat in my head for months, spinning around. I wasn't able to dismiss it. I spent time thinking about it while bouncing my head. I would dismiss it, but then the subject reintroduced itself into my thoughts again.

I thought, 'I like masturbating, and the feeling it gives me.' Hearing this statement caught my attention and curiosity. I decided a tenfold experience was hard to pass up. Knowing it was a possibility if something went wrong, I could die. I bounced my head on that thought, then I thought, 'I won't die.' I continued bouncing my head.

Drawn to the experience of masturbating and anticipating a tenfold feeling, I laid in my bed on my side listening to my heart beat, thinking, 'This conversation wasn't even directed towards me. Why did I hear this?' I kept thinking, a tenfold experience. I wondered, 'If this was true, would it be worth the risk?' I thought, 'If I tried it, I need to do it right!' I knew if I failed, I could die. I puzzled over this, developing a strategy. What does an escape plan look like that's foolproof? I continued bouncing my head.

I never calculated in the least that I could pass out, lose brain function, slow or stop my heart from beating as a result of a lack of oxygen into my body. The thought never entered my head. Besides, it would only be for a short moment anyway. I figured I could consciously execute my plan, then allow air back into my lungs, restoring my body's natural desire to breathe in short order.

I felt whatever additional euphoric feeling it gave me beyond the normal feeling was worth the risk. I had to have this experience for myself. I thought about where to do this. Maybe the tree? I continued bouncing and thinking, 'I need to find out for myself. If it truly was a tenfold experience, or not.' If it was, I wanted to experience it. The thought of a tenfold experience overrode any sense of fear or thinking something could or would go wrong. I was cautious about it to some extent, knowing that death was possible if I cut my breathing off for too long, but I reasoned out the complications in my head by thinking it wasn't going to take me that long to masturbate.

I bounced my head, thinking, 'How skillfully can I pull this off, without losing consciousness for any length of time, even accidentally?' I didn't want to be found dead with my pants off and a noose around my neck, exposing my naked body to whoever found me. I felt for a moment how embarrassing it would be to be found naked and hanging lifeless. I wouldn't be able to

367

defend my actions. I continued bouncing my head, feeling uncomfortable with my thoughts, but I kept thinking about it just the same.

Bouncing my head this time seemed more like bouncing my head on a bag of bricks, but it didn't deter me as uncomfortable as it was to bounce. I stopped with my head to the side of my pillow, thinking, 'If I was found dead, they would know what I was doing in my last moments of life!' Feeling embarrassed with that thought in my head, I envisioned myself dead. I continued thinking, 'I need to devise a foolproof plan not to die.' I stopped bouncing for the night with that thought in my head. I had a lot to think about.

By morning I figured out how and where I could pull this off. The old box elder tree came to my mind. It seemed to be the go-to tree for climbing and building tree houses in. It had sturdy limbs which reached high into the air, so no one would see me there. Setting a ladder up against the tree, I climbed the ladder twenty feet up to find a location to execute my plan. It didn't take me long as I stood on the old platform looking up into the tree.

I found what I thought was the right place, just above a makeshift area I had built for the beginning of a tree house years ago but never finished. Seeing many heavy limbs above me, I spotted one limb in particular I felt would work, not only for the hanging, but thinking, 'it had a limb I could use against my back, and that limb might aid in my survival.' I was diligent processing all the worst case scenarios, knowing there was no room for error. I felt better about this already! In addition, there was a safety limb just below my proposed area. My confidence began to grow, feeling a lot more comfortable about this perspective experience. I climbed up onto the safety limb, giving it a few jumps. It was plenty strong enough to hold my weight.

With an upper limb to hold the noose and a lower limb to step up on as an escape, relieving the pressure from around my neck, and a limb against my back, I was ready for this experience. It seemed to be exactly what I was looking for. If the tale was true, and as long as everything went as I planned, this experience would be incredible. My anticipation built, but the thought, 'I don't want to get caught in any way, shape, or form' kept running through my head. I was driven to try this experience, but not die. Keeping every sexual thought and desire to myself, I just needed to make sure no one was around when I did it.

In my bedroom, I tested a strap around my neck. I didn't want a rope burn, and a strap seemed more comfortable anyway. I tried it on as if I was being fitted for a suit. It fit as comfortable as it was going to be, giving the strap a tug above my head, preparing myself mentally for the moment I hung. I found a rope in the garage to hold the strap. I knew I could adjust the height as I needed for the length of my body.

After gathering the materials, I draped the rope and strap over my shoulders to keep my hands free as I climbed. My hands trembled against the ladder's edge, but I kept taking another step upwards. Reaching the platform, I looked up at the location I selected, climbing higher into the tree to tie the rope around the upper branch. Still feeling a little nervous, I threaded the strap through the rope and buckled it down. I was convinced it was put together properly, and decided to give it the weight test. The ropes hung lifelessly, waiting for me to test it out. Next was my height, in coordination with the safety limb. My calculations were close enough to be safe with any margin of error.

I wanted to put together the framework ahead of time while it was still light. I put the strap around my neck and held my hands on the strap against my jaw as I stepped carefully off the limb for a brief moment. My breathing was obstructed from what I was used to, but I continued. The trunk against my back pressed a little against my spine through my shirt. I stepped back up onto the safety limb. I felt everything was set, including the onset of dusk. I climbed down from out of the tree. I wanted to see where everybody was located.

It was Friday night. I went in and watched TV to pass the time away, waiting for mother and Daddy to leave to go dancing. I figured nobody else would be around. I paid no attention to what was on the TV. I was simply passing the time, making the evening seem normal. Finally mother and Daddy were about to walk out the door.

Mother said, "Goodbye, we're on our way!"

I happily said, "Have a nice time dancing!"

Everything was going as planned. I was home by myself. I waited about ten minutes to be sure mother and Daddy didn't return home, forgetting something. Mother usually didn't miss anything, but I wasn't going to take any chances.

I decided I had waited long enough. Feeling they were gone for the evening, I turned off the TV, and walked out the door to climb the ladder.

The closer I got to this event, the higher my anticipation built, and more random thoughts went through my head about the safety of my plan. I felt the nervousness in my legs with each step up the ladder. My mind scrambled for any negative repercussions over and over again, thinking about any downfalls like, 'would I pull my neck out of place and paralyze myself?' I immediately told myself, 'no, that wasn't going to happen!' I never saw any of the old films where somebody who got hung had their head come off as a result of hanging, so I eliminated that thought from my mind. My imagination still wandered.

Paralysis might take place, but I felt that would only be in the case of a sudden jolt in the neck, separating my head from the spine. That was not going to happen either. Nonetheless, it gave me a squeamish feeling which passed though my body and down my legs as I continued climbing. I felt for people I had seen hanging in old black and white photographs from history class in school. People who had that happen to them, even if I had never met them. I felt as if it was me in the photo. Reason took over my imagination. 'I'm not going to be on a platform which drops out from underneath me. I'm not going to die! I'm not going to become paralyzed!' I told myself this over and over again. I just wanted a euphoric experience.

I felt more confident with each step of the ladder although my legs were still shaking with each step. I kept climbing. I tried thinking of every other possibility that could happen, except passing out, becoming unconscious, dying from asphyxiation, or any other complications associated with hanging myself.

I told my brain again, 'Death is not going to happen!' I believed in myself. Besides, I never heard of anyone dying from doing this. I focused on the anticipation of a higher sensation which outweighed the risk of dying, thinking, 'it's going to feel incredible!' I couldn't think of any other stories to tell myself, I didn't have any reason not to believe it wouldn't work.

Drawing myself to feel the heightened sensation, I took another step up the ladder. Anticipation continued to build in me. My legs seemed a little more wobbly the higher I climbed. At the end of the ladder, I climbed up into the tree, taking another step up to reach the platform. The platform would become my staging area to undress, but not yet.

I stood still, listening to my heart beat, and feeling the stillness around me. My breathing seemed a little faster and deeper than normal. I climbed up another eight feet to the location then back down to the platform to undress. I was ready to do what I planned on doing from all the preparation, undoing my belt buckle, unzipping my zipper, pulling my pants down from off my body, and from around my heels, setting my pants in a pile. I heard a slight clunk when my pants hit the platform. It was probably my keys. I slowly pulled my underwear off, hesitating in the moment.

My body was ready with an erection to make this happen. I kept looking and listening again to be sure nobody was around. Convinced I was alone in the canopy of the tree, I took my shirt off, leaving my socks on to protect my feet. I started my climb again, then stopped. I thought my shirt would protect the skin on my back against the rough bark of the tree. I was still convinced the tree would act as an additional safeguard to my survival rather than hanging completely free. I returned to the platform to put my shirt back on. My anticipation heightened. Still listening for any sounds which were out of place, I climbed back into the location on the safety limb.

Convinced I was well hidden from anyone on the ground, between the leaves of the tree, and the cloak of the evening's light, I carefully placed the strap around my head, adjusting the strap underneath my chin and against my throat, just as I had practiced in my bedroom. I was thinking, this is going to work out!

With everything in place as I had planned, I stepped off the limb, testing my body weight against the strap once again. I choked a little, but I expected that from my test run. I stepped back onto the limb, salivating even more. This time I took a deep breath and stepped gently off the limb to proceed as I had planned.

I felt the lack of air in my lungs that my body desired, but I didn't reverse course. The air from the deep breath had to sustain me for the moment.

Brian drove up in his truck in that moment of no return.

I wasn't going to stop for nothing now. I couldn't, I was too far along in my feelings! I knew he wouldn't see me in the tree anyway. I didn't let his arrival distract me. I kept going. I had so much suppressed energy, I had to spend it now.

In a short moment, the experience I was hoping for didn't deliver as my imagination portrayed the feeling of a tenfold experience to be. In fact, it was no heightened experience at all. I immediately stepped up onto the safety branch. I thought to myself, 'This was a lie!' I felt really dumb.

Standing on the limb in a precarious situation, I listened to Brian get out of his truck and ring the doorbell. I could hear the ring from where I was standing in the tree, trying to control my heavy breathing from the quiet evening air. I waited, holding still, waiting for my body to settle down. Standing motionless, I wasn't going to hurry and get dressed with my pants off, or holler to Brian, 'don't leave, I'm in the tree!'

Since nobody answered the door, Brian got back in his truck and drove away. I watched all this take place from inside the tree. Seeing Brian's tail lights fade from my sight, I resumed my thoughts. 'There wasn't even a little bump in the feelings my body gave to me from this experience!' I knew what to expect when I masturbated without a rope around my neck, but I risked my life for nothing. I was still feeling, 'This was dumb!'

For all the effort I spent planning out this event to get a heightened sensation as I was expecting, the experience went down in flames. I was thinking, 'I'm glad I didn't lose my life over it!' It wasn't worth the worry, time, or effort to even think about doing it again. I was definitely feeling dumb, but I was alive. I thought, 'if I wasn't up in the tree playing with myself, I could have gone out on the town with Brian.' He always made fun things happen in life.

I went back to my thoughts. 'If I had to get any closer to death then the way I planned it, forget it!' I fortified my resolve never to try this again. I climbed down to the platform to get dressed as if this never happened. I was still lamenting, 'I could have gone with Brian.' He lived about ten minutes away. I thought of calling him, but I had a tendency to explain myself, so I decided to go back into the house and resume watching TV as if nothing ever happened at all. I was disappointed, knowing I could have been doing something fun.

Every time I heard of a suicide from that day forward and it was a boy, I wondered in my heart of hearts did he die from an unintended death, masturbating due to a lie which was passed around like candy, rolled in anticipation? I would never dare ask such a personal question to a family who lost a loved one due to suicide, but I felt the pain of their death with such great magnitude in my heart.

Years later I found out the name: 'auto-erotic asphyxia.' It's a lie that takes the life of many beautiful souls. It was reported as 'history's best kept secret.' When I did research on this while writing this book, I found out that about 1,000 people die each year trying this stunt.

Seeing Brian the next day, I never said a word to him about seeing him at my house.

Brian commented, "I saw your truck on the road, but you weren't home. I thought we could go do something?"

I said, "I'm sorry I missed you!" I didn't say anything further.

The day had come for Brian to leave on his mission for his church. He said his good-byes and left for the airport.

A few months later, Brian sent a letter from England. I knew it was from Brian, because of the unique envelope, and it had his name on the upper corner of the post. I was excited to open it up, thinking, 'This came all the way from England!'

Except for my kindergarten teacher Mrs. Petty, congratulating me for graduating high school, no one had ever sent me a personal letter before.

Brian explained how cold and cloudy England was compared to Utah. He continued, 'England's summers were six weeks long. I saw that message on a billboard at the beginning of summer, and it was right, summer was short!'

I continued reading.

He wrote, 'I told a friend who was with me, "Look, a blue cloud!" I could hear him laughing as if I was walking down the hall behind him. I hadn't considered looking up at a cloudy sky and seeing a blue cloud before, but Brian was a very positive person. I always looked at a blue cloud and thought of Brian thereafter. It was a positive way of seeing an overcast day.

Brian concluded in his letter with a personal note from his heart, writing, "The church's teachings are true." He added, "I love you whether you become a Mormon or not." He signed his name as 'Elder Brian.'

I thought, 'That was so nice of him to write, 'I love you whether you became a Mormon or not.''

A feeling of calmness and peace overshadowed me, a different feeling that I had never felt before in my heart. I thought, 'if this is what love feels like, it feels really nice. I pushed out the uncomfortable thought that I had never told Brian what attracted me to him in the first place, walking down the hall seeing his beautiful body. It no longer seemed to matter anyway. Afraid of saying anything about my same sex feelings, I resolved to keep them to myself, as I had promised. I kept reminding myself, 'I'm taking my feelings of attraction to my grave.' I decided to enjoy our friendship together. It was enough to know I had a friend who liked me, at least as he knew me.

CHAPTER TWENTY-NINE

SO GORGEOUS

I decided to enroll in a trade tech college to avoid a possible draft. That draft never seemed to materialize in Congress in the early 1980s, but I was committed to learn more about carpentry. I immediately became comfortable in my surroundings. The teacher Mr. Davies and two fellow students became important people to me.

After some carpentry pre-testing, Mr. Davies made a comment. "I think you're capable of more than you're leading on!"

I was shocked at how quickly he had come to this observation. His comment resonated with my brain immediately. I had thought that I thoroughly hid my behavior in the background of my brain and far away from the people around me. I knew he was right. From then on I felt comfortable in Mr. Davies' presence, knowing he could recognize my capabilities through my façade.

Mother's predicated words were deeply ingrained into my head, 'smart people are dumb and dumb people are smart.' I thought that I should always stop myself from appearing smart because that would make me dumb. Yet here Mr. Davies saw my smarts, my intelligence, and honored that, dismissing any illusion I imposed on myself from mother's belief.

He won my respect immediately. I saw that he was keen in his observations and brave enough to say something. I knew then and there he was a good teacher for me. I had only met a few teachers in my life that I

377

felt were true educators for my mind. Otherwise I spent most of my time figuring out how to beat the system. That in itself had its own value, but not always.

I knew I was capable of more, not just in building construction which I had already studied for over 10 years, but intellectually, too. I didn't know what to do with the information I had stored in my head, but I had the confidence that in time I could organize it. Empowering myself in the moment, I chose to exercise my intelligence, based on what I had envisioned, and had conceived in my head, and how it aligned in my future. Mr. Davies' comment was more valuable than he would ever know to my mind.

I thought that few people would expect a lot from me if I was dumb. Disempowering myself, depending on the moment, I picked and chose accordingly.

I also felt inadequate about my looks, so I gravitated to beautiful people to fill in the holes I felt I lacked in my physical appearance. My self-esteem was in disrepair, so I mimicked everything I felt was a miss to me, copying them nearly in their entirety. In the lunchroom, I saw a gorgeous student sitting at the lunch table eating his sandwich by himself. My heart seemed to intensify in its rhythm, beating a little faster than moments earlier. Seeing him sent butterflies to my stomach, then I felt the butterflies bumping into one another. He looked so nice; it was love at first sight. I found the courage to ask him, "Can I sit with you?"

He said, "Yes."

I said, "My name is Robert."

He said, "My name is Ryan."

I fell in love with his name, too.

Ryan was everything I wanted to look like and more. He was my age, soft spoken, had a cute laugh, clear skin, a beautiful face, long blond hair, blue eyes, fit as a fiddle, and clean in how he dressed. The butterflies kept flying! Ryan got up out of his seat to go to the candy machine. He said, 'Put sugar on shit, and people will eat it.' He laughed, and so did I. I never heard that before. I thought of my sweet tooth and felt he was right. His comment became etched in my mind, along with mother's: 'if you eat like a diabetic, you'll never become a diabetic.' I liked that Ryan was health conscious. It resonated with my health beliefs.

Attracted to his looks at first, I completely became enthralled with the rest of Ryan's personality. I really wanted to be his friend and to get to know him a lot better. Ryan seemed to be okay with me being his friend as well. In short order we talked about everything, well almost everything. I had a crush on Ryan I couldn't talk about. We worked and studied well together on college projects in the classroom and out in the field. He told me he was sexually active with girls. I couldn't tell Ryan, I was only sexually active with myself. I was very surprised at how honest he was with me. Except for mother sharing her intimate moments with Daddy, which I dismissed the best I could out of my head as if I didn't hear it, no one had ever shared something so personal with me.

I kept my feelings to myself and controlled my thoughts. I couldn't bring myself to say a word to Ryan about the feelings I had for him. I left my thoughts in my imagination, enjoying his presence and our camaraderie together.

I immediately mimicked Ryan's actions though not his character, processing his life into mine. I wanted to be anybody but myself, so it felt good to mimic people's attributes I found appealing. In a short order, I became the people I admired inside my mind. With little effort on my part, I mimicked multiple styles at once, being anybody but me. I grew and parted my hair to look like Ryan's hair.

I changed my laugh to sound like Ryan's laugh. I postured my body the way Ryan postured his body. I bought clothes, dressing myself like Ryan did. I mimicked everything about Ryan, except his car and how he thought. Ryan came across to me with confidence. I mimicked his confidence. It was nothing but a charade deep inside of me. I pressed on.

Our camaraderie connected well together at school and socializing in the city. Ryan invited me to his home. He showed me his motorcycle and a 1969 apple green polished Dodge Charger that screamed, 'Come get me!' I drove a 30-year-old 1950 Chevy pickup truck that hadn't been washed in 20 years or at least since the last time it rained. It didn't scream. It spoke softly, 'Old man driving down the road!'

Talking about his motorcycle, he said, "It's fast!"

I told Ryan, "I've only been on a motorcycle once before with my brother when I was a little boy."

Ryan said, "Do you want to go for a ride?"

I said, "Yes!" I hopped on the motorcycle sitting behind Ryan. I said, "Where do I hang on?"

He said, "The strap on the seat or hang onto me."

The thought of putting my arms around him gave me such an incredible feeling, but I was afraid. I grabbed the strap as we took off, headed for the freeway. I waited until we were out of the subdivision to take him up on his offer. I put my arms around him. The feeling was everything I had anticipated and more.

Ryan loved the speed of the bike. Feeling the momentum press against me, as the wind tousled my hair with a snap. I decided to take Ryan up on his offer, putting my arms around his body as we approached 90 mph. My eyes teared from the wind and the thrill.

My energy shot through the roof. I had no idea it would feel so good. I didn't care now if anyone saw us. I never thought to be so fortunate. My chest against Ryan's back was better than any thought I felt was possible. The ride took second place to the feeling of my arms tightly wrapped around his body. It was as if I was hanging on for dear life, and I was.

The energy from that one moment never dissipated from my feelings and never stopped producing butterflies. I didn't want to dismiss that moment out of my mind for anything. Thinking about my arms around Ryan's body increased my energy long after the ride was over. The thought brought a shortness of breath, a faster beat to my heart, a feeling which never abandoned me, never tired, nor left my soul. It was etched in me.

After the motorcycle ride, feeling comfortable in one another's presence, Ryan said, "Let's go pick up some girls at the mall. I got just the place to take them to overlook the city."

I said, "Girls?"

Ryan said, "Ya!"

I said, "Um…what mall do you want to go to pick up girls?"

Ryan said, "I know just the mall."

We switched vehicles to his gorgeous apple green Charger.

I figured he had done this before. I envisioned what Ryan wanted to do with the girls, since he had explained to me in details earlier.

I immediately became nervous. I'd never gone on a date before, let alone if anything else might happen. I didn't know what to say or what to do with a girl in my presence, except to be polite. My thoughts raced inside my head, sending concerned feelings to my stomach, uncomfortable feelings that I couldn't dismiss. These butterflies were not flying the same way as when I saw Ryan for the first time. I became more nervous inside my mind, particularly as we got closer to the mall. I figured Ryan would do all the talking; I had no idea what to say. Ryan would make all the right moves; I didn't know how to present myself. Ryan would say what needed to be said. I didn't know where to begin. I followed along, trusting Ryan and observing his actions closely.

When we arrived, we saw two girls leaning against a planter box inside the mall.

Ryan said, "Let's check them out! You take that one on the left, I'll take the one on the right."

With each step towards the girls, my thoughts scrambled, trying to find

381

confidence to overcome the fear I was hiding within myself. My nervousness increased as we approached. My mind emptied of all thought. I had to find confidence or this experience wasn't going to go so well.

Ryan did all the talking as I expected, asking the girls, "Do you want to come with us?"

Both girls were eager to go, almost simultaneously saying, "Yes!" It was as if they were waiting for two boys to pick them up.

I asked her name. She told me. I forgot it immediately.

Holding my girl's hand, we walked to the car beside Ryan and his girl. Ryan had this down. This was a completely new experience for me. It was more than I ever expected or imagined would take place with my friendship with Ryan. I knew through personal experiences orgasms were nice, but, in all the millions of bounces, hard or soft, comfortable or uncomfortable, irritated by wrinkles or not, I had never processed or prepared myself emotionally to be with a girl I was dating, let alone have sex with one of them. I had only imagined being with my future wife. I was letting my imagination get ahead of me though. I thought, 'maybe it would be okay! What will I do when the moment of truth is exposed?' I was scaring myself.

We drove from the mall parking lot to the upper avenues overlooking the city lights. I sat in the backseat with my girl expressionless, very nervous. My mind raced. I saw Ryan waste no time kissing his girl in the front seat. I had never kissed a girl before. I didn't know what to say or where to start or what to do. Uncomfortably sitting in the back seat, I waited on myself to take Ryan's lead. Filled with fear, paralyzed in a stupor of inactions and thought, I felt my arms squished up against her body. It started losing its feeling, because I did nothing to create circulation in my arm.

Ryan stopped kissing long enough to take a tiny swig from a little bottle he showed me earlier. It was his bottle of Everclear, 190 proof. I didn't drink, but I knew 200 was pure alcohol. I watched Ryan take a swig, then re-engaged his lips onto hers again. I didn't think he would drink while on a date.

My girl seemed bored, sitting next to me with no action. She spoke up. "I want some pudding."

My mind didn't go empty with what she just said. 'What did she say?' I thought, 'She wants my sperm?' I looked towards Ryan as if to say, 'Did you just hear what she said?'

Ryan took another swig and continued kissing his girlfriend.

I thought, 'I don't think he heard her.' I didn't know what to do with her request. Again, Ryan took another swig. I was pretty sure Ryan was out of it at the moment.

Convinced Ryan heard nothing, I abandoned her request, unable to act out on anything my thoughts played out inside me.

Ryan said shortly thereafter, "I don't think I can drive. Do you want to drive?"

That was good news for me. I said, "Yes, I'll drive." From the backseat to the driver's seat was a good escape for me. I felt so uncomfortable staying there any longer.

Driving the girls home was a relief. Both were going to be dropped off together. Yet this only brought another concern for me. Would she expect a goodbye kiss? Out of the car, Ryan wasted no time putting his arms around the girl's body, kissing her passionately. I nervously attempted to kiss my girl, mimicking what I observed Ryan doing, thinking, 'I don't know how to do any of this stuff.' I couldn't mimic what I saw Ryan doing, and it only made me feel more uncomfortable.

I flashed back, seeing Daddy put his arms around mother and giving her a peck on the lips. It was nothing passionate. None of my brothers were married, kissing was never talked about at the kitchen table, so I had no clue. Watching TV didn't teach me about kissing. It wasn't real anyway. I had nothing in my head. I felt no passion or excitement in my pucker.

I was concerned about getting germs and wondered if I had bad breath

383

besides. Mother's words bolstered this thought process from the many times she had said, "You were made with germs!" Mother's comment didn't make me feel any better. This moment was like the entire evening, I was putting a square peg into a round hole. This experience was much more than I wanted to take in.

I had too much to think about that didn't fit me. In spite of my uncomfortable state of mind, I tried kissing her. Feeling I had the talent of a watermelon I stopped, fortifying how uncomfortable I felt. Ryan continued kissing his girl. I walked to the driver's door, waiting for Ryan to stop kissing her, thinking, 'I'll be glad when this is over.' I waited again for Ryan to stop kissing her so I could drive us home. I waited patiently until he was finished. At his home, I got out and met Ryan at the back of his car, and I handed him the keys.

I asked Ryan, "Did you not hear what that girl said who I was sitting with in the back seat?"

Ryan said, "No!"

I said, "She wanted my pudding!"

"What?!"

Ryan said, "Why didn't you say something! Oh, I can't believe I missed that!"

He expelled air quickly through his lips, circling in disbelief of the missed opportunity.

I replied, "I just figured you ignored what she said."

Ryan said, "No, I didn't hear her." Still frustrated, Ryan said, "That was the whole purpose of picking up the girls tonight."

I thought, 'I'm glad it's all over.' I didn't say it out loud. We talked for a few more minutes before I left.

I knew Ryan was upset from the missed opportunity. I would have loved to have seen more of Ryan's body. I changed my thoughts to what I could control, thinking about the opportunity I had to drive Ryan's apple green

Dodge Charger. I hopped in my old unkempt pickup truck, closing the door and hearing the metal scrape against its frame in the jamb. It screeched in my ears. With the door tightly closed, I knew with a surety I was going to bed still a virgin.

I walked into the house after the evening was over. A picture on a piece of paper caught my attention as I walked by. I stopped and picked it up. It turned out to be an anti-Mormon flyer. I knew immediately it was mother's. Looking at the picture, the words faded from my view. The literature depicted an unflattering picture of a black woman wearing strange underwear. They were like nothing I had ever seen before. I thought, 'I'm glad I'm not a Mormon.' The clothing hid her body and looked confining and uncomfortable to me. I liked wearing the least amount of clothes possible for the sun to touch my body, tanning everywhere my imagination took me.

The latest news from the Mormons was that the leader had had a spiritual revelation that blacks should be allowed to receive the priesthood.

Mother was outraged, saying, "They're just trying to avoid a lawsuit. That's what this is all about! A message from God! Who would believe that bullshit!"

The fact that mother had this flyer didn't surprise me. I thought about mother's disgust with Mormons, Mormonism, and religion in general. It didn't matter to mother if the leader of the Mormon church allowed black people to receive and hold the priesthood. It didn't matter if they allowed black people to join the church some 12 months earlier or yesterday or 100 years ago. Yet mother was happy to use it against them if she could. Mother was as defiant as ever towards Mormons. Mother passed out the literature to specific people who had joined that religion, trying to persuade them to think otherwise.

I knew Ryan and his family weren't Mormons or Jack Mormons. Based on what Ryan told me, I picked up the literature to take to Ryan's mom. Looking at the picture more closely, it was no less unflattering the

385

second time I viewed it. That was okay with me. I didn't care. I wanted to follow mother's lead. I didn't read any of the words. I didn't know how to comprehend what I read anyway, and I didn't bother trying. As long as it was anti-Mormon literature, that's all that mattered to me.

Handing the paper to Ryan's mom, I said, "I got this from my mother. It might be interesting to you?"

She looked it over intently. I stood waiting for a response. She flipped the paper over to see if there was anything on the other side. There wasn't. She asked me, "Did you read this?"

I told her, "No, I didn't read it."

Ryan's mom summarized its message for me. Whatever she said dissipated about as fast as it entered my mind. Only the picture remained in my head. I was still thinking, 'I'm glad I'm not a Mormon!' After a nonchalant response from both his mother and me, I dismissed myself to be with Ryan. I didn't know who else to pass the literature out to, so I didn't.

Ryan and I left his home to drag State Street, hoping to pick up some more girls and show off his car. It turned out to be a fairly uneventful evening. Once it ended, Ryan took me back to his home. We talked for a short time before I left to go to my house.

I hopped into bed, turned over on my stomach, stretched out over my pillow and clasped my left hand on my right wrist in preparation to bounce my head. I paused to feel the coolness of the pillow case against my face until it dissipated into the thoughts of the day. I connected one experience to another, finding any commonality between them. I bounced, thinking of all the events of the last several weeks: my friend Ryan's gorgeous body, wrapping my arms around him on the motorcycle, the girls he wanted to pick up, the awkward moments overlooking the city lights. One thought after the next bounced through my head. I thought of the girl wanting my pudding. I wondered what I had missed. I bounced non-stop. Maybe it didn't matter. I bounced with more intensity, wondering about having sex with a girl, I bounced with an intention to understand life, thinking everything was possible. I bounced, wondering what sex would be like with Ryan. I bounced feeling the energy of that thought which only participation surrendered to. Bouncing felt so good for my mind to feel. I had unlimited energy.

I bounced, invigorated by the sensation of my face hitting the pillow, followed by calming thoughts of life. It felt so good to imagine life's fullness. I continued processing specific conversations and thoughts which had bothered me the most. I answered questions which rotated in my head from questions people asked of me years earlier, thinking about them as if they just happened in the moment. I replayed my answers out loud as if it was yesterday. I bounced thinking, as better answers occurred to me, I thought before bouncing again, 'I should have answered that question a different way.'

With that thought in my mind, I turned my head to the side, using my nose and my finger to open a pocket in my pillow to breathe clearly. Satisfied with the amount of air I was inhaling, I took a deep breath through my nose, pausing for a moment before exhaling. I listened to the night's silent sound before taking another breath. I laid still, listening to the messages which whispered in my mind. I asked myself, 'what is my mind trying to tell me?' I laid still, hearing the feeling of my heart beat. My heart's rhythm echoed in my ears, beating into my bed. In the stillness of the moment, I listened for the messages to whisper in my mind. I waited for the answer like osmosis. I knew an answer would come out of thin air to enter my mind when I was ready to hear it. I replayed another conversation, re-answering the same question over again differently. I really liked my thoughts of Ryan.

My mind switched thoughts like gears in a complicated transmission. A persistent thought resurfaced, interrupting my thinking. I asked myself, 'why am I irritated with that thought? Why did I say it that way? What other way could I have said it?' Feeling uncomfortable with the new answer I came up with, I repeated the process until I found an answer I was comfortable with.

387

Once I found no misunderstandings with a new answer, I began bouncing again, moving to another thought, stopping again and allowing a flood of new thoughts to enter my head. I continued bouncing, then stopped.

With my eyes closed, I held my head above the surface of my pillow, listening to my mind. Suddenly I farted. It made me laugh. My thought dissipated, and a new thought entered my mind. I thought of the spacecraft going to the moon, using air as a lubricant. I connected that air with my body. As far as I was concerned, my body was functioning the way it was supposed to in order to stay healthy. I liked being healthy. I flung the sheets to clear the air. I resumed watching images float across the insides of my eyelids. My eyes moved around, like watching an action seen in a movie. My eyes caught different shades of black floating across the backs of my lids. I resumed bouncing my head for what seemed hours. It felt so good. I knew I could do a thousand bounces in a little over eight minutes. I didn't care about the time, I just enjoyed bouncing my head. Satisfied with my conclusions of thought, I adjusted my body to fall asleep and did so.

CHAPTER THIRTY

THE AMERICAN WAY

AJ was the third person that became important to me in college. He wanted to get to know me. I assumed he was attracted to me in some way like I was attracted to Ryan, but I didn't know what yet. I was not attracted to AJ at all. He didn't look anything like Ryan. Married with a child on the way, AJ had a big head. He was short and stocky, about ten years older than me. He was from upstate New York, and he talked in a monotone New York accent about girls and fast cars. Both subjects were unimportant and boring to me. We were as opposite as opposites could be.

I visually gravitated to people who filled in holes I felt I had in me, holes that kept me from feeling complete. I imagined AJ had holes in himself that I filled. I didn't know what holes I could fill for someone else.

AJ didn't fill any holes in me until he asked an unlikely question. He asked, "Do you want to become a millionaire?"

The unlikely friendship between the two of us began with that simple question. It became clear to me that AJ's interest in me was as a friend in business. That suited me well. Becoming a millionaire was a hole I was looking to fill, one that originated in my childhood dreams as a ten-year-old boy. I had spent hours bouncing my head, formulating how to become one. I felt deep within me that if I was going to go anywhere in life, or if I was going to be important, I needed to become a millionaire. Then I would be important. As I matured, I realized that wealth wasn't what made a person important, but the goal remained as a part of a full life.

AJ called me one evening.

I said, "Hello."

He said, "This is AJ."

I said, "Hi AJ!" I hoped that he was going to talk to me about becoming rich. In the back of my mind, I worried that it might be another solicitation for sex. I was willing to risk it. I needed someone to teach me how to become a millionaire.

He said, "Do you want to hear about all the cars I once owned?"

As soon as the word cars came out of his mouth I became tired. I said, "No." I had no interest in cars. I thought for a brief moment that the sex phone calls weren't as bad as I thought. At least they weren't boring.

AJ said, "What! You don't want to hear about my cars?"

I replied, "No, I have to go to sleep." I was thinking, 'I'd rather dream about eating peaches then listen to a list of cars AJ once owned.' I wanted to end the call as soon as possible.

Despite our different interests, AJ and I grew in our friendship. Ryan appealed to the beautiful side I wanted to be on the outside. AJ appealed to the entrepreneur side I needed to become on the inside. I wanted to learn more, to understand wealth.

AJ, a part-time entrepreneur, finally said something I wanted to hear. "Can I show you a business opportunity where you could become a millionaire?"

That was a hole I'd been waiting to fill since I was a little boy. I'd bounced my head millions of times thinking what life would be like being a millionaire. I had my answer to AJ's question in no time flat. I said, "YES!"

Interested and anxious to see what AJ was excited to show me himself, I prepared myself mentally, making sure I kept an open mind. I knew that it would take a lot of work to become wealthy. I just needed to see or hear the pattern of how to get there. I was willing to work hard to make life happen for me the way I needed it to work for me.

As early as elementary school, I had been determined to reach my goal. When my so-called friends would reject me, I saw their actions as a stepping stone to my becoming rich. I would sometimes think out loud, "They don't want to invite me to anything? I don't care! I'm not going to let them distract me! I'm going to go to work and work harder than I've ever worked before! My friends are going to make me rich!" I was trying to fill the hole of abandonment that was rooted deep inside of me with my pursuit of success. Eventually I learned my friends weren't going to make me anything. I would make myself by molding my mind to fit my destination.

I told myself over and over again that I would be a millionaire, tapping my destination into me, calculating every move. I would buy land, build a house on a hill, drive a Cadillac, become a mom. I may have been masking the pain of feeling unwelcome and unvalued by my friends and family, but it motivated me. I worked harder, putting in long hours in my lawn business, and I built relationships with my lawn customers instead of worrying about personal relationships. My adult customers talked to me kindly. I asked them questions about their lives. My interactions with them gave me the freedom to treat them the way I wanted to be treated. I served them hand and foot, giving them value for what they paid me to do. I appreciated that they worked hard in their lives to afford me to be there. I didn't take advantage of their money. I felt privileged to work for them. I wanted to learn how they got where they got in life, in order to afford my services.

I recalled Mr. Johnson, my high school construction teacher, telling me once, "A barber can learn how to become a very wealthy person."

I said, "How is that?"

He said, "All he has to do is ask the person who is sitting in his chair, 'how did he earn his money?'" Mr. Johnson smiled. "Yeah, he has a captive audience for about an hour. Most people will tell you how they made their wealth in life if you ask them." He continued, "They'll give you stock tips, advice in investing, business ideas, real estate, even their financial secrets."

I said, "This is really simple."

I was impressed. I bounced my head on that piece of advice throughout my life.

I didn't cut hair, but I did cut lawns. I gained their trust, and asked each of my lawn customers, 'How did you earn your wealth?'

They were happy to talk to me, and I listened.

I was very open to understanding financial principles more than I would ever know.

I just needed someone to show me more than what I knew to help me understand wealth as a reality outside of my imagination, far beyond my upbringing. The evening came for me to see what AJ was talking to me about.

AJ said, "I'll pick you up from your house around 6:30 tonight and take you to the meeting with me."

I said, "Okay, I'll be ready."

AJ did what he said he would do. He picked me up at my house and took me to a meeting place, somebody else's home. There were other people at the house besides me. I tried not to feel shy or uncomfortable being around so many people I didn't know. I trusted AJ.

AJ introduced me to a man by the name of Richard. After a pleasant introduction and welcome, Richard began the meeting.

He asked all of us, "If money was no object, what would you do with it?" He followed this by asking the next question, "What is your dream?"

People answered.

I raised my hand.

"Robert, what is your dream?"

I thought, 'he remembered my name.'

That aside, nobody ever asked me that question before!

I had a myriad of dreams that I had thought of doing while bouncing my head all those nights. I had an answer for him. I said, "I want to be a millionaire, I want to buy acres of land and a red 1959 Cadillac convertible, with its big flared tail lights! It has been a dream for me ever since I saw one driving down the road!" I thought the '59 Cadillac had a flair which seemed to garnish my personality, representing my flamboyant style that I had yet to fully express. I also wanted so badly to be noticed, to be seen as valuable and unique. I continued, "Yeah, the '59 Cadillac is one of my dream cars!"

Richard said, "That's good! It's important to have a dream!"

Others answered with what was in their heart of dreams.

Richard wrote everybody's dreams on the paper, moving on in the meeting and talking about commerce. He explained the flow of goods and services in our economic system. I understood commerce. I thought back to 7th grade when my economics teacher wanted to know how much the class understood about commerce. The teacher gave each of the students homework to give an example in the front of class. I decided to use a pencil as an example. From cutting down a tree with a chainsaw to driving trucks delivering the finished product to market, I knew there was a lot that went into a product like a pencil from conception to reality. I explained everything in detail from my understanding to the class, even with such a simple product.

Richard caught my attention, drawing circles at the top of the paper, saying at the same time, "This is 'YOU."

I envisioned myself there as he said, "YOU."

He then drew out six circles under the word YOU, saying, "You sponsor six people and they sponsor four and they sponsor two people. If everyone buys a little, it adds up to a lot."

I could see this happening. I felt really excited.

Richard asked, "Who buys everyday products like toothpaste and laundry detergent? Everybody does!" Richard continued, "Who are some people you think would be interested in using products, buying from themselves in their own business or making some extra money on the side?"

That was an easy question for me. I spit out some names.

Richard wrote down the names of the people in the circles, saying, "They have the opportunity to build a business as big or bigger than you. There are no limitations!"

My mind soared with possibilities. This all made sense to me. I became more interested as he talked about the company and how it was founded.

Richard continued telling about the business in detail. It seemed to go on a little long as the meeting approached 2 hours. He explained how the company took the term 'American Way' and shortened it to 'Amway,' writing AMWAY on the paper and circling it several times.

I had no reaction to this part of his presentation. I remember seeing some Amway products around the house that mother used. I had no preconceived idea that this was what Amway was all about. With what Richard just showed me, I thought 'this seems too simple, but I like it!'

I said, "I think I'm interested in signing up! What does it cost to get in?"
Richard said, "$99."

I thought to myself, 'I can afford that!'

Richard said, "We can talk tomorrow. It will be just as good then!"
I said, "Okay."

I felt good about AJ's friendship and these new people I just met. I had a good feeling it was going to work out really well.

Richard said, "All you have to do is talk to other people and encourage them to live their dreams, and in return it will help you, too!"

Seeing this plan reminded me of Daddy telling me to save 10% of everything I earn, and my comment back to Daddy, 'I'll just make a lot of money.' I thought, 'This would be the financial vehicle I could earn a lot of money with.'

This business seemed easy. Except I learned in short order not everyone was as interested as I thought they would be in living their dreams. I was rejected over and over again, but I pressed on, talking to people. I knew I needed to break out of my silent cocoon which I had tended to gravitate to and hibernate in. I knew if I was going to live my dreams, I had to overcome my tendency to withdraw from people.

I practiced my lines over and over again. I struggled with self-esteem, buying an endless loop tape and recording a message I came up with. Playing it while I slept I told myself, 'I can do it! I believe in myself! I'm successful!' I played the tape in my ears throughout the night, jamming my subconscious mind with positive affirmations, only to find myself irritated after a while, feeling unrested. I turned off the tape so that I could sleep. Still, I played the tape night after night.

I was successful in bringing other people into the business, people who were already millionaires and those who were not yet established in life. Once I sponsored them, I didn't know what to do with them. In short, they fell away. I wasn't having financial success in particular, but I was learning about financial principles, along with better judgment with the use of money. I had to learn how not to suppress the feeling to run and hide from people which I innately had to fight within myself. I learned to look people in the eye when I talk to them. Both of these skills were very difficult for me to learn.

I listened to positive clichés, reading books on success principles, except I couldn't get past the first chapter because I couldn't comprehend what I read. I lost interest in reading. It was no different than high school for me. I couldn't figure out how to beat the system I committed myself to. Success seemed to be surrounded by very tall walls. People aren't able to penetrate the walls, dig underneath them, or even parachute over them. Success takes time.

I became drawn back to my lawn business. I didn't give up on my Amway business, but I found walking behind the lawnmower, cutting lawns with its back and forth pattern, was stimulating and rewarding to my mind. I also received immediate gratification through compliments of a job well done. And I got immediate compensation, motivating me to work even harder. I pressed on with Amway in the evenings. After a long day cutting lawns, I dedicated time to go with AJ and Richard to weekend seminars and rallies monthly. Little by little, pieces of information entered my head. I never gave up the feeling I would succeed in becoming a millionaire.

I realized the business opportunity was an ingenious idea, but it had a problem. Yet that problem was also the solution to the problem–it was people. Not every person had the same idea on how to get to their dream or goal. People didn't understand how choosing their goals wisely would lead them to their dreams. I decided to become a student of success principles with the intent to become important and serve people. I realized that earning money was the wrong dream, the wrong goal. I was missing several steps. I needed to focus on being of service to people, and the money would automatically follow. I also realized that becoming a millionaire was going to be harder than I thought. It was going to take a lot of hard work. I learned that just because someone goes into business for themselves doesn't mean a truckload of money is going to back up at their doorstep and dumped at the door.

To keep motivated, I needed to focus on something tangible. I wrote down my dreams, finding posters of my dream car. I was going to buy a brand new Cadillac. It was on the top of my list.

The people in the Amway business were all Mormons, including AJ, yet neither AJ nor anybody else ever tried to push their religion on me. I didn't think of them as 'Jack Mormons,' but people who lived their religion. Unlike what mother had said about Mormons, they didn't have an agenda and they didn't reject me because I wasn't Mormon. I never felt threatened or that they were out to get me to be one of them. Even though I passed out anti-Mormon literature, I had no feelings of intimidation or coercion with the group.

396

AJ asked me, "Would you be interested in driving back east to Missouri to attend a seminar and rally?" He continued, "It'll be an 18 or 20 hour drive one way."

Sitting in a car for that many hours made me think of mother sitting in her old rattle trap. Still, it sounded interesting to go to the rally. I said, "I'll go."

Feeling uneasy and outside my comfort zone, I knew I was venturing into unknown territory by going on this trip. The first fear which came to my mind was using a public toilet to poop in. I became paranoid about what to do. I decided to prepare my mind and not allow my body to do a bowel movement. I scared myself from doing what was so important for a body to do. Nonetheless, in spite of my fear of pooping, I adjusted my schedule in my body, mind, and the lawn accounts in order to accommodate this event, only allowing myself to use the toilet to pee in.

Other bodily functions concerned me too, like, 'What if I had to fart?' I thought it was a disgusting sound, not to mention the smell. Even if I let it out quietly, the stench could be unbearable. I had few options. I'd never been around people in such tight quarters. It was like I didn't allow myself to be human. It wasn't okay for me to fart. Mother always let out big farts that squeaked, and it was disgusting. I plugged my ears as fast as I could so as not to let the sound waves hit my ear drums! Between mother showing off her poop and the sound of mother farting, I seemed to be somewhat paranoid about the subject. Mother would have no idea of the long term effects on me personally.

Other than these issues, I was excited to go and learn valuable principles of becoming wealthy.

Leaving early Thursday morning, we drove into the sunrise, driving all day so that we would arrive before the first event Friday night. We rented one room with two beds near the conference center. I was told we would separate the bed from the mattress so that we could cram more people into

397

the room and make it cheaper to rent.

Friday's function began. I nervously checked in on my body to be sure all bowel movements would stay on hold for the next two to three days.

There was a lot of excitement in the air. There were numerous speakers, motivational music, and big screens sharing messages of positivity and inspiration. I found a seat along with 15,000 other people who also made the long trip to Missouri from all over the world. We were all there to get pumped up so that we could return home and build our businesses with renewed enthusiasm!

Saturday's function was no less packed with people, excitement, and activities. The feeling of camaraderie was electrifying. After a break Saturday night it was announced that there would be Sunday services by the evangelical preacher Mac Evans.

I asked Richard, "Are we going to go home before or after the service?" I was thinking, 'I'm not interested in sitting through church services when we could be driving home.' Besides, I had a schedule to keep up with my lawn business.

Richard said, "We'll leave Sunday after church services are over."

I said, "Okay." I reminded myself not to have any bodily bowel movements or sounds, preparing my mind not to use the toilet on the way back home. I wanted no emergencies! Sunday morning the music blared, introducing Mac Evans for the beginning of Sunday services. It seemed to me to be more like a part of the rally. The audience roared with a loud cheer of excitement and respect, just as they had done with the previous speakers.

Mac praised Jesus. I immediately tuned out, at least partially. I didn't understand anything about the Bible or the verses he talked about. I understood very little about Jesus. I did enjoy the pop song "Jesus Christ Superstar" and I heard Lonnie's dad use the name Jesus as a cuss word. Other than that, nothing specific followed in my mind to connect me with what he was saying. I listened, being little more than a captive audience.

Still, the more he talked, the more I found his stories of Jesus interesting.

Mac talked about being saved. That caught my attention. He spoke of repentance. I thought of my past, stealing from the lumber company, from mother, and other people. I thought of how I would change price tags in the store to reduce the prices I paid. He said that I could be forgiven of all these past sins to clear my conscience.

Mother's repeated statement to me came into focus: "You have a brain and a conscience. Use it."

I wanted to have the peace of a clear conscience Mac talked about.

Mac said, "I invite all who are ready to come down to the front of the stage in Jesus' name, to be at the foot of Jesus, realizing with a humble prayer that you are a sinner in need of a savior, and a desire to let Jesus into your heart and soul to be saved. In Jesus' name, Amen."

Soft reverent music played as I watched people walk step by step down to the front of the stage. Even people from the top of the arena where I sat filtered down one by one. More sat in their seats like me.

I sat forward in my chair with my elbow on my knees, my arms reaching up to hold up my head. My chin was coddled in between my two thumbs and my clasped hands were over my mouth.

I watched people continue to walk down to the stage. The music continued playing softly while Mac encouraged people saying, "Let go of the toils of life. Let go of your sins and let them be washed away. Allow Jesus to heal your troubled soul."

I watched the people walking to the stage while my mind processed what I had heard. I habitually stole stuff, and I knew it was wrong, but I had never considered myself a sinner before. For the first time, I thought maybe I was, and maybe I should repent and make right what I had done wrong.

I removed my head from my comfortable position, turned to Richard sitting next to me, and said, "I think I'll go down." Right away I felt a little awkward with what I had just said. I didn't expect those words to come out of my mouth, but I felt it was a good decision. I felt it was the first step in making right on the wrongs I had done.

Richard said, "I'll go down with you."

We walked down the stairs towards the stage. I didn't know what to expect. This was all new to me. Yet I knew it was right.

Mac talked tenderly as people gathered, saying, "Let Jesus into your life. Feel his presence!"

More people in the coliseum got out of their seats and filtered toward the stage, walking towards their salvation.

I walked to the stage, too, feeling like I was allowing Jesus to expand the firmament of my being with each step I took towards him. I felt a peace within my soul I had never felt before. It felt so comfortable, so good.

Standing amongst others who made the track down, I allowed the feeling of Jesus to fill my soul. I felt Jesus was there to help me make things right. I still didn't 100 percent understand the idea of being a sinner, but I was contrite in my spirit and I knew I needed Him. I felt Him there with me.

Mother's rants on religion never entered my thoughts. I had a lot to be forgiven for, thinking of all the thefts I committed. I felt I needed to make right with those I stole from.

Mac offered a prayer to those who stood before him. He spoke in Jesus' name, saying, "Feel the fullness of forgiveness with the acknowledgment of Jesus into your life. Let go of your sins and feel the love of Jesus!"

I stood before Mac and a number of other people. Some wept openly, feeling the joy of forgiveness. Others felt their hearts filled with the fullness of Jesus' spirit. I didn't tear up, but I fully embraced this new experience of peace in my soul. I hadn't expected to find peace at an Amway rally, let alone find God.

After the prayer, I returned to my seat, feeling Jesus had entered into my life somehow. I didn't understand everything in that moment as I processed my feelings, but I appreciated it. I especially appreciated that Richard had accompanied me.

After the service, it was time to leave. Sitting in the car on the way back, I listened to others in the car tell stories about Mormonism, God, and temples. I added nothing to the conversation. I just listened. The experience was reminiscent of how I used to sit and listen to the old Germans.

One story of building a temple in Hong Kong grabbed me. Richard's dad Everett, a soft spoken man, said in a very deliberate voice, "In Hong Kong, if your building cast a shadow on another owner's building and they filed a complaint from your proposed building, you couldn't build it." Everett continued, "When the church decided to build in Hong Kong, an ad was put in the paper. The church had a 45 day waiting period for complaints to be filed. If there were no complaints or protests the church would be allowed to build their building."

Everett continued, "After the 45th day no protests had been submitted. The government officials couldn't understand it. They said, "There must be something wrong." Another 45 day waiting period was required before a building permit would be issued. Another 45 days passed with no protests! The permit was issued for the church to build its building. The next day a complaint was filed, but it was too late. The permit was issued and the church was granted its building permit." Everett added, "It was absolutely astonishing that there was no protest. It was a miracle for this to happen the way it turned out. God's hand had to be involved."

I was more fascinated than ever with Everett's story, thinking about God, Mormonism, and Jesus. I don't know today if the story was true, but I believed it.

Religion became a phenomenon to me that was like a sixth sense. I likened it to sitting at the kitchen table, listening to mother's friends escape Germany or survive Nazi concentration camps. A silent dialogue played out in my head. I didn't hear the same radical tones I heard from mother's voice, the ones that played like an endlessly looping tape of complaints and vile feelings.

Everett's voice had a calmness I hadn't heard before. It was the tone in his voice which told the story inside of me. Everett's voice resonated with what I heard when I was six years old, the day I was riding my bike and kept falling off the edge. It was the day I closed my eyes and heard the voice in my head, saying, "I am watching over you." I knew it to be God's voice. The two voices were very much alike, that of Everett telling stories on that drive home, and that of God the day I heard Him speak when I was young. I couldn't dismiss Everett's words. They whispered a calmness to my soul, a calmness I needed to feel.

Arriving home safe, I finally relieved myself. Feeling physically better, and feeling spiritually better than ever, I went to bed. I recalled the stories I had heard while bouncing my head with fervency. I stopped only to scratch an itch on my nose. I embraced the soft feathers with each bounce of my face. I replayed the conversation over and over again in my head, thinking about my experience of allowing Jesus into my life, thinking and processing a mix of conversations with each bounce of my head until I had satisfied my need to repeat the events of the day with each bounce. Finally, shifting my body, I faded out to sleep, allowing my experience of the weekend to fade into the recesses of my soul.

CHAPTER THIRTY-ONE

A FAINT HEART

After Mike, Brian, and Greg left on their missions, I began a weekly tradition on Monday night where I would leave a rose at the doorsteps of each of their families. The parents of my friends were so nice to me, I felt the need to give back to their families what I felt in my heart they had given to me. I would always leave a real rose, coordinating the color with the season or holiday of the week. The exception was Halloween when I laid a black rose at their doorsteps. I had to spray paint them, because black roses don't exist anywhere in nature. I also had to use silk roses instead of real ones so that the paint didn't destroy the roses.

I had never had so many people show their generosity as my friends' families had. I didn't care if they were Mormons. I didn't classify them as such. I classified people as nice and not nice. I had no reason not to like them. In my mind, we just happened to live in 'Mormon country' so a lot of people were Mormon. It was simple and straightforward. I had learned at mother's knee that religion should be despised, and the Mormon influence was a big part of why mother hated Utah. Religion in general agitated mother, but I found as I reached my maturity that religion did not agitate me. Religious people were nice to me, and that's all I needed to witness. That's all I needed to feel, and I felt it.

Anticipation coursed through my veins as I planned out the roses for the week's tradition. It went on for months. I made the decision as long as they didn't know it was me that was leaving the roses, I would continue. I bounced my head at night, thinking about how I had laid the roses that night, how I had rung the doorbell and ran to my car, feeling my heart beat fast and the rush of adrenaline as I opened the car door. Each time, I thought, 'I didn't get caught.' I bounced with energy and delight as I recalled my mysterious gift-giving.

With most of the homes, it was fairly easy to lay the rose down and run. I could conceal myself nearby fairly quickly. That was not the case at Mike's home. Mike's parents lived deep at the end of a cul-de-sac. There was one way in and one way out. Laying the rose at the doorstep meant running from my car down the street, laying the rose, and running the same distance again up the block to make my getaway. I felt if I was going to get caught I would get caught at Mike's house. I planned accordingly.

Each time I parked my car down the road, leaving my door unlocked, knowing a quick getaway was important. I trained myself to start the car fast. I mentally rehearsed the feel and shape of the key in my fingers so that when I needed to start the car I could do it without having to look for the correct one or fumble for it as I put in it the ignition. Mike had older brothers still living at home.

A few times after laying down the rose and running away, I could hear them hollering "HEY!" as I ran down the darkened road. I ran faster to my car when I heard them, feeling more exuberant than ever. As I turned out of the neighborhood each time, I would think, 'I got away!' I knew they had become curious as to who was doing this and I sensed they were trying to catch me.

This continued for months, until the fateful day when I was finally caught. It was at Mike's house, as I figured it would be. On this Monday, I did what I always did, leaving my car down the block unlocked and nonchalantly walking to the house with the rose held tight to my side. I wanted to be sure I didn't have a recognizable silhouette from any neighboring porch lights. My heart beat fast as it always did upon approaching the doorstep. It seemed no different than any other time, except this time they left their porch light on. I hesitated for a moment but decided to stay consistent. I laid the rose down and ran.

I ran to my car, hearing a little rustling from the bushes behind me. I thought nothing of it. One step shy of reaching the sidewalk, I felt two arms around my stomach. I flung forward. I was stopped dead in my tracks. I never reached the sidewalk. My mind said quickly, 'you've been caught!' Mark and Mike's other brothers had been hiding in different parts of the front yard behind the bushes. They all came out at me at once to be sure I wasn't going anywhere. Mark held me until I relented from my attempts to escape. He was bigger and stronger than me so it was no use. After I relented, he released me. The pursuit was over.

I stood upright, turned around, and the light from their porch lit my face.

Mark said, "We thought it was you!"

He was right of course. I smiled, laughed and said, "You caught me!" I was grinning from ear to ear.

With the soft porch light in my eyes, David said, "We've been trying to catch you for weeks, but you were too quick. That's why we decided to hide in the bushes, waiting to catch whoever was doing this."

I said, "I appreciated how your parents treated me."

They were very appreciative of my gesture.

I cut the conversation short. I had more roses to deliver. They went into their home, confirming to their parents it was me. They told them what I said about appreciating them, explaining why I was doing this.

I stopped delivering roses after that evening, satisfied with the amount of time I was able to pursue my appreciation for their love. I felt fulfilled in my heart.

I quit college with one semester left to go to pursue my lawn business during the day and build my Amway business at night. I was working harder than ever on myself. I was stepping out of my comfort zone to talk to people I didn't know, setting up appointments, and showing them the plan only to spring on them at the end, "It's Amway." I felt squeamish about telling them it was Amway, because Amway had developed negative connotations with many people.

Each time I prepared myself as if I was going to get flogged for saying the word Amway. Many times I would feel as if I had convinced them this was the best thing since sliced bread, only to hear, "I'm not interested!" In the Amway meetings, I was taught to tell myself, 'One more no to go,' and to keep going, which I did. With my friends gone on their missions, I had plenty of time in the evenings to spend on my pursuit of mental development and wealth.

Reaching deep inside of me, I stepped through many doorways of fear and frustration. I trained my mind to keep practicing. I believed I was more than a lawn boy. I didn't want to be cutting lawns for the rest of my life. I imagined people asking me in the future, "How long have you been cutting lawns?" I imagined that I would sound like an old man, answering, "I've been cutting lawns for 40 years!" At that moment I decided that I didn't want to ever say that. I would cut lawns for the purpose of getting out of cutting lawns. I didn't know when my final year would be, but I knew it would come.

One night one of the most successful Amway business partners, Jerry, was coming into town to show people 'the plan.' In Amway's multi-level marketing system, people who had sponsored others were referred to as "upline" from those they had sponsored. I found myself sitting in a meeting that lasted the better part of two hours. I was trying to stay awake, but I felt like I was being serenaded to sleep. I struggled to stay awake. My body was used to running all day long. Sitting and listening was difficult, but I persisted in order to listen and participate.

Richard's wife Marilyn, one of my uplines, recognized a behavior which was noticeably different. She noticed that I mimicked the people around me. I knew she was right. I chose some people like Ryan because I found them beautiful to my eyes. More often than not, I just mimicked people's mannerisms. One day I mimicked the mannerisms of Casey and other upline sponsors. Another day it was Jerry or Richard or anybody else I admired. It depended on my environmental thoughts of the day. It could be anybody; anybody but Robert. Although sometimes I was Robert, though I didn't really know what that meant. I rotated through people mimicking their style, behaviors, voice or mannerisms. Like spinning a blackjack wheel, 'where the ball stops, nobody knows.' 'Who is Robert today, nobody knows.' Neither did I.

I still don't really know. Identity is relational. It isn't something that exists just inside like society teaches. It is something that we recognize only when we are observing ourselves in relation to something or someone else. It might be that we are relating to another person ("I am introverted" or "I am a good friend") or we might be relating to a place ("I am from Utah" or "I am a city person"). We identify with whatever it is that we choose to relate to or that we feel compelled to relate to. In God's creation, Adam and Eve were created to be in relationship with God and each other. It is the same for us. Maybe the bottom line is that no man is an island.

My upline friends, Richard and his wife Marilyn, had given birth to two girls years earlier. Ashley and Camille both were hearing impaired, and as an additional challenge Ashley was severely autistic.

They were the first to observe possible signs of autism in me.

Their lives were quite an adventure because of the girls' special needs, particularly with Ashley's autism. One Sunday morning as the family prepared for church, Ashley insisted on visiting the location where the city parked its buses overnight. The family was preparing to take the family to church, but Ashley had other plans. In the blink of an eye Ashley disappeared.

Ashley had studied a map of the city's bus routes, locating the exact spot where the buses were parked. It was a hundred blocks north of their home.

Nobody knew what was going through Ashley's mind. Ashley had never visited the location, except on the map. Unbeknownst to her parents, Ashley took off on her bicycle, pedaling away, and prompting an emergency search of the neighborhood. Ashley was found hours later after visiting the bus yard. A highway patrol officer spotted her riding her bicycle down the freeway in the fast lane. She was safely returned to her family.

Marilyn was determined to learn more about autism so that she might understand her daughter. She read many books on the subject. Later, she told me that while she was reading, the name 'Robert' kept coming to her mind because she saw so many behavioral traits in me that were being explained in the books.

Mimicking was one of these behaviors. Mimicking is normal to a certain degree, sometimes known as 'copycatting,' but mimicking people heavily is something different. Ashley studied maps; I studied people.

Marilyn said to Richard, "I think Robert might have autism." She cited the mimicking and other behaviors like unusual questions and statements which were noticeably unusual. These were all very different from their experiences with other people they interacted with.

Unbeknownst to me I was being observed! Until Marilyn and Richard, nobody had paid such close attention to my behaviors. They didn't share any of their observations with me at the time, but later they would become an instrumental piece of the puzzle that is me.

I received a phone call from Greg's parents that let me know that Greg was returning home from his mission that Saturday. I was excited to see him. I thought, 'The time flew by so fast.' Greg's return signified to me that my other friends would be returning home soon as well. Greg and I picked up almost where we left off. We hung out, and I visited with his family, hearing stories about his two years away. I noticed Greg seemed a little different in his countenance after returning home. Two years seemed to have increased his maturity from when I saw him last. There was something else, too. I didn't know how to express it exactly, but I could see it in his aura.

Shortly after his return, Greg invited me to a baptism at the local Mormon church. I said I would attend. Never having attended a baptism before, I was curious.

Greg asked, "Do you have a suit you could wear when you come to the baptism?"

I said, "Yes." The suit I had was the one I dressed up in when I showed people the Amway plan. It was a dark Navy blue suit with a white shirt and a red tie. I didn't know I would fit right in, looking like a Mormon boy.

Nearing the time of the baptism, I finished my lawn route, jumped in my 1950 Chevy pickup truck, and changed into my suit while driving down the road. I enjoyed the challenge. I made it to the baptism with a few minutes to spare. Tilting my chair against the back wall, minding my own business, two missionaries introduced themselves to me. They were from other parts of the U.S. and had been assigned to Utah for their missions. They sat next to me, tilting their chairs too. We chatted about nothing.

One missionary asked me, "How long have you been a member of the church?"

I said "I'm not a member!"

Both missionaries dropped their chair on all fours.

The other elder, Raymond, said, "You're not? You look like you're a member!"

I said, "No, I'm not."

Raymond said, "Can we set up an appointment and talk to you about the Plan of Salvation?"

I said, "Yes." I didn't know anything about a Plan of Salvation. My only experience associated with salvation was going down to the front of the stage at the Amway seminar. I had accepted Jesus into my life, but I hadn't heard the Mormon Plan of Salvation.

Mike had returned home shortly after Greg. Raymond, my friends, and I made arrangements to meet at Mike's house. I was very familiar with this house since this is where I was caught. The missionary taught me the lessons of the church, challenging me to be baptized.

While being taught, I thought, 'This stuff is too crazy not to be true. How would you make this up?' This was all so fascinating to me from what I was taught at home in my upbringing.

I reflected on my upbringing in contrast to what I was learning. I had grown up in an extremely eccentric home against religion. It made me wonder if people who grew up in an eccentric religious environment leaned away from religion the same way I leaned towards religion. I wasn't planning on having anything to do with religion in my life. I planned on following mother's suit, except religion fascinated my mind. I realized, 'I could learn about religion, practice it, live it, and not be a fanatic about it.'

A baptism date was set. I asked, "Can I have Brian baptize me before he is released from his mission?" I was told, "Yes!" With a confirmed date, all was set.

I started attending church.

I was still living at home.

Mother started noticing my weekly excursions from the house on Sunday mornings. She asked me, "Where are you going?"

I said, "I'm going to church."

Mother asked, "Why are you going to the Schoffstall? Do you believe that bullshit?"

I skirted mother's question. I said, "There might be people I could sponsor in my Amway business."

Mother was satisfied with my answer.

I decided not to tell mother or Daddy about my baptism date. The day

410

came. I became baptized and confirmed in the Mormon church, starting a new life. I had one big question for myself, 'How do I make it to the Celestial Kingdom being attracted to the same sex?' I didn't tell anybody about my attractions in my heart, mind or soul. My attractions for the same sex didn't go away after baptism. I didn't think they would, nor did I want them to. I figured the answer would come to me. Becoming a mom was still very empowering and important to me. I had never lost sight of my purpose. I had a lot to figure out in my head.

Sometimes I wonder if I was baptized unworthily, thinking about my years of being a thief, knowing I needed to make restitution with those I stole from. I feared being thrown in jail. My misdeeds parked themselves in the middle of my stomach like a rock, sending signals to my conscience. A voice within me said, 'you need to take care of the people you stole from.' This was the right decision whether I was a Mormon or not.

Mother's words kept flowing through my head: 'you have a brain and a conscience; use it.' I couldn't dismiss my conscience no matter what, nor did I try. As uncomfortable as it was, I needed to dismiss the thought that I was baptized unworthy, but I knew I had to do something to make right in my life for my own peace of mind, one day. Eventually, I did make restitution to the lumber company for the materials I stole.

Months later I decided to tell Daddy I was baptized.

He didn't have a lot to say.

Daddy said, "All right."

I asked, "Don't tell mother."

Daddy agreed not to tell mother. I continued going to church, learning from people and the Scripture. I found out the latter would be known as 'scriptoriums.' I soaked up their knowledge and experiences like sitting at the table listening to the old Germans. I had new people to mimic, styles and behaviors to learn from, as I listened to them talk at the pulpit.

411

While I was cutting a lawn in a commercial area of town, a motorcycle stopped not far from me. It was Ryan from college. I was surprised to see him. He recognized me cutting the lawn and stopped to say hi.

I said, "Hi Ryan!" I was smiling from ear-to-ear. He was as beautiful as the first day I saw him. I noticed was that he wasn't driving his Charger. "Whatever happened to your green Charger?

Ryan said, "I wrapped it around a tree. It wasn't even that big." He showed me with his hands about a four or five inch trunk.

I said, "Oh, I can't believe that happened. It was such a nice car!"

Ryan said, "Yeah, it was!"

Laughing, Ryan said, "Have you dated any horny girls lately?" His laughter was as cute as the first time I heard him.

I smiled, surprised at his question. I said, "No." I thought about how I had dated a few girls who were introduced to me by matchmakers, but I wasn't interested and didn't pursue them. I stood still on the lawn, trying to decide whether I should tell Ryan I became a Mormon or not. I was reminded of the anti-Mormon literature I had passed to his mother not long ago.

I knew Ryan didn't care for the Mormons or their religion from past conversations, and that made me even more hesitant. I decided not to tell Ryan I was a Mormon.

Ryan needed to leave, saying he had to go to a job interview. I had a lawn to cut anyway.

Ryan said, "I'll see you around."

I said, "Sounds good!"

Ryan hopped on his motorcycle, driving a few doors down.

I thought about our experiences together, thinking about the girls we picked up at the mall. I was glad nothing happened in the car that night.

I never saw Ryan again.

Raymond served his mission faithfully, returning home to Oregon from Utah to be released from his time serving as a missionary. While on his mission in Salt Lake, he met a girl he wanted to marry. They married shortly thereafter and settled in Salt Lake City. He made living arrangements in Salt Lake, getting a job as a cashier at a local drugstore.

It just so happened that mother went to that drugstore. Two years later she was standing in his line, ready to check out. He greeted her and bagged her items. Mother wrote out a check, handing it to Raymond.

Raymond read mother's name on the check and asked, "Do you know a Robert Bautner?"

Mother said, "Who are you?"

Raymond said, "I was one of the missionaries who taught Robert the missionary lessons!"

Mother said, "YOU DID WHAT?"

Raymond didn't know I hadn't told mother about my baptism two years earlier.

Mother said in a huff with an unpleasant tone, "Why don't you Mormons leave us non-Mormons alone!" She gathered her purchase from my friend, the bewildered cashier.

She stormed out of the store, furious at what she just heard. 'Robert became a Mormon!'

Racing home, mother wasted no time questioning me upon her return, interrupting my TV program. "I just found out you became one of THEM!"

I lost all attention for what I was watching. I immediately knew what mother meant.

She launched into telling me the story of how she found out I was a Mormon.

I told mother, "Yes, I was baptized 2 years ago." I said, "I told Dad, and told him not to tell you!"

Mother said, "I thought you were just doing it to find people for your

413

Amway business."

I said, "Yeah, I said that. But I believe in it!"

Mother snarled, "How you could believe in that bullshit, I'll never know!"

I dropped the subject. There was no reason to discuss my decision any further. I knew it was a passionate subject for mother, and I wanted no part of any conflict with her over it.

I bounced my head fervently that night as I had since I was 7 years old, enjoying every bounce. I thought about mother, Mormonism, and her disgust for me since I was born. I wasn't baptized with a faint heart.

CHAPTER THIRTY-TWO

THE JERK

"Did your mom have any kids that lived?" Dick sat across from me at the diner, hands wrapped around his coffee cup. He was smirking, as he always did when he asked me this.

I was dumbfounded. This was the umpteenth time he had asked me the same question. I was just as perplexed as the first time he had said it. I knew he knew my mother, and I knew he knew she had five boys, and I was one of them. Why would he repeat himself over and over again? I kept thinking, 'of course my mother had kids that lived.' I thought and thought, but I couldn't figure out what he meant. I didn't understand his motivation. I furrowed my brow and answered hesitantly, "Yes."

Even though I knew this was the only sensible answer to the question, I didn't know if that was the answer he was looking for. I would bounce my head at night, trying to figure out what he meant. I thought, 'what does he mean?' I recalled all the good times I had with Dick. He told me often that he met me while rabbit hunting. I thought, 'Can't he remember we met at the swap meet? It wasn't even that long ago.' Yet he perpetuated the story.

It was five years before I figured out that he was kidding. I had always known he had a crude sense of humor, but I hadn't realized that these were his jokes, too. Later still it occurred to me that my dad had never joked with me. Combining that with my autism meant I had no context to understand his sense of humor. We grew to be good friends, even like father and son.

One time while traveling with Dick, a load of lumber and other building materials fell out of somebody's truck, landing in the middle of the intersection by the Kentucky Fried Chicken on State and 39th. Dick swerved around the mess. He said, "That was a close call." It was dead center for both east and west, north and south travelers. Dick continued driving northbound on State.

A short distance away I told Dick, "We should go back and pick up those materials."

He said, "They're not ours."

I said, 'I know, but it's out in the middle of the intersection. It's a dangerous situation."

Dick must have thought it was a good idea because he turned around.

I told him, "When I worked at the lumber company, I witnessed people not securing their load after putting it in the bed of their truck. I would often see building materials on the side of the road while I was driving home." Many of them had lost their load after they pulled through an intersection when the light turned green. Eventually I figured out what had happened. Going from a dead stop to accelerating caused the load to shift significantly, meaning if it wasn't safely secured it would slide out. The material seemed to be secured by its own weight, but it wasn't at all. They often came back to the lumber company complaining, claiming we didn't put their materials in their vehicle, but we did and they signed off on it. They were responsible for tying down their materials, but they left it to gravity to keep their load in place. They didn't think about centrifugal force, a force that overrode their sense of security. This was clearly the case with the plywood, lumber and other materials that we had come across dead center in the middle of the road, a hazard for drivers in all directions.

By the time we had turned around, another man was loading the material up into his truck.

Dick said, "Somebody else is already loading it up."

I said, "He doesn't know it's not ours." I smiled.

Dick grinned. He was gregarious enough to push his weight.

We pulled up next to the man loading the material. Dick said, "Thanks for loading up the material, but it's ours."

The man said, "No, it's not."

Dick turned to me and said in a low voice, "What do we do?"

I said, "Tell him we'll call the police."

Dick said to the man, "Let's call the police." There was no whimper in his voice.

The man agreed.

Dick and I got out of the truck to help clean up the littered building materials. While Dick and the other man picked up the scattered plywood and 2x4s, I gathered a handful of the 16 penny nails that had scattered after the 50 pound box hit the road and split its guts. The wounded box lost some of its tire piercing contents on the road. It occurred to me that the nails would have done wonders for Dick's tire shop at the time, but it wasn't in the right location. If we'd been closer to the tire shop, those nails might have made for a good business day for Dick.

When we finished cleaning up the mess, all of us got into our vehicles. The man met us in a nearby parking lot to call the police. By the time we had gotten there, cooler heads had prevailed. Dick and the man discussed the matter, but neither had called the police yet.

We knew he was doing the same thing we were doing. By the end of the discussion, Dick had prevailed. Really, he was just a better actor. The man surrendered the material and put it into Dick's truck. Dick and I went on our merry way with somebody else's building materials. I never thought about the poor man who made it to his home with an empty truck bed. To our knowledge he never returned to gather what had fallen out of his truck.

We justified our actions by claiming it was a safer intersection without the box of nails, plywood, and lumber in the middle of the road.

I learned a lot from Dick. Maybe too much.

"It's time for you to leave the house," Daddy said.

"What? What do you mean, it's time for me to leave the house?" I asked.

He said, "You're almost 25 years old. It's time for you to be on your own."

I thought, 'I've been a good son.' I participated in chores, took care of the yard, built a pond, landscaped the yard, and built a gazebo. I caused no trouble in or out of the house. I had a job working my own business. I thought I was pretty orderly, and now I was being asked to leave. I never thought of myself as a mama's boy, but I did find myself in a comfortable environment. Maybe too comfortable. I endured mother's wrath, beatings, insults, and insinuations because it was comfortable. It was what I knew.

I bounced my head that night thinking and processing, processing and thinking about the new life ahead of me. Daddy didn't give me a time frame, but I knew down deep it was the right decision. I needed to be pushed out of the nest.

Daddy asking me to leave reminded me of when I was 15 turning 16. He had taken me up the hill to my customer's house with all my lawn equipment and told me, "I can't pick you up this time."

I was shocked. "How am I supposed to get back home with all my equipment 8 miles away?"

Daddy replied, "That's for you to figure out."

My feathers were never ruffled, but I felt awkward.

I kept bouncing. I kept thinking. I had helped Dick fix up his basement a few years ago. He was renting it for $200 a month and the renters were moving out. Maybe he would rent it to me for the same amount. I continued, thinking of other exit plans in case renting from Dick did not work out.

The next day, I told Dick what my dad asked me to do. I said, "I need to make plans and leave the house."

He laughed and laughed. Dick said, "My old man had to burn the house down to get me out."

I smiled, not fully understanding what he was talking about or if he was serious.

Dick continued to laugh.

My imagination didn't want to go any further. But that was like not thinking of a red ball.

When he was finished laughing, he said, "I'll rent the basement to you for $250 a month."

I was surprised he raised the price $50 a month more than the last tenants. I thought, 'maybe he was trying to soften me up with his joke. Or maybe he knew I worked hard and could afford the extra $50.' Even though I was surprised, I agreed to $250.

That night I bounced my head, knowing that I had a roof over my head. The pillow felt comfortable and smooth as I had become accustomed to in times of turmoil.

My mind shifted, thinking about my lawn equipment. Now my feathers became a little more ruffled. I needed to ask Daddy if I could keep my equipment at his house. This would solve a big problem. I bounced until I felt satisfied, shifting my body to fall asleep.

I asked Daddy the next day if I could keep my lawn equipment at his house. He agreed I could for the time being. I just had to live somewhere else. This took a lot of pressure off of me. My lawn equipment was my bread and butter.

That night, like I did every night, I bounced and bounced, thinking about both my past and my future. With a little pit in my stomach, I thought about the new life I would be living soon. I wondered what my space would look like. I took inventory inside my head of what I would need to collect for furniture. I had some, but I knew I needed more than I had already acquired. I had been ratholing it. I learned that term from Dick. I retired for the day after thousands of soft strikes against my pillow. I had a plan lined up for what to do in the coming days.

I followed through with the plan. I started looking through newspaper ads for light fixtures, couches, chairs, and even a microwave oven. Mother's setup seemed to be efficient. I liked her setup. That night I returned to my pillow, jogging every detail into my head as if I was drawing out a schematic of the next day. I did this for the week and even bounced out a schematic of my future. I did it again and again until I was satisfied that I was moving in the right direction. Then and only then was I ready to fall asleep.

The first thing I found was a Strass crystal chandelier. It was beautiful. It sparkled with the colors of the rainbow. I decided I would put that in the hallway of the place I was renting. That night, I continued setting up my new place inside my head with each bounce, feeling the comfortable feathers against my face. I felt I had made peace with my past and now my new future through those feathers. I started to feel excited about this new chapter in my life. It was the next step in achieving my dream of building a house on a hill and being a mom. And I was very excited about the decorating.

I knew more than ever that Daddy was right. I needed to move out. Living under Dick's roof was a good transition out of the nest. I would make it on my own. I found the confidence I needed within each bounce night after night. Daddy was good not to give me a time frame. This gave me time to develop an accurate plan for my direction.

I grew in confidence with my lawn customers, too, feeling that they would keep me year after year. Eventually I grew my business to the point that I was cutting 73 lawns a week by myself. I believed I would be okay on my own, but it helped so much to bounce confidence into me, to create a surety.

I wanted to become more efficient in my work and thoughts so I could serve them better with extra time and effort. I looked for back roads to take me to my customers' locations, shaving 5 to 7 minutes off by driving a shorter route to the next customer's house. I applied a lesson I learned from my principal in the fourth grade, Mr. Sullivan. He stood about 10 feet from the classroom door. He said, "If I walk halfway to that door, and then halfway again and continue going halfway, mathematically I'll never reach that door." He told us that if we do things halfway, without giving 100% of our effort, then we'll never reach our destination. This was a valuable lesson to me. Whether he knew it or not, I applied it to my life's work.

Because of this practice, my time added up a few minutes here and a few minutes there. I took on a few more clients and catered even more to each one of them. I had a rent payment to make, a future to live for, and a world to create.

My lawn customers were more than people who paid me to cut their lawn. They became people I cared about. Relationships were forged; friendships were fostered. I met my customers' expectations more than ever. It was a pleasure to serve them. They had trusted me to take care of their yards. They made me feel important, and I made them feel valued.

I bounced everything into my head, thinking about their loyalty, how they treated me with kindness, and how they truly cared about me. I felt the softness of the feathers against my face until it was time to stop. I adjusted my pillow then shifted my body and fell asleep.

Jim was one of my favorite customers. He was a man whom I learned to admire for his charitable goodness and honesty towards people. He asked me one day to purchase a particular shrub for their yard. Jim and his wife Leslie were planning a wedding for a relative in late September and wanted to lengthen the row of shrubs in their backyard. They also wanted the new shrub to mature a little bit before the wedding. I remembered a local nursery in town that sold plants. It seemed a natural solution to a minor problem. With diligence to serve, I cut off a sprig of the bush and followed through doing what I said I would do.

Walking in with the sprig, I was directed towards the right area. An employee weeding the area under the bushes on her hands and knees stood up as I approached. She was very friendly and asked what she could do to help me. I showed her the plant in my hand.

She immediately said, "It's a snowberry bush."

I said, "Thank you. Where do I find them?"

She walked me to the location. I recognized her from high school. She drove a little yellow MG midget everywhere she went including school, and she always parked in front of the store. The car was very recognizable. It seemed to be one of a kind.

I commented, "You've been working here for a very long time. You must own the place."

She said, "I don't own the place."

I was just bringing up small talk, but she seemed to be taking me seriously.

It didn't matter. She was so handsome. Her voice hit an octave that my ears found very calming and soothing. With a short boyish haircut, flat chest, slender build, and a pleasant disposition, I was enamored with her beauty. The other girls were beautiful, pleasant, and very feminine. I could see now how they competed with my own feminine mind. They didn't hold a candle to the type of beauty in front of me, the type that I was attracted to.

I didn't feel it was appropriate to be forthcoming, but my heart felt a connection I didn't expect when I went there to find a shrub.

I bounced my head that night with energy to spare. I immediately felt God had put all the answers here on Earth for people like me who were attracted to the same sex but who wanted to marry the opposite sex, rear a family, and be faithful. My mind went to work immediately to resolve how I was going to get to know her. I didn't know her name or anything about her except her employment. At the time I was too shy to ask her for her name directly, but I wanted to get her name and contact number. I thought this would be a good reason to go back into the nursery. I didn't feel it was a good idea, important, or appropriate, to tell her I was gay. Anway, I had promised myself I would keep my secret just that–a secret. I had vowed never to act out on it. Besides, it wasn't something you mentioned in that day.

I had bounced into me the desire to be a husband, a daddy and a mom, night after night, year after year. It would have been too complicated to explain to her or anyone, so I kept it to myself. I had no idea it would be so simple to find a woman I was attracted to despite my same sex attraction. I was delighted to find somebody whom I could pursue that would fill the consciousness of that 10-year-old boy. To me, she was a godsend. I now had the means to have a productive, meaningful, and a completely fulfilling relationship.

That night, I had a lot to think about. I planned to plant the bushes later in the week, but that wasn't the main thing on my mind. I reached my left arm above my head, grabbing my right wrist and bouncing my head fervently. I thought of the handsome woman I had met. It seemed like a short time, but it could have been the better part of an hour. I enjoyed each bounce as the softness of the feathers on my face penetrated my heart. I bounced her handsomeness into my mind, body, and soul. I bounced every word she said, every feeling I felt, and every thought I remembered into my pillow. I bounced and bounced to my heart's delight. I expended every ounce of my energy until I was ready to fall asleep.

I now understood why I didn't bounce my head for the other girls I dated, and why I wasn't motivated to get to know any of them like this woman. They didn't reach the bounce of my soul.

A gnaw in the back of my head reminded me that I promised to take my feelings of gayness to my grave. I kept the promise I made to myself. I knew there were other people like myself that were gay, who wanted to marry, and rear a family. The feminine qualities I harbored deep in my heart were not a freak of nature, but a gift, and not just a gift to me. I felt this was a gift for her too, if she liked me.

I thought of that 10-year-old boy who had failed to kill himself the day after his overbearing mother had punched him in the face. I remembered wanting to die but choosing to live. The feelings that underlay that experience were ones I had acquired at that time, and they had never sat idle. The decisions I made to live, be a mom, a dad, and become somebody important, and to create a positive impact on the future of this world through my children, my legacy. If she liked me and had any fatherly or masculine instincts like I had motherly instincts, that 10-year-old boy's failed attempt to kill himself was not in vain.

I never realized how marrying a girl who (to me) looked like a boy was the perfect solution. I thought, 'if this girl liked me enough to marry me, we both could make it to the Celestial Kingdom.' This was from what I had learned and come to believe in the Mormon religion. I truly had figured out a way to become a mom. All the time spent bouncing my face into my pillow, nodding my head in a yes motion, may have had more internal connections to the depth of my soul than I had ever realized. Until that moment, I had had no idea of the value, long-term consequences, or immediate gratification of that simple behavior. The millions of bounces spent were on the verge of becoming complete.

Now I just needed to know if she was a Mormon since marrying within my faith was important. Living in Salt Lake City, I assumed she was a Mormon. I hoped she was, but I didn't know for sure. I wanted to find out without sounding like mother who was always asking people whether or not they were Mormon. I revisited the store to inquire about her. I also wanted to get her phone number. I asked a woman who seemed to be the keeper of the store if I could have her number.

She seemed to be suspicious of my intentions. She began interrogating me. At the time, I didn't know that this woman was the girl's mother. Of course, she would feel particularly protective of her.

I dutifully answered her questions as she interviewed me in depth as to why I wanted the girl's phone number.

The storekeeper finally said, "I will talk to her first and get her permission before giving you her number."

I was satisfied with what she said, so I returned to the store the next day to find out the answer. I hoped the girl had said yes.

The storekeeper gave me her name and phone number. I was thrilled. I learned her name was Esti.

I drove home, thinking about how to call her, practicing a number of possible responses.

'Hi, hello, this is Robert, um, you don't know me…'

My mind went back and forth, practicing, sitting on the couch, staring at the phone. I thought of something I learned in my Amway business. My trainer had taught me, 'If you feel uncomfortable in the moment, just tell the person, "I'm really uncomfortable; I'm new at this." They will understand and respect your sincerity.' The idea was that it would settle down a person's nerves, making it more comfortable for both parties.

I liked the idea of using what I had learned in Amway. Setting aside the fear of intimidation and tribulation, I picked up the phone and dialed her number. Her mother answered the phone. After being questioned as to the intent of my call, as if I was at my next interview, her mother seemed satisfied with my answers and handed her the phone.

She answered, "Hello?"

I wasted no time telling her, "It took a lot of guts for me to call you." I continued, "I'm very uncomfortable at this moment!"

She seemed flattered that I had pushed through my discomfort to call her, in spite of my fears. What I learned in Amway worked. I was still nervous, but the conversation seemed a little more comfortable. She had a beautiful voice, making it easier to listen.

Out of respect for her feeling safe, I made arrangements to meet her where she was employed. She seemed excited and agreed to meet me there.

I met her at her desk after I finished my lawn route for the day. We talked for a few minutes. She was sitting at her desk, but I talked to her while standing in the doorway.

She said, "There's some requirements for somebody to date me."

I said, "What are your requirements?"

She said, "You have to be a Mormon!"

I said, "I just got baptized a couple of years ago."

She said, "Okay, one other requirement, you have to be taller than I am!" She stood up for a brief moment, then sat back down immediately and said, "You'll do!"

My heart felt hopeful for the two of us.

I pondered on whether or not I should tell her I was attracted to the same sex. I decided, 'I'm going to keep my commitment to myself. I'm going to take my feelings of my same-sex attraction to my grave.' I also thought, 'There's no reason for me to say something about it. She might not like me if I did. Besides, I'm not going to act out on my feelings anyway, so why was it necessary to say something at all?' I dropped the subject, ending the conversation in my head.

I bounced my face into my pillow, thinking a thousand thoughts. Every bounce was worth the hit. I wondered if she married me how she would handle that I liked to bounce my head, if she did marry me. I thought, 'Would I still bounce my head? What if I had to fart while in bed? What would happen if I snored? What if she snored? What would sex be like instead of masturbating?' I didn't have any answers to my questions. I thought, 'I'll ask Dick. He'll tell me the answer to some of my questions.' With that thought of talking to Dick, I adjusted my pillow to fall asleep.

I worked harder than ever keeping the lawn accounts fulfilled, cutting them with integrity and following through with exactly what the customer asked me to do. I believe I learned this from obeying my mother. When she told me to go to your room, I did what she asked me to do. I knew the consequences if I didn't. I worked hard to satisfy each lawn I groomed and save my money. I knew one day I would need to support a wife and children. I worked very long hours, 15-16 hour days, developing patterns in my lawn route, making it faster for me to be more efficient. All the while, I was thinking about how I was building the foundation for my fortune, to reach my goal of becoming a millionaire.

At this time, a new movie with Steve Martin came out in the theater called The Jerk. I found Steve's humor funny so I wanted to see it. I went to the theater to watch the movie. I watched it intently, having no idea that this movie would be disturbing to me.

Navin, the protagonist played by Steve, was poor in the beginning, but he ultimately invented a gadget which made him a fortune. With his newfound wealth, Navin spent his money on a Trans Am, enjoying the good life, topped with a feathered cap. Navin was set for life. I identified with Navin, and I imagined myself as him in the future. But then, as is common to Steve Martin's sense of humor, the invention became a huge problem when it started deforming people's faces. Navin was sued, and he lost his fortune by the end of the movie. He ended up the same poor jerk he was at the beginning of the movie. I knew it wasn't real, but the movie impacted me immensely. I didn't want to lose the fortune that I was working so hard to build.

I returned home, disturbed from watching the movie. I called AJ up. "I said, "AJ, I just saw a movie with Steve Martin called The Jerk. Essentially he made a fortune and lost it by the end of the movie!" I continued, "I'm worried I will become like what Steve Martin did in the movie and blow my money on a Trans Am, driving around the city wearing a feather in my hat! I know if I don't do something with this money I've saved, I'll be just like Steve Martin and waste it."

AJ, unattached to the movie or my mimicking characteristic behavior,

427

said in a calm voice, "Come out here. There's lots of land for sale where I live!"

AJ lived on the outskirts of town, so I decided to take him up on his offer the next day. AJ and I drove around looking for land.

AJ said, "Turn down that road."

I did. After a couple of minutes, I spotted a sign high in the air painted with a broad brush in red lettering. The sign stood independent of the realtor sign. It read, '17.5 ACRES AND HOUSE $250,000!' I thought, 'The farmer who painted that sign must want to sell his property real bad.' I decided to inquire at the house.

I stopped the car to talk to the owner, to ask him directly. I introduced myself to him. I said, "I'm interested in your farm."

He said, "Okay," adding, "I'm firm on the price!"

I asked him, "When will your contract be up with the realtor?"

He said, "In two weeks."

I figured that was probably why he painted the sign. He was sick of people asking the question, 'How much do you want for your land?' I could tell in the few minutes after meeting him, he was a no-shitting-around kind of guy!

I thought about the land over the next two weeks, thinking, 'I can't afford a quarter of a million dollars!' But I was making a mistake. There was a difference I didn't catch at first. I was telling myself, 'I can't afford a million dollars!' All I could focus on was the 'million dollars,' not realizing the mistake in my head. I was avoiding the real price: $250,000. I had a self-imposed threshold, and I had a choice to step over it or not. Although the fact was I couldn't afford $250,000 either. But it didn't scare me away. I wondered if he would break the farm off from his house, making the price cheaper for me to buy the land. Then he could sell his house independent of the farm and maybe I could afford that. I decided to ask him that question the next time I saw him.

Unmarried, I felt I could live the good life from the money I earned in my lawn business, like Steve did in the movie. I could have chosen to live a flamboyant lifestyle with no limits. But my instincts told me a different story. I couldn't live Steve's lifestyle. The more I thought about it, the more I needed security in my life. I wanted to build a legacy and be a success. I thought, 'If I buy the land and it goes up in value, becoming more valuable over time, people would value me for owning land.' I believed my future would be set when I got old.

I devised a plan in my head to ask the owner the next time I met him. I thought, 'If he could break the farm off from his home, it would still be 14 acres.' This was what I said I would buy when I was younger: 'acres of land!' I also thought, 'If I could make one payment a year in the fall, and do it over the next 10 years, it would be paid for in short order. I had learned this principle in my Amway business about duplication. I could afford to buy this piece of land if he agreed on one payment per year.

The next time I met him, I asked him if he would agree to the plan I had worked out in my head. "Would you be willing to break the house off from the farm and accept one payment a year over the next ten years?"

He said, "I'll ask my brother. He owns the other half of the farm. But it sounds doable." He continued, "If my brother agrees, I'll charge you simple interest."

I said, "I can afford simple interest over compounding interest."

I had also learned the difference between the two through Amway. Even though I didn't know how much it would be, it still sounded affordable.

He said, "My brother and I inherited the farm from our parents when they died. It's been up for sale for five years and nobody has made me an offer until now." Taking a breath, he added, "Utah is getting overrun by people. I want to get the hell out of here!"

His comment reminded me of mother's sentiments. I understood his feelings.

The owner talked it over with his brother and got back to me.

He said, "My brother agreed on one payment a year over the next 10 years, and we'll split the farm from the house, making it more affordable. Since it's been up for sale for over 5 years, maybe the house would sell quicker and for less money. We'll sell you the 14 acres for $10,000 an acre."

I was happy with his decision.

He said, "I'll go to the bank on Monday and draw up the paperwork. You can deposit the payment directly into my account."

I said, "I can do that!" My down payment would be $20,000, and it would be $17,500 a year after that, starting in the fall.

I kept the down payment in my pocket for safekeeping until it was time to pay him. Carrying the money on my person lent itself to my sense of importance and responsibility. I wasn't worried at all about getting mugged. I felt it was safe with me, and I felt in control of the money.

I gave him the down payment on Monday as agreed. I was the new owner of the farm! At age 25, I now owned 14 acres of land, and I could do whatever I wanted with it.

I thought about my neighbor Judy, telling me I would never make money in the lawn business. I was also reminded of Dick saying, "Talk, talk, talk. Talk is cheap. You'll never buy land."

I thought, 'I did what I said I would do!' They had inspired me to turn their negative statements into positives and then into reality.

With the down payment on the farm, my work was cut out for me.

Simultaneously I had been dating Esti for several months. I felt very uncomfortable with dating. Not because of her, but because of years of mother telling me, "Don't get married, don't have children, and for hell's sake, don't come around here if you do! Move to China!"

None of my brothers had married. They had all acquiesced to mother's demand. They never married nor had children. I had nothing to go by as an example of how to date. I was never taught. I learned by watching others I saw in public, mimicking what I viewed. I had nothing in my head to mimic. This caused my mind to venture into territory I was unfamiliar with.

Esti let me know that I wasn't romancing her like she expected. She wrote me a letter hinting at her feelings.

At first I didn't understand the letter. She wrote, "A faint heart never caught a fair woman!" I couldn't comprehend why she was trying to tell me. My heart was on fire for her! But if that's how she felt, then I simply didn't know how to express myself correctly. I knew how to be respectful and polite, but I didn't know anything about romance. Years of abuse had taken an unforeseen toll on my mind. Additionally, my autism made it difficult for me to pick up on social cues and expectations. I wasn't able to communicate what was in my mind to another person, let alone a woman I was interested in marrying.

I salvaged the misunderstanding in the moment by telling her, "My heart isn't faint. It's on fire for you!"

I hadn't realized the depth of what mother had left behind in me. I wasn't of how damaging it was within. 'Mother, one of a kind.' I felt mother was just that. I lived in the innocence of ignorance, thinking, 'life will work out. It always does.' I never attributed her treatment towards me as traumatic abuse.

Yet it was almost costing me my future.

Still, I persisted, and my relationship with Esti grew.

A short time later, my younger brother Walter was looking at the possibility of marriage, too. Mother reminded us together, "Whoever gets married first will get the gold flatware Omi owned."

When it looked like I might be married first, mother said to Walter, "I'll buy you a bigger and nicer gold flatware set then Omi's." Mother did what she said she would do. The last thing she wanted was for me to have anything nicer than my brothers. She never passed up an opportunity to let me know how little I meant to her. She said to Walter, "I bought you a nicer one than the one Omi had. I'll give Omi's to Robert and give you the better one when you get married."

I knew this was just how mother was. I remembered it, and I will until my dying day, but I didn't let it bother me.

I decided it was time to pop the question. I needed to ask my girlfriend to marry me! One night after we were returning from an Amway seminar and rally, it occurred to me that it was the right moment. It was late, around 11:30 at night. We had pulled in front of her house. We were sitting in the car.

I was very nervous with a dry cotton mouth. I asked, "Have you ever considered becoming Mrs. Bautner?"

She said, "No!"

Feeling turned down in cold blood, I took the rejection like all other rejections from mother–in silence. I said, "Okay."

I went to church the next day. Life went on. I worked hard in my lawn business the following week with little fanfare or thought about being turned down.

Two weeks after the crash of my proposal, I got a phone call from Richard, my Amway upline. "What's going on?"

I said, "Lots of good things!" I had learned to say lots of good things because 'lots of good things' repeatedly happened in my life.

Richard said, "That's good!" He paused. "What's going on between you and Esti?"

I said, "Nothing. I stopped seeing her. I proposed to her and she turned me down."

Richard said, "She did?"

I said, "She did."

Richard decided to probe deeper, asking, "How did you propose to her?"

I said, "In the car in front of her house after the seminar and rally last month. I asked her if she had ever considered becoming Mrs. Bautner, and she said no."

Richard said, "That's how you proposed to her?"

I said, "Yes."

Richard said, "That's not how you propose to a woman!"

I said, "It's not?"

Richard said, "No, it's not."

Apparently, Esti had figured something was wrong when I stopped calling her and making any contact with her in any way. Sensing I had proposed to her, she went to Richard to talk to him. She told Richard her side of the story. Richard recognized that my way of proposing marriage wasn't a very good way to go about it. Richard decided to call me and verify.

Richard said, "When you propose to a woman, you take her to a nice restaurant, you have a ring available to give her. Bring some flowers if it's not too obvious. While you're eating, you surprise her by hopping down on your knee, asking her in a very romantic way, 'Will you marry me?' That is how you propose to a woman!"

I said, "Oh, that's how you do it?"

Richard said, "Yes, that's how you do it. Not in your car coming home from an Amway meeting, late at night."

I said, "I didn't know that's how you did it!"

I was happy to have another chance. I bounced my head on my pillow for what seemed like hours that night, thinking about what Richard was telling me about how to propose in a more romantic way. I thought, which restaurant would I choose? Where would I get a ring? How would I know her ring size? What kind of food would she like? What kind of flowers should I buy her? I bounced my head in comfort, thinking of all the possibilities.

After a bouncing marathon, I stopped, perched my torso on my left elbow, shuffled my pillow to comfort, laying my body down into my pillow, feeling it sink deep into the feathers. I stretched out my body with my head to the side. Listening to the casualness of my body inhale, then exhale, the

433

rush of air sounded peaceful to my ears.

I was determined to propose in a better way. I would follow through on my commitment to myself and my relationship with Esti.

Yet I was torn between the world I was entering and the world I had been raised in.

'The mind can't see what the eyes don't know.'

With the observational part of my mind, from the earliest moments of life, I saw mother follow through on what she said she would do. Mother never offered even a faint threat that she didn't carry out. Her consistent brutality was what my eyes and body knew.

On the positive side, she had taught me to do what I said I was going to do. On the negative side, my conscious mind had interpreted the brutality of mother as normal. My mind could only see what my eyes knew. But I was now learning that it wasn't normal. I had mistaken her brutality, her attitudes, and her way of looking at the world as normal, because of the inevitable education process that children experience, taking everything they witness in their homes as the foundation for their perception of reality. What my subconscious mind perceived and interpreted became a scrambled series of messages inside my head about the nature of life.

I had to decipher mother telling me and my siblings 'don't get married, don't have children, and don't come around here if you do.' It was a selfish comment, only said to serve herself. Mother didn't want to be put into a nursing home to rot, and she feared she would be forgotten if her boys had families outside of her. She wanted her children to herself, unencumbered by spouses.

Seeing the world outside the walls of mother's house helped my mind and eyes see the world for more of what it really was, instead of seeing what mother wanted me to see, isolated and overwhelmed by her manipulative power. My growing life outside of mother's home began to break the Stockholm Syndrome I had unknowingly been subjected to.

434

For the first time, while in my church classes, I learned that God put the desire in man to procreate. This was a confirmation of the dream I had had since I was ten years old, to be a mom.

My mind began to see differently, because my eyes knew new things.

It helped me to understand how powerful mothers are. Mother had overrode God with her brutality toward her God-given children, but I would override mother by returning to God, getting married, and fulfilling my God-given gift of having children.

Sifting through these traumas of life and making my own pathway out of them helped me identify who I was: who I was as a child, who I was in this moment, and who I would be in the future. I was a traumatized child with dreams of being a mom, I was a man with same-sex attraction who was finding a way to achieve all his dreams, and I would soon achieve those dreams, being a husband, a daddy…a mom.

With stillness, I listened to the beat of my heart, thinking once again, 'The mind can't see what the eyes don't know.' With a few breaths left in consciousness, I fell asleep in innocence.

CHAPTER THIRTY-THREE

SCABS FORM, HAIR GROWS

"Hans, someday we're going to baptize you." It was Tom talking to Daddy. He was Daddy's boss. Tom probably only told this to Daddy once, but when Daddy told mother, she took offense. She was so singularly insulted that she repeated it on a regular basis. Mother hijacked the story and told it over and over again at the dinner table, always flinging her arm out in disgust. I could only imagine what thoughts went through Daddy's head when Tom told him he would be baptized in the Mormon church. I knew that Daddy would have to be dead before that took place, or at the very least, mother would be dead. Just to be baptized at all was unthinkable.

Daddy's 90th birthday was approaching. Time was not on his side.

I told Daddy, "If you could make it to 100 you would be in very good shape, because very few people die over 100."

Daddy just looked at me with his deep blue eyes and smiled.

My joking was just my way of covering up a dull persistent ache in my gut that never seemed to leave me over the years. The inevitability of his death was a reality in the back of my mind I wanted to dismiss but couldn't.

I couldn't forget Daddy telling me that when he got so old he couldn't take care of himself, he would go off into the woods, lean up against a tree and die. With Daddy 48 years older than me, I knew one day in the not so distant future, Daddy was going to die. I could see he was slowing down. I hoped to the deepest part of my heart, Daddy wouldn't follow through on what he said he would do.

Daddy read positive books associated with the mind. He read books on keeping the body healthy on a regular basis. He read the newspaper daily. Every morning Daddy had a routine where he exercised without fail, spending his time keeping himself on an active regimen to keep his body fit through physical movement. He would jump on a mini trampoline and do other exercises, even taking cold showers. Every night Daddy briskly walked Richard Street, walking up and down the dead end road.

Daddy lived the better part of the 20th century, with the 21st century knocking on his door, and he always kept moving. I paid attention to Daddy's actions. I wanted him to stay healthy, to stay alive as long as possible.

I often reminisced, thinking about Daddy's life in Germany as a little boy, born in 1913. I pictured his home in a quaint village, a cottage with a thatched roof. I imagined smoke drifting from the chimney, with a fire in the fireplace keeping his home warm and comfortable. The fire cast a warm glow, radiating from the windows and offering an invitation to passersby, 'you're welcome to my home.'

I pictured chickens scratching the ground, pecking the bugs they unearthed, clucking with pleasure. Omi would gather the eggs from hidden nests for breakfast. A cow was out in the pasture, waiting to be squeezed for morning milk. The smell of flowers blooming under the window sills. A stone pathway led to the front door lined in beautiful shrubs. A flock of geese flying overhead broke the silence of the morning. I pictured Daddy's upbringing in the German countryside as a very quaint, calm, quiet, and peaceful existence.

But this was my imagination.

Reality offered a hard freeze.

438

History tells a different story. In Germany the car was still in its relative infancy. Airplanes were still a fairly new invention. Walking was the main form of transportation. World War I broke out nine months after Daddy was born. Germany was bombed, left in ruins. By the time the war ended in November of 1918, Daddy was 5 years old. Germany was ravaged by the war. Few resources were available. There was no cow in the pasture to milk, which Omi felt contributed to Daddy's small frame. There were no chickens laying eggs to eat. It was a constant struggle just to keep food on the table and a roof overhead.

Daddy spent his most formative years in a war torn nation, followed by an adolescence in a depressed German economy. The economic plight followed Daddy into his adulthood, shaping his life's decisions.

Daddy took me to his work now and again. We drove down narrow roads with old abandoned buildings with broken windows alongside the roadway. Daddy knew all the back roads to his work. Eventually we made it to the factory where they printed the daily newspaper. Daddy showed me his office in the middle of the plant. I sat in his chair and swiveled it side to side in front of his desk.

Eventually Daddy walked me around the printing company where big printing presses roared. Big drums spun quickly. The machines clicked and chattered. Spools of paper on one end flew through the machine, coming out as newspapers on the other. I was left in astonishment at how quickly this machine worked seemingly without fail as it printed the paper for distribution in the city in a few short hours. An array of workers kept the whole process running smoothly.

Daddy walked towards the finish section of the operation and pulled out his loop from his pocket. The loop was a 50x magnifier. He randomly pulled a paper from the printed pile to check for the dots in the picture. His job was to make sure the pictures were recognizable in the final print. Daddy let me look through his loop. The dots were fuzzy under the magnifying glass. The fuzziness faded into a sharper picture the further away you got.

He took me to another part of the plant where they printed books. Daddy was the main craftsman to make sure the photos had the right color content, pigment, and that the dots were close enough together to make a clear, crisp, and clean picture.

Daddy said, "You have to have magenta, cyan, and yellow to make up a color picture." He checked through his loop regularly to make sure the prints were crisp, clean and professional. He used his lithography expertise that he'd learned from so many years ago when he was a journeyman. Daddy won the Lithograph Craftsman of the Year Award in 1973.

Aluminum sheets with backward print spun on those big spools of the machine. Once the aluminum sheets were used, they were discarded and another sheet was put together for the next printing. Outside on the dock, pallets of spent aluminum sheets were stacked. Daddy was able to take them home. He gathered the aluminum sheets for years, amassing a large collection. He had the idea that if he could have them cut into smaller manageable size pieces, he could turn them into shingles and re-roof his home.

Eventually Daddy retired from the Desert News where he worked the better part of 20 years. When Daddy wasn't working in the garden, he was busy sliding the aluminum sheets under the old wood shingles. Mother always worried he would fall off the roof, but Daddy never did. Little by little over many years Daddy re-roofed his home using the old aluminum sheets that were once slated for the scrap pile.

When Daddy was 85 years old he told me, "I'm running away from home."

I asked him, "Where are you going to run away to?"

He said, "I'm going to go to California."

I thought, "What's in California?"

I didn't blame him for wanting to run away from home. I figured he had had enough of mother and wanted to live the rest of his life in peace and harmony. It was a peace and harmony that was not available at home. Eventually, I found out Jenny, who lived in Omi's house for a while, talked Daddy out of leaving. I always appreciated her doing so.

Another time, I asked Daddy, "How come you never divorced mom?" I truly wondered what his answer would be.

He said magical words to me. "I thought it was important enough to keep the family together so I stayed married." I loved Daddy even more with that answer.

I watched Daddy go from briskly walking up and down Richard Street to walking back and forth in the driveway. It was hard for me to see Daddy slowing down. Eventually Daddy was walking back and forth at the foot of his bed. It pained me to see his decline. We celebrated his 90th birthday in September of 2003. I knew time was short.

Daddy had a small stroke. Mother was nearly blind from cataracts and was not able to care for Daddy. The doctor in the hospital suggested Daddy go to a rehabilitation center to regain his strength. While in the hospital, his faculties were intact. He was still coherent. I had a pressing question I couldn't let go, a question I needed to ask. I said to Daddy, "Why didn't you say something to me growing up about the way mother treated me and the other boys? Why didn't you pull us aside, and say something, anything at all? Why didn't you tell us to get married, have as many children as you can afford, and have a good life?"

Daddy laid in his hospital bed, pausing before answering my question. He said, "I didn't think it would affect you."

My mind paused, comprehending his answer. I couldn't understand what I just heard. I didn't expect this answer. He must have had some inkling that it was a torturous upbringing. I couldn't identify one specific thing he should have noticed, because it just seemed to run together inside my head. All of mother's comments, beatings, and overbearing beliefs—they ran

441

together. I said calmly, "Good hell, it affected me a lot!"

I had to really ponder on Daddy's answer for a very long time in order for it to make sense to me. I had to understand Daddy's perspective, putting myself in Daddy's upbringing to comprehend his answer. Remembering he was born just before World War I, he didn't take it for granted he had a roof over his head or food on the table. Daddy put food on the table for us. He kept a roof over our head. We never had to worry about where to find the next meal or if we had shelter. Daddy provided all that for us, something that he didn't have when he was a child.

Maybe mother was an anomaly to him, a distraction, a function of his desire to have children? Maybe he just ignored her, and he expected us to do the same. He wasn't mean-spirited; he was innocent. He was innocent of how mother's wretched ways would affect his young sons. He had only known love growing up with Omi, and he was ignorant of the effects that verbal, emotional and physical abuse had on children. No one in his generation really knew. Answering the question the way he did, 'I didn't think it would affect you,' became easier for me to understand the more I considered it. Still, it was sad.

I visited Daddy as he continued to deteriorate, standing by his bedside in the hospital. I had worried for years that this day would come sooner than it had. But it was here now.

I recalled the one time Daddy had ever told me he loved me. I was 19 at the time. Daddy was 68. I had been wanting to hear the words, 'I love you' from him.

I was in the kitchen with him one day and I asked, "Could you tell me that you loved me?" I continued, "I'd like to hear those words at least once before you die."

He said, "I love you."

I was satisfied, hearing him answer my request.

I said, "Thank you."

Hearing those three little words, 'I love you' was what I had needed. One time was more cherished than if he had told me 'I love you' throughout my life.

I continued reminiscing, taking a seat beside his bed. I recalled the one Christmas present Daddy gave me growing up. It was a pair of night lights, one was a Santa Claus and the other a Christmas tree. They were wrapped in white tissue paper very roughly. Daddy didn't make sure the edges were trim and neat, clean and sharp. It was a very rough wrapping of two gifts. That made it more memorable, more treasured, more hallowed than if he had given me Christmas presents throughout my life. It was to me as if it was the train set that he received as a Christmas present year after year.

I was grateful more than words could express for his love for me and his subtle way of showing it. Even when he disciplined me. I cherished the thump on the head when I was bouncing my head in my crib and knocking against the wall. I even treasured the scar I had gotten from Daddy when he had tried to gently slap me for being naughty but had accidentally dug his fingernail into my chest. It was the only time Daddy laid his hand on me, but it was memorable and beloved because his gentleness, even in the accidents, was such a stark contrast to mother's harshness.

I more than appreciated the countless times my daddy touched my feet and massaging my back. I appreciated the simple talks we had. It was no accident that I belonged in this family, no matter what mother said. There was a purpose beyond the surface of life itself. Daddy was the glistening edge of an otherwise bitter cold denseness that would otherwise have kept all sunlight from penetrating its mass.

He was trying to talk. I struggled to understand exactly what he was saying and wanted. He muttered the words "ice cream." I was warned by the hospice nurse that he could choke and die because his body was shutting down. I couldn't bring myself to give Daddy ice cream. I could sponge his lips and put water on his mouth with a sponge, but no direct liquids for his internal organs to process.

I took Daddy's socks off and massaged his feet with love and tenderness. It was a love and tenderness that he had given me for so many years growing up. It was a small way of giving back to him what he'd given to me.

Eventually they sent him home. I was relieved that he could die at home and not in a nursing home or hospital.

Years earlier I had asked Daddy, "Could I have that gun that you brought with you from Germany before you die?" He had answered, "We'll see." I had interpreted that as a yes.

Now I knew time was short. Very short. Daddy was no longer coherent but breathing erratically on the couch. I ran into his bedroom to retrieve the gun. I decided to pray to God to take him. It was okay. I could let go. In a prayer circle with my wife, she shook my hand to indicate to hurry up and finish praying. Daddy was taking his last few breaths. In a beautiful moment, Daddy passed. I knew he was gone after his jaw dropped.

Mother made arrangements to bury Daddy. She put Billy in charge of carting her to the funeral home and cemetery and to carry out her instructions. She made the comment, "I wonder if Tom will show up at the funeral." President Thomas S. Monson, an apostle for the Church of Jesus Christ of Latter-Day Saints, was Daddy's boss at the Desert Press. I only knew him as Tom growing up around the dinner table. I wasn't in his circle of influence to let him know when Daddy's funeral was. But like clockwork, President Monson showed up. I asked President Monson if he would speak for a moment about Daddy and their time together at work. President Monson graciously accepted my request. He commented on what a fine craftsman Daddy was, saying he was the best in his field. He praised him for the work he did for the Church.

President Monson's comments reminded me of a story mother told me every Christmas. After Daddy retired from the Desert Press, mother and Daddy were invited to the annual Christmas party for the retirees on the top floor of the church office building. Mother said, "I always went in a tank top to make sure there was no misunderstanding." Mother wanted everyone to know she was not a Mormon.

It was ironic that the organization mother hated with a passion provided her and her family an income for so many years. The church was mother's bread and butter so she could live unencumbered. Yet she showed them nothing but contempt.

When it came time for the funeral, mother wouldn't go. Mother refused to go when Billy showed up to take her. I couldn't understand why she would do this after 56 years of marriage. I can only speculate that she wanted to live in denial. But I wasn't surprised at mother's behavior. It was indicative of mother. She had to control the last thing she could with Daddy.

I asked President Monson if he would bless Daddy's grave.

He said, "That's generally reserved for a family member."

I said, "I think it would be okay if you did it."

He agreed and blessed Daddy's grave.

Facetiously, I thought to myself, 'mother will be pleased.'

"Where do you want the magazines that came in the mail?" I asked mother.

"Put them on my bed," mother replied.

I walked into her bedroom. She clearly hadn't slept in it in years, even before Daddy died. The bed had long been abandoned to an ever-growing pile of unread magazines and advertising flyers. The space between the last magazine and the ceiling became smaller and smaller.

I returned to the living room where she sat, day and night, on the same worn couch that she had had most of my life. It was the same couch that Daddy had died on four years before.

It was a pleasant Sunday afternoon. I visited mother often, knowing one day in the not too distant future mother would be passing. She no longer had

445

the vim and vigor she once had. I never wondered for a moment to ask her if she felt her and Daddy would be reunited in the hereafter.

I remember this visit in particular.

Mother spoke up, "You can have the china cabinet when I'm dead."

I nearly laughed. The last thing I wanted was that china cabinet. I looked over at the wooden object that had so often been the source of beatings and threats. It was also the scene of my failed suicide attempt at age 10. That mother thought I would want it, me, her least favorite child, getting her prized possession that was so completely unappealing to me. The offer itself spoke to the chasm between us.

As my eyes moved over the cabinet, I was surprised to see it was broken. The bottom right side of the curved glass was missing. "What happened to your china cabinet? The glass is broken!"

She said, "A pillow was irritating my feet at the end of the couch. I kicked the pillow off of the couch, the pillow hit the statue next to the cabinet which fell into the glass and broke the cabinet."

The statue was a life size owl sitting on a stump. I had bought it for her as a Mother's Day present at the swap meet when I was 20 years old. It was heavy and about 2.5 feet tall. "You must have kicked the pillow pretty hard."

Mother said nothing.

She had said all my life that I would get nothing of hers. Spitefully, she would say over and over, unsolicited, that she wanted me to have nothing. Only now, when the cabinet was broken, was I worthy to receive it in her eyes.

I didn't want it.

Every threat mother had uttered growing up passed through my mind. I stared at the broken glass, hearing the scream of her voice in my mind. 'Get away from my cabinet! If you break the china cabinet you have to deal with me!' No threat was veiled, even in my adult mind. Mother acted on her ultimatums.

Yet here she was with only herself to blame. It was ironic after all this time mother was her own victim. I thought of asking her if she had any regrets in beating me up for turning her priceless possessions upside down in the china cabinet when I was four years old, even after she found out it was Billy who set me up. Even after she had decided this was one of her favorite stories that she would tell and retell whenever I was around.

I couldn't bring myself to mention this or any stories of the past. I was, after all, my father's son, committed to turning negatives into positives.

In a way, maybe it was my fault that the cabinet was broken since I had bought her the statue some 20 years earlier. But she didn't bring it up and neither did I. Let sleeping dogs lie.

Instead, I asked if I could have the Japanese bowl. It was a gilded porcelain bowl with an intricate scene of Japanese life. It had been given to my mother by her best friend's mother while she was still living in Chicago. I don't know where it came from before then. I don't know if it was worth anything. I wanted it because Lutta, mother's friend, was a very nice woman. She was always kind to me. I didn't want anything else, because it all reminded me of mother.

Mother waved one hand weakly in the direction of the cabinet. "I don't care."

I immediately stood and took it out of the china cabinet, setting it on a side table so that when I left I could take it with me.

I expected her to rescind her gift, but I set it there anyway. It reminded me of when I asked mother for Oma's chest of drawers. She had said no, but Daddy intervened, and I took it home…only to receive an angry call the next day to bring it back. I refused.

Mother said, "What the hell is that noise?"

I heard nothing. I listened carefully, very carefully. Far off into the distance I could barely hear a lawn mower roaring. Her body may have lost

447

its spunk but her ears never lost the sound of irritation.

I said, "Do you mean the lawn mower?"

"Yeah, is that what it is?"

I said, "Yes, it's a lawn mower."

She grumbled about how irritating it was.

She had completely forgotten about the bowl, to my benefit.

Mother passed shortly thereafter.

As I look back, I see the irony in my mother's irritation with the lawnmower. The roar of a lawn mower has been an immensely positive one in my life. It was how I first earned a living. It was the beginning of my earthly success. It was the source of many valuable lessons of life, learned from my customers. Things like the importance of showing up on time and that two wrongs don't make a right. My clients showed compassion and love for my family. Each time we had a child, many of them would give gifts. I learned that people worked hard early in their lives to afford me in their later years. I never took it for granted they had lots of money or no money. I learned to dance with my lawn mowers, my customers, and the people who serviced my equipment.

Likewise, I found the positives in my relationship with mother. I had no misconceptions about her and hadn't had any since the day she punched me in the face when I was ten.

And now she was gone.

Mother and I danced to a tune that had no rhyme or reason, no fanfare, no expectations, no glitz. She never found love within herself to love me, but that didn't stop me from loving her. Her desertion of God inspired me to find God. Her disdain for Jesus Christ brought me to Jesus Christ. Mother's contempt for religion brought me to religion.

To this day, I can't imagine surviving my life without God to protect my mind, my body and my soul. He protected me, guided me and directed me.

The relationship between mother and me had its challenges. They weren't over, despite the fact that she was dead. In fact, I would find in the months and years that followed that they were just beginning. It has taken a lot of faith to look past the harshness of the life she created for me as a child. I have learned to find the positives of life's future and purpose despite her.

The experiences between mother and me were meant for something bigger than me. I came to believe some spirits come to this life to experience every difficulty imaginable to be taught. I was one of those spirits. If all I went through with mother was just about me, it would be a loss of a relationship. With a positive attitude, I was tempered for a bigger purpose than viewing my life as a loss. Weathering life's turbulence as Daddy did with mother taught me more than I gave Daddy credit for. It's hard to believe that I would validate these experiences in order to become the person I became.

I would do it all over again.

At her death, I found myself emotionally unsettled for the first time in many years.

The evening of June 1st, a Thursday, I received a call from Billy.

He didn't greet me. He said, "Mum is dead. The mortuary has already picked her up."

I was still working. I told Billy I would be there as soon as I could.

By the time I got there, it was almost dusk. I knew she was already gone. I paced back and forth in the driveway thinking about all our experiences.

I had been robbed of the opportunity to find closure. I didn't get to ask mother any 'why' questions. I didn't get to tell her 'I love you,' at least the way I understood what my love for her was. I had learned to love myself, to love mother. That was my understanding of love. It was a lesson mother had taught me unintentionally.

Frank came out of the house. "Why are you pacing?"

I replied, "Mother affected me a lot and I never got closure with her."

Frank stopped for a moment and said, "Mommy didn't affect me."

449

I said, "You've got to be kidding me, mother didn't affect you? Your life was altered deeply because of the way she treated you."

Frank ended the conversation by walking away. He went back into the house.

Billy lived across the street. He must have seen me pacing outside, because he came over. "I'm taking care of mum's funeral arrangements." Billy continued, "I was disgusted by how Daddy's funeral went. At mum's funeral there will be no prayers, no mention of God, and no religious connotations at her services. There won't even be a service. We're going to have a wake."

I said, "What is a wake?"

Billy ignored me and kept talking. "There will be food at her funeral."

I thought that was a good idea. That sounded like mother's style of a funeral. I envisioned beer, bratwurst and sauerkraut. Billy left. I went home.

I never entered the house.

The day came for the funeral. There was no bratwurst or sauerkraut, but lots of beer and a little bit of finger food. While my brothers visited with one another in another room, I sat next to mother's casket, ruminating about our life together and observing how beautiful she was inside her casket. I was certain it was a place she had never envisioned being. Her jewelry was delicately placed, her dress was pressed. Mother's wig had fresh curls, her hands were meticulously in place. Mother of course would have it no other way. I was very pleased at how beautiful she looked. I thought of taking a picture, but I could not bring myself to do it. I wanted my memory of what I thought our relationship could have been, not what it was.

I walked out of the room to see where everybody was. My brothers were eating and drinking beer. Mostly they were drinking. I wasn't interested in that, and most of all I didn't like that mother was all by herself. I returned to her side. I wanted to be with her for what little time I had left with her.

While our living relationship was over, a new relationship had begun. I didn't know what that looked like at the moment. As time passed, I found that this new relationship empowered me to set the conversation and control the outcomes. She could no longer tell me I was wrong or that she should never have had me. That allowed me to process and begin to heal.

I didn't know at the time I would become a writer to find the closure I sought. I discovered that it was not the finding of closure but the seeking that was the most revealing. I didn't know the depth of my love for her then, as I do now. I didn't know that the biggest hurdle (and the greatest reward) with our relationship was yet to come.

I returned to her home a few weeks later. It didn't have the same pizzazz it once had with mother. Her home seemed stale and incomplete. I decided to take a small electric frying pan.

I didn't know that would set off a fury in Billy. There was nothing unique or special about it, but that didn't matter to Billy. Billy immediately called me up and asked, "Did you take the frying pan?"

I said, "Yes, I did."

Billy angrily said, "You return that frying pan now!"

I said, "I won't be returning the frying pan. Mother's dead. She doesn't need it anymore."

In short order, the locks were changed, permanently barring me from returning into the house.

I was reminded of Oma's dresser that mother tried to claw back after Daddy convinced her to let me have it. She didn't need the dresser, but she didn't want me to have it.

Billy was his mother's son.

I didn't press the issue nor ask if I could have anything else. Billy and the rest of my brothers kept the doors locked. The home became a shrine for the next two years. Once they decided to turn it into a rental, they pilfered it for whatever they wanted.

Now with Daddy and mother both gone, I saw more than ever that these wounds of life from the relationship between mother and me had formed scabs on my soul. The scabs were evidence of the consequences of life's wounds yet they were the body's way to begin to heal. At the same time, hairs of forgiveness had grown underneath the scabs, pushing off the scabs, to reveal the beauty of the soul. In my life, mother's narcissistic rage was the weapon that created the wound, but God put the protection over me in the scabs that formed to heal me, and Daddy's legacy of forgiveness and love allowed the hair to grow, pushing off the scabs and ushering in new healthy skin. Daddy's legacy minimized the scars of abuse and trauma, and now more than ever I was grateful.

CHAPTER THIRTY-FOUR

WRITING TO REMEMBER

I wrote my first sentence for my book and sent it to a former neighbor Jan, a woman who had become a dear friend. I said to Jan, "What do you think of what I wrote?"

Jan said, "You wrote a nice bullet point sentence!"

I was encouraged by her comment to keep writing. She responded to me, and that was enough to encourage me to go back to the drawing board. Of course, those who didn't respond also encouraged me, because I saw their lack of feedback as a sign that I needed to make it more interesting. Either way, I was focused on writing the book, and I absorbed everything I experienced from others into the process of writing in the most positive way I could. I see now, from talking with others, that this is a uniquely autistic way of responding to feedback…it is what I call innocence. It is the innocence of that singular focus on the object of my attention, the book. That innocence is essentially my natural inclination to interpret my environment within the scope of my objective.

I rewrote the sentence from her feedback. I said, "How do you like what I have written, now?"

Jan was such a dear friend. She said, "Now you've written a nice bullet point paragraph! Where are all your feelings and emotions?"

I said, "My emotions were beat out of me as a child. I don't have any."

She said, "You better go back into your childhood and think about them then!"

I did, bouncing my head at night, thinking of everything in my past.

I had a lot to think about. I continued writing about my childhood, writing page after page. Because I didn't want to overstep my friendship with Jan, I asked Christian to read my new pages, too. He was a nurse by trade. One of his tasks was to read prescription bottles to make sure the medicine that was administered to his patients was accurate. Christian read each word specifically and carefully on the bottle. He applied these skills to my work, too, giving me great feedback. Before I asked him to read my pages, I didn't know that having a friend who read pill bottles for a living would become so important in my writings. His attention to detail was invaluable. It kept me focused. Christian had a different understanding of life than I did, and that helped, too.

I continued to write. Christian continued to support me.

After reading what I wrote, Christian said, "It's going to need a lot of editing."

I was frustrated at his comment. I asked, "What does editing look like?" I needed to see what editing looked like so that I could learn to edit my own work.

He gave me the framework I needed to understand how writing should be structured.

Our friendship continued to deepen throughout my writings.

Christian had an interest in seeing someone with autism succeed, because two of his children were autistic. He knew that so many people with autism seemed to be left behind and labeled as incapable. He knew that autism was a gift. In fact, sometimes he wished he had such a gift. Christian knew autistic people had a lot to offer the world from a unique perspective. He wanted to see more autistic people tell their story.

Christian hoped what I was writing would be a contribution to the world of autism, to show people that autism works as a legitimate way of

454

functioning in society, even if it is unique. Christian provided the feedback I needed so desperately to feel relevant. He helped me slow down my brain so that I could capture memories that I had forgotten.

I had wanted to forget them. What I didn't know then was that I needed to remember in order to heal. Those memories were the keys to unlocking a new life that was healed of the trauma of my childhood. Until that moment, I didn't even know I had experienced trauma.

Looking at it now, I can see that my autism diagnosis was the catalyst for healing. I also learned that it had protected me throughout my life. It was a coat of armor of innocence, a way of looking at the world, that shielded me from internalizing the abuse. Mother's verbal and physical beatings never soaked into my inner being, my identity, my soul.

Yet I didn't want that diagnosis. I didn't want to think of myself as defective. I knew I wasn't broken. So I still wasn't convinced that I really was autistic, but as I wrote I found myself considering the possibility more and more. I was conflicted, because I still didn't believe I was broken. How could I be autistic if I wasn't broken? How could I have accomplished so much in life if I was defective?

I even asked my editor if she thought I was autistic. She came back with a resounding "Yes!" She added that being autistic didn't mean I was broken. It meant I was different. I was neurodivergent.

I began to change how I thought about autism. I could be autistic without believing I was broken. Even if others thought I was, that didn't mean they were right.

Thinking, then writing, I began to dig deeper. I began to understand how my mind had numbed my emotions as a result of my upbringing: all the beatings, feeling devalued as a human being, and as a boy hearing mother's repulsion of me.

As I wrote I began to realize that my same-sex attraction and my desire to be a mom kept me alive. It gave me purpose. But I wondered if I should write about everything. I didn't understand the role of autism in my life at the time, but I understood my attractions. Awareness was growing in me about how much I had missed in life, how much I hadn't understood about what was going on around me.

Yet I continued to battle the autism diagnosis.

Christian was telling me to write about autism.

I told Christian, "I can only write about the effects of autism if I have autism. If I really am autistic, it will come through my writings."

I continued to write.

When I was writing about being seven years old, I got stumped. I said to Christian, "I can't write about what is going through my mind!"

Christian said, "Why?"

I said, "I was doing sexually perverted acts that were too uncomfortable for me to write about!"

Christian said, "Like what?"

I said, "Like humping cars, my friends, and inanimate objects. After that, I'd say, 'now there's going to be two of them!'" I continued, "I can't write about that stuff!"

Christian said, "You need to think about this as you go to sleep tonight. Something happened in your life that you're hiding!"

I took his information, thinking nothing would come of it, but I did as he asked. That night as I was going to sleep, I thought, 'What am I hiding from?'

In the morning I woke in disbelief! I remembered everything about Rick sticking his penis in my face. I remembered everything in detail about what had happened, as if it had just happened. Although I remembered it clearly, it still didn't seem significant.

Although I remembered it clearly, it still didn't seem significant. I told Christian later that evening what I had discovered, but I still did not give it any importance. I simply thought, 'Things like this happen to everyone in

456

life. So what if he stuck his penis in my face?' It was just a part of my life. On the other hand, it helped me understand why I exhibited early sexual behaviors like humping things and fascination with erections as a child, but I thought the importance of the event ended there. As I recounted the event to Christian, I reiterated my sentiment, "So what?!"

Christian's reaction was simple but profound. "I think this is important to your story."

I wasn't yet convinced, but I took note of his response.

Later, as I was heading toward the door at the end of a session, I told Dr. Bellings about the incident. "Did I tell you about Rick sticking his penis in my face?"

Dr. Bellings was shocked. "No! What are you saying?"

I quickly told her, knowing my time was up. I thought that would be the end of it.

Dr. Bellings continued the conversation even though our session was over. She asked me a question before I opened the door. She said, "Did Rick have an erection when he stuck his penis in your face?"

I said, "Yes, he did."

Dr. Bellings said, "This is a lot more complicated than you think. You're not giving it enough credence!" She continued, "When the sexual switch is turned on, particularly in a boy's head, it's turned on for the rest of his life. It can't be turned off."

I left her office with that thought stirring in my head. That was why I was humping cars, boys, and inanimate objects as a young boy. It was starting to make sense why I had uncontrollable erections so early in life. My conscious mind had shrouded this experience from my awareness, keeping me in innocence. My subconscious mind wasn't so innocent. The following week Dr. Bellings and I talked about Rick in more detail.

More and more issues arose in my conscious mind as I wrote and continued working with Dr. Bellings: past trauma, conflicts in my marriage, same sex attraction, to name a few. A few weeks later, talking about Esti and me, Dr. Bellings said, "Robert, it's not uncommon for people to marry to resolve an issue they have with one of their parents."

I said, "I don't doubt that's true for some people, but that's not my case!" I had known since I was ten years old that I needed to get married, because becoming a husband was the gateway to becoming a mom.

Dr. Bellings continued to press home this theory.

I didn't change my mind. Each week she kept reiterating the same comment, but I felt no different. For six weeks she repeated this idea, making the same comment, and each time I reiterated the same response, "That's not my case!"

Dr. Bellings said, "That's okay, people do it subconsciously all the time."

I still disagreed, frustrated at the end of these sessions that she consistently made the same comment, and me giving the same answer. After six weeks of this, I closed the office door behind me, determined to resolve this one way or the other in my mind. Walking to my car, I thought, 'What if I reword her question?' I said to myself, 'What did I get married for? To resolve what issue with whom?'

The answer came to me almost instantaneously, before I even touched the car door! I pondered my conclusion, dumbfounded. I realized at that moment that all my life I had been competing against mother to be a better mom than she was.

I hadn't been consciously aware of this competition until that day. Because I had no other example of mothering than hers, I could only go on what I had learned from watching her. I realized that I had cherry picked her behaviors in my own parenting. In my mind, not all of her behaviors were unreasonable, so I chose the good and discarded the rest.

My thoughts were transformed immediately. I suddenly understood why I had always wanted to be a mom. I was awestruck. I opened the car door, still in shock at my conclusion, thinking faster than the speed of light.

I had just unraveled this mysterious riddle in me. The thought that had been motivating me all along was: 'I can do a better job of being a mom than mother ever thought of being, without hesitation!'

I realized that this was why I had paid attention to every nuance of mother's behavior, words, and patterns. I had been processing everything she was doing, saying, and being so I wouldn't become like her. I knew without a doubt I would become a legitimate mom. Mother wasn't, and never would be, and mother would never be me. The words 'know before you who I am' repeatedly went through my mind, but I didn't know why until that moment. Wanting to be a mom was my reality standing before me.

I sat in the seat, closing the door, hearing it snap closed. I thought, 'This is making more sense in my mind the more I think about it.' I began to unfold other riddles. Now I understood why I paid attention to every behavior, taking mental notes of every thought, action, and behavior which went through my mind. I wasn't going to emulate mother or her extremes while raising my children. I liked how she raised us to be obedient, and I wanted my children to be obedient. But I wanted my children to know they were loved and valued.

As I look back, I believe I did succeed in curtailing most of mother's harshness though my kids say I was sometimes extreme. I never hurt them, but I could be harsh. We have good relationships now, and they always knew how much they were loved and valued, but in listening to them I see how I would do things differently if I had the chance to do it all over.

I started the car, thinking, 'This is why I had been raising my children in detail at ten years old, so my children wouldn't have to masturbate to find the feeling I was missing out on.' I had touched myself to find a crumb of emotional security which mother couldn't give me, to fill the inner void where her love should have been.

Mother would never surrender her emotions to me. They were buried so deep underground inside of her, far from her heart and even further from me. Never mind the charade she paraded to others. I couldn't prove it, but based on mother telling me she never had an orgasm and how she spoke against men, I wondered if she had been a victim of incest as a girl. Some of the things, in my mind, that pointed to this were that she only wanted girls, she always said she should have stopped with one, and she never spoke of her father. She kept so much of her relationship between her father and her a secret, only telling me two stories about him. First, he died of obesity, and two, she was his favorite. It made me wonder if she wasn't raped by her father as a child. Of course, I'll never know, and the evidence is thin, but something had to explain her cruelty.

All this information was awe-inspiring to understand. As my mind unfolded more of my past, I realized there was so much more that was happening in my mind, and I needed to write this information down.

More and more realizations tumbled forth. My deep unfulfilled need for emotional connection was why I remembered so fondly when Daddy touched my feet. It gave me some emotional connection towards Daddy. I also concluded that men were nice and women were mean. This subliminal connection may have contributed to my decision to become gay, though it was my decision to become a mom that kept me from living as a homosexual.

I understood why touching my children's feet was so important to me. I would give my children the emotional support they needed because of my experience with Daddy touching my feet. This was all coming together in my mind, so I continued to write.

I realized then that I had become addicted to masturbation as a surrogate for the emotional security that had been so lacking throughout my childhood. Without that emotional security, I had felt worthless. Touching myself gave me the sense that I had control over my value, without guile, guilt or remorse. Through self-gratification, I had a sense of being, a sense of belonging, and a reason to live. It was all coming together in my mind.

I thought, 'I could write this.'

It was more than that.

I needed to write this.

I also began to understand why I mimicked others. It was to hide what I felt were maladies, to fit into a life when I felt so uncomfortable being inside myself. I wanted to be a 'somebody,' but I wanted that 'somebody' to be anybody but me. This was making more sense than ever in my mind. I didn't want others to be tempted to reject me when I felt so depleted already and so devalued by mother. I'd given mother too much of my power already! Masturbating at least helped me find my identity and discover a feeling of love I so desperately needed within me. Even though that self-gratification was a misinterpretation of love, it was through the innocence of this act that I found love for myself.

I hadn't second-guessed the value of it when I was young. I had safely guarded this information inside my mind, and I was determined to create a better reality for my future children. I knew I could give my children what they needed, so they wouldn't have to search this world for replacement for the sense of belonging everyone needs. This is why I had been paying attention to all my behaviors, so that I could create a better world for my children. I was still in a state of awe, sitting in my car in the parking lot processing this information.

I knew in my mind I would build a relationship and a trust with my children, so my children wouldn't have to find a solace with their body, like I had to find solace living in an environment filled with loud noise, screaming, feeling and witnessing the beatings of my brothers, wooden sticks to the back, knuckles to my face, hearing hated words towards children, uncontrollable outrage, anger, malice, slurs towards others, and most of all, a contempt for God!

I knew I would never tell my children, 'I should have never had you! I'm giving you away! I should have left you in the cart at the store, or drowned you in the tub when I had the chance!' Those words would never pass through my lips or become a thought in my mind to control my children because of my insecurities!

Mother had been teaching me more than she thought. It was all in the riddle inside my head, and now it was unraveling quickly. I captured my thoughts to write them down. It was all because of a good question asked the wrong way, when Dr. Bellings had suggested, "People marry to resolve issues with their parents. What unresolved issues are you trying to resolve through your marriage?" I knew this was the wrong question, but it was a good question nonetheless. I had turned this around and asked myself, 'What did I get married for? It wasn't to resolve issues with my mother. So why did I get married? What issue was I trying to resolve and with whom?'

This sequence of thoughts was all it had taken for my mind to unravel from its irritation. I wanted to turn around and go back into Dr. Bellings's office, but I had to wait a week to tell her my breakthrough! I drove home thinking, 'I've spent nearly 50 years trying to understand this riddle in me!' All that time, I had been trying to resolve the issues with myself. I had been competing with mother to be a better mom, and perhaps I had extended that into my marriage.

It continued to surprise me how competitive I was with mother. I began wondering if I was competing against my wife, too. Thinking, 'If I was competing against mother, why wouldn't I compete to be a better wife than my wife?' I was just as awe struck, if it was true, I realized it was so. I didn't know how to apologize. I was stuck in competition, competing against me, myself and my thoughts. It wasn't all in my imagination. It was my reality. Now I understood what I had been missing, but these realizations begged the question: what else had I been missing? Was this the mental illness Esti had been talking about? It would mean that the 'illness' wasn't my autism but my traumatic past and its effects on my mind.

Mother competed against God, telling her boys 'don't get married, don't have children, and don't come around here if you do! Move to China!!" It was all hyperbole! It was all about her being number one, bigger than God, more important than everyone else. She wanted to be the queen of her world and the most important person in the worlds of her sons and husband for all time. This was even why she guilted us about sticking her in some nursing home and letting her rot until death. She couldn't control aging or death, so she settled for trying to control how we treated her when she was old. She divided her boy's interest, and even tried to manipulate us from getting married so we would never place anyone above her on the pedestal of her own making. She succeeded with my three older brothers. Mother tried to make us into her own image. I felt she succeeded with my three older brothers.

It was born out of a mirage of insecurities in her head. Mother overrode God. But I overrode mother! I had been competing against mother's beliefs out of a state of innocence, a state that I didn't understand but was guided to act on naturally. I believed there is a God; He is a reality I couldn't deny! Mother pushed her anti-religious beliefs from an extreme point of view. Recognizing these extremes was valuable information that I applied to history. Mother's extremes were front and center with me. I valued this information more than I let on in life.

I noticed and recognized more truths, understanding why America broke away from England, because of England's extremes in leadership and religion. England had a monarchy, but America had elected a president. England worshiped God through the government's 'Church of England,' but America separated church from state, and allowed a person to worship as they pleased. Englander's traveled one way down the streets, and America chose the opposite side. Right side versus left side and vice versa. It was making more sense to me how extremes played out in people's lives.

Mother had filled me with so many extremes. I was just realizing how extremes play out in a person who wields power and mixes insecurities with authority. Mother was a very powerful woman with powerful extremes.

Now I also understood why God had said, 'I'm watching over you' at six years old. Had I needed the protection of innocence through a perpetual state of autism? I needed the accompaniment of God throughout my life, and most importantly in my childhood and in my marriage. It was at this point that I began to consider that perhaps I really was autistic.

That night I bounced my head for a few moments, thinking these thoughts as they played out from my past. I needed to guard against becoming like mother. I bounced my head thinking, 'I had no interest in being a mommy. I thought that was too manipulative, because mother had always demanded I call her "mommy." To her the term 'mother' was too distant. I wanted to be a mom, neither manipulative nor distant.

Seeing Dr. Connelly, I told her about the breakthrough I had had as a result of Dr. Bellings's question. Dr. Connelly was surprised by my breakthrough and by how deeply I was competing against mother and Esti.

Dr. Connelly then said, "I had heard enough of your upbringing and noticed a constant positive attitude towards your mother, despite your experience at home." Dr. Connelly said, "Do you know you have not said anything negative about your mother? You've expressed no animosity, no hatred, no ill will feelings towards your mother at all? You came in here wanting to have your autism rescinded, but there's more up inside of your head then you realize, Robert."

Dr. Connelly continued, "I've never heard you say one thing about your mother which would indicate you didn't love her."

I said, "You're right, I have no negative feelings towards her. I do love her, even to this day."

I had plenty of experiences to find failure, and I had legitimate reasons not to succeed in my life. I knew I wasn't going to let failure win. I am a success story. I knew what was in my mind and who I am. I created an importance by my working to satisfy customers expectations, and they in return appreciated what I did for them. I succeeded for me. Even if nobody else noticed, I would succeed for myself. The chasm left by the absence of mother's love was so deep that I had to fill it if I was ever going to be okay. It only added to my ambition.

I understood more why I protected and valued my feelings with the utmost importance, with my attractions, holding them sacred. I did this not to exploit them, but to hold them in high self-esteem, feeling the beauty they gave me inside my mind. It gave me the chance to feel my emotions which had been buried so deep inside of me, surrounded by pain from life's exposures. I needed these feelings to live! Acting out on my feelings would have created a metamorphosis in my mind, completely changing the composition and devaluing the sacredness of the feelings I had for my attractions. The more I wrote, the more I understood why I valued anticipation over participation.

I learned that telling a story is far different through writing. I had no idea the level of abuse I'd gone through until I wrote my words down with feelings which I hadn't known existed inside of me. Only then did I begin to understand the experiences I went through growing up, and the depths of the details. I was continually surprised by what I had gone through with mother and how the similarities in your wife lay in the making.

After finishing the first draft of the book, I began to see that my autism had kept me in a state of innocence. The unique perspective of autism, that lack of comprehension of social contexts and cues, had afforded me a sort of blindness to the reality of the abuse that I had endured. That blindness had protected me from the rage and victimization that normally results from the type of abuse and rejection I had experienced in childhood. To this day, I do not believe I was a victim of anything. I don't identify with words like "victimization" or "suffering" or even "endured." Yet I know intellectually that these words are relevant to my experience, particularly from a non-autistic perspective.

I came to an innocent understanding about the beauty of pain which I had gone through with mother. The next time I worked on the manuscript, I wrote as if I was penning a letter to mother, speaking to her from my heart, in a way I would never have done when she was alive: "Mom, you were doing me a favor! You had a mission in life to teach me differently, to teach me in a meaningful way I couldn't have learned under any other circumstances."

"I didn't change the innocent love I've always had for you inside of me after writing down my story about us." With a swell of tears in my eyes, in the innocence of love, I can say, "I love you, Mom. Thank you for gifting me this life's experience!"

"Now I get to find legitimate forgiveness for you through the innocence of my being, and heal my soul to love you even more, so I can start crying. So I can start healing. So I can start living."

The end in this case is the beginning...the beginning of a new life in the fullness of who I am, who God created me to be.

A LONG GOODBYE
A TRIUMPHANT SEQUEL TO *STOP YOUR CRYING*
COMING TO BOOKSTORES
FALL 2024

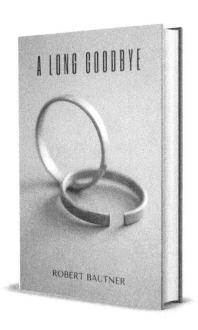

For Robert, being married under God, for eternity, meant everything. That eternity was cut short. His wife began a long goodbye six years into their marriage. He saw it in her eyes, her actions, and felt it during intimacy. A silent barrage of 'I should have never married you' swept through him. His mother had routinely said, "I should never have had you" and now his wife, "I should never have married you." His childhood was a long goodbye of heartaches and distress, and now so was his marriage. The memories and the emotions of both demanded to be released. Not an easy task, especially when one is autistic, where it is difficult to understand those who are not… and where it is difficult to be understood. Yet this isn't a tale of desolation. Instead, it's a story of transformation, a testament to the resilience of the human spirit. From the heartrending struggle to comprehend his reality, emerges an understanding of the profound tenderness of his soul. This tale exposes the delicate balance between the past and present, the pain of leaving behind and the power of moving forward. Thirty-six years later, the papers are signed, and a new chapter for Robert begins. This is that story. It is *A Long Goodbye*.

THE WOLF CYCLE
A UNIQUE LOOK AT HOW TO BE HUMAN
COMING TO BOOKSTORES
SPRING 2024

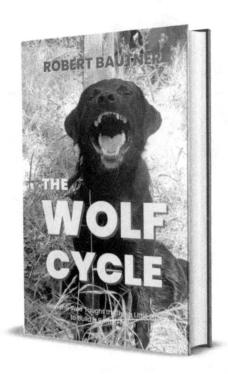

Inspired by The Three Little Pigs, this book asks you the question: which house did you build? In the original fairytale, one built the straw house, one built the stick house, and one built the brick house. The truth is that no house was superior: each of the three pigs built their homes based on how their brains were wired, not on the materials that were available. You know the end of the story, but do you know the beginning? The beginning of your story started before you arrived. Written to save civilization. The Wolf Cycle, how the wolf taught us to build a better house. It is a book about how your innocence defeats any and all evils you will ever face.

ABOUT THE AUTHOR

Robert Bautner is an author, father of five, and a horse farmer who was born autistic and dyslexic, who endured a childhood of abuse, and who emerged from it with a lifelong commitment to turning negatives into positives after a failed suicide attempt at age 10. During that same period, he discovered he was gay and that he wanted more than anything to be a mom. As a young man, he came to know Jesus Christ as his Savior and joined the Church of Latter Day Saints. To reconcile his seemingly irreconcilable traits, he decided to always be gay but never homosexual, and he set out to find a woman who would be a good match. He found her and they married, having five children over 36 years of marriage. Unfortunately, their happily-ever-after wasn't. He began writing when his wife filed for divorce, using the feelings of overwhelming loss and grief to channel the pain of his childhood, starting him on a journey of healing. He is forever grateful that on that fateful day when he was 10, he was saved, ironically by the brother that tormented him the most. In his immutable style, he continues to turn negatives into positives, and his sole desire is to inspire and encourage you, dear reader, and perhaps save a life.

Printed in the USA
CPSIA information can be obtained
at www.ICGtesting.com
CBHW080301090424
R15066200001B/R150662PG6341CBX00001B/1